Doomsday: Iran
The Clock is Ticking
By James G. Zumwalt

A NONFICTION IMPRINT FROM ADDUCENT
www.Adducent.co

Titles Distributed In
North America
United Kingdom
Western Europe
South America
Australia

DOOMSDAY: IRAN
The Clock is Ticking
By James G. Zumwalt

Doomsday: Iran
The Clock is Ticking
By James G. Zumwalt

Copyright © 2012 All rights reserved. No part of this book may be reproduced or transmitted in any form or by any means, electronic or mechanical, including photocopying, recording or by any information storage and retrieval system, without written permission from the publisher, except for brief quotations as would be used in a review.

ISBN 978-1-937592-25-7

Published by Adducent (under its *Fortis* Nonfiction imprint)
Jacksonville, Florida
www.Adducent.Co

Published in the United States of America

All statements of fact, opinion, or analysis expressed are those of the author and do not reflect the official positions or views of the publisher. Nothing in the contents should be construed as asserting or implying authentication of information or endorsement of the author's views. This book and subjects discussed herein are designed to provide the author's opinion about the subject matter covered and is for informational purposes only.

DEDICATION

To my first grandchild, who hopefully will come to know a world free of hatred, intolerance, and violence.

TABLE OF CONTENTS

Introduction — 1
   Setting the Doomsday Clock — 1

Chapter 1 — 6
   Understanding the "Sins of the Father" — 6
   The Mullahs' Grudge Against America — 6

Chapter 2 — 16
   Discontent with the Shah Opens the Door to the Islamic Revolution — 16
   Ayatollah Ruhollah Khomeini the Magician Pulls an Islamist Theocracy Out of His Turban: Now You See Democracy, Now You Don't! — 17
   Khomeini Claims Bakhtiar as a Casualty in the Fight Against Democracy — 27
   Khomeini's Roadmap to Theocracy Continues — 29
   Bazargan Becomes an Unwitting Vehicle Traveling Khomeini's Roadmap — 29
   Khomeini's Sleight of Hand Sneaks the Constitution Through — 30
   Khomeini's Last Minute Constitutional Manipulation Paves the Way for a New Supreme Leader — 34
   It May Be God's Constitution, Law & Koran but Supreme Leader & Guardian Council Interpret Them on God's Behalf — 37
   Interpretation by Islamists is not just Limited to the Constitution — 38

Chapter 3 — 40
   The Mullahs' Hypocritical Oath — 40
   Supreme Leader's Rubber Stamp Assembly of Experts — 43
   Perception Clouds Reality As Ayatollah Ruhollah Khomeini Grabs the Reins of Power — 43
   Khomeini Approves U.S. Embassy Takeover and Seizure of U.S. Diplomats — 45

Improving Educational Access for Men by Decreasing It for Women	49
The Satanic Verses	50
Khomeini's Haunting	53
Understanding Islam's Rise and Split	56
The Two Faces of the Koran	66

Chapter 4 — 78

Concept of Supreme Leader Unique to Shia in Iran; Khomeini Introduces the "Fear Factor"	78
Iran's Presidents: The Perceptions and the Realities	81
Ahmadinejad: "The Catalystic Converter"	85
Stolen Election	90
Rafsanjani's Confrontation with the Supreme	93
Ahmadinejad Ruffles the Supreme's Feathers?	96
Iran's Next President	100

Chapter 5 — 102

Iran's Dangerous Nuclear Mix	102
Iran's Nuclear Program: Getting Started—and Stopped	103
Getting Started Again	105
The P5+1-2 Confronts Iran and Sanctions Slowly Flow; Iran Announces It Has Achieved Completion of the Full Nuclear Fuel Cycle	122
The Contentious IAEA-U.S. Relationship	127
NCRI Exposes Iran's Nuclear Program to the Light of Day	130
If One Bomb Can Destroy Israel, Iran Must Be Talking About Nukes	131
Iranian Early Bird Failed to Catch the Computer Worm	132

Chapter 6

Iranian Officials Indicted for Exporting the Islamic Revolution	139
Hezbollah—The Arms of the Octopus Extend to 9/11	141
Iran Takes an "All Talk/No Action" Approach to Negotiations; President Mahmoud Ahmadinejad Takes Office Creating International Incidents as Distractions	158
The Role of the Islamic Republican Guard Corps, Qods Force and Basij	161

Chapter 7 — 166

Analyzing the Iranian Leadership's Mindset: "We Will Bury You"	166
Understanding Iran's "Path"	169
The "Belief" and the "Goal"—Crossing Over from Reality to the Spiritual World of the Mahdi	171
Beware of the Imposter—Awaiting "the Mountain of Gold?"	179
Ahmadinejad Manifests his Belief the Mahdi is Coming	183
Three Stooges of Evil—the Movie: Coming Soon to a Theater Near You!	186
Iran Won't Be Kept from its Appointed Rounds—Not Even by MAD	191

Chapter 8 — 194

Iran's Leadership Spreading HIV	194
Not Everyone is Invited to Humanity's "Pool Party"	194
When Shiites Need Not Play "To Tell the Truth"	202
Even Islamic Extremists Need Love	207
Iran's Gender Pecking Order Hidden Under Cover of the "Wicked Double Helix"	210

Chapter 9 — 217

Iranian Mullahs Destroying Persia's Roots	217
Actions Which Have Reeled-in Iran's Conduct	220

MEK: An Iranian Lion in Iraq	222
When a Counter-Intelligence Operation Goes Well	236
When a Counter-Intelligence Operation Goes Too Well	236
Did Iran's Counter-Intelligence Operations Dupe the U.S.?	238
The MEK Pawn	240
MEK Update	241
Chapter 10	**244**
Is It Already Too Late for the West—Has Iran Already Duped the World?	244
Turning Shiite Brother Against Shiite Brother: The Iran-Iraq War	250
Who Wants to be a Millionaire?	262
Chapter 11	**267**
"Assad" State of Affairs in Syria	267
Iran's Motto: "What You Said is not What I Know I Heard"	281
Iran's Influence In Iraq	289
Khamenei Seeks to Mirror in Iraq Khomeini's Success in Iran	294
Iran Gaining Ground in Iraq	297
U.S. Turnover to Iraq—Tehran Was Ready But Was Baghdad?	299
Iraq's Prime Minister Maliki—Friend or Foe to Iraq?	301
Is Iraq Being "Saddamized" by Maliki—The Man Who Would Be Dictator?	302
The Day Baghdad Died and No One Would Listen	308
Al-Sadr—Iraqi Nationalist or Shiite Islamist?	311
Where Do Their True Loyalties Lie?	316
Chapter 12	**317**
Shiites and Sunnis: Using Different Roadmaps But Heading to the Same Destination	317

The Cordoba Initiative—Symbol of Islam's Greatest Victory	318
Sunnis Take the Fork in the Road for the Mahdi's Return	323
Islamist Sunnis' Holy Grail Undermining Democracy—Opening the Door to Shariah "Creep"	323
Iran Fans the Flames of Violence in Afghanistan	331
The "Wild Cards" in Iran's Future	339
Conclusion	353

INTRODUCTION

Setting the Doomsday Clock

Sixty-five years ago, a universally recognized means for assessing global vulnerability to self-destruction based on man's development of weapons of mass destruction was established. As of 2007, that vulnerability assessment began to include man-made catastrophes related to climate change and emerging technologies. Dubbed the "Doomsday Clock," it is monitored by the Bulletin of the Atomic Scientists (BAS) in Washington, D.C. When these scientists determine man's actions or inactions either increase or decrease the global vulnerability, the minute hand of the clock is adjusted accordingly. An adjustment closer to midnight reflects increasing danger while a movement farther away symbolizes the opposite.

Over these past six and a half decades, the minute hand has covered a fifteen minute spread, springing precariously close to midnight before easing back. The decision on any adjustment is made by the organization's Board of Directors, after consultation with their Board of Sponsors—a group that includes 18 Nobel Laureates.

In 1953, the hand made its closest approach to midnight—at two minutes before the hour—when the U.S. developed a hydrogen bomb. The hand retreated to its furthest point—17 minutes before midnight—in 1991 when the U.S. and Russia penned their Strategic Arms Reduction Treaty.

Adjustments to the Clock are not made annually but on an as-needed basis. When an adjustment is required—which, as of October 2012, has occurred twenty times during the Clock's existence—normally it is made in the month of January. In 2010, the minute hand stood at six minutes before midnight but was moved forward one minute in January 2012, signaling an increased vulnerability.

The 2012 adjustment was attributed to three developments: (1) The narrowly avoided disaster at Japan's Fukushima nuclear plant triggered by the March 11, 2011 earthquake and tsunami; (2) the transition of power and control of North Korea's nuclear weapons to another generation of the Kim dynasty; and (3) Iran's designs on developing nuclear weapons.

It is the third development that is most worrisome as a theocracy in Tehran, which has proven itself to be ruthless and brutal, communicates to the civilized world exactly what violent intentions it has for the future—all while refusing to clarify whether those intentions include building a nuclear weapons capability. The message Tehran sends on this issue is being transmitted in so many ways, both directly and indirectly, to the West. But recipients of the message choose not to give it credibility in spite of the sinister tone in which it is being conveyed.

This message continues to fall on deaf ears.

In sports, the team that comes out on top is usually the one that has studied the other's strengths and weaknesses. Winning turns on avoiding an opponent's strengths and taking advantage of his weaknesses. Iran's Supreme Leader Ali Khamenei has identified a crucial weakness of the West in dealing with his country—ignorance. He has said:

> *"An enduring problem of our enemies is that they do not know our nation well and are not familiar with our people. They cannot appropriately discover the way spiritual and Islamic ideas affect people. They cannot understand the element of the clerics, its position and effect and quality of that effect. Therefore, the strangeness of these facts to them has always been problematic to them...a military encounter is a very expensive and dangerous way for any country."*

This book is written to help turn this weakness into strength. It seeks to explain the message Iran is—very openly—conveying to the West, the tone in which it is being conveyed and why the message should be heeded based on the underlying beliefs of the messenger. It seeks to leave one with a comprehensive understanding of the Iranian leadership's mindset as it has played out and continues to play out on a wide range of issues—how it worked to implement Islamist doctrine into Iran's constitution;

how it worked to use the U.S. hostage crisis in Iran as a means of unifying domestic opposition behind the theocracy; how it could have ended in two years an Iran-Iraq war that took eight (failing, contrary to the Prophet Muhammad's teachings, to accept an earlier peace offer); how it was willing to sacrifice its most valued asset—its children—in an effort to defeat Saddam's army; how it thrives on hypocrisy and its people's willingness to accept it; how it utilizes the extraterritoriality mandate of its constitution to justify terrorist attacks anywhere in the world; etc.

The world community stands on the threshold of a nuclear holocaust, yet turns a blind eye as to why, what is happening in Iran, is happening. It needs fully to understand how and why Iran is seeking out and determined to experience its own version of the "Big Bang Theory."

To understand the message requires one first to understand the mindset of the messenger. What follows will attempt to provide insights into that mindset by tracking its evolution and the foundation upon which it has been built.

It will cover the evolution of Iran's Islamic Revolution during the three plus decades since it toppled Shah Mohammad Reza Pahlavi in 1979, bringing to power a theocracy, initially headed by the late Supreme Leader Ruhollah Khomeini, and continuing up through the country's leadership under Ali Khamenei, who replaced Khomeini as Supreme Leader upon the latter's death in 1989, and Mahmoud Ahmadinejad, who was elected president in 2005 and "re-elected" in 2009 as the election was stolen from the Iranian people by their mullah masters.

History is replete with examples of world leaders communicating threats to an enemy. There have been those who subsequently failed to make good on them (such as Iraqi leader Saddam Hussein's warning to the U.S. prior to the Persian Gulf war that conflict would be the "Mother of all Battles") and those who do make good on them (such as Osama bin Laden's warning in 1996 he was declaring war on the U.S.).

Hussein's threat fizzled on the battlefield for many reasons, but one of those was the U.S. and its allies fully understood what they were facing and how best to defeat it. Despite Saddam's bravado, the Persian Gulf ground war became the shortest war in modern history with the U.S. taking very few combat casualties.

Osama bin Laden, on the other hand, made good on his threat with devastating effect. As is customary in Islam, he openly conveyed that threat to the enemy—but that enemy then failed to heed it. As a result, the shocking events of 9/11 subsequently stunned the Nation.

A similar and potentially much more devastating threat has been communicated to the U.S. by Iran as it continues to move forward with its nuclear program in violation of international law. While Tehran claims its program is for peaceful purposes, its actions—such as its covert construction deep underground at numerous sites—strongly suggest otherwise. Therefore, it is imperative one focus on understanding the Iranian leadership's mindset to assess whether its threats should be dismissed as false bravado or dealt with as very viable.

The U.S. paid a heavy price for its failure to assess accurately Osama bin Laden's true intentions. It will pay a much heavier price should it fail to accurately assess Iran's.

It is imperative the intentions of Tehran's mullahs be fully understood—and as soon as possible. Some nuclear issues will be discussed herein and a timeline provided—but the book's main focus will be on understanding the Iranian mindset and motivation—and why there is but one way this crisis can be resolved to remove a danger to the world community. This also requires understanding how that mindset has come to impact on other countries in the region such as Iraq, Syria, Lebanon, and Afghanistan.

Is Iran's leadership's mindset one capable of reasonable negotiation? Why would it not be fully transparent about the nature of its nuclear program if, in fact, its intentions are peaceful? If Tehran has been deceiving the world and its true intention is to develop nuclear weapons, the international community must no longer be lulled into a false sense of security as Tehran moves closer to achieving its sinister goal.

Over 2500 years ago, the brilliant Chinese military strategist Sun Tzu wrote a treatise entitled "The Art of War." In it, he espoused certain principles a military commander should master before engaging an enemy on the battlefield.

Among the key principles listed by Sun Tzu was, "Know your enemy." That is what this book seeks to do—i.e., enable the reader to know the enemy. While there may be those critical of using the word "enemy" to describe Iran, it must be realized Iran has already declared war against the U.S. Iran has been fighting an America that refuses to recognize it is at war with a country that has claimed more American lives than any enemy since the war fought in Vietnam. (For those still critical, please note in the quote by Supreme Leader Khamenei above, he refers to the U.S. and Israel as "enemies.")

To understand the conflicts at play between Washington and Tehran, one cannot begin with the nuclear crisis—one has to understand Iran's history and how it first came to cross paths with America's. That requires embarking upon a journey that will share "the good, the bad and the ugly" of the policies the parties involved have pursued over the past six plus decades and how they gave way to a relationship and differences today that some experts suggest may simply be insurmountable diplomatically, absent a regime change.

Supreme Leader Ali Khamenei is correct as to his claim of Western ignorance in understanding what drives Iran. Because of that ignorance, the West continues to apply a "reasonable man" standard to an Iranian leadership locked into the mode of an "unreasonable man" mindset.

Not understanding the Iranian leadership's mindset gives credence to Supreme Leader Khamenei's claim. Understanding it should give one pause to wonder whether the Doomsday Clock is running slow!

It is imperative to understand this time difference before it becomes too late to act.

The Clock is ticking...

Chapter One

Understanding the "Sins of the Father"

A primary reason cited by Iran's theocratic leaders today as to why it regards the U.S. as "the Great Satan" stems from Washington's interference in Iranian affairs in 1953. In the interests of fairness, it should be acknowledged that what happened in Iran at that time clearly constituted interference in that country's domestic affairs—with little justification for the actions of the Western powers involved other than wielding control over Tehran's oil resources. The democracies involved clearly overstepped their bounds, imposing their will upon the expressed will of the Iranian people.

Today's leaders in Iran, however, strongly believe "the sins of the father" are visited upon the son. Despite the passing of three generations since the interference by the U.S. in Iran's domestic affairs, the theocracy in power today chooses to hold "the sins of the father" against the son. Tehran's mullahs seek the destruction of the Great Satan as they are unwilling to forgive and forget a U.S. transgression reversing their people's will as expressed in a democratic election—the result of a covert U.S. Central Intelligence Agency (CIA) action. Yet, there is irony in the mullahs' lack of forgiveness toward the U.S. as, 56 years later, in 2009, they were guilty of committing the same sin—imposing their will over the expressed will of their own people in what was to be a democratic presidential election.

The Mullahs' Grudge Against America

To understand the 1953 incident giving rise to the Mullahs' "Grudge" against America requires a brief refresher on Iran's history and how its relationship with the West evolved. As Iran's (Persia's) history goes back thousands of years, perhaps the best place to start is the late eighteenth century.

In the late eighteenth century, Iran, then still known as "Persia," was ununified—a nation ruled by tribes. (Persia did not officially become known as "Iran" until March 3, 1935.) In 1779, a Turkmen tribe, known as the "Qajars" and led by Agha Mohammad Khan, reunified the country, establishing the Qajar Dynasty, which would rule until 1925. Agha Mohammed Khan made Tehran—then but a village—Iran's capital. Although crowned "Shah" in 1796, his reign was cut short when he was assassinated a year later, to be succeeded by a nephew, Fath Ali Shah.

A large portion of the territory unified by Agha Mohammed Khan was lost by Fath Ali Shah as he found himself on the losing end of wars fought with Russia over the next 37 years. These losing conflicts with Iran's northern neighbor prompted Fath Ali Shah to increase contacts with Europe, some of which led to diplomatic rivalries over Iran. It also led, with the subsequent continuation of the Qajar Dynasty under Naser-e-Din in 1848, to significant Western influence within Persia.

Considered the most successful leader among the Qajar dynasty, Naser-e-Din was instrumental in modernizing Iran and introducing Western technology, science and education. But competing influence between Russia and England enabled both countries to encroach upon Iranian independence by the late nineteenth century.

Naser-e-Din's rule ended in 1896 when he was assassinated, and his son, Mozaffar o-Din Shah, succeeded him. But the son proved to be an ineffective leader who wasted the country's assets due to his extravagant tastes. In exchange for allowing the expansion of European influence in Iran, he and other government officials received lavish payments. The spending and corruption raised a public furor, heightened by increased foreign influence.

Mozaffar o-Din initially agreed to address some of the people's complaints but, failing to do so, they began protests in 1906. These protests finally led to a constitution, severely restricting the Shah's powers, which he signed on December 30, 1906. Five days later, the Shah died, succeeded by his son, Mohammad Ali Shah.

The constitution led in 1907 to the Supplementary Fundamental Laws which provided for various rights, with some restrictions, comparable to those in the U.S. Constitution, including freedom of speech, assembly, press, etc. But the new Shah opposed the constitution, claiming it was contrary to Islamic law. With Russian assistance, Mohammad Ali Shah suspended the constitution in 1908 and initiated a violent effort to arrest and kill its supporters. Civil war erupted. Pro-constitution forces marched on Tehran in July 1909 and deposed the Shah, who fled to Russia. (That Shah, Mohammad Ali Shah, died in Italy in 1925, setting a precedent for every successive Shah of Iran—dying in exile.) The pro-constitution legislature reinstated the constitution, voting to maintain the Qajar Dynasty by replacing the exiled Shah with his eleven year old son, Ahmad Shah.

The exiled Shah, however, in a failed attempt, sought to regain his throne the next year. Russia and England—pursuant to a 1907 agreement—divided Iran into two spheres of influence. Those spheres took into consideration the locations of oil deposits that had been discovered in Iran in 1908. Russia had exclusive influence in the northern sphere; England had exclusive influence in the southern and eastern sphere; both had free competition in a neutral sphere established in the center.

Tensions arose again, however, in 1911. An Iranian government attempt to send a tax collector into the Russian sphere led to a Russian ultimatum to dismiss the collector and Tehran's refusal to do so. As Russian troops in Iran sought to march on Tehran, a southwestern Iranian tribe known as the "Bakhtiari" took control of the government, accepting the Russian ultimatum. The Bakhtiari maintained control of the government for a period of time during which the constitution was again suspended.

As one might imagine, the eleven year old Ahmad Shah was incapable of dealing with the myriad of interests, foreign and domestic, vying for influence within his country. Further compounding this was the advent of World War I and his country's occupation by Russian, English and Ottoman forces. Even as he aged, Ahmad Shah still proved incompetent. A 1921 coup by a military officer, Reza Khan, who later ruled as Reza Shah Pahlavi, left Ahmad Shah in control by title only. During a trip to Europe in 1925, Ahmad Shah was formally deposed by parliament, ending the rule of the Qajar Dynasty and starting the shorter rule of the two generation Pahlavi Dynasty. Like father, like son, Ahmad Shah too died in exile—in 1930 in France.

Reza Khan joined the Iranian army as a private. His positive attitude and intelligence helped him rise through the ranks as he quickly gained the attention of impressed senior officers. Unhappy with the chaos in the country created by the Qajar Dynasty's lack of leadership which allowed foreign power influence to thrive, he led a force of 1200 men in the previously mentioned 1921 coup.

Initially taking command of the army, Reza Khan recognized that the key to any initiative to improve conditions in the country turned on effective and strong leadership. He also recognized Ahmad Shah was not providing it. Reza Khan's footprint increased as he later became prime minister, launching various reforms as he continued to consolidate power. Adept at playing political chess without revealing his intended moves ahead of time, he effectively isolated opponents, gradually gaining control of the reins of power. The Shah, ill and seeking treatment in Europe, was eventually deposed by parliament in 1925, with power formally vested in Reza Khan as he became Shah in 1926, establishing the Pahlavi Dynasty.

Continuing the reforms he started as prime minister, the new Shah focused on ending domestic turmoil by breaking the power of the various tribes and minimizing foreign influence. Recognizing the equality of women, he empowered them to vote and abolished the requirement they wear veils. He terminated the unique privileges of foreign influence groups, including their influence, wielded for decades, over Iran's finances and communications. He put the country on the road to democracy, establishing the country's first university, recognizing education was vital to paving that road properly.

Although Reza Khan (now Reza Shah) maneuvered to end foreign influence in Iran, World War II disrupted that effort. Concerned with Reza Shah's friendly relationship with Germany, English and Russian forces—which had allied themselves to fight the Germans—occupied Iran in 1941. The allied forces demanded Reza Shah abdicate, although they allowed his eldest son, Mohammad Reza Pahlavi, to replace him to keep the dynasty in power. Living a life in exile, Reza Shah died in 1945 in Africa.

It is against this historical backdrop of Iran's history, with Reza Shah's son (Mohammad Reza Pahlavi who would later be ousted by the 1979 Islamic

Revolution) coming to power that the stage was set for an incident involving the Western powers that became the basis for the mullahs' Grudge today.

After becoming Shah in 1941 at the age of 21, Mohammad Reza Pahlavi continued to march forward with reforms in the same direction set by his father. As the country was beset by numerous domestic challenges—political, economic and social—in the wake of World War II, the new Shah also found himself challenged for power by a popular, professional politician, Mohammad Mosaddeq, who almost proved successful in deposing the young Shah.

It was this near success by Mosaddeq that triggered the CIA's 1953 coup, with the assistance of co-conspirator Britain, thus making it necessary to understand Mosaddeq's background. While the plot had first been proposed, and rejected, by the Administration of President Harry Truman in 1952, it was implemented by Truman's successor—Dwight Eisenhower.

Western educated, Mosaddeq was elected to parliament in 1923. Although Reza Khan had affected a coup in 1921, Mosaddeq was determined to serve the country, until Reza Khan was crowned as Shah in 1925—a move he opposed, resulting in his voluntary retirement from public office. When Reza Khan abdicated in 1941, Mosaddeq ran again for parliament as a diehard nationalist, winning the election in 1944.

It was Mosaddeq who led the charge to nationalize the oil industry as its resources were being controlled and exported by foreign companies—primarily by the British owned company today known as British Petroleum (BP)—which then pocketed most of the profits to the exclusion of Iran. BP's oil contract with Iran represented England's greatest foreign asset—one it was unwilling to relinquish voluntarily. But to Iranians, the overbearing contract was a symbol of British imperialism that had to be severed.

The Iranian parliament overwhelmingly voted to nationalize the industry in March 1951. With Mosaddeq's popularity growing, the parliament elected him as premier, further intensifying the rivalry with Mohammad Reza Shah Pahlavi for control of the government. Mosaddeq's international impact was evidenced by Time magazine's selection of him as its "Man of the Year" for 1951.

Mohammad Reza Pahlavi had also backtracked on his promise to serve as a constitutional monarch whose powers were limited by parliament. This brought the Shah and his prime minister into further conflict as Mosaddeq continued to challenge the Shah's authority.

England did not react well to Iran's nationalization legislation, organizing an international boycott to pressure Iran economically. London's complete withdrawal from the Iranian oil industry left a vacuum for Tehran as it fought to find alternative buyers but could not quickly do so. As a result, the Shah saw Iran's economic downturn as providing a convenient excuse to fire Mosaddeq as premier. He did so in August 1953. But the Shah's action prompted an outpouring of public support for Mosaddeq, forcing the Shah to flee the country.

It is at this point that the U.S. CIA implemented a plot to bring the Shah—considered a valuable and malleable ally of the West—back into power by interfering in Iran's domestic affairs.

A 1954 classified CIA report written by one of the coup plotters and detailed in a New York Times article provided insights as to what actions the agency, along with Britain's intelligence agency SIS, took to topple the elected Iranian government of Mohammed Mosaddeq. It would take two attempts, four days apart, to be successful.

Without getting into specifics of the CIA's plan, a few quotes by Professor Mark Gasiorowski—a Louisiana State University professor considered to be a prominent scholar of the coup—should suffice. He notes in an April 19, 2000 article he wrote in response to an April 16, 2000 publication of the aforementioned 1954 CIA by the New York Times:

> "Perhaps the most general conclusion that can be drawn from these documents is that the CIA extensively stage-managed the entire coup, not only carrying it out but also preparing the groundwork for it by subordinating various prominent Iranian political actors and using propaganda

and other instruments to influence public opinion against Mossadeq. In my view, this thoroughly refutes the argument that is commonly made in Iranian monarchist exile circles that the coup was a legitimate 'popular uprising' on behalf of the shah...The most intriguing new tidbit here (i.e., in the 1954 report) *is that the CIA's agents harassed religious leaders and bombed one's home in order to turn them against Mossadeq."*

The result of the CIA's actions in contravention of international law was to bring the Shah back into power. After the Shah's return, Mosaddeq was imprisoned and tried for treason. At his trial, Mosaddeq gave a remarkably eloquent justification for his actions seeking to reform the country and curb foreign influence:

"Yes, my sin... my greater sin and even my greatest sin is that I nationalized Iran's oil industry and discarded the system of political and economic exploitation by the world's greatest empire...This at a cost to myself; my family; and at the risk of losing my life, my honor and my property...With God's blessing and the will of the people, I fought this savage and dreadful system of international espionage and colonialism...I am well aware my fate must serve as an example in the future throughout the Middle East in breaking the chains of slavery and servitude to colonial interests...If I sit silent, I have sinned."

Spending three years in prison, Mosaddeq was later released and put under house arrest, where he spent the remaining eleven years of his life. He died in 1967 at the age of 85. Although his domestic charge in support of nationalism was blunted, he did help Iran succeed in retaining control of its oil industry.

There is little doubt that the 1953 CIA intervention into Iran planted the seed of suspicion as to U.S. intentions in the decades afterward, not only in Iran but throughout the Middle East. That seed has blossomed into more of a "weed"—from the U.S. perspective—in need of elimination in a new era of enlightenment. But it is one Iran's current government seeks to grow and nourish in furtherance of its own goals today.

Although Mohammad Reza Pahlavi would continue to serve as Shah for 26 more years, like his three predecessors, he would eventually be forced to abdicate, pressured to do so by President Jimmy Carter as the Islamic Revolution of 1979 swept a new—and much more brutal—group of authoritarians into power.

Recognizing the lingering effect of the Grudge on Tehran, in March 2000, during the U.S. presidency of Bill Clinton and the Iranian presidency of Mohammad Khatami, the U.S. extended an olive branch, which Tehran rebuked. U.S. Secretary of State Madeleine Albright came close to apologizing to Iran for U.S. involvement in the CIA plot.

What Albright had said was, "It is easy to see now why many Iranians continue to resent this intervention by America in their internal affairs." The Iranians immediately criticized the U.S. for not offering a full apology. Supreme Leader Khamenei announced any effort at reconciliation with the U.S. would be "treason."

Some Iran observers believe the Grudge is actually promoted as a ploy by Islamists who want the West to buy into this argument as being responsible for the conflict with Iran today. They suggest it is a ploy as Ayatollah Khomeini and many of Iran's other leading clerics in 1953 had actually supported the Shah's return and the removal of Prime Minister Mosaddeq. Such observers suggest this ploy diverts the West's attention from examining the real source of conflict after 1979, which is Iran's revolutionary ideology and global ambitions.

While the 1953 CIA plot remains a sore spot among the Iranian leadership today, it is by no means the only one. In a letter, dated May 8, 2006 from Iranian President Mahmoud Ahmadinejad to U.S. President George W. Bush, other grievances were aired as follows (insertions in parentheses are Ahmadinejad's):

> *"The brave and the faithful people of Iran have too many questions and grievances, including the coup d'état of 1953*

and the subsequent toppling of the legal government of the day, opposition to the Islamic Revolution, transformation of an Embassy into a headquarters supporting the activities of those opposing the Islamic Republic (many thousands of pages of documents support this claim), support for Saddam in the war waged against Iran, the shooting down of the Iranian passenger plane, freezing the assets of the Iranian nation, increasing threats, anger and displeasure vis-à-vis the scientific and nuclear progress of the Iranian nation (just when all Iranians are jubilant and celebrating their country's progress), and many other grievances I will not refer to in this letter."

The references above pertain to the following:

- "Transformation of an Embassy into a headquarters supporting the activities of those opposing the Islamic Republic (many thousands of pages of documents support this claim)" alludes to the claim by Ayatollah Khomeini that the U.S. Embassy seized in 1979 was a "Den of Espionage." The documents were those found afterward by student militants which, had either not been destroyed by U.S. Embassy officials, or had been shredded but pieced back together by those militants.

- "Support for Saddam in the war waged against Iran" was the U.S. assistance, mostly in the form of intelligence, provided to Iraq's Saddam Hussein during the Iran-Iraq war—a conflict the U.S. was committed to not seeing Iran win.

- "The shooting down of the Iranian passenger plane" pertains to an Iranian civilian passenger plane with 290 people onboard shot down over the Straits of Hormuz while still in Iranian airspace by the guided missile cruiser USS Vincennes (CG-49). The incident occurred on July 3, 1988 as the aircraft headed toward the ship but refused to identify itself after repeated U.S. warnings. Tensions in the area were already high due to a combination of violent incidents such as the May 17, 1987 Exocet missile attack by an Iraqi aircraft against the guided missile frigate USS Stark (FFG-31) and subsequent attacks involving Iranian boats and mines. The Vincennes' crew mistakenly believed the aircraft to be a warplane. (Claims against the U.S. were settled in the International Court of Justice, with the U.S. making monetary payments to each victim's family—although the U.S. did not admit responsibility or give an apology.)

- "Freezing the assets of the Iranian nation" was an apparent reference to those assets frozen in the aftermath of Tehran's actions in seizing the U.S. Embassy and taking its staff hostage on November 4, 1979.

- "Increasing threats, anger and displeasure vis-à-vis the scientific and nuclear progress of the Iranian nation (just when all Iranians are jubilant and celebrating their country's progress)" relates to U.S. objections to Tehran's nuclear program which the U.S. believes involves weaponization.

CHAPTER TWO

Discontent with the Shah Opens the Door to the Islamic Revolution

Since his restoration to power was the result of actions by Western powers, Iran's last Shah, Mohammad Reza Pahlavi, was left with an appreciation for maintaining a healthy relationship with his American "Big Brother." While continuing to make domestic changes such as land reform, extending rights to women, improving education, etc., he also ensured Iran became a stalwart ally to the U.S. in the Middle East. To reinforce this, he opened the floodgates to Western culture.

But, while reforms for his people made him friends, it also made him enemies. Some were created by the Shah's opulent and self-aggrandizing lifestyle; some by outraged Islamic extremists disgusted that Western culture was so easily accessible to Iranians. The Shah's actions, such as his 1967 coronation as the "King of the Kings (Emperor of Iran)" with his wife as Empress and the replacement of the Islamic calendar in 1976 with an imperial one starting 2500 years earlier based on the Persian Empire, caused a massive public outcry.

Other factors were at work in wearing down support for the Shah—his continuing violation of the constitution, Iran's role as an American puppet in the region, his suppression of the people by his hated intelligence agency, the SAVAK, etc. His acceptance of Western influence and expansion of women's rights was not taken well by clerics, who saw their power diminishing, or by Islamic extremists. Despite the efforts of his father to put Iran on the road to democracy, Mohammad Reza Pahlavi added detours as he continued to exercise full authority over his people while minimizing the constitution's impact.

The Shah initiated a reform program in 1963 known as the "White Revolution"—called such as it was bloodless. It sought to curry favor with the poor through land reform as Iran's middle class became more vocal in its opposition to the Shah. The thinking behind the White Revolution was by doing so, the peasant class and workers would become more tolerant of the Shah's leadership. But as it was also a step towards westernization, it was criticized by a cleric named Ayatollah Ruhollah Khomeini. His criticism led to his being exiled in 1964, initially to Iraq and later to France.

As discontent with the Shah festered until erupting in the late 1970s, Islamic leaders began spouting their populist propaganda that "benevolent" Islam was the answer to their prayers for a human dignity denied to them by the current government. Leading the propagandist songbirds from his exiled perch was Ayatollah Ruhollah Khomeini, who encouraged a popular uprising against the Shah. The protests that erupted in Iran in 1978 ousted the Shah in 1979.

Of all the adjectives to describe Khomeini after his rise to power in Tehran, his "benevolent" interpretation of Islam would be one never witnessed by the Iranian people.

Ayatollah Ruhollah Khomeini the Magician Pulls an Islamist Theocracy Out of His Turban: Now You See Democracy, Now You Don't!

It is essential to understand Ayatollah Khomeini's background and the direction he ultimately led his nation as he was instrumental in manipulating the Islamic Revolution to his personal benefit. He did so in a tsunami of change that was able to sweep through the nation before the Iranian people truly understood what had hit them.

Born September 24, 1902, Ruhollah Khomeini would clearly become Iran's most influential political and religious leader. It could well be argued, almost a quarter century after his death, he was internationally one of the most influential as well since the political fallout generated by his Islamic Republic continues to impact on the world today. This influence was reflected early on by his selection as Time magazine's "Man of the Year" for 1979. He was described in Time as the "virtual face of Islam in Western popular culture." His ghost still lingers over a region of the world more chaotic now than when he was among the living, sowing those seeds of chaos.

Khomeini's family is said to have descended from the 7th Imam of the Ahl al-Bayt. He suffered the impact of violence early in life: his father was murdered when he was but a year old. He began studying the Koran (Islamic holy book also known as the "Quran") and the Persian language at six and learning religion the following year. His religious studies continued with assistance from his family.

Still in his teens, Khomeini attended seminary in the city of Arak. He later became a student of the Grand Ayatollah Abdul Karim Haeri Yazdi, joining him later in the holy city of Qom. The Grand Ayatollah was a fervent "Twelver"—one believing in the return of the "Twelfth Imam" or the "Mahdi" (a concept discussed later in a chapter entitled "The Belief and the Goal"). While Khomeini would be influenced by Yazdi's Twelver beliefs and his role as a teacher, he would not be influenced by his teacher's "studied disinterest in politics." Khomeini would become an extremely well-studied political activist.

Even if Islam did not prohibit it, Khomeini was probably not a person to whom one would be attracted as a "drinking buddy." He believed time not spent studying or to further the cause of Islam was time wasted. He once noted, "There is no room for play in Islam…It is deadly serious about everything." That probably explains the consistently dour expression always observed on Khomeini's face.

While Khomeini's studies extended to Islamic law, known as "shariah," and jurisprudence, he also dabbled in poetry, philosophy and mysticism—these last two subjects rarely taught at seminaries. His poetry reflected some surprising thoughts that he never expressed during his lifetime—poetry that oddly seemed to offer some limited criticism of spirituality and religion.

As a teacher himself, Khomeini stressed the interrelationship of religion to social and political issues of the day. In 1963, his political activism took flight as he began speaking out against the Shah. Members of the Shi'a clergy (Islam is divided into two sects—Sunni, and Shi'a—both of which are discussed in a later chapter entitled "Understanding Islam's Rise and Split") were well respected by the people for their stand against the Shah's efforts to Westernize during the Shah's White Revolution initiative. Such an initiative met with the mullahs' opposition. While the mullahs deemed the White Revolution dangerous, their opposition was probably tied more to the threat Westernization posed to their own personal power by offering an environment of independent thought, as opposed to one in which the mullahs did the thinking for the people.

As Khomeini continued to deliver speeches critical of the Shah, he was arrested in June 1963, triggering three days of riots. Put under house arrest, he was later released. But when the Shah held lavish celebrations in October 1964 to celebrate 2500 years of rule by the monarchy, Khomeini went on a verbal attack against the government again. His attacks were directed against the Shah's opulence and his capitulation to the U.S. government which he had allowed to retain jurisdiction over crimes committed by U.S. military personnel stationed in Iran.

This time Khomeini was arrested and held for six months, before being released and brought before Prime Minister Hasan Ali Mansur. Furious over Khomeini's failure to apologize, Mansur slapped Khomeini. Fourteen days later, Mansur was assassinated. Khomeini quickly departed Iran for a life in exile.

First stop for Khomeini in exile was the holy Shi'a city of Najaf, located in Iraq. This was followed by a one-year stay in Turkey before returning to Iraq in 1965. There he remained for 13 years until 1978, when he was asked to leave. His last stop in exile was the outskirts of Paris, France, for four months. Nearly 15 years after leaving Iran, his exile ended as the Shah's began.

Of more than forty books Khomeini authored during his lifetime, the most influential was one discussing his theory entitled "Vilayat-e faqih"—translation: "Guardianship of the Jurisconsult"—published in 1970. (Jurisconsult means clerical authority.) It represented a turn-around in his thinking from the 1940s when he accepted the concept of a limited monarchy under Iran's 1906 Constitution.

Thirty years later, however, any government built around a monarchy was unacceptable to Khomeini as "all human affairs" had to be strictly governed by shariah. It was his rationale that, since anyone holding a government position should have knowledge of shariah, then only those most knowledgeable about it should hold such positions. Unsurprisingly, he next reached the conclusion that only clerical authorities, such as himself, should rule the government. He clearly excluded government by monarchy or parliamentary body as he claims such was disavowed under Islam.

While Khomeini wrote about his clerical rule vision, he well understood it would not fly in the face of an informed Iranian people. Therefore, he limited publication of it to those within his circle of clerical thinkers who also were opposed to the Shah. Fortunately, for Khomeini, the Shah continued to ratchet up his people's anger against his rule, giving rise to their quest for change regardless of the personal sacrifice they had to make to get it—and, as would be evident in the end, one about which they were not all that well informed.

The 1977 death of Islamic reformist and philosopher Ali Shariati did much to propel Khomeini to the front of the political revolutionary leadership pack. Since Shariati had done a great deal to popularize an Islamic revival, with him gone and Khomeini now in the driver's seat, followers were drawn to him. Almost like a feeding frenzy, people began attributing mystical qualities to Khomeini. A late eighth century prophecy by the 7th Imam was circulated which claimed, "A man will come out from Qom, and he will summon people to the right path." It was said this prophecy pertained to Khomeini. Then people began to claim they were seeing Khomeini's face in the moon and other locations. As sighting reports increased, Khomeini became the Islamist equivalent of "Where's Waldo."

An Iranian scientific (allegedly) paper joined in to promote Khomeini's messianic image and criticize doubters such as the U.S. claiming:

> "Our toiling masses, fighting against world-devouring imperialism headed by the bloodsucking United States, have seen the face of their beloved Imam and leader, Khomeini the Breaker of Idols, in the moon. A few pipsqueaks cannot deny what a whole nation has seen with its own eyes."

Needless to say, the Iranian government never produced a photograph of "the man in the moon" sighting.

Khomeini, despite having a dour personality, knew how to play his image. The title of "Imam" in Iran was reserved for the twelve imams mentioned in the Koran by Muhammad, of which the twelfth was the Mahdi. Yet Khomeini's followers called him "Imam," propelling his mystical image, which he then made no effort to correctly modify. Other titles followed, such as "Deputy to the Twelfth Imam." Rumors spread that maybe Khomeini was, in fact, the Mahdi and when asked if this was so, again rather than correct a misconception, Khomeini would neither confirm nor deny it.

Unfortunately for most protestors against the Shah who joined the cause in hopes of paving a road back to democracy in Iran—perhaps through a transitional Islamic government—they quickly learned the road to Hell is paved with good intentions. What many Iranians believed would be a more benevolent government than that under the Shah would turn into a nightmare.

With Khomeini's popularity gaining ground and the Shah's fading, an onslaught of news media interviews sought to gain insights into what the soon-to-be leader of Iran had planned for his country. Only hindsight would reveal an eerie similarity between those 1979 interviews and ones the media had done with the soon-to-be leader of Cuba, Fidel Castro more than two decades earlier in the Sierra Maestra Mountains. Both leaders spoke about great promise for their countries; both left their listeners filled with hope; both spoke of democracy and both disappointed after coming to power by then instituting a system of government that only ended up replacing one dictatorship with another.

The deception Khomeini knew was necessary to play the media for fools was evident when he responded to an interviewer in November 1978 who inquired whether the Ayatollah would participate in a post-Shah government. Khomeini's response was:

> *"Personal desire, age, and my health do not allow me to personally have a role in running the country after the fall of the current system."*

After his return to Iran, however, an apparently rejuvenated Khomeini was verbally abusing those seeking to form a new government, saying:

> *"I will strike with my fists at the mouths of this government. From now on it is I who will name the government."*

An apparently much healthier Khomeini then embarked upon a killing rampage for the next decade that would see thousands of his countrymen, women and children executed in the name of Islam—a version of Islam as interpreted by him.

Khomeini did not hesitate to tell some "whoppers" in deceiving those hoping for a better life in Iran, as he did in sharing his beliefs with a London Times reporter:

> *"My belief and those of other Muslims are the issues that the Quran contains or those that have been uttered by the prophet of Islam and by rightful authorities after him. The root and essence of all those beliefs which are our dearest and most valuable beliefs is monotheism. According to this principle we believe that the creator of the world and of all beings in the universe including mankind is the one and only Exalted God who knows all and is capable of all things and to Him belong all things and objects.*
>
> *"This principle teaches us to be submissive only before the power of God and to obey no man unless obeying him be tantamount to obeying God. On the basis of this principle, no individual has a right to force any other man to bow to him. Furthermore, this principle of faith teaches us the principle of human freedom that is, no man has a right to deprive an individual or community of liberty, to legislate for them, to regulate their conduct according to his own*

understanding of it which is generally defective, or regulate the conduct of others according to his wishes or desires.

"Still more, from this principle we come to believe that legislation for man's progress is with God alone, just as the laws of creation and being are willed by Him. Man's happiness and perfection and that of the communities, are pawned to obedience to divine laws of which, mankind is informed through the Prophets...

"Man's degradation and fall is due to deprivation of his rights and his submission to other human beings. Therefore, we must rise in opposition to these shackles and chains of bondage and to challenge those who invite us to servitude, and to liberate ourselves and the community, so that we may all be servants of God and submit ourselves to Him.

"It is for this reason that our social rules and regulations begin with opposition to dictatorial and colonialistic powers. Also, from this principle of faith, and belief in monotheism, we get the inspiration that all men are equal before God, who has created them all. And all are His creatures and servants. This is the principle of equality of men and that man's only distinction and preference to one another rests in his virtue and freedom from perversion and sin. Therefore, all the things that upset this equality, and institute vain and nonsense distinctions in the community must be fought."

Khomeini's dictatorial rule would make the words he spoke above complete hypocrisy. By claiming "to obey no man unless obeying him be tantamount to obeying God," he was equating himself to God. By claiming Islam opposed dictatorship, the theocratic dictator was the pot calling the kettle black. By claiming Islam recognizes the principle of the equality of men, he deems himself as a man-of-the-cloth the most equal among all men. And while he believes in no equality for non-Muslims, he believes some Muslims (men) as being more equal than others (women).

On January 16, 1979, suffering from lymphatic cancer and recognizing he could no longer control his people's desire for new leadership, the Shah left for exile in Egypt, where he would die six months later. The Pahlavi Dynasty's run in Iran had come to an end. The "benevolent" Islamists, led by Ayatollah Khomeini, would let no grass grow under their feet in quickly filling the power vacuum. The world's first Islamic state came into being with the creation of the Islamic Republic of Iran on April 1, 1979.

The change the people wanted was about to happen, but the change that would happen would not be what they wanted.

There was an exceptionally large disconnect between Khomeini and his people—emotionally, politically and religiously. What they needed then in early 1979, he was incapable of delivering. The first sign of this was given when he was en route from Paris to Tehran by plane on February 1, 1979. Interviewed onboard the aircraft by ABC News reporter Peter Jennings who inquired of Khomeini: "What do you feel in returning to Iran," Khomeini responded: "Nothing."

As one observed film footage of Khomeini being greeted by millions of Iranians upon his return, one saw him express no emotion. One saw no smile of satisfaction cross his face. Occasionally one would see him reach out to touch a child—an act in such contrast to the fate he would bestow upon so many young children in the months ahead. The expressionless face Khomeini exhibited as he journeyed through the streets of Tehran that day would not be too different from the one frozen on his face a decade later as his body was transported along those same streets during his funeral procession. But, during that decade, tens of thousands of Iranians would be put to death by Khomeini's regime, given a far less ceremonial burial than he would receive.

After 15 years in exile, Ayatollah Khomeini had arrived home in Tehran, greeted by the cheers of millions of his countrymen who two weeks earlier celebrated the Shah's departure.

Khomeini quickly left no doubt who was in charge after his arrival. Once the Shah had left Iran, a provisional government was established, under the leadership of interim Prime Minister Shapour Bakhtiar. Khomeini said of that interim government, showing a *tender* side, "I shall kick their teeth in. I appoint the government." He immediately appointed an interim prime minister of his own, Mehdi Bazargan. Then, draping himself in the title equivalent of "God on Earth," he advised what he was establishing was, "God's government... since I have appointed him, he (Bazargan) must be obeyed." To underscore what he was saying, Khomeini made clear any challenge to his authority or that of his prime minister constituted a "revolt against God." (This became a favorite claim of Khomeini and his successor—any effort by the people to question Iran's clerical leadership was treason against God.)

Ayatollah Khomeini was well on his way to establishing an Islamic Republic. In March, a referendum was put to the people on an issue which they overwhelmingly approved:

> *"...the people's sovereignty to be replaced by the absolute sovereignty of God, and that Khomeini's concept of the 'government of the legal scholar' (Vilayat-e Faqih) be made the principle of the constitution."*

An initial draft of the constitution incorporated not only Khomeini's Islamist thinking based on a book he had written earlier ("Hukumat-e Islami") but was also modeled after the Constitution of the Fifth French Republic of 1958. It provided an almighty position to which was attached the title "Leader"—and to which the word "Supreme" would later be added by Khomeini. "Supreme Leader" was to be the highest ranking authority in the country both on a political and religious level. It was a position Ayatollah Khomeini would assume and hold until his death in 1989.

Perhaps it proved confusing for Iranians to understand their proposed constitution included implementation of elements both of an autocracy of theocracy and a democracy of the French constitutional government model. It may have been their belief the mix of these two was providing more of the latter and less of the former. If so, they were badly mistaken. They failed to realize by making the latter subordinate to the former, democracy was dead. Sadly, the only taste of democracy the Iranian people got out of their sacrifice was a democratic vote for a complete theocracy disguised as a partial democracy serving to open a door through which an autocratic monster would walk to replace the Shah.

While a democratic tune was heard by voters embracing one article of the constitution providing for the president of the Islamic Republic of Iran to be elected by popular vote, they failed to hear the autocratic dirge drowning democracy's tune out. In effect, the constitution that would giveth would also taketh away. While the constitution gave the people the right to vote for their president, it specified elsewhere in the document that sovereignty was vested in God, with said sovereignty to be exercised by the Supreme Leader and the "Guardian Council of the Constitution" appointing him.

Thus, the combination of these two constitutional provisions, which the public failed fully to grasp, was that their right to elect the president would be severely limited by the Supreme Leader's right to decide who could even run for office. As would later be done, while hundreds of candidates might seek to run for the office, Supreme Leader Khomeini had the right to deny almost all of them the right to do so, only allowing a select few of whom he personally approved.

The new constitution sought to replace Iran's 1906 Constitution. It was passed on October 24, 1979 in another public referendum, becoming law December 3, 1979 (later amended on July 28, 1989).

With the advantage of hindsight, one wonders whether voters really understood what it was they were voting for in the referendum. The Iran of pre-1979 would be decidedly different from the Iran of post-1979. It is doubtful the people, with the benefit of the post-1979 experience of mullah rule under their belt and with the benefit of another vote, would have willingly given such an endorsement.

Just like most Americans affected by the U.S. Patient Protection and Affordable Care Act enacted by President Barack Obama in 2010 (known as "Obamacare"), it is doubtful most Iranians affected by a new constitution proposed by Ayatollah Khomeini in 1979 took the time to read what, after their approval, would become law.

In the end, Ayatollah Khomeini played the Iranian people for fools. He led them to believe they were entering into a democracy, with the mullahs only playing a transitional role to achieve it. As would be demonstrated in the months ahead, however, the mullahs were there to stay, implementing a rule of law under which no one—man, woman, child or even those who originally led the revolution against the Shah—was safe as no one knew against whom Khomeini would turn next.

Khomeini Claims Bakhtiar as a Casualty in the Fight Against Democracy

To understand Khomeini's disdain for the interim government of Prime Minister Bakhtiar set up with the Shah's departure and whether or not that disdain was warranted (which certainly turns on whether one was an advocate for democracy or theocracy), it is important to briefly explain who Bakhtiar was and his eventual fate. Doing so will help one further understand Khomeini's mindset and his devious transition plan to power. It also provides further insights into the unique environment of the power vacuum in which men—some reasonable, some not—were operating at this time in Tehran.

Shapour Bakhtiar had served under the democratically elected Prime Minister Mohammad Mosaddeq who was toppled by the CIA in 1953, becoming the subject of the Grudge. When the Shah was then reinstated, Bakhtiar not only became a vocal critic of the monarchy but was actively involved in underground activities, of a peaceful nature, against it. A supporter of democracy and nationalism, he was imprisoned, off and on, for a period of six years although his moderate demands to effect change always remained peaceful.

It was Bakhtiar's longtime dedication and commitment—which had him leading the fight in the trenches for democratic rule—that won him an invitation by the Shah to create a civilian government as the Shah's regime was gasping its last breath. As one who had made immense personal sacrifice in a peaceful struggle for democracy, Bakhtiar was the right choice to help transition Iran from dictatorship to democracy.

Bakhtiar became prime minister—a position he accepted in hopes of preventing civil war from erupting in Iran as the mullahs and the communists teamed up to steal democracy from the people. Little did he know he would only have five weeks left as prime minister—without being given much chance to attempt a transition.

As the new man, (temporarily) in charge, Bakhtiar did all the right things: he lifted martial rule, allowed freedom of the press, released all political prisoners, dissolved the SAVAK, etc. He promised to hold elections to decide Iran's future. Despite the right things Bakhtiar did, he made one fatal mistake in his effort to be fair with the Iranian people—he allowed Khomeini to return to Iran. Unfortunately, it was Bakhtiar's history of fighting **for** democracy that sealed his fate with Khomeini for whom democracy was the furthest thing from his mind.

From his Paris perch, Khomeini refused to support Bakhtiar in his efforts to democratize Iran, tagging his prime ministership as illegitimate. With Khomeini worship at its height, the military defected to his side, and Bakhtiar proved unable to rally support to his. (Khomeini declared "jihad" against those soldiers who failed to join him.) When the Shah left Iran in January 1979, Bakhtiar was not far behind, leaving three months later for Paris.

Being a die-hard supporter of democracy, Bakhtiar continued to fight for democracy in Iran—although from France. Accordingly, Ayatollah Khomeini, now in control in Tehran, issued orders for Bakhtiar to be eliminated. An assassination attempt in July 1980 failed.

Although Khomeini would not live long enough to see it happen, Bakhtiar was assassinated 14 months after Khomeini's death. Bakhtiar and his personal secretary were murdered, with a bread knife, in Bakhtiar's home, in a Paris suburb. It was determined four assassins were involved. Two ultimately escaped to Iran; two were arrested in Switzerland–one of whom was the great grandnephew of former Iranian president Hashemi Rafsanjani and both of whom were extradited to France to stand trial.

Of the two who stood trial, Rafsanjani's great grandnephew was acquitted while his cohort received an 18 year jail sentence—serving 16 years before being released. Just like the hero's welcome given to Lockerbie plane bomber Abdelbaset al-Megrahi upon his return to Libya in 2009, Bakhtiar's assassin received a similar welcome upon his return to Iran in 2010.

Khomeini's Roadmap to Theocracy Continues

As mentioned, with Khomeini's return to Tehran on February 1, 1979, and despite the fact Bakhtiar was serving as prime minister, Khomeini appointed his own prime minister, Mehdi Bazargan. Bazargan's appointment was yet another cleverly disguised move by Khomeini to give the appearance Iran was moving towards democracy when it was not. When all was said and done, Khomeini the Magician would pull out of his turban, not the anticipated democracy, but the long-planned theocracy he had envisioned in Iran for years. Therefore, a brief background about Bazargan is needed, again to understand how certain personalities fit into Khomeini's game plan.

Bazargan Becomes an Unwitting Vehicle Traveling Khomeini's Roadmap

Bazargan was a prominent Iranian scholar and well respected intellectual who, while having grown up in Tehran, had been educated in France. Upon graduation, he joined the French army and fought in World War II. Like Bakhtiar, he went on to serve under the democratically elected Prime Minister Mohammad Mosaddeq, subject of the Grudge, and was imprisoned for some of his political activities. It was not long, however, after becoming Khomeini's prime minister on February 4, 1979, Bazargan—as an advocate for democracy—found himself locking horns with Islamists, including Khomeini himself.

Bazargan fought against an Islamic state, but was repeatedly defeated in his efforts to do so by Khomeini and his minions. Although he believed a democratic Muslim state was possible, this was totally contrary to

Khomeini's thinking. The more Bazargan pushed for democracy, the more he witnessed that the government evolving in Iran wreaked of theocracy.

Nine months after his appointment as prime minister, Bazargan resigned in the aftermath of the seizure by student militants of the U.S. Embassy and their taking of the personnel there hostage. Bazargan knew the initiative had been personally approved by Khomeini and also knew it stood in direct contravention of international law. His hopes for democracy dashed and witnessing Iran's total disregard for the rule of law, Bazargan could no longer support a renegade regime.

Even out of office, the courageous former prime minister, remaining in Iran, continued to oppose Khomeini's establishment of a theocratic state. He was harassed by young Islamist revolutionaries for doing so. Despite this, he took the government on. He objected to the economic disruption implementation of Islamist principles was causing, the "fear factor" it was introducing to citizen's daily lives as one never knew if and when one would suddenly run afoul of the government and the persecutions for committing a sin against God, etc. (Between 1979-1985, Khomeini's economic policies—or lack thereof—would increase poverty by 45%.)

Bazargan sought to run for the presidency of Iran in 1985 but, due to his strong anti-Islamist attacks against the government, he was one of those denied by Khomeini from running. Despite his concerns about the direction the Islamic Revolution had taken, Bazargan believed in the concept, "my country, right or wrong." He remained in Iran, committed to fighting Islamism and did so until his death ten years later in 1995.

Khomeini's Sleight of Hand Sneaks the Constitution Through

With Khomeini's players in place and a draft constitution giving the appearance he favored a hybrid democratic-theocratic government, a plebiscite supporting replacement of the monarchy with an Islamic government passed in late March 1979 with 98% vote approval. Few Iranians understood what had hit them: the mullahs would have full control over all governmental assets and responsibilities to the point of impacting, on a daily basis, the life of every single Iranian citizen.

As Khomeini's henchmen gathered steam, they reversed the actions taken by Iran's earlier democracy-motivated Prime Minister Bakhtiar. The newspapers to which he had given freedom of the press were shut down; those critical of various government actions were beaten; political parties were banned; etc. Khomeini's fear of democracy was made clear by his statement:

> *"The club of the pen and the club of the tongue is the worst of clubs, whose corruption is a hundred times greater than other clubs."*

Khomeini well knew freedom of speech was the biggest threat to his theocracy and could not be tolerated.

The draft constitution was re-written to incorporate additional Islamist controls (e.g., creating a Supreme Leader ruler) and limiting democratic freedoms for the people. In a telling sign by those who recognized the danger of "one man, one ayatollah rule," many mullahs failed to support Khomeini's end run to establish a theocratic government.

The Constitution of 1979 was passed but, unfortunately, for those Iranians hoping for democracy, it was nothing like the constitution at the turn of the century that preserved some measure of human dignity.

Two aspects under the new constitution were extremely noteworthy for the impact they would have domestically, on one hand, and internationally, on the other.

First, Ayatollah Khomeini became the all-powerful "Oz" from whom all decisions flowed. He would be known as "the Supreme Leader" whose decisions were not appealable and whose authority was only terminated by his death. He controlled the daily activities of each and every citizen.

Second, the Constitution was written to be extraterritorial. Ayatollah Khomeini emphasized this point in many of the speeches he delivered—even before the constitution was passed. In January 1979 he lectured:

> "The governments of the world should know that… Islam will be victorious in all the countries of the world, and Islam and the teachings of the Koran will prevail all over the world."

In March 1980, he encouraged followers:

> "We must strive to export our Revolution throughout the world."

That is exactly what Iran's Constitution of 1979 mandated.

The extraterritoriality of the Iranian constitution and mandate to spread the Islamic Revolution globally did not give one a "warm and fuzzy" feeling it was love and joy Khomeini sought to spread. The extraterritoriality aspect of the Constitution took on a much more sinister meaning when reflected upon within the context of the following instruction given by Khomeini to his followers:

> "Islam makes it incumbent on all adult males, provided they are not disabled or incapacitated, to prepare themselves for the conquest of (other) countries so that the writ of Islam is obeyed in every country in the world. . . . Those who know nothing of Islam pretend that Islam counsels against war. Those (who say this) are witless. Islam says: 'Kill all the unbelievers just as they would kill you all! Does this mean that Muslims should sit back until they are devoured by (the unbelievers)?' Islam says: 'Kill them (the non-Muslims), put them to the sword and scatter (their armies).' Does this mean sitting back until (non-Muslims) overcome us?... Islam says: 'Whatever good there is exists thanks to the sword and in the shadow of the sword!' People cannot be made obedient except with the sword! The sword is the key to Paradise, which can be opened only for the Holy Warriors!"

Iran has the only constitution in the world that mandates such extraterritorial applicability—i.e., that the Islamic Revolutionary wind that brought shariah to Iran must continue to spread throughout the world. Khomeini saw Iran as the catalyst by which Islamic law would become effective in both Muslim and non-Muslim nations under a global caliphate. Under this caliphate, non-Muslims would have the choice to convert to Islam or be put to the sword.

Ironically, while Iran's leadership whines about the Grudge and U.S. actions contrary to the will of the Iranian people, it sees nothing wrong with its extraterritorial mandate to impose shariah in other countries contrary to the will of their populations.

Gradually, Khomeini revealed his true disdain for democracy. At a speech at a school in Qom in August 1979, he said:

> "Those who are trying to bring corruption and destruction to our country in the name of democracy will be oppressed. They are worse than Bani-Ghorizeh Jews, and they must be hanged. We will oppress them by God's order and God's call to prayer."

As a "man-of-the-cloth," Ayatollah Khomeini's constant thirst for violence was particularly telling about the role he foresaw Islam playing.

It is clear from Khomeini's remarks above he believed a particular ill, by definition, attached to democracy: corruption. His rationale for this was given in an exchange with intellectuals clamoring for greater freedoms:

> "Yes, we are reactionaries, and you are enlightened intellectuals: You intellectuals do not want us to go back 1400 years. You, who want freedom, freedom for everything, the freedom of parties, you who want all the freedoms, you intellectuals: freedom that will corrupt our youth, freedom that will pave the way for the oppressor, freedom that will drag our nation to the bottom."

Those Iranians who had been loyal to the Shah but decided to stay behind would soon regret their decision. Islamic revolutionary "kangaroo" courts left many of those accused not knowing the basis of the charges against them, even after being sentenced to death. The crime of which many would eventually learn they were guilty was "fighting against the Twelfth Imam"—another crime equivalent to treason against God.

Also, targeted were fellow revolutionaries, such as communists, with whom Khomeini had allied himself out of necessity then but for whom he had no need now. Sent to the executioner as well were citizens, including children, upon whom the strict lifestyle dictated by shariah had been imposed so quickly, they had no knowledge they were violating the law.

Iran proved to be a harsh environment in which ignorance of shariah was no defense. Khomeini became an "equal opportunity" executioner as the bodies of men, women and children piled up. The body count under Khomeini continued until his death on June 4, 1989, at the age of 86.

Unfortunately, his successor as Supreme Leader, Ayatollah Ali Khamenei, would prove to be just as blood thirsty under his own brand of "spiritual guidance"—guidance which would see Iran become one of the world's most prolific executioners.

Khomeini's Last Minute Constitutional Manipulation Paves the Way for a New Supreme Leader

Just like Harry Truman found himself nominated for the first time to run for Vice President of the U.S. on the Democratic Party ticket with President Franklin Delano Roosevelt who was making what would be his fourth and last run for that office before his death, Ali Khamenei benefitted from a similar situation. He saw Khomeini live long enough to change his "Will" as to who would succeed him.

Grand Ayatollah Hossein Montazeri had previously been approved by Khomeini and the Assembly of Experts in 1985 to succeed Khomeini as Supreme Leader. Montazeri was the only cleric with the religious credentials to so serve. But in early 1989, just months before his death, Khomeini received a letter from Montazeri calling for greater freedoms for the people, criticizing prison and police conditions as being far worse under Khomeini than under the Shah—attacking Khomeini's intolerance and brutality and the executions of thousands of Iranian citizens. Montazeri said in his letter:

> "The world is slowly gaining the impression that we in Iran are concerned only with killing people."

The letter was leaked to the European press. Furious, Khomeini immediately sought to change the Supreme Leader succession, making Khamenei his beneficiary instead. However, Khamenei lacked the requisite level of scholarly credentials to rank as a "Grand" Ayatollah, as required by the Constitution. Not to be denied, Khomeini called for a constitutional change, which was rammed through, denying Montazeri the coveted position, but never silencing him. (To date this is the only constitutional amendment—dated July 28, 1989—to be made.)

Although having been a founder along with Khomeini of the Islamic Revolution, Montazeri did distance himself from Khomeini on an important issue—the return of the Twelfth Imam. He said:

> "Using this belief as a political means for deceiving people of leading them to certain decisions is wrong."

The reference to deception suggested Montazeri well recognized Khomeini was seeking to secure power for himself by claiming people had to empower him in order to prepare the way for the Twelfth Imam's return.

Still respectful of Montazeri as "the fruit of my life," Khomeini—put him out to pasture—suggesting he retire to teach in Qom. Khomeini's death and replacement by Ayatollah Ali Khamenei did not silence Montazeri. He continued to criticize the new Supreme Leader as well. It was Montazeri's firm belief too much of a political role was undertaken by the Supreme Leader and that Khamenei was much too junior to be issuing fatwas.

Khamenei was not as tolerant as Khomeini towards Montazeri, eventually putting him under house arrest for a six year period between 1997-2003. Upon his release, Montazeri's license to teach was restored. In that capacity, he endeavored to teach a moderate generation of theologians. He continued the fight for human rights on behalf of his people, also issuing a statement in support of protestors of the 2009 presidential election after Khamenei stole it from voters.

Montazeri objected to the government practice of stealing elections. He warned:

> *"Either officials change their methods and give freedom to the people, and stop interfering in elections, or the people will rise up with another revolution."*

Before his death, later that same year, Montazeri issued two fatwas on issues that required tremendous courage to do so.

One pertained to the Baha'i Faith. This is a religion which originated in Iran in 1844 and one of the world's newest religions. It was founded by a Persian merchant who suggested he was a figure prophesized in the Koran. The religion promotes three things anathema to Islam—equality, education and science. Today, one of the largest populations in the world of its followers resides in Iran. For decades, followers have been persecuted for their teachings—running contrary to Islam—so that they are accused by the Iranian government of being apostates. As such, they are subjected to harassment and/or death.

Montazeri was the first respected religious leader who dared address this issue, requiring all to respect the rights of Baha'I Faith followers as equal to those of Iranian citizens. What makes this fatwa so remarkable is that it is considered un-Islamic to support a religion other than Islam. (When Muhammad did this recognizing the Meccan religion, he later renounced it suggesting "the Devil made me do it"—giving rise to "the Satanic verses," discussed in a later section entitled with the same name.)

The second fatwa was just as remarkable. In August 2009, four months before his death, Montazeri issued a fatwa stating the regime team of Supreme Leader Khamenei and President Ahmadinejad lacked legitimacy as "all violence against the people violates the principles of Islam." Interestingly, what adds to the impact of this fatwa is that the concept of velayat-e faqih, which Khomeini used as a basis for justifying his rule, was the brainchild of Montazeri who, with this fatwa, criticized its use in this manner.

Getting a fatwa issued is similar to playing the television game show "Jeopardy." In the game, contestants are required effectively to formulate a response as a question. It appears to be a similar drill by which fatwas are issued. An article entitled, "Merciful God Hears the Cries of the Oppressed" by Katajun Amirpur details this drill.

Fatwas must be properly formulated in response to a question (i.e., a fatwa cannot be issued without a "source of emulation" raising the matter). Thus, the fatwa must begin with, "What is to be done if..." Accordingly, the "source of emulation" for Montazeri was a question posed by a well-respected theologian and student of his, Moshen Kadivar, about a ruler's legitimacy if the trust of the people has been abused. Amirpur notes the gist of Montazeri's response was:

> *"If a ruler has neglected his secular and religious duties and abused the trust of the people, then his rule is illegitimate. Then he must step down of his own accord without being asked. Should he attempt to retain power through violence, lies and deception, the faithful have a duty to depose him using all legally permitted means. No believer may shirk this obligation for any reason whatsoever."*

Hopefully, Montazeri's fatwa will prove valid as a future revolutionary vehicle to overthrow a brutal regime.

It May Be God's Constitution, Law & Koran but Supreme Leader & Guardian Council Interpret Them on God's Behalf

At this point, it is necessary to understand the role of the "Guardian Council of the Constitution" in which constitutional sovereignty was to be jointly exercised with the Supreme Leader.

As mentioned, while the Constitution's sovereignty was vested in God, it was to be exercised by the Supreme Leader and the Guardian Council appointing him. The Council consists of twelve men who, as a single body, exercise a great deal of power. The relationship between the Supreme Leader and the Guardian Council sounds, and is, somewhat incestuous as, either directly or indirectly, the Supreme Leader wields significant control over a group that is supposed to have the authority to remove him.

Of the twelve Guardian Council members, six must be experts in Islamic law "conscious of the present needs and the issues of the day," but are to be selected directly by the Supreme Leader. Of the remaining six, they must be jurists "specializing in different areas of law." Although not selected by the Supreme Leader, they are elected by Iran's parliament from among those nominated by the head judge—who is appointed by the Supreme Leader, thus providing him with indirect influence over the other six members.

While the Guardian Council has responsibility for interpreting the Constitution, it is obvious from the members' selection process, the Supreme Leader maintains a steady "hand on the till" concerning any impact the Guardian Council can have. It also plays a role in approving presidential candidates and laws passed by parliament, ensuring that only those laws reinforcing the country's values, as interpreted by the Guardian Council, become effective. This ensures only a single set of Islamic values is permitted to progress. But, again, the influence of the Supreme Leader is absolute.

Manned by Islamists, the Guardian Council—implementing the Supreme Leader's guidance—maintain a tight cap on how the Constitution is interpreted and the direction in which the government moves domestically.

Interpretation by Islamists is not just Limited to the Constitution

Islamists are also able effectively to use the Koran and teachings of the Prophet Muhammad to control followers. Teachings and verses favorable to reinforcing the Islamist's belief are often selected and given interpretations most supportive of those beliefs. Islamists inform followers they are prohibited from making their own interpretations as they are mere "mortals," unsophisticated and lacking the knowledge to interpret the meaning of Muhammad's messages. Therefore, Islamists argue, followers must accept the Islamist's meaning without question.

But what happens when something in the Koran is ambiguous or otherwise unclear—such as two verses seeming to say different things? As a religious scholar or leader, the Islamist apparently is qualified to make that interpretation, possessing the appropriate knowledge to know what Muhammad meant. But, arguably, there is a disconnect here, suggestive of a double standard and hypocrisy. By providing his own interpretation, it would seem the Islamist—as a "mortal" without any specific elevated spiritual status—runs afoul of the very prohibition he imposes on his followers.

CHAPTER THREE

The Mullahs' Hypocritical Oath

An uninhabited South Atlantic island for centuries has served as a breeding ground for the albatross; lacking predators, the population has thrived.

A few years ago, mice made their way to the island. The mice began preying upon the much larger albatross chicks that outweigh them 200-fold. Now, it is the mice population that is thriving.

Observers are surprised that despite being outweighed, the mice do not hesitate to attack the larger chicks. Even more surprisingly, however, is the fact the albatross parents do nothing to protect their offspring. As the mice attack, the albatross parents appear totally oblivious to the fact that a serious threat to their offspring even exists.

There is an explanation for this, scientists say. The albatross parents, having never known predators on the island, have become "ecologically naive" as to the existence of any threat to their chicks. Sadly, in a few more years, such naivety may well result in the devastation of the albatross population.

An ecologically naive parent—in this case the albatross—is a freak of nature. All through the evolution of the animal kingdom, offspring have depended on parents to protect them from and teach them about danger. Absent such protection, species would disappear from the face of the Earth.

One need only look at recent photographs of the remarkable rescue of her puppies by a mother dog in Santa Rose de Temuco, Chile. As firefighters worked to put out a burning house fire, the mother repeatedly braved smoke and flames to rescue her puppies. As she brought each one out, she placed it in the safest place she could find—on a step on the fire truck at the scene. She refused to stop until her entire brood was safe.

This natural instinct to protect offspring is just as true of mankind as it is of the animal kingdom.

It is tragic, then, when a child, obviously dependent upon a parent for survival, fails to receive the necessary nurturing to be able to recognize and understand when a threat to the child's survival exists.

The mullah who preaches to a child the glory of sacrificing one's life as a suicide bomber—an indoctrination in Iran beginning at the tender age of four or five when they are shown animated videos glorifying the act—clearly represents such a threat to that child.

It is difficult to understand how Iranian parents can simply stand idly by, allowing their children to be convinced the short-term "livelihood" of being a suicide bomber is acceptable as falling within the natural order of things. Islam has served to make such parents ecologically naive and freaks of nature. If love for a child cannot cause parents to rethink whether what a mullah, who says he speaks on behalf of Islam, teaches, what can motivate parents to question such unnatural teachings?

Several years ago the on-line publication "6th Column Against Jihad" summed up the impact of Islam on Muslims:

> *"Islam kills Muslims off in the worst possible way, by destroying their humanity at the earliest possible age in life...their lives are a living hell."*

Caught between one's natural instinct to live, imposed by God, and an unnatural one to die, and imposed by religious zealots claiming it is the path to God, children being instructed in Islamism find "their lives are living hells." In effect, children are put early in life into the bind of being a "good Muslim"—by taking the life of a non-believer—or being a "bad Muslim" and preserving it.

How can one's religious teachings convince parents any God responsible for creating human life is so willing to see it destroyed in a manner glorified by man in the name of God? How can one's religious teachings blind any sane adult to the danger such thinking represents to a child?

How can one's religious teachings prevent a parent from challenging the hypocrisy of a mullah who casually teaches someone else's child to sacrifice his life but has never been known to teach his own child to do the same?

These mullahs, while electing to "talk the talk" have failed to "walk the walk." They are perfectly happy to promote the hypocritical theme of "do as I say, not as I do." Unlike doctors who take a Hippocratic Oath to preserve life, Islamist mullahs take a "Hypocritical Oath" to destroy it. The safest job a Muslim can have to avoid the "suicide bomber's draft" is to become a cleric as there is no reported case of a mullah applying for the job.

Of course, hypocrisy serves as no deterrent to the Islamist as long as his followers continue to accept such an obvious double standard.

The mullahs' mindset stands in stark contrast to that of "The Four Chaplains" of World War II fame, known as the "Immortal Chaplains."

During World War II, four chaplains—two Protestant pastors, a Catholic priest, and a Jewish rabbi—were serving onboard the USAT (U.S. Army Transport) Dorchester in the North Atlantic, when it was torpedoed at night by a German submarine. With insufficient lifejackets for all, the four surrendered theirs so that others might live. As the ship went down, survivors recalled seeing the four men-of-the-cloth, standing arm-in-arm, each praying in his own faith for the survival of the others onboard fighting for their lives. The four "walked the walk" and—having preached about the value of human life—sacrificed, in a final tribute to their fellow man, their own lives to save the lives of others.

In the card game of an Islamist's life, mullahs succeed in teaching others to play the suicide card by manipulating followers not to play the only card capable of defeating such Islamist hatred—independent thought. Denied independent thought by his Islamist teacher, the follower is left unable to recognize hypocrisy even when it stares him in the face.

Supreme Leader's Rubber Stamp Assembly of Experts

Iran's Constitution makes mention of an "Assembly (or Council) of Experts." This is a body, first elected by direct public vote to serve in 1983, of more than eighty Islamic cleric scholars who are vested with the authority either to elect or dismiss the Supreme Leader. Members serve for eight year terms. Today, the Guardian Council approves eligibility for all candidates through either written or oral examination.

Only if the Assembly cannot find a qualified candidate for Supreme Leader is it permitted to elect one of its own members. The public elects members to the Assembly from among a list of candidates who have previously been vetted by the Guardian Council. Those members serve for eight year terms, meeting two times each year for a minimum of two days.

The first successor selected to follow Supreme Leader Khomeini was his hand-picked choice of Ayatollah Montazeri in 1985. When Khomeini informed the Assembly in a letter dated 69 days before his June 4, 1989 death dismissing Montazeri and replacing him with Khamenei, the Assembly moved expeditiously to do so. There should be one conclusion drawn from this quick replacement and the fact the Assembly has never acted during the history of its existence yet to remove a sitting Supreme Leader: the Assembly is essentially a rubber stamp of the Supreme Leader.

After the June 2009 presidential election, some Iranians hoped that the Assembly would make an effort to question decisions made by Ayatollah Khamenei that have moved the country towards increased authoritarianism. But the body has never tried to do so. Undoubtedly, one contributing factor to this reluctance is that Khamenei has made several members of the Assembly very wealthy.

Perception Clouds Reality As Ayatollah Ruhollah Khomeini Grabs the Reins of Power

The perception by the Iranian people when Mohammad Reza Pahlavi became Shah in 1941 had been Tehran would edge toward democracy, with the reinstatement of its earlier constitution. That perception proved wrong. The reality was the Shah led the country into a dictatorship.

Similarly, the perception of Ayatollah Khomeini by both the Iranian people and the international community was that of an enlightened leader—a Mahatma Gandhi who would peacefully lead the fight for human rights. Again, perceptions proved wrong. As Ayatollah Khomeini established himself as Iran's "Founding Father," he quickly built a reputation for himself quite contrary to the one built by America's Founding Fathers. Everything America's Founding Fathers treasured as a basic human right vested in its citizens, Khomeini stripped away from Iranian citizens.

The unfortunate reality for Iranians was it was not a Mahatma Gandhi they got, but a Pol Pot. He turned on the very people whose hopes he had ridden to power—imposing upon them the will of Allah as written in Islam's teachings, but only as he interpreted that will. He would rule Iran for a decade with an iron fist as thousands of Iranians would die under his brutal leadership.

U.S. perceptions of Khomeini proved wrong, as well. As Khomeini came to power, the U.S. Ambassador to the UN under President Carter, Andrew Young, had gone so far as to suggest the cleric was "some kind of saint." But, supporting the Shah's abdication and Khomeini's accession to power has proven to be the worst U.S. foreign policy disaster of the 20th century—one for which America continues to suffer the consequences today. In supporting Khomeini, President Carter clearly backed the wrong horse, triggering the Islamofascist nightmare that now confronts the international community.

Anointed Supreme Leader (a more appropriate title would have been "Dictator for Life"), Khomeini launched a bloody purge the likes of which have not been seen since the reign of terror unleashed by the French Revolution's Maximilien Robespierre almost two centuries earlier. In the early days of the French Revolution, some outside observers saw an evolution that would lead to the birth of liberty; others—such as the 18th century statesman Edmund Burke—quickly saw a France descending into anarchy and tyranny followed by despotism. The same would become true for Iran as well.

Unfortunately, President Carter was no Edmund Burke. It was soon realized the repression under the Shah paled in comparison to that under Khomeini—as did the tally of its victims—with Khomeini eliminating all opposition to ensure his theocratic rule. Within months, the Iranian people were perhaps wishing the Shah's "kinder, gentler" SAVAK intelligence agency, they had so come to hate, would return. But it would not return as, this time, it was Khomeini's brutal minions dehumanizing them.

Shariah justified the executions by Khomeini of underage girls who innocently violated tenets of a religion about which they knew very little, if anything. Eventually, even those in Iran who had helped bring Khomeini to power felt the sting of the religious leader's arbitrary rulings, many of whom were executed as well.

Nothing would drive the point home better to Americans than the U.S. Embassy hostage crisis. In dealing with Iran's theocrats, negotiators would find the Iranians far beyond the realm of reason, refusing to honor even the basic tenets of international law.

Khomeini Approves U.S. Embassy Takeover and Seizure of U.S. Diplomats

To fan the flames of the Islamic revolution against the U.S., Khomeini personally approved the takeover of the U.S. Embassy in Tehran on November 4, 1979 by Islamist students and militants who seized 52 U.S. diplomats as hostages. (Although never proven, several of these hostages later swore current President Mahmoud Ahmadinejad was one of those students.) While the motivation for the seizure was tied to the U.S. granting a visa to the Shah to receive medical treatment in October 1979, it may have simply been the triggering event of prior planning by the militants.

Khomeini labeled the U.S. Embassy a "Den of Espionage." The Islamist students scoured the embassy, obtaining reams of classified documents, either salvaged from shredders or not destroyed, which they then made public.

Following the seizure of the U.S. Embassy, Ayatollah Khomeini bragged, "The Americans can't do a damn thing." He was right. This clear violation of international law resulted in the only loss of U.S. territory since World War II. It was this act that proved a wake-up call for President Carter who, although recognizing the hostages were "victims of terrorism and anarchy," proved incapable of acting. Ironically, his paralysis was caused by an Iranian government which he had helped secure power.

Due to the unpopularity of the U.S. caused by its close relationship to the Shah, the seizure of the U.S. Embassy and taking of its hostages received popular domestic support. Khomeini saw the incident as pulling his divided people together. He also saw the popular excitement as dimming domestic focus on the constitution Khomeini wished to ram through. Again he proved right.

As Iranian confidence in its ability to confront the Great Satan increased, U.S. confidence in its President to end the crisis decreased. Carter authorized a secret rescue attempt of the hostages that was initiated on the morning of April 24, 1980. The effort, known as "Operation Eagle Claw," would do little to restore the American public's confidence in its President.

The operation involved eight RH-53D helicopters from the aircraft carrier USS Nimitz (CVN-68) flying to a remote road serving as an airstrip in eastern Iran. Of the eight, only six helicopters were able to continue on to the second operational phase, landing at the "Desert One" site where C-130 transport and refueling aircraft awaited their arrival. Due to radio silence, the helicopters were unable to request authorization to fly above a blinding sandstorm, resulting in mechanical problems that caused one aircraft to return to the carrier and the other to be abandoned.

As the mission required a minimum of six helicopters, the Desert One operation continued on. However, upon arrival at their second site, yet another helicopter developed problems. The Desert One commander, therefore, requested and received authorization from President Carter to abort the mission.

Unfortunately, it was after the mission was aborted that things only got worse. As the helicopters were getting into position for refueling, one clipped a refueling tanker aircraft, killing all eight servicemen onboard. The remaining aircraft made it back, but only after attempting one of the most disastrous rescue attempts in U.S. history.

One can only imagine what Iranian Islamists felt at this point. Having seen their revolution topple the Shah, having seen the Shah suffer from cancer and in the throes of death, having seized the U.S. Embassy with the U.S. unable to respond, and now having witnessed an attempted rescue turn into an unmitigated disaster, the Islamists had to believe Allah was "running interference" for them—undermining any U.S. effort to challenge them. Khomeini wasted no time in running with this, claiming "divine intervention" was taking place in his favor. This claim fit in beautifully with his strategy of playing up the Twelfth Imam card with the Iranian public.

While the exact details of the Desert One rescue plan still remain unclear, it is deemed unlikely to have succeeded—even with the full complement of aircraft—since the hostages were no longer held in one location together but scattered about.

There had been some Iranian leaders, like President Banisadr, who—for supporting the release of the hostages—fell out of favor with Khomeini when the Supreme Leader claimed "divine intervention" caused Desert One to fail. The failed rescue attempt contributed toward ending the careers of two presidents—Banisadr (who was impeached) and Carter (who lost his re-election).

The Iranian Hostage Crisis lasted for a total of 444 days, ending in the diplomats' release on January 20, 1981, only moments after a new U.S. President—Ronald Reagan, who had vowed to undertake stronger action if the hostages were not released—took the oath of office.

It would have been interesting to do a psychological profile of Khomeini. There were clearly hot buttons that drove his thirst for the violence and the brutality accentuating his rule. He became judge, jury and executioner for so many Iranians who probably never understood the offense of which they had been accused; similar to Stalin's slaughter of millions of his countrymen who simply found their names one day on an executioner's list.

Khomeini held nothing but contempt and hatred toward the U.S. and Israel, which explained his decision to violate international law and incur international condemnation by seizing the U.S. embassy. It was as if the Supreme Leader lived in a schizophrenic daze, making outlandish claims that the root of all Iran's woes stemmed from these two countries.

Apparently unable to distinguish between the woes for which the U.S. was responsible and those for which Israel was, he offered the outlandish generalization:

> *"All our calamities and all our problems are from America and all our calamities, and all our problems are from Israel…Iran's economy is in the hands of America and Israel. Iranian markets are outside the hands of Muslim merchants."*

He repeatedly asserted in his speeches Iran's commitment to the destruction of both countries.

Khomeini talked about the failure of the West to "allow the establishment of a single leader in Iran's secular and Islamic universities because they fear the ideas of Iranian men" (making no mention of women)—as if Western states even controlled Iran's educational centers. He voiced no problem with the education he promoted for young Iranians, which focused strictly on Islam and rote memorization of the Koran. Ironically, while promoting the "freedoms present in the Koran," he expected none of those so-called freedoms to be exercised in challenging his authority and decisions. It was either blind obedience to the Supreme Leader or death.

The Supreme Leader never allowed facts to interfere with his own accounts of history. Even the split under Islam between Sunnis and Shiites, he professed, was due to Western influence. This would have been a remarkable feat for Western influence which, at the time the split occurred more than a millennium earlier, was anything but influential.

Improving Educational Access for Men by Decreasing It for Women

In a country where the number of female college graduates exceeds the number of males, there should be praise for its Department of Education in influencing such a high graduation rate. But, if that Department of Education is situated in Iran, no such praise is warranted—instead, the Department is instructed to decrease the number of female graduates by limiting access to university courses.

In a country where religion strongly favors men over women, it is deflating for men who fail to do as well scholastically as women.

For years now, women have been outperforming men—outnumbering them by 3-to-2 in passing recent university entrance exams.

Three dozen universities in Iran have given notice that a combined total of 70 degreed courses will be limited to "single gender" classes in a clear act of government-sanctioned sex discrimination to reduce the number of female graduates to fall below that of men.

Hardline clerics have registered their concerns about the social impact in a country where the men may not be smart enough to get the message: as the educational level of women in Iran rises, the number of women marrying Iranian men has decreased.

Although Iran boasts the highest ratio of female-to-male graduates in the world, it is not a statistic of which Islamists are proud.

One university attempted to justify a need to exclude women since 98% of female graduates are left jobless. Whether this is just a ploy by the university at the government's request to justify reduced course levels for women or not, the claim would only seem to add flames to the fire of sex discrimination by suggesting employers are heeding Islamist leaders who discourage giving jobs to women. It is clearly an effort by Tehran to deny female equality.

It is interesting that women joined the men in the 1979 protests against the Shah, supporting the return of the Ayatollah Khomeini. Just before the Shah fell, he was in the process of westernizing education in the country—which included improving rights for women. That effort ended in 1979 as the mullahs' influence focused on the Islamization of the school curriculum. Little did women realize at the time while their rights had increased under the Shah, they would decrease under Khomeini.

The damage done in Iran by the Islamization of the curriculum has taken its toll. A 2003 independent study by China of the top 500 universities in the world did not list a single Iranian (or Arab) college.

The Satanic Verses

Just as Khomeini had no concerns about violating international law at the beginning of his rule by seizing the U.S. Embassy, international law caused him no concerns towards the end of his life either.

In February 1989, never at a loss to embrace hatred and violence, Khomeini issued a death sentence against a citizen of another country—the British author, Salman Rushdie. Rushdie had written a book entitled "The Satanic Verses" which Khomeini claimed disparaged Islam. A novel published in 1988, the book was inspired, in part, by the life of the Prophet Muhammad, with the title referring to a group of pagan verses—initially part of the Koran—but later deleted when their interpretation was questioned by Muslim believers.

Before discussing Rushdie's book, one need understand the origin of the Satanic verses within its religious context.

It is said the Prophet Muhammad was seeking to convert the people of Mecca to Islam. He was reciting verses revealed to him by the Archangel Gabriel, when he suddenly began reciting additional verses he never before had recited. The Meccans were pleasantly surprised upon hearing these verses as they suggested Muhammad was saying other religions, in addition to Islam, were acceptable.

The essence of the additional verses appeared to be a renunciation by Muhammad of his earlier uncompromising position Islam alone was the only religion, and there was but one God. This renunciation arose when Muhammad's recital suggested the goddesses worshiped by the Meccans were real and responsive. The Meccans, therefore, rejoiced in the renunciation, joining Muhammad in prayer by ritualistically prostrating themselves.

It is said the Angel Gabriel then castigated Muhammad for reciting the additional verses, which had not emanated from Gabriel but from Satan, who had spoken to Muhammad, pretending to be Gabriel. Accordingly, Allah abolished the revelations, which Satan had proposed to Muhammad, who then recanted these Satanic verses himself, thereby continuing the persecution of Meccans.

Interestingly, one interpretation of Muhammad's Satanic verses error according to some scholars was an attempt by the Prophet to equate females (goddesses) to males, perhaps in an effort to lay the groundwork for Muhammad's sole heir—who was female—to inherit his leadership. While Muhammad had sired many children, only one—a daughter named Fatima—would survive him. Fatima bore children, providing the only direct line for Muhammad's descendants.

Rushdie used characters in his book, allegedly portraying Muhammad, Satan and the Angel Gabriel. He also used parallels, alternating between dream and reality sequences, incorporating the same focus of the Satanic verses. The use of these characters and parallels raised the ire of Muslim believers who saw it as blasphemy, even though the Satanic verses are mentioned in the Koran itself.

Riots occurred over the book in Pakistan, England and India prompting the Ayatollah Khomeini to act. Interpreting the book as mocking Islam, he issued a fatwa ordering all Muslims to kill the author and his publisher or to identify the blasphemers to others who could carry out the death sentence. Despite the violation of international law due to its extraterritorial application, Khomeini claimed the fatwa had universal jurisdiction, allowing the author to be executed wherever he could be found.

Khomeini's fatwa has also been criticized by Muslim scholars as it failed, as required by shariah, to provide an opportunity for the accused to defend himself and also because a Muslim can only be required *"to kill anyone who insults the Prophet in his hearing and in his presence"* (of the Muslim hearing the offending statement).

Although love may mean "never having to say you are sorry," Rushdie did. But, apparently, the apology was insufficient for Khomeini to "feel the love" as he refused to withdraw the fatwa. Khomeini's unforgiving wrath was made clear by his statement:

> *"Even if Salman Rushdie repents and becomes the most pious man of all time, it is incumbent on every Muslim to employ everything he has got, his life and wealth, to send him to Hell."*

One critic of "The Satanic Verses" notes the irony of the author's intended message in the book and the reaction it received by Islamists such as Khomeini, writing:

> *"Rushdie seems to have assumed that diverse communities and cultures share some degree of common moral ground on the basis of which dialogue can be pieced together, and it is perhaps for this reason that he underestimated the implacable nature of the hostility evoked by 'The Satanic Verses,' even though a major theme of the novel is the dangerous nature of closed, absolutist belief systems."*

In Khomeini, Rushdie clearly had an "absolutist" Islamist believer as a book critic.

Although Iran suggested it would not support the fatwa against Rushdie in 1998, the government backtracked in 2006 by claiming fatwas can only be terminated by the person issuing them. As Khomeini was dead, the fatwa, therefore, is "irrevocable."

On September 16, 2012, only four days after the posting of the 14-minute, anti-Muslim YouTube film "Innocence of Muslims," it was announced the reward for killing Rushdie was being increased from $2.8 million to $3.3 million. The increase was due to the belief his survival in the aftermath of his book's publication had encouraged others, such as the producer of the YouTube film, to insult Islam.

While Rushdie has avoided his date with the executioner thus far, others associated with his book have not fared so well. Several of those who have translated the book into various foreign languages have been murdered or the targets of attempted murder. Khomeini may no longer be among the living, but his fatwa is.

Khomeini's Haunting

Khomeini's brutal theocratic rule lasted for ten years before he Passed away on June 3, 1989.

Unfortunately, Khomeini failed to live long enough to receive an international court's condemnation of his brutality.

In October 2012, a moral victory—although not a legally binding one—was obtained in favor of victims of the Iranian mullahs' rule during "the bloody decade" of Supreme Leader Khomeini's reign.

A three day hearing at The Hague resulted in an interim judgment on the matter which held the Islamic Republic of Iran had committed crimes against humanity and gross violations of human rights against its citizens.

In an article published October 30, 2012 entitled "Iran 1988: Judgment Time," the author provided the following details:

> "The tribunal was set up in 2007 by survivors and families of victims living in exile and comprises leading jurists from around the world. It heard statements from experts and witnesses on how the Islamic Republic systematically crushed political and religious dissent in the decade following the 1979 revolution, executing 20,000 of its citizens. During the summer of 1988 alone, 5,000 political prisoners were hanged from cranes or shot by firing squad

under a direct fatwa issued by Ayatollah Khomeini, the supreme leader. The victims were leftists, students, members of opposition parties and ethnic and religious minorities—many originally sentenced for non-violent offences, such as distributing leaflets or taking part in demonstrations.

"The tribunal's ruling builds on 'a formidable corpus of evidence,' which includes the report of a Truth Commission held in London in June. The Commission heard 75 witnesses, who were either tortured and imprisoned themselves or are the family of executed prisoners. Around 100 witnesses in total submitted evidence, describing the same pattern of arbitrary arrest and detention without trial, of rape, death sentences issued by kangaroo courts, children as young as 11 being executed, families made to pay for the bullets used to kill their relatives. They recalled how torture was routinely used to break prisoners, make them recant their religious or political beliefs, or denounce others: they described flogging, beating, being suspended in the air by their arms twisted behind their backs, made to sit blindfolded for months in tiny boxes known as 'coffins' and being tortured in front of their children or spouses.

"'The evidence speaks for itself. It constitutes overwhelming proof that systemic, systematic and widespread abuses of human rights were committed by and on behalf of the Islamic Republic of Iran,' the judges said.

"The Iran Tribunal is now calling for the Iranian regime and the Human Rights Council of the United Nations to investigate these crimes and bring the perpetrators to justice. That is unlikely to happen. But for the survivors and the bereaved, the tribunal is a victory in itself: it has allowed their voices to be officially recorded and heard in court for the first time in 25 years.

> "Bits of the proceedings were seen inside Iran, despite the government's attempts to block foreign broadcasts. 'We have been inundated with calls from people in Iran saying they wanted to record the deaths of loved ones, which they had never told anyone about,' says Pardis Shafafi, a legal assistant with the tribunal.
>
> "'For the first time, people in Iran—especially the younger generations—are finding out what happened in the '80s and can see how the past still informs the present,' says Shokoufeh Sakhi, who testified at the hearing. She was arrested while still in secondary school, spent six years in prison where she was tortured and survived the 1988 massacre. She is now a PhD student in Canada. 'What happened in the '80s doesn't belong to the people of the '80s. It laid down the foundations of where these young people were born: they were born in a climate of fear and oppression, and they are used to it and accept it, but the roots for the present situation have to be found in the massacres of the '80s.' The judges are expected to deliver a full judgment in November.
>
> "In Iran, the age of criminal responsibility is 9 for girls and 15 for boys. This is one of the factors that results in Iran being the country with the world's highest juvenile execution rate. At least five juvenile offenders were reportedly put to death in 2009."

Fourteen years after Khomeini's death, in 2003, a cleric in Iran made a statement that, had it been anyone else, would have resulted in their arrest and possible execution. He said:

> "Iranians need freedom now, and if they can only achieve it with American interference I think they would welcome it. As an Iranian, I would welcome it."

Later the same year, the same cleric visited the U.S. where he met with the son of the late Shah. Unsurprisingly, the Shah's son endorsed the cleric's statement.

In 2006, back in Iran, that cleric again called for a U.S. invasion of Iran to topple its Islamic Republic. In an interview, he explained:

> *"If you were a prisoner, what would you do? I want someone to break the prison (doors open)."*

In a totally unexpected "haunting," the comments above were made by a cleric named Khomeini. They were not the words of the deceased Supreme Leader, but those of his grandson, Husain Khomeini.

Ironically, the Islamic Republic that the grandfather had built, the grandson now sought to destroy. Having witnessed the absolute brutality of a draconian system of control by mullahs more interested in personal power than humanity, a Khomeini—two generations removed—has now stepped up to become an advocate for democracy.

The late Supreme Leader Ruhollah Khomeini must be rolling over in his grave.

Understanding Islam's Rise and Split

Just as there are different sects of believers within other religions, there are two main sects of believers within Islam. While Islam was a unified religion under the Prophet Muhammad during his life, it became divided soon after his death. It has given rise to one of the most intense, violent and deadly religious rivalries in history.

While most Muslims perceive the real threat to their existence comes from outside their religious community, their sectarian hatred blinds them to the fact the threat to their own real undoing lies within it.

Historically, most problems contributing to the miseries of the Middle East have been self-inflicted, leading to a lengthy tally of Muslim-on-Muslim victimization. More recently, wherever the Arab Spring has landed in the region, Muslim-on-Muslim violence has continued as tyrants refused to go quietly into the night.

For the Muslim-on-Muslim tally, one need only look to Darfur; the Iran-Iraq war; Iraq's invasion of Kuwait; the massacres in Algeria; the slaughter of his own people by late Syrian leader Hafez al-Assad in the Hama massacre; the slaughter of a similar number of Syrians by al-Assad's son, Bashar; the use of gas against Yemen by Egypt in the 1960s; the Taliban control of Afghanistan; the deaths of thousands of Iranian children "volunteers" encouraged by Tehran to clear minefields during the war with Iraq; the executions of thousands of Iraqis by Saddam Hussein; the continuing death tolls in Iraq inflicted by Muslim militants; etc. The list—and the suffering—is endless. The word "massacre" attaches itself to many of these acts by Muslim leaders, yet the people fail to focus on their leaders as the real source of their victimization.

Instead, such leaders—such as Khomeini, Khamenei and Ahmadinejad—have preached during their lives that the source of all their trials and tribulations is Israel and the U.S. Their people, blindly accept this, unwilling to exercise the independent thought that would enable them to deduct it is not Israel or the U.S. holding the fate of Muslim nations in their hands, it is the Muslim people who have the power to determine their own fate.

The lemming is a small rodent, mouse-like in appearance, found in the Arctic region.

Like many rodents, lemmings experience periodic population booms and busts. There is a popular misconception the animal is driven to commit mass suicide as a means of population control.

While the lemmings' behavior may appear to be suicidal, it is really its effort to survive that occasionally results in a death of the masses. As a large population grows, food becomes scarce and the lemmings' migratory instinct kicks in—at times driving it to cross large bodies of water. Simply following the leader, as one lemming jumps in, the others do the same. If a body of water is extremely wide, many drown in the process of crossing.

But due to this behavior, the lemming is used as a metaphoric reference to people who blindly follow popular opinion, with often deadly consequences.

There is an obvious difference in this metaphor in that, unlike the lemming, man has the capability to exercise independent thought as to whether or not he should blindly follow.

But nowhere is the lemming mentality more apparent than in the Middle East.

It takes a courageous person to question what others choose blindly to follow and accept. One such person has emerged—in the form of a senior Saudi military leader—to question the Arab world's blind belief Israel is its "public enemy No. 1."

Retired Commodore Abdulateef Al-Mulhim, who served in the Saudi Arabian navy, wrote the following in an article entitled "Arab Spring and the Israeli enemy" published October 7, 2012 by the Arab News—an article highlighted two days later in the U.S. by author Gadi Adelman:

> *"The Arab world wasted hundreds of billions of dollars and lost tens of thousands of innocent lives fighting Israel, which they considered is their sworn enemy, an enemy whose existence they never recognized. The Arab world has many enemies and Israel should have been at the bottom of the list. The real enemies of the Arab world are corruption, lack of good education, lack of good health care, lack of freedom, lack of respect for the human lives and finally, the Arab world had many dictators who used the Arab-Israeli conflict to suppress their own people."*

Al-Mulhim went on to share what prompted him to write the article:

> *"(I)...decided to write this article after I saw photos and reports about a starving child in Yemen, a burned ancient Aleppo souk (market) in Syria, the under developed Sinai in Egypt, car bombs in Iraq and the destroyed buildings in Libya. The photos and the reports were shown on the Al-Arabiya network, which is the most watched and respected news outlet in the Middle East."*

The former Saudi military leader proceeded to ask the kinds of questions Muslim leaders and their followers have failed to ask for over six decades:

> *"The questions now are: What was the real cost of these wars to the Arab world and its people? And the harder question that no Arab national wants to ask is: What was the real cost for not recognizing Israel in 1948 and why didn't the Arab states spend their assets on education, health care and the infrastructures instead of wars? But, the hardest question that no Arab national wants to hear is whether Israel is the real enemy of the Arab world and the Arab people."*

The answers al-Mulhim provided were conclusions at which any educated person exercising independent thought would arrive:

> *"The common thing among all what I saw is that the destruction and the atrocities are not done by an outside enemy. The starvation, the killings and the destruction in these Arab countries are done by the same hands that are supposed to protect and build the unity of these countries and safeguard the people of these countries. So, the question now is that who is the real enemy of the Arab world?"*

What al-Mulhim came to realize is what history has borne out in modern times—i.e., far more Muslims have been killed by fellow Muslims than by non-Muslims. The real threat to Islam lies within.

He noted as well how, with the Arab Spring having sprung, no mention has been made of an issue so many Arab governments have repeatedly raised to isolate Israel—the issue of Palestinian refugees.

He observed how Israel has turned into an economic dynamo, an educational powerhouse, and a leading developer of high technology. Perhaps most importantly, he recognized the extent to which Muslims have been welcomed into Israeli society as equals:

> *"Many Arabs don't know that the life expectancy of the Palestinians living in Israel is far longer than many Arab states, and they enjoy far better political and social freedom than many of their Arab brothers. Even the Palestinians living under Israeli occupation in the West Bank and Gaza Strip enjoy more political and social rights than some places in the Arab World. Wasn't one of the judges who sent a former Israeli president to jail an Israeli-Palestinian?"*

Al-Mulhim concluded with a declaration never before heard because it comes from one truly motivated by improving the welfare of his fellow Arabs:

> *"Now, it is time to stop the hatred and wars and start to create better living conditions for the future Arab generations."*

Could al-Mulhim's article represent the equivalent of "the camel's nose under the tent" on the issue of Arab's misplacing the blame for their suffering? It is doubtful.

Al-Mulhim's article is an encouraging exercise of independent thought. But, as such, it is contrary to the teachings of religious leaders whose power rests with Muslim lemmings who entrust their independent thought to such leaders. Thus, so long as real bullets are not flying, these religious leaders will lead the assault against reasoning such as that expressed by al-Mulhim.

The trend of the 21st century follows that of the 20th as Muslim-on-Muslim violence continues today.

Understanding the Islamic sectarian split is but another factor in the equation in understanding the Iranian mindset. To explain the split and how it impacts on the Iranian mindset, one must understand how Islam appeared onto the world stage and the evolution of its subsequent split into the Sunni and Shi'a sects.

Abū al-Qāsim Muḥammad ibn ʿAbd Allāh ibn ʿAbd al-Muṭṭalib ibn Hāshim—later to be known as the Prophet Muhammad—was born in 570 A.D. in Mecca. Born fatherless and left motherless at the age of five, he was raised by his paternal grandfather until his death three years later. It was only after being put into the care of his fraternal uncle that Muhammad finally enjoyed some long term stability in his life. He often traveled with his uncle—a merchant—well into his teenage years.

In his twenties, Muhammad came into the employ of a wealthy, older woman merchant, Khadija bint Khuwaylid, who eventually proposed marriage to him. Wed in 595 A.D., he was 25 at the time, and she was 40. It was a monogamous marriage, lasting until her death at age 65 in 620 A.D.

After Khadija's death, the six year old daughter, Aisha bint Abu Bakr, of Muhammad's close friend, Abu Bakr, was betrothed to the Prophet. Aisha continued to live with her parents until the age of nine, when her marriage to Muhammad, 53, was consummated.

Muhammad would go on to take between eleven to thirteen wives, several of whom were women widowed by husbands killed in battles with the Meccans.

It would not be until the age of 40 that Muhammad would experience, in 610 A.D., his first epiphany. Troubled by the worship of idols rather than a single God, he often made sojourns to a cave outside of Mecca to fast and meditate. It was on one such trip he experienced an overpowering presence. Muhammad suddenly found himself reciting words of such eloquence and meaning, he and others determined they had to have derived from a heavenly source. Muhammad and his close confidants believed the revelations came from Allah, who used the Angel Gabriel as a communications medium.

It would be three years, however, before Muhammad shared this experience publicly, only after the revelations started coming with greater frequency. Illiterate and unable to write down what Gabriel shared with him; Muhammad had tribe members serve as scribes to write down these revelations. These later became the substantive text of Islam's holy book—the Koran. Based on his unique communication access, Muhammad became known as the messenger of God and founder of Islam.

As Muhammad revealed his divine messages to others, he was persecuted by, and his tribe caused to suffer by, nonbelievers. An attempt on his life resulted in a revelation that Muhammad should move to Medina, which he did, in 622 A.D. (This event—and the year it occurred—later led to the start of the Muslim calendar.) There, he gathered many more followers. Fighting ensued between the Muslims and Meccans over the next several years, resulting in a treaty in 628 A.D., by which Muslims were given freedom of movement for the first time.

Hostilities with the Meccans broke out again, however. Declaring jihad, Muhammad, joined by several other tribes and his followers marched on Mecca in 630 A.D., forcing the Meccans to submit to Islam or be put to death. Victorious, Muhammad and his followers returned to Medina, consolidating most of Arabia under Islam.

Muhammad made his last pilgrimage to Mecca in 632 A.D. Three months later, in June, he died in Medina, where he was buried.

Muhammad's death sparked immediate controversy as to who should succeed him as leader. Until Muhammad's death, all Muslims looked upon themselves as being cut from the same cloth. It was a disagreement among Muslims on the succession line, however, that resulted in a subsequent split and the creation of two separate sects—the Sunnis and the Shiites.

The Shi'a Muslims, or "Shiites," were of the school of thought that leadership of Islam should remain within the family of Muhammad. As Muhammad had no surviving sons when he died, it was believed his closest male relative—his son-in-law Ali bin Abu Talib—should succeed him.

Ever since Muhammad's death, Shiites have consistently determined the right of succession based strictly on family lines. They believe placing leadership in the hands of those mullahs who follow such a line best reflects Muhammad's or God's personal choice. "Shi'a" means a group or supportive party of people, shortened from "Shia-t-Ali" or "the Party of Ali." Shiites are the smaller sect, representing only 10%-15% of all Muslims worldwide.

Iran is one of four Muslim countries in which the majority of the population is Shi'a—with neighboring Iraq a second. (From an Iranian's perspective, if one is a Sunni, one is an Arab—not an Iranian.) Additionally, it is a derivative sect of Shi'a—the "Alawites"—which has come to power in Syria, where they represent a minority (10%-15%) in a Sunni majority country, ruled for decades by the Assad father/son dictatorship. Alawites take their name from Muhammad's son-in-law, Ali bin Abu Talib. The practice of their faith involves several non-Islamic beliefs.

It is the Shia majority presence in Iraq and the Alawite minority leadership in Syria that has generated a close bond in both countries with Shia majority Iran.

Unlike the Shiites, the Sunnis were of the school that familial lines should not be controlling on the matter of Muhammad's succession. They believe it is "sunnah" or "custom" which should control. It is a reference to the naturally smooth and easy flow of water and meant to embark upon a clear and well-trodden path of following the customary flow of practices.

Sunnah consisted of Muhammad's beliefs as recorded by transcribers into "hadiths." These hadiths were the result of customs related by Muhammad either implied or by tacit approval as understood by the transcriber. Based on Muhammad's life, hadiths encouraged believers to live their life as did the Prophet—who lived life in constant remembrance of God.

A verse from the Koran stating, *"Verily in the messenger of God you have a good example for him who looks unto God and the Last Day and remembers God much,"* underscores the fact Muhammad's mission was to teach and exemplify the holy book—not simply to relate its verses and depart. He was not to be worshipped but to pass on wisdom preserved in the sunnah, which came directly from God.

For Sunnis, the wisdom of sunnah was that leadership should flow to he who is most wise rather than he who is closest related. Accordingly, Sunnis elected a close advisor of Muhammad's, Abu Bakr (whose six year old daughter was betrothed to Muhammad), as his successor, making him the first Caliph of the Islamic nation.

"Sunni" means "the people of Sunna"—a term to describe those who follow exactly in Muhammad's footsteps, doing everything as he did it. Sunnis represent the much larger of the two main sects, comprising between 85%-90% of all Muslims.

Interestingly, neither sect considers the other Muslim and, therefore, does not even consider the other to exist. Yet, when it comes to counting followers of Muhammad, they are more than willing to recognize each other in the global count.

The dynamics of hate between the two sects has reared its ugly head most recently in Lebanon, following the October 19, 2012 assassination of the intelligence chief, Brigadier General Wissam al-Hassan, a close ally of Sunni leader Saad Hariri. Believing the Shiites of Hezbollah are responsible, Sunnis have vowed revenge.

Lebanese Sunnis make it clear "only Sunnis should live in this country," "if a Shiite is passing by, we are going to kill him," and "I was born to kill Shiites." As history has demonstrated, the hatred the Muslim sects have toward each other continues into a new era.

While initially the main difference between the two sects was how successors were determined, over the ensuing centuries the divide between them has widened as other differences have manifested themselves. For example, traditions of Islam evolving through the hadiths to establish Islamic customs were not embraced by Shiites unless related by one falling into the family lineage, thus creating a tradition gap between the two sects.

Shiites also believe, since the imam leadership chain that descended reflected both Muhammad's and God's personal choices, their leaders are sinless and, as such, are to be venerated. Sunnis, on the other hand, believe their leaders, if they deserve veneration, as a 1970's television commercial for the Smith Barney investment firm once advertised, they have to make it "the old fashioned way…they earn it." Thus, if Sunni leaders fail to perform, Sunni followers retain the authority to remove them since leadership is not a birth right.

Understanding the evolution of the sectarian split in Islam, the following Sunni joke may register.

As the larger sect, Sunnis refused to acknowledge the existence of Shiites. This was obviously very frustrating to Shiites so their scholars suggested their Sunni counterparts hold a meeting with them to discuss the issue. A time and place was established for the meeting. The Shiites arrived at the appointed time.

But the Sunni scholars failed to show up. One hour went by and another. Still the Sunnis failed to arrive. Finally, after a third hour passed, a single Sunni scholar appeared, arriving with his shoes under his arms.

The Shiite scholars were shocked to see only one Sunni scholar show up. They inquired as to why he was late and why he had his shoes under his arms. The Sunni reported the other Sunni scholars were not coming.

He then explained why he had his shoes under his arms. He said it was because that was how Muslims during Muhammad's time carried them whenever they attended a Shi'a meeting. The Shias responded (since the sectarian split did not occur until after Muhammad's death) with, "But Shias did not exist during Muhammad's time."

With a smile on his face, the Sunni scholar exclaimed, "That is exactly what we have been saying all along!"

(Note: If the above failed to at least elicit a smile, the author takes full responsibility for failing adequately to explain the difference between the two sects.)

The Two Faces of the Koran

In 1957, a book entitled "The Three Faces of Eve" was made into a movie. It was a true story about a woman and mother named "Eve" who suffered from multiple personality disorder.

Each of her three personalities was distinctively different. Only two of them—Eve White, timid and self-effacing, and Eve Black, her "alter personality," wild and fun-loving—are initially revealed to her psychiatrist, Dr. Luther. Eve Black knows about Eve White's existence but Eve White does not know about Eve Black's. At one point, Eve Black—acting independently of her other personality—attempts to kill her daughter, for which she is committed to a mental hospital.

Dr. Luther considers both Eves to be incomplete and inadequate personalities. Under hypnosis, a third personality emerges—a rather stable personality calling herself Jane. Only after getting Eve to remember a traumatic childhood experience that caused a personality split does Dr. Luther succeed in curing her by getting all three personalities to merge into one.

As one reads the Koran, there are parts that seem to conflict with each other—almost as if it, like Eve, had multiple personalities; there can be no dispute for anyone who has read the holy book that different interpretations can be applied, opening the door to confusion.

It is almost as if the Koran were written in two parts. The first discernible break point seems to cover the first twelve years of Muhammad's life after the Revelation in 610 A.D. It is this part that conveys a more peaceful side of the Prophet (Part 1). The next ten years, representing the last decade of the Prophet's life, conveys a darker, more violent side (Part 2). This generates considerable confusion when something read in Part 1 conflicts with something read in Part 2.

There were changes in Muhammad's life that could have influenced this "change in life" transition.

It is known Muhammad did lose his first wife in 620 A.D. It is also possible, although no records are available, he may have lost his very close confidant and mentor, Waraqa Bin Nofal, the cousin of his wife, who was quite elderly at that time. Waraqa was an Ebionite priest—who, as a Jewish Christian, regarded Jesus as the Messiah and insisted on following Jewish rites. He studied Christian scriptures, thoroughly mastering them. He accepted poverty voluntarily. He served as a steady and guiding hand for Muhammad.

It is known too that between June 21, 622 A.D. and July 2, 622 A.D., Muhammad embarked on the "Hijra"—his departure from Mecca and relocation to Medina. Having lived all his life in Mecca, Muhammad had been told by Allah through Gabriel of a plot to assassinate him and, therefore, the need for him and his followers to migrate to Medina.

The impact of Muhammad's Hijra on the Koran's content was shared by religious scholar Richard Bonney:

> *"The Qur'an was revealed to the Prophet in two distinct periods of his mission; the first part (85 chapters), which emanated from Mecca, being mainly concerned with matters of belief...while the second part (29 chapters) comprised legal rules and regulated various aspects of life in the new environment of Medina."*

In "Jihad and the Qur'an: The Case for a Non-Violent Interpretation of the Qur'an," Jeremiah J. Bowden explains the shift in tone:

"The reactions to Muhammad's initial proclamations progressed from mockery to malicious hostility and finally to murderous plots on his life. During this period, it was revealed to Muhammad that he ought to be patient and avoid direct confrontation with the nonbelievers:

"Bear, then, with patience, all that they say, and celebrate the praises of thy Lord, before the rising of the sun and before (its) setting. (Qur'an 50:39)

"We created not the heavens, the earth, and all between them, but for just ends. And the Hour is surely coming (when this will be manifest). So overlook (any human faults) with gracious forgiveness. (Qur'an 15:85)

"With the increased opposition of the Qurayshi oligarchy (a non-Muslim tribe of Mecca with whom Muhammad signed the Treaty of Hudaybiyya only to break it as soon as he felt strong enough to do so), some of Muhammad's followers desired to strike back against those who opposed them. God enjoined Muhammad to remain patient, but allowed the Prophet to confront the non-believers by means of argumentation:

"Invite (all) to the Way of thy Lord with wisdom and beautiful preaching; and argue with them in ways that are best and most gracious: for thy Lord knoweth best, who have strayed from His Path, and who receive guidance. (Qur'an 16:125)"

"And dispute ye not with the People of the Book, except with means better (than mere disputation), unless it be with those of them who inflict wrong (and injury): but say,

"We believe in the revelation which has come down to us and in that which came down to you; Our Allah and your Allah is one; and it is to Him we bow (in Islam). (Qur'an 29:46)

"After Muhammad and his followers fled prosecution in Mecca and emigrated to Medina, things changed dramatically. Muhammad took on the roles of judge, civic leader, general, soldier, and diplomat. Several of the refugees wanted restitution for the goods they had to leave behind. Having only a few resources at their disposal, and wanting to regain some of the goods that had been lost, God allowed the Muslims to raid caravans destined for Mecca: 'To those against whom war is made, permission is given (to fight), because they are wronged; and verily, Allah is most powerful for their aid.' (Qur'an 22:39)"

"In March of 624 C.E., events started to unfold that would eventually lead to the Battle of Badr. The Medinans learned that a rich Qurayshi caravan was on its way from Syria to Mecca. Muhammad began planning his attack. The Meccans, aware of Muhammad's plan, sent a thousand-man army to annihilate the Muslim contingent. Muhammad, inspired by a God-given dream, announced that the Medinans would engage the much larger Meccan army. Several members of Muhammad's army saw his mission as futile and decided to desert their leader.

"According to some Muslim traditions, Muhammad wrote to the Qurayshi elites informing them that although he was prepared to do battle, he would prefer it if the armies would disengage. The Qurayshi, having the upper hand, and seeing this as the perfect opportunity to eradicate the Muslim nuisance, declined.

"Some able-bodied and willing men were delegated to remain in Medina to keep order and maintain worship. The Muslim army consisted of some 70 emigrants and approximately 230 Medinan converts against a thousand. If victory were to come, it would be a miracle granted by God."

"It was during this time that Surah 8 was revealed. In it are several verses that pertain to the waging of jihad.

"One of which speaks directly to the discrepancy in numbers between the two warring factions, 'O Messenger, rouse the Believers to the fight. If there are twenty amongst you, patient and persevering, they will vanquish two hundred: if a hundred, they will vanquish a thousand of the Unbelievers: for these are a people without understanding.' (Qur'an 8:65)"

"Further, Surah 8 provides believers with the proper way to go about waging war:

"Say to the Unbelievers, if (now) they desist (from Unbelief), their past would be forgiven them; but if they persist, the punishment of those before them is already (a matter of warning for them). And fight them on until there is no more tumult or oppression, and there prevail justice and faith in Allah altogether and everywhere; but if they cease, verily Allah doth see all that they do. If they refuse, be sure that Allah is your Protector - the best to protect and the best to help. And know that out of all the booty that ye may acquire (in war), a fifth share is assigned to Allah, - and to the Messenger, and to near relatives, orphans, the needy, and the wayfarer, - if ye do believe in Allah and in the revelation We sent down to Our servant on the Day of Testing, the Day of the meeting of the two forces. For Allah hath power over all things. (Qur'an 8:37-41)."

"But if the enemy inclines towards peace, do thou (also) incline towards peace, and trust in Allah. For He is One that heareth and knoweth (all things). (Qur'an 8:61)"

"The Battle of Badr established at least four important precepts pertaining to jihad. First, it is God who commands a jihad. The waging of war must occur under the direction of an authorized leader. Second, God is

responsible for ensuring victory. Even when the odds are stacked against believers, they can still have hope that God will provide. Third, jihad is limited in its scope and must cease once the enemy inclines toward peace. Fourth, prisoners of war were not to be slaughtered or abused..."

(Note: In further support of how Islamists pick and choose which of Muhammad's teachings they follow, the third precept above requires jihad "must cease once the enemy inclines towards peace" has not been followed not only during the Iran-Iraq war but is not being followed in Afghanistan as Afghan government and Coalition forces seek to have peace talks with the Taliban.)

The medieval jurist Shamseddin al-Sarakhsi (1010-1090 C.E.) proposed an evolutionary view of revelation, which held that Muhammad was commanded to engage in jihad in four developing stages:

1) To spread the Islamic message and faith peacefully (early Meccan period);

2) To confront and argue with unbelievers in a wise and fair manner (mainly pre-Hijra and early Medinan period);

3) To fight the Umma's enemies if Muslims were unjustly wronged, and such fighting was not to be undertaken in the sacred months; and

4) To wage war against unbelievers unconditionally and constantly to bring about the victory of Islam.

One of the conflicts arising in Parts 1 and 2 of the Koran has to do with whether military action ("jihad") against non-believers is sanctioned. Some scholars argue verses from the Koran sanction it both during and after Muhammad's life, reading, "fight in the name of your religion with those who fight against you." But others disagree, arguing these verses are taken out of context and clearly prohibit aggression when read in context, by only allowing military action in self-defense.

Some of those supporting the former position of jihad explain why:

> "...while Muhammad was in Mecca, he 'did not have many supporters and was very weak compared to the Pagans...it was at this time he added some 'soft,' peaceful verses,' whereas 'almost all the hateful, coercive and intimidating verses later in the Quran were made with respect to Jihad' when Muhammad was in Medina...This interpretation of events is strongly disputed by other scholars...claiming an intention of encouraging self-defense in Islamic communities."

> "...(Scholar) Yohanan Friedmann has argued that the Quran does not promote fighting for the purposes of religious coercion, although the war as described is 'religious' in the sense that the enemies of the Muslims are described as 'enemies of God.'"

Where conflicting verses appear in Part 1 and Part 2, the Islamic doctrine of "abrogation" arises whereby those "revealed later in the Prophet's life supersede verses revealed earlier," with Qur'anic verse 2:106 often given to support this position:

> "None of Our revelations do We abrogate or cause to be forgotten, but We substitute something better or similar: Knowest thou not that Allah Hath power over all things?

> "The doctrine of abrogation rectifies seemingly contradictory statements in the Qur'an. A classic example of this is the Qur'anic position on drinking wine. In Surah 2:219 the reader is told there is some profit in drinking wine, however, the bad outweighs the good, 'They ask thee concerning wine and gambling. Say:

> 'In them is great sin, and some profit, for men; but the sin is greater than the profit.'

"This verse is later abrogated by verse that states worshipping while intoxicated (a mind befogged) is not allowed, 'O ye who believe! Approach not prayers with a mind befogged, until ye can understand all that ye say.' (Qur'an 4:43)"

"Finally, the believer is admonished to forgo intoxicants altogether, 'O ye who believe! Intoxicants and gambling, (dedication of) stones, and (divination by) arrows, are an abomination, of Satan's handwork: eschew such (abomination), that ye may prosper.' (Qur'an 5:90)"

"(Author Robert) Spencer wants to argue that according to the doctrine of abrogation, Surah 9 overrides all of the more peaceful and tolerant verses of the Qur'an because it was revealed at a later time… the sources of most of the verses of peace and tolerance above are all Meccan. That means anything they teach must be considered in light of what was revealed later in Medina… The last Sura revealed, Sura 9, is Medinan. Thus it is in effect the Qur'an's last word on jihad."

"However, Spencer is not merely spouting off in an echo chamber, he does his best to cite Islamic scholars to substantiate his position. Spencer references Ad-Dahhak bin Muzahim (d. 723 C.E.), Ibn Juzayy (d. 1340 C.E.), and Ibn Kathir (d.1373 C.E.) amongst others, who all aver that the Sword Verse abrogated every agreement of peace, every treaty, and every term between Muhammad and non-Muslims. Spencer ends this section by claiming, 'In other words, Muhammad gave peace a chance with the specific suras, and then understood that jihad was the more expedient course.'"

The website "AnsweringIslam" notes the following about the referenced "Sword Verse" above:

> "One of the most frequently quoted Quranic verses is chapter 9 verse 5. This verse is known as 'The Verse of the Sword.' Muslim terrorists cite it to justify their violent jihad. Correspondingly, critics of Islam claim that it commands Muslims to act with offensive aggression towards the non-Muslims of that period, and contributes to Islam's final theological doctrine of aggression towards all non-Muslims of all times. Apologists for Islam claim that 9:5 is purely defensive. Which side is right?
>
> "As the Islamic source materials are examined it will become evident that verse 9:5 is part of the theology of jihad and is meant to be both offensive and defensive. It is directed against Pagans living both near to and far away from Muhammad.
>
> "Understanding 9:5 in context requires an examination of the passage in which it is found. This passage consists of 29 to 41 verses or so (depending on which scholar's view you hold)...
>
> "Islam's final theological position regarding the use of violence to further its domain does not rest upon one verse or passage. Rather the entire Quran, other Islamic source materials, and Muhammad's actions and lifestyle (Sunnah) must be examined and evaluated..."

Most Muslims believe as follows:

1) The Koran represents "the literal word of Allah" as given between 610 A.D.-632 A.D. to Muhammad through the Angel Gabriel. As Muhammad could not read or write, he immediately memorized the words given to him by Gabriel and then recited them to a transcriber.

2) Since these transcriptions took place soon after they were revealed to Muhammad and were recorded during his lifetime, how the

Koran reads today is extremely close compared to how it read in Muhammad's time.

3) The last revisions to the Koran were started under Caliph Uthman only twelve years after Muhammad's death and were completed 24 years later. Thus, the revisions were checked by people who already had memorized Muhammad's version of the Koran, resulting in an extremely accurate revision.

The majority of modern day scholars who have studied Islam do not seem to question the Koran's authenticity.

However, as "Muslims: Their Religious Beliefs and Practices: Volume 1, London, 1991" indicates, there does seem to be some style variations suggesting "an evidence that many different hands have been at work therein, and caused discrepancies, adding or cutting out whatever they liked or disliked."

"An Introduction to the Quran," Edinburgh, 1977, by R. Bell and W.M. Watt, suggested such variations may have involved text revisions during compilation. They noted there were, "abrupt changes in the length of verses; sudden changes of the dramatic situation, with changes of pronoun from singular to plural, from second to third person, and so on." They believe, however, there probably were not any substantive changes or a "controversy would almost certainly have arisen."

There is debate over whether the Koran is a complete book—i.e., whether it can stand on its own to teach one how to practice the faith. Those arguing against it suggest some practices are mentioned such as "The Five Pillars of Islam" (paying witness to Allah—"there is no God but Allah;" prayer; alms-giving; fasting; and pilgrimage) but without sufficient detail on how to perform each.

Another example is that there are other practices, not even mentioned in the Koran, but which are still performed such as stoning adulterers; dogs being deemed as unclean animals; wearing of the hijab; listening to music; playing competitive games (unrelated to military exercise, such as chess; etc.).

It has been noted by some critics "the morality of the Quran, like the life story of Muhammad, appears to be a moral regression." They focus on the fact that a more moral Muhammad is reflected in Part 1 than in Part 2.

A basic precept of Islam is the ethic to which it adheres "of originality or superiority." While finding value in some Islamic ethics, as to these the Catholic Church finds, "There is none." This "ethic" of superiority is one immediately putting Islam at odds with all other religions.

Those holding this ethic close are basically Islamic supremacists—who believe in their supremacy as members of a specific religious sect. What they see and promote as a positive ethic is really a negative. What they see and promote is no different than the thinking of any supremacist— "Because I am a member of a defined group, ergo I am special." It is an ethic that creates an immediate divide between Muslims and non-Muslims at the outset.

The lesson to be learned from this chapter is that it is impossible for religious scholars to walk away with the exact same interpretation of the entire text of the Koran. The problem then becomes, who has the last say on what a verse means.

Unlike the Catholic Church—led by a Pope who, as the sole authority for all Catholics, can provide uniformity on church doctrine—Islam has no single "Pope equivalent." This explains the reason for so much confusion within Islam—for the meaning of specific verses can be given multiple interpretations by multiple religious scholars. Nor is there a system, like the American legal system, by which a Muslim can submit to a higher authority for a ruling on two conflicting interpretations.

Muslims are told by their religious leaders man cannot interpret God's words. Yet that is precisely what these religious leaders do by issuing their own individual interpretations. (This raises the question how Supreme Leader Khamenei can issue a meaningful fatwa—as he supposedly has done—declaring nuclear weapons not permissible under the Quran as, obviously, the subject matter did not even exist until more than thirteen centuries after the Quran came into existence.)

This is what leaves an Islamist free to give to any verse of the Koran a violent interpretation of his own choosing.

Just as Dr. Luther combined the three faces of Eve into one, only by merging the two faces of the Koran into one—its original face as a truly peaceful religion to be voluntarily accepted, or not, by non-believers, is there any hope of bridging the great divide existing between Muslims and non-Muslims. From the Muslim perspective, no such bridge-building will occur, with the only alternative, therefore, for non-Muslims to convert.

CHAPTER FOUR

Concept of Supreme Leader Unique to Shia in Iran; Khomeini Introduces the "Fear Factor"

As indicated earlier, Sunni Muslims heavily outnumber Shiites by a margin of almost 9:1. Unsurprisingly, therefore, there are far fewer Shiite-majority countries than there are Sunni-majority states. In fact, there are only four—Iran, Iraq, Bahrain and Azerbaijan.

Each of these Shia-dominant countries has implemented a different form of government. Azerbaijan is a presidential republic; Bahrain a constitutional monarchy; Iran, as we have seen, is a theocratic republic; and Iraq a parliamentary democracy. Thus, there is no mandate among Shiites that one form of government is ordained by Muhammad's teachings to be superior to another. None, save for Iran, however, not only believes its form to be superior to all others around the globe but also believes its theocracy will become the vehicle for imposing a new world order upon all earthly inhabitants.

Basically, what each of these four Shia-dominant states has done is to come up with its own vehicle for retaining power in the hands of an influential few.

While Azerbaijan holds public elections for president every five years with the president able to run as often as he wishes, political machinations allowed manipulation of the existing governmental infrastructure to establish a father-son dynasty—along with the assistance of an election that international observers noted had serious irregularities.

In Bahrain, it is the monarchy that wields influence and will continue to do so—as have dynasties throughout history—until dying out or their people, having finally had enough, revolt. (Interestingly, as the monarchy has attempted to increase rights for the people—such as giving the vote to women—clerics, opposed to such rights, have gained greater power.)

While the 2003 U.S. invasion of Iraq released Iraqis from the brutal rule of the dictator Saddam Hussein and a parliamentary democracy was gradually established, that democracy is showing some signs of erosion as Prime Minister Nouri al-Maliki, influenced by his brother Shiites in Iran, has reneged on political power-sharing promises, thus centralizing control in his own hands.

In distinguishing the "power plays" involved in these four Shiite-majority states, it is important to note why Iran, alone, stands out. While the theocracy card has not been involved in power plays made in the other three Shia-dominant countries, it has been played to the max in Iran. But it is control that has been the ultimate prize in all four states—permanent in all but Iran whose religious zealots see it only as a temporary measure to make way for an apocalyptical prophecy.

Tehran's leadership has factored into its control equation the fulfillment of a religious prophecy. But the equation remains incomplete without the means for achieving the end being sought—a means that involves not only the acquisition but the use of nuclear weapons. What should concern the world community most is the theocracy card has not been played simply to gain control of the Iranian people; it has been played specifically to fulfill a deadly global prophecy.

There has even been limited criticism among Iran's own clerics that Khomeini may have gone too far in the structure of the theocracy he very stealthily instituted. As a student in Qom, Khomeini was taught by the highly respected Ayatollah Haeri Yazdi. Yazdi was just as committed to the same prophecy as was Khomeini but believed, as a religious figure, clerics should maintain a "studied disinterest in politics." That is, Yazdi believed clerics should maintain an arm's distance from politics and limit themselves to religious counseling. There were also those who believed Khomeini had embarked upon an ego trip, having elevated himself to the revered position in a theocracy of "Supreme Leader"—a position rightfully reserved for only the Mahdi.

Interestingly, even among the majority of Shiites, Khomeini's theocratic formula for control represented a minority position. Historically, among Shiites, as long as an existing government is just, there is no basis for interference by mullahs. Theoretically, any unjust regime, whether theocratic or not, represents a "usurpation and betrayal of God, the Imams and the people." It constitutes oppression to which justice is the right response. "That justice must prevail is almost the only norm that Shi'ite governance theory has established. It follows what the founder of their faith, Imam Ali, proclaimed to be normative."

This was why most Shiite mullahs supported Iran's 1906 constitution as it helped to reign in an unjust regime.

Author Katajun Amirpur notes:

> *"The worst that can happen to a nation, unavoidably summoning the wrath and vengeance of God is tyranny over God's creatures. Ali (Imam Ali, the founder of the Shia faith) warns that the ruler must be on his guard against that because 'merciful God hears the cries of the oppressed.'"*

Khomeini understood in the building of his theocracy, without the "glue" to bind it together, it could come crashing down on top of him. The glue he opted to use was not new—it has been used by dictators long before him and will continue to be used in the future. But Khomeini was able to make this glue stick because it was part and parcel of the ideology of Islam as he promoted it in Iran. That glue was fear.

Even if one was a Khomeini team player, one never knew how long he would continue in that capacity. High level Iranian government officials who sang Khomeini's praises one day were running for their lives the next. Such fear proved toxic. Serving in government was like musical chairs as one did not know when he would be out of a job—or a life.

Toxicity either stimulates or poisons one's will to fight oppression. The toxic effect on the Iranian people after their government stole the 2009 election from them was what caused them to rise up against their mullahs; however, the brutal way it was put down by their government proved even deadlier.

It remains to be seen whether the entire well holding the Iranian people's will to resist oppression has now been poisoned or whether they still retain sufficient reserve empowering them to rise up again.

The "fear factor" Khomeini instilled in Iran was one to be maintained at all costs. It permeated all aspects of daily life. It was why he never liked to give any indication he would negotiate or soften his positions with enemies for fear it would be perceived as weakness. Khomeini even worried his decision to release the U.S. Embassy hostages right after President Reagan took office might be perceived in this light. Perhaps motivated in part to reassure followers any perception of weakness was inaccurate, he gave his blessing three years later to bomb the U.S. Marine Barracks in Beirut. For Khomeini, it was imperative for him to demonstrate he had no fear about taking the Great Satan on.

That was a lesson the U.S. failed to learn in its dealings with Iran.

Iran's Presidents: The Perceptions and the Realities

Supreme Leader Khomeini's reign of terror witnessed brief tenures for Iran's first two presidents. It was he who approved all presidential candidates in advance. While hundreds of candidates signed up to run, the Supreme Leader quickly culled the list down to include only those whom he believed would not challenge him. Even with such an advantage, Khomeini proved to be wrong in his selection.

In Iran's first post-Islamic Revolution presidential election held on January 25, 1980, Abulhassan Banisadr was elected to a four year term with 78.9% of the vote, taking office on February 4. While he would survive two helicopter crashes, he would not survive serving his term.

Within 16 months, Banisadr had fallen out of favor with Khomeini, allegedly for attempting to curtail the authority of clerics in power. Khomeini relieved Banisadr as Commander-in-Chief on June 10, 1981 and charged parliament with responsibility to impeach him, which was done eleven days later while Banisadr was absent. As the deposed president learned Khomeini had also issued orders for his execution, he fled to France.

After Banisadr flew the coop, Khomeini held a Provisional Presidential Council meeting attended by six people—one of whom was the ex-president's Prime Minister, Mohammad Ali Rajai. The prime minister nominated himself for the presidential election, winning office with 91% of the vote. He was sworn into office on August 2, 1981.

Four weeks after taking office, on August 30, 1981, Rajai attended a meeting of Iran's Supreme Defense Council. In an assassination effort reminiscent of one made against Adolf Hitler during World War II, a briefcase left in the room exploded. However, unlike the attempt on Hitler's life, this one proved successful, killing the new president and others present. It was believed the assassin was a member of the Iranian opposition group MEK (an organization that is discussed later in this book).

Iran's third president, Ali Khamenei, born in 1939, was the first of three clerics in a row to serve. Although he had been the victim of an assassination attempt in June 1981 that paralyzed his right arm, he ended up faring better than his predecessors by serving two full terms (1981-1989) as president. Having survived, the attempt gave rise to a reputation for Khamenei as the "living martyr." (When Supreme Leader Khomeini died in June 1989, it was Khamenei who replaced him as Supreme Leader.)

Originally opposed to clerics holding the office of president, Khomeini believed Khamenei's religious credentials made him more of a player as president within a regime where a theocratic government head of state was answerable to a spiritual Supreme Leader.

The perception of Khamenei was a toned-down Khomeini; the reality—he was cut from the same cloth. In a telling sign of the violence he supported, president Khamenei often appeared in public with an AK-47 rifle at his side—an odd accessory for an avowed spiritual leader within the safe confines of his own country. But the weapon was symbolic of the violence Khamenei espoused originally as president and later as Supreme Leader.

In 1989, six months before his death, Khomeini—now armed with a nation-state with which to further Islam's goal of global domination—

made a brazen suggestion to the Soviet Union's Mikhail Gorbachev. As Moscow was witnessing the collapse of its East European satellite buffer and the collapse of communism, Khomeini encouraged the Soviet leader to consider replacing Marxism with Islamism.

Khomeini wrote in a letter to Gorbachev:

> "I strongly urge that in breaking down the walls of Marxist fantasies you do not fall into the prison of the West and the Great Satan. I openly announce that the Islamic Republic of Iran, as the greatest and most powerful base of the Islamic world, can easily help fill up the ideological vacuum of your system."

The letter to Gorbachev was the first one Khomeini wrote to a foreign leader since the Islamic Revolution toppled the Shah. It was clear he believed Allah to be on his side as communism was on the decline. That left only the Great Satan standing in the path of Islam's further advancement around the globe.

After Khomeini's death, another of his confidants, Akbar Hashemi Rafsanjani, became Iran's fourth president (1989-1997)—this time selected by the new Supreme Leader Ali Khamenei. The perception of Rafsanjani was a man of the people; the reality—he brutally sought to eliminate opposition to Iran's theocracy. He managed to amass a personal fortune for himself in office while leaving his nation's economy in shambles.

Hundreds of intellectuals were purged under Rafsanjani—imprisoned, tortured or simply disappeared; some dissidents were beaten to death. Iran's borders posed no obstacle to Rafsanjani's brutal reach as he authorized numerous terrorist attacks abroad, including the 1994 bombing of a Jewish community center in Argentina. This resulted in the issuance in November 2006 of a warrant by an Argentine judge for Rafsanjani's arrest. (This was in addition to a 1997 German criminal court's conviction of an Iranian hit squad for murdering four dissidents, ruling they had acted upon orders from a special committee of which the controlling members were Rafsanjani and Khamenei.)

Most telling about Rafsanjani's mindset were comments he made displaying callousness for human life. In 1989, reflecting on the targeting of foreigners for terrorist attack, he observed:

> *"It is not difficult to kill Americans or Frenchmen. It is a bit difficult to kill (Israelis). But there are so many (Americans and Frenchmen) everywhere in the world."*

And, more forebodingly, was a 2001 comment alluding to the future use of nuclear weapons by Iran, a statement made when it was not yet known Rafsanjani had already initiated a secret nuclear weapons development program:

> *"The use of even one nuclear bomb inside Israel will destroy everything. However, it will only harm the Islamic world. It is not irrational to contemplate such an eventuality."*

Such comments by a "man-of-the-cloth" are most telling about how such clerics and other Islamic fanatics view their religion to be committed to the destruction of non-believers.

For Mohammad Khatami, Iran's fifth president (1997-2005), the perception was he was a reformist; the reality—he was ineffectual. He came into office with a public mandate, representing 70% of the 1997 vote, for reform. Hard-line resistance from ultimate decision-maker Ayatollah Khamenei made any such progress impossible. And questions endure in the aftermath of Khatami's tenure as to whether he really was committed to reform or merely served as a foil for Khamenei. Reports surfaced that Khatami too was involved in ordering extra-territorial assassinations against Iranian dissidents.

While Khatami would initiate many reforms, few succeeded. As mentioned, a question mark remains as to whether he truly was a reformist or simply played the role of one. Based on a U.S. policy giving Iran more than the U.S. received in return, it would not be surprising if Khatami was instructed by Khomeini to play the role for this purpose. It is also supported by the fact Khatami, well aware of the country's nuclear program, did much to continue to keep it under wraps while moving it forward.

Khatami has been critical of the man who followed him into office, Mahmoud Ahmadinejad, at one point accusing him of promoting a "Taliban-like fundamentalist movement" in Iran. However, if Khatami were truly reform minded, Mahmoud Ahmadinejad has proven the complete opposite.

For Iran's religious leadership, there was no turning back. The country, under its tutelage, was locked into the conservative principles of an Islamic Republic which were to be used as a springboard for infecting the world with Islamic fundamentalism. With the term of each successive Iranian president, the Islamic Revolution was gaining ground both inside and out its borders to spread it.

Ahmadinejad: "The Catalystic Converter"

It is Iran's sixth and current president, Mahmoud Ahmadinejad, who generates the greatest worry for the international community. His Islamist beliefs are coupled with his belief it is he who has been personally selected by the Prophet Muhammad to help create a global caliphate—i.e., a new world ruled by an Islamic successor to the Prophet.

Born in 1956, Ahmadinejad believes he is in a race in which he is running the final leg. He believes he has been ordained to cross the nuclear finish line in order to trigger a world-changing event to establish this Islamic global dominance. He believes he is the "catalyst" in a prophecy that will convert the entire world to Islam. One might call the role he envisions for himself that of the "catalystic converter."

In 2005, Ahmadinejad became president—the first non-cleric in 24 years to do so as Supreme Leader Khamenei decided he no longer wanted a spiritual competitor serving as president.

The election was noteworthy for two reasons. First, there was a very low voter turnout, probably due to dissatisfaction over Khatami's failed reforms. Second, that low turnout is probably what led to most reform-minded senior government officials being turned out of office, providing Ahmadinejad with a mandate to press forward with his initiative for further Islamization of the country. The 2005 election results and Ahmadinejad's hardline conservative approach have been called by Western observers the start of the "Second" Islamic Revolution.

Supreme Leader Khamenei, attempting to suggest the conservative and reformist clerics provided balance for Iran, once said the existence of the two factions serves the regime, like the two wings of a bird. Based on Khamenei's endorsement of conservative-leaning Ahmadinejad as president, one gets the impression the reformist wing of this symbolic bird—like Khamenei's right arm injured during an assassination attempt before he was Supreme Leader—was paralyzed.

It has been difficult for the West to try and pin labels on Iranian leaders.

Professor Fouad Ajami of Johns Hopkins University has warned America about its obsession in trying to identify "moderates." He noted during President Reagan's term:

> *"The Reagan officials have fixed the radical label onto the Ayatollah Ruhollah Khomeini's designated successor, Ayatollah Hussein Ali Montazari. The moderate label has been assigned to the Speaker of the Parliament, Hashemi Rafsanjani. But this is all guesswork."* (Ironically, time would show Montazari was more the moderate while Rafsanjani was more the radical.)

After all, it was under alleged "moderates" like Rafsanjani and Khatami that Iran's nuclear and missile programs respectively made tremendous advances. Part of the difficulty too in identifying moderates was created as one time radicals, like Montazari, came to recognize how extreme some radicals were becoming, thereby throttling back on their own to a truly more moderate position.

The 2005 election mandate enabled Ahmadinejad to amass more power in a shorter time. Because his thinking and that of Khamenei was so aligned, he was often given leeway to undertake issues normally falling within the realm of the Supreme Leader. However, such leeway would later come back to nip Khamenei as Ahmadinejad would take on wealthy (read that as corrupt) officials and clerics. This created problems for the Supreme Leader who, in many cases, had doled out wealth to these clerics to buy their loyalty.

The perception of Ahmadinejad by Iranian voters was a populist who promised to improve the economy and care for the poor; the reality—he has neglected both, committing resources to pushing forward with Tehran's nuclear weapons program to the detriment of the nation's economy. With drastically increased oil revenues, Ahmadinejad should have been able to improve conditions for the poor but that proved not to be his priority. And, by the time Iran's economy did become a priority for him, it was too late for him to stop a free fall caused by devastating sanctions.

Ahmadinejad seems to have no appreciation for economic matters. His failure to improve Iran's economy may well stem from the influence of Supreme Leader Khomeini who once said, "economics is for donkeys." Ahmadinejad holds a similar disdain, saying he wears "his contempt for economic orthodoxy as a badge of honor."

His perception by U.S. observers was that of an extremist; the reality—he is a religious zealot who will stop at nothing to achieve his goals in the name of Islam. Just how extreme Ahmadinejad really is became apparent when former president and dissident-slayer Rafsanjani, running against him in the 2005 presidential campaign, was viewed, comparatively, as a "moderate."

And, the fact Ahmadinejad considers hardline cleric Ayatollah Mohammad Taghi Mesbah-Yazdi—a fervent opponent of any dialogue with the West—to be his ideological mentor further underscores Ahmadinejad's extremist views and leanings. It should put one on notice that serious negotiations with the West are simply not an option for him.

To better understand Ahmadinejad's mindset, one must first understand his career path.

When the Islamic Revolution came to Iran in 1979, Ahmadinejad, then 23, became a member of an ultra-conservative faction of the Office for Strengthening Unity (OSU) Between Universities and Theological Seminaries, established by a Khomeini minion to organize Islamist students against a rapidly growing opposition group known as the People's Mujahedin of Iran (PMOI). PMOI was later dubbed the "Mojahedin-e Khalq" (MEK), meaning "traitors of the people," so called as the Khomeini government sought to depict the group in a negative light.

OSU was the group that formulated the idea of seizing the U.S. Embassy in Tehran. Interestingly, when the idea was first proposed, Ahmadinejad suggested seizing the Soviet Embassy as well. His idea was rejected by other students, perhaps out of concern a more forceful or joint U.S./Soviet response might be triggered by a simultaneous seizure of both embassies. However, it gives one early insight into Ahmadinejad's thought process in taking aggressive action against enemies, either without rational reflection on the consequences of those actions or with a total lack of concern for same.

When the 1980 war with Iraq began, Ahmadinejad joined the fight, later becoming a member of the Islamic Revolutionary Guard Corps' (IRGC) special operations Qods Force, responsible for launching attacks outside Iran's borders. (Now about a quarter the size of the regular army, IRGC was formed in 1979 as Iran's mullahs questioned the loyalty of a military that had just served the Shah.)

Ahmadinejad became a senior commander of the Qods Force (a group which conducted covert operations in Iraq during the U.S. occupation and which is conducting the same in Syria to bolster its ally's failing regime there), directing assassinations of Iranian dissidents in the Middle East and Europe. He went on to serve as governor of cities in northwestern Azerbaijan province and took other governmental appointments before returning to university life as a teacher. In April 2003, he was appointed mayor of Tehran—a position from which he reversed many of the progressive changes made by his predecessors.

After being elected president of Iran in 2005 by an electorate reflecting a relatively small group of eligible voters, Ahmadinejad worked quietly to install several of his IRGC cronies into key political positions within the government as well as industry. His continued close relationship with the IRGC is evidenced by the wealth of state contracts its construction arm has been awarded.

The prominence of former IRGC commanders now serving in the government has given the IRGC added confidence and a loud voice in foreign policy decisions. This was evidenced in February 2007 when the overall IRGC commander, General Yahya Safavi, boasted the U.S. would be unable to make any security changes in the Middle East without Iranian cooperation. (It is important to remember this bellicose group is the same one with its "finger on the button"—i.e., operating Iran's ballistic missile and satellite facilities.)

With his fellow Qods Force and IRGC comrades serving in high government positions and development of a nuclear weapon well on its way, Ahmadinejad was feeling his oats. In 2006, he sent a somewhat rambling letter to President Bush and the American people, the purpose of which, to Western readers, was unclear.

A close reading of the letter by those familiar with Islamic tradition suggested a sinister motive—i.e., offering an enemy, before initiating war, the opportunity to embrace Islam which, if refused, then justifies the enemy's destruction. If so, this again strongly suggests Ahmadinejad envisions nuclear war as paving the way for the Mahdi. And, at the moment of Mahdi's return, Ahmadinejad unabashedly proclaims he will become heir to the Prophet Muhammad—perhaps explaining a "vision" he told others he saw of himself engulfed in an "aura" while speaking at the U.N. in 2006 that supposedly left those in the audience spellbound.

There are other statements Ahmadinejad has made suggesting his hostile intentions and that war is near. In an October 20, 2006 speech to mark the Iranian holiday of "Quds," he urged all Muslims to prepare for a "great war" to destroy Israel. This statement was made just a year after his notorious declaration "Israel should be wiped off the map."

In a most definitive act of his ultimate intentions, Ahmadinejad has purchased 18 BM-25 long range, land-mobile missiles from North Korea—missiles ONLY capable of accommodating NUCLEAR warheads.

Confident he is basking in the Prophet Muhammad's glow, Ahmadinejad does not limit his contempt to the West, displaying disdain, as well, towards his regional Sunni neighbors. When these Sunni states sent representatives to meet with Ahmadinejad to express their concerns about Iran's nuclear program, he dismissed them as "yarns woven by Jews," claiming the nuclear facilities were so safe "he would build his own offices on top of them."

As Ahmadinejad jockeys for a showdown with the U.S. on the nuclear issue, Sunni moderate states, lacking confidence in U.S. military protection, are increasing their defense budgets—considering too the option of starting their own nuclear programs. Iranian nuclear irrationality is clearly breeding a regional arms race!

Stolen Election

As relations between the West and Iran continued to deteriorate during Ahmadinejad's first term as president, the international community hoped the 2009 presidential election in Iran might lead to a new president. Three candidates opposed Ahmadinejad: former Prime Minister Mir-Hossein Mousavi, former IRGC commander (for 16 years) Mohsen Rezaee and reformist politician and former Speaker of the Parliament Mehdi Karroubi.

Domestic dissatisfaction with Ahmadinejad was so great it translated into a ground swell of support for Mousavi who, from all poll indications, would plummet the sitting president in the election.

Initially, the primary challenger to Ahmadinejad was former President Mohammad Khatami. However, he withdrew before the election, throwing his support behind Mousavi.

The election took place on June 12, 2009. Despite a huge turnout, which did not favor Ahmadinejad, Supreme Leader Khameini declared

Ahmadinejad the winner the next morning by an overwhelming margin of almost 63% over the favored Mousavi who only received about 34%. The minimal balance of the vote was split between Rezaee at 2% and Karroubi at 1%.

Claims of fraud arose just as quickly as the results were announced.

Mousavi's supporters, wearing the campaign color green, poured out onto the streets to protest what was widely perceived to be a fraudulent election. The demonstrations were met with a crackdown by the Iranian police and military, plus the Basij militia loyal to Iran's Supreme Leader. The bloody crackdown ignited protests around the globe, and prompted Iran to issue harsh rebukes against any country voicing criticism of its actions as meddling in Iran's private affairs. Shockingly, among those nations intimidated by this threat was the U.S.

There was extensive phone communications jamming on election day and of BBC broadcasts.

The New York Times reported:

> "...the (Iranian) *government had been preparing its fraud for weeks, purging anyone of doubtful loyalty and importing pliable staff members from around the country... dissident employees of the Interior Ministry... have reportedly issued an open letter claiming the election was stolen.*"

Six days after the election, two Iranian film makers presented electoral commission documents purporting to show Mousavi had actually won the election as Ahmadinejad had only received 12% of the vote.

Protestors included many high profile people from Iran's entertainment industry, religious leaders, former members of the Basij and IRGC. Iran's entire national football team wore green wristbands to voice their support for protesters, many of whom were arrested and sentenced to prison.

Mousavi joined in the protests, issuing a statement urging followers to demonstrate peacefully. However, it was not his followers who turned to violence but the Basij. Meanwhile, Khamenei suggested the unprecedented large voter turnout coupled with Ahmadinejad's re-election victory was a "divine assessment." Ahmadinejad added his "two cents worth," claiming the election was "completely free" and the result "a great victory" for Iran.

A video captured one of the first victims among the protesters—beautiful, 26-year old Neda Agha-Soltan who was peacefully marching with others. Suddenly, a bullet cut her down, believed to have been fired by a member of the Basij. The video was quickly circulated on the internet and resulted in international condemnation of Tehran's violent response to peaceful demonstrations. As her name meant "voice," she became known as the "voice of Iran."

The protests lasted from June 13, 2012 through February 14, 2013.

When Ahmadinejad was sworn in on August 5, 2009, many high-profile government figures, who usually attended such events, refused to do so. These included former Presidents Khatami and Rafsanjani.

Mass trials of arrested protestors (more than 4,000) followed, with long prison sentences for those convicted.

In perpetuating Ahmadinejad's and Khamenei's "Belief" concerning the Twelfth Imam's return, many Iranian government newspapers claimed the victory represented the official end of the Islamic Republic and beginning of the Islamic emirate or an imamate (caliphate) regime of the Mahdi's reign.

Reza Kahlili is a pseudonym for a former CIA operative in Iran's Revolutionary Guards and author of "A Time to Betray." He noted concerning the aftermath of the 2009 election:

> *"By appeasing the Islamic Regime we turned our back on the Iranian people's aspirations. We had a golden opportunity in 2009 to help the Iranian people to*

overthrow this regime. This regime could have collapsed within weeks. Internal intelligence reports later showed that had the demonstrations continued for several more weeks the regime could have collapsed."

Rafsanjani's Confrontation with the Supreme

Ahmadinejad has proven to be a "loose cannon." Those around him with influence have been unable to reel him in as he continues his race to prepare for the Mahdi's return. No one, perhaps, was more eager to do this than former president Rafsanjani, particularly since he had lost out to Ahmadinejad as a candidate for a third term in the 2005 presidential election.

Rafsanjani was appointed chairman of the Assembly of Experts in September 2007. This was a significant development as it suggested criticism of Ahmadinejad was rather broad-based.

As described before, the Assembly of Experts is a political body charged with responsibility for assessing the Supreme Leader's performance and, if dissatisfied, potentially has authority to replace him. Chairmanship of the Assembly was an important position. Basically a rubber stamp for the Supreme Leader, Khamenei wanted a "yes" mullah in that position to follow his lead. But, as a critic of Supreme Leader Khamenei, Rafsanjani was not that mullah. Therefore, for him to have secured the chairmanship position meant there had to be other important players who also were critical of the Khamenei/Ahmadinejad team.

The appointment of Rafsanjani to chairman raised hopes hardline leaders would throttle back on the chokehold they had on the people. It had no impact. The same was true on the foreign policy level. Any hope for change was dashed by the fact many of the hardliners who elected Rafsanjani were the same ones who cheered on Ahmadinejad earlier. They were the same ones who issued an unprecedented fatwa "sanctioning the use of atomic weapons against (Iran's) enemies" and ruling "the use of nuclear weapons may not constitute a problem, according to sharia." Such a fatwa only served to encourage Ahmadinejad to continue his outlandish and aggressive behavior.

The chairmanship position came up for re-election in 2009 with Rafsanjani prevailing again as his discontent with the Khamenei and Ahmadinejad team still lingered. But he lost his seat two years later in the 2011 re-election campaign, suggesting Khamenei and Ahmadinejad had managed to regain their support.

Rafsanjani's replacement as chairman was Khamenei's close ally Ayatollah Mohammad-Reza Mahdavi Kani. All previous chairmen before Rafsanjani, along with Kani, had been elderly clerics lacking any real political clout. Rafsanjani was the noticeable blip on the radar screen that had the only opportunity to check the Supreme's power. His failure to do so makes it unlikely anyone else will be able to do so either.

Kani's health issues also rule him out as any possible threat to Khamenei. At age 79 and wheelchair bound, Kani only took the position as Khamenei had requested he do so. It is doubtful, however, he will survive too many more years, which will only raise the chairmanship issue again in the near future. Kani's replacement with another Khamenei supporter will make it clear the Supreme Leader is still in the driver's seat.

(Note: Kani heads the "Combatant Clergy Association"—a political party in Iran founded in 1978 by clerics seeking to overthrow the Shah. Among its founding members were both Rafsanjani and Khamenei. Selection by the clergy of the words "combatant clergy" is an interesting choice for men-of-the-cloth. It suggests such religious leaders of Islam equate themselves to "warriors of God" in the true sense of the word "warrior," underscoring Islam's violent side.)

It is difficult to determine whose drumbeat it is to which Rafsanjani marches. After his two term presidency, and perhaps knowing he would run again in 2005, Khamenei was probably beating the drum, which would explain Rafsanjani's 1999 speech at Tehran University endorsing the use of force to suppress student demonstrations.

When he ran for parliament the next year, Rafsanjani came in last place but later the Council of Guardians voided enough ballots of his opponents to enable him to qualify for a seat. As would be seen ten years later when Ahmadinejad ran for re-election, voter fraud was yet another arrow in the

Islamists' political quiver. However, in Rafsanjani's case the resulting uproar caused him to resign.

Ten years after Rafsanjani's speech endorsing the use of force, he did a turnaround, giving a speech critical of the government's suppression of the media and activists. His fluctuating positions make it difficult to tag him as either a hardliner or reformer.

This "tagging" exercise was made no easier by Rafsanjani's stand in the aftermath of the June 12, 2009 presidential election in which Khamenei reported an overwhelming victory for Ahmadinejad that was highly disputed. Rafsanjani seemed to straddle the fence on the issue, remaining silent—until July 17, 2009.

It was during Friday prayers that day, Rafsanjani broke his silence, for once expressing a modicum of sensibility. He said:

> *"All of us—the establishment, the security forces, police, parliament and even protestors—should move within the framework of law...We should open the doors to debates. We should not keep so many people in prison. We should free them to take care of their families... It is impossible to restore public confidence overnight, but we have to let everyone speak out...We should have logical and brotherly discussions and our people will make their judgments...We should let our media write within the framework of the law and we should not impose restrictions on them...We should let our media even criticize us. Our security forces, our police and other organs have to guarantee such a climate for criticism."*

It was a much different human rights environment Rafsanjani was calling for than Iranians had experienced for the previous three decades. Whether he meant it or not, his words fell on the deaf ears of the Khamenei/Ahmadinejad leadership team. Yet again, the Iranian people felt a sense of hope slip away.

Ahmadinejad Ruffles the Supreme's Feathers?

It appears that by early 2011, an over-confident and over-zealous Ahmadinejad may have gone too far, thinking, perhaps, as the Prophet Muhammad's "fair haired boy" he could even challenge Supreme Leader Khamenei by whose authority he served as president. Perhaps Ahmadinejad had forgotten but, as only the third non-cleric president of Iran, today he stands on the edge of either continuing a precedent or ending one as, to date, no non-cleric president of Iran has ever completed the full term for which he was voted into office.

As previously mentioned, the first non-cleric president to serve was Abulhassan Banisadr in 1980 who was impeached and tagged for execution by Khomeini after challenging Iran's clerics, escaping to France.

Banisadr's replacement, Mohammad-Ali Rajai, also a non-cleric, became Iran's second president on August 2, 1981, only to be assassinated less than a month later.

Fate now awaits Ahmadinejad, as the third non-cleric president, who completed one term in office, to see if he will fully complete his second. He has already made history by becoming the first Iranian president to be called before parliament to answer questions for his conduct, the answers to which could provide a basis for possible impeachment.

It appears Ahmadinejad is running afoul of the same "red line" that did President Banisadr—by arrogantly challenging the clerics' authority.

Iran observers feel there have been issues brewing between Khamenei and Ahmadinejad for a while. However, the challenge to Khamenei's authority did not become public until April 2011.

It was at that point in time Ahmadinejad dismissed his intelligence minister, Heydar Moslehi, who had been personally selected for the position by Khamenei. The Supreme Leader reinstated Moslehi. In protest, Ahmadinejad refused to attend Cabinet meetings, only returning after an eleven day hiatus. His refusal to support Khamenei's reinstatement of Moslehi was viewed as disobedience, which caused members of the Iranian Parliament to demand Ahmadinejad's impeachment.

Perhaps not wishing to impeach Ahmadinejad in the midst of Iran's confrontation with the West on its nuclear program, Khamenei opted to take a different tack to demonstrate his displeasure with the president. He arrested Ahmadinejad's chief of staff, Esfandiar Rahim Mashaei, whom Khamenei supporters believed to be the real power behind Ahmadinejad and whom Ahmadinejad was grooming to become the next president. Arrested too were two dozen other Ahmadinejad supporters.

Ahmadinejad enjoyed a close relationship with Mashaei who is Ahmadinejad's son's father-in-law. He had generated criticism among clerics for promoting Iranian nationalism (rather than Islamism) and cavorting with a movie star. But it was the nature of the crime of which Mashaei and the others stood accused that was most telling.

The Ahmadinejad supporters were all charged with sorcery—i.e., magicians who have invoked the spirits to act against Khamenei and his followers. One of the accused was described as "a man with special skills in metaphysics and connections with the unknown worlds." While such claims are reminiscent of the Salem witch hunts of the 1690s in America, three hundred and twenty years of evolution have enabled America to recognize what is myth and what is not. Apparently, over a thousand years of evolution under Islam have been insufficient for Persia/Iran to similarly mature. Such claims of sorcery suggest perhaps Iran's leadership has been spending too much time watching the "Sci-Fi" channel!

In Mashaei's case, the charges stemmed from evidence gathered by government listening devices of private meetings he held to discuss "designs to supplant the clergy." Allegedly, Mashaei has told supporters he too is in contact with the Mahdi (in addition to Khamenei and Ahmadinejad who have made similar claims). Making this claim was sufficient for Mashaei to be charged with being a member of a "deviant current" seeking to subvert the clergy's role. (Apparently, only the clergy can be in contact with the Mahdi.)

The basis for the charge of "deviant current" arose because clerics claimed the Mahdi's return cannot be predicted. Trying to predict it gives rise to the charge. As Khamenei and Ahmadinejad have been claiming the return is "imminent," one wonders why they then are not part of the same deviant current.

Apparently, the clerics are not too fond of non-clerics having spiritual contacts that should be reserved only for religious leaders. It is surmised since both Ahmadinejad and Mashaei are non-clerics and both have claimed communications with the Mahdi, they maintain a very close bond based on a mystical, as well as a familial (through the marriage of their children) level.

For a Mahdi who was supposed to maintain a very low profile, revealing himself just to one who has been chosen to assist in the return, one wonders how many more people are yet to see the Twelfth Imam. With so many people laying claim to being visited by the Mahdi, one wonders how the Twelfth Imam is sorting this all out on game day.

Additional signs of a power struggle between Khamenei and Ahmadinejad were manifested in November 2011.

Ali Akbar Javanfekr, described as "one of the most powerful figures in publicizing Iran's government policies and messages to the outside world" and who also served as the presidential advisor for press affairs was arrested during a raid of his office.

Put on trial, Javanfekr received a one year sentence and three year suspension from journalism for "publishing materials contrary to Islamic norms" and "insulting to the Supreme Leader." His crime was publishing a series of articles questioning the compulsory dress code for women as not being an Iranian practice but an imported one.

But, it is believed Javanfekr's real sin was in having supported Ahmadinejad. When Javanfekr was quoted in a newspaper for saying the president had come "to serve the people…(and) will stay till the end, till martyrdom," the newspaper was shut down for two months for "disseminating lies and insults to officials in the establishment."

Javanfekr appealed his one year prison sentence, which was then reduced to six months. He was re-arrested in September 2012—as President Ahmadinejad was addressing the U.N.—to begin serving his time.

Upon Ahmadinejad's return to Iran after his U.N. speech, he attempted to visit Javanfekr at Evin Prison, but was denied access by the head of the country's judiciary branch, Ayatollah Sadeq Larijani, for not seeking authorization from him first. When Ahmadinejad claimed he did not have to do so as president, Larijani responded Ahmadinejad failed to understand the limits on his constitutional powers.

Ahmadinejad's conflict with the clerics has not gone well as it has undermined his authority and resulted in the defeat of many of his supporters in the March 2012 parliamentary elections. While there is little disagreement between the president and Supreme Leader on the nuclear program, the dispute seems to be limited to Ahmadinejad's challenge to authority and internal politics.

Unlike the U.S., which has instituted various checks and balances among its three governmental branches to prevent overreaching by one over the other, Iran centralizes control of all three under the Supreme Leader. For this reason, Larijani informed Ahmadinejad he needed to obtain either Larijani's or Khamenei's permission for the visit.

Iran's state prosecutor, supporting the position of the clerics who oppose the president's visit for being politically motivated, encouraged Ahmadinejad to drop the matter and focus his attention more on the country's economic problems.

The Ahmadinejad versus Supreme Leader power struggle only further contributes to the complexities of trying to resolve Iran's nuclear issue.

But, the claims of contact with the mystical Mahdi by Mashaei, Khamenei and Ahmadinejad and the outlandish charges against only Mashaei for possessing metaphysical skills and contacts with "unknown worlds" does not give one a particularly "warm and fuzzy" feeling that men such as these may soon have access to nuclear weapons.

One wonders if, in Iran, it is the patients who are truly in charge of the insane asylum!

Iran's Next President

Since Iran's Constitution limits the office of president to two terms, it will be a new president who takes office in August 2013, following a June election. As it gets closer to that presidential election, the less likely it becomes Ahmadinejad will be dismissed before his term is up and the more likely it is he will become a "lame duck" president—his leash somewhat tightened by Khamenei. But, even if he were terminated, no change in direction concerning Iran's nuclear program would be expected. Ahmadinejad's replacement would just become yet another in a line of presidents under whose tutelage Tehran will continue nuclear weapons development as a president who stops the program now would be perceived by hardliners as weak-kneed.

And, just like Ahmadinejad and his predecessors in office, the new president will have confidence a divided world community will do little to stop Iran. A new president undoubtedly will, as has Ahmadinejad done, continue to engage in meaningless discussions with the P5+1 (label given to the five U.N. Security Council states plus Germany) simply to buy more time to complete the program's ultimate objective.

Regardless of whether Ahmadinejad is terminated or not, realistically, the next president to receive the blessing of Iran's senior clerical leadership will have to adhere to the same fundamentalist Islamic beliefs as has Ahmadinejad—to include lying to non-believers in furtherance of Islam's cause.

Clearly, however, Khamenei will work feverishly to ensure Ahmadinejad's handpicked successor and fellow Mahdi communicator, Mashaei, does not get the nod to replace Ahmadinejad. Should Khamenei be unsuccessful in blocking Mashaei, it would be an indicator Khamenei is struggling for control again. In any event, it will be interesting to see if the new president will adopt Ahmadinejad's confrontational style with clerics, assuming he himself is a non-cleric.

Sadly, the only constant for the West ever since the Islamic Revolution came to Iran has been its miserable failure in trying to understand the mindset of the Iranian leadership. Misperceptions of the past continue to cloud the realities of what the West is truly facing in an Iran now ruled by Islamofascist theocrats. Ahmadinejad's fate still hangs in the wind, but regardless of what the next year brings in Iran's presidential sweepstakes (controlled by the Supreme Leader), the West cannot afford to allow past misperceptions to cloud future realities in understanding what to expect from a new leader.

It would be naïve to believe one can sit down with Iran's next president, whoever he is, and achieve what has been unachievable through negotiations to date with previous Islamist presidents. While every Iranian president may appear to be their own man, each—in reality—maintains a very similar mindset on the nuclear issue.

Chapter Five

Iran's Dangerous Nuclear Mix

President Mahmoud Ahmadinejad

As much of Iran's talk about its nuclear program has been devoted to convincing the world community its focus is strictly on a nuclear program for peaceful purposes, it is important to understand the evolution of the program. What follows will explain how Iran evolved into becoming a member of the nuclear club and where it is now headed.

In assessing a nation's threat to others, there are two components that make a dangerous mix when combined. One is its possession of nuclear weapons; the other is its propensity to use violence in total disregard for the consequences of its actions.

How do these components measure up for Iran?

As to the first, Tehran is running a race to possess nuclear weapons, with the finish line visible somewhere on the horizon. How far Tehran is from that finish line is uncertain. Some Iran observers suggest a definitive decision has not yet been made by Iran's leadership to make the final dash across the finish line to weaponize its nuclear technology. One should assume, however, that Tehran has made the decision and that mad dash will be made, with only the timing unknown.

Lessons learned tell us such an assumption has to be made.

It should not be forgotten, prior to the Persian Gulf War, U.S. intelligence estimated Iraq was at least four to five years away from being able to develop enough fissile material for a bomb. This proved to be a significant underestimate as inspectors discovered, after the war, Baghdad was only 12-18 months away from that goal. Such an underestimate now with Iran could prove deadly—and would be a suicidal assumption.

As to the second component—the propensity to use violence—one must examine Iran's past acts to determine if Tehran, armed with a nuclear weapon, is more likely than not to undertake a future act of violence.

Repeated past acts of an extra-territorial nature in furtherance of a violent ideology is a strong indicator of one's potential to initiate an act of violence in the future. If Iran has ignored its own borders before to undertake such acts, it is fully capable of so acting in the future—to include the use of a nuclear weapon.

The incidents below are telling as they demonstrate no concern or fear by Iranian leaders at the highest levels of government to resort to violence against their ideological enemies. Decision-makers acted blindly out of a belief they had a religious mandate to do so. Their acts, in some cases, earned international arrest warrants for Iranian government officials serving in a dual role of executioner and man-of-the-cloth—a role completely foreign to the Western world but perfectly acceptable in an Islamic one.

Iran's Nuclear Program: Getting Started—and Stopped

Although Iran's nuclear program has been the focus of much attention early in the 21st century, it is a program that got its start almost a half century earlier. (Note: The following timeline was developed with the assistance of "Timeline of Iran's Nuclear Activities" published by Semira N. Nikou in "The Iran Primer" by the United States Institute of Peace.)

In a 1953 speech, President Dwight Eisenhower, perhaps with encouragement from Albert Einstein, sought to promote the "constructive" rather than "destructive" nature of nuclear power by launching the "Atoms for Peace" program. Under the program, the U.S. would provide, on an international basis, equipment and information on the peaceful uses of nuclear technology to help educate people and conduct research into such applications. It was under this program the first two non-nuclear nations received nuclear reactors—Iran and Pakistan.

In 1957, Iran executed a cooperation agreement with the U.S. under this program to obtain U.S. technical assistance, lease enriched uranium and conduct research on peaceful energy uses.

The nuclear program in Iran was slow to get started. It was not until 1967 the Tehran Nuclear Research Center (TNRC) was established and then equipped by the U.S. with a 5-megawatt research reactor. In 1968, Tehran signed the Nuclear Non-Proliferation Treaty (NPT), ratifying it two years later. It is this act that still makes Iran subject to verification by the International Atomic Energy Agency (IAEA) today. The Shah envisioned building up to 23 nuclear facilities to make Iran energy independent of its own oil with two reactors to be installed at Bushehr to supply energy to the city of Shiraz.

On May 15, 1974, Iran and the IAEA signed the NPT's Safeguards Agreement which allowed inspections to verify non-diversion of nuclear enrichment material for military use. A West German company agreed to build two light water reactors at Bushehr with construction beginning in 1975.

In April 1976, although President Ford supported helping the Shah to build 23 nuclear reactors, he refused to approve independent reprocessing capabilities, for which the Shah continued to press.

In January 1978, both countries signed an agreement for safeguards beyond the NPT requirements.

By 1979 and the fall of the Shah, all work on Iran's nuclear program ceased—not only because the U.S. terminated cooperation but also because Ayatollah Khomeini allegedly believed such technology to be evil in accordance with Islamic teachings. The two Bushehr plants were only 50% and 85% completed respectively when construction came to a halt under Khomeini.

Getting Started Again

Whatever non-Islamic concerns influenced Khomeini's decision not to develop its nuclear technology in 1979 seemed to disappear in the years after the start of the 1981 Iran-Iraq war. (It's fascinating how something deemed "un-Islamic" by an Islamist one day can become "Islamic" the next.) Towards the end of that conflict, perhaps motivated by Iraq's nuclear program at Osirak (which, in 1981, came to a screeching halt in an Israeli air attack), Iran sought to jump-start its nuclear program again in 1984 when German engineers conducted a feasibility study to complete a reactor at Bushehr. That plan had to be temporarily abandoned on March 24, 1984 when Iraq attacked Iran's facility, inflicting heavy damage. But in December, with Chinese assistance, Iran opened a nuclear research facility at Isfahan, which received a training reactor in 1985.

Former IRGC member Kahlili explained Khomeini's change of heart towards developing nuclear weapons as follows:

> *"When Iran began its nuclear program in the mid-1980s, I was working as a spy for the CIA within the Revolutionary Guards. The Guards' intelligence at that time had learned of Saddam Hussein's attempt to buy a nuclear bomb for Iraq. Guard commanders concluded that they needed a nuclear bomb because if Saddam were to get his own, he would use it against Iran. At that time, the two countries were at war.*

> "Mohsen Rezaei, then chief commander of the Guards, received permission from the Ayatollah Ruhollah Khomeini to start a covert program to obtain nuclear weapons, so the Guards contacted Pakistani generals and Abdul Qadeer Khan, the Pakistani nuclear scientist.
>
> "Commander Ali Shamkhani traveled to Pakistan, offering billions of dollars for a bomb, but ended up with a blueprint and centrifuges instead. The first centrifuge was transferred to Iran on Khomeini's personal plane."

By the late 1980s, German intelligence reported Iran conceivably could develop nuclear weapons in a matter of years if Tehran was able to obtain uranium from another country, such as Pakistan. Even so, progress on its nuclear technology seemed to move very slowly as Iran sought ways of lining up suppliers and obtaining technical assistance. (While the decision to re-start Iran's nuclear program represented a reversal in Supreme Leader Ayatollah Khomeini's thinking in 1979, it is interesting to note it came at a time when the president was Ali Khamenei, who would succeed Khomeini as Supreme Leader upon Khomeini's death in 1989. There should be little doubt if the mandate was given to President Khamenei directly by Khomeini that Supreme Leader Khamenei would be committed to continue to move forward with the former's marching orders after his death.)

In May 1987, following 18 months of negotiations, Argentina signed an agreement with Iran to provide a new core for the TNRC to operate the reactor on only 20% enriched uranium rather than 90%.

By 1989, Argentina replaced the TNRC core.

On October 9, 1990, Iran made the decision to start rebuilding its damaged Bushehr nuclear power plant.

On August 25, 1992, Iran signed a cooperation agreement with Russia on the civil use of nuclear energy, including construction of a nuclear power plant.

By 1993, Argentina delivered the 20% enriched uranium (fifty pounds worth) to Iran.

In January 1995, Iran signed a contract with the Russian Ministry of Atomic Energy to build a light water reactor at Bushehr under IAEA safeguards. Russia was under a contractual obligation to complete the plant within 55 months. The project's completion was delayed until August 2010.

In May 1997, by adopting the Additional Protocol, the IAEA expanded the Safeguards Agreement by which inspectors conducted short notice inspections and were provided multiple entry visas. Iran did not sign it until 2003—perhaps motivated to do so by the U.S. invasion of Iraq.

On February 23, 1998 President Clinton opposed Iran's nuclear energy program on the basis it had sufficient oil and gas reserves for power and work on the nuclear power reactor could indirectly contribute to a weapons program.

On March 6, 1998, the Ukraine refused to sell two turbines for the Bushehr reactor after pressured by the U.S. not to do so.

On May 7, 1999, Moscow reported Iran wanted to expand nuclear cooperation.

On May 19, 1999, Iranian President Khatami visited Saudi Arabia where the countries issued a joint statement to turn the Middle East into a WMD-free (Weapons of Mass Destruction-free) zone, claiming that Israel's WMDs posed a serious threat to peace.

On March 14, 2000, President Clinton signed the Iran Nonproliferation Act, allowing the U.S. to sanction individuals and organizations providing material aid to Iran's nuclear, chemical, biological and ballistic missile weapons programs.

During March 12-15, 2001, Russian President Vladimir Putin and Iranian President Khatami signed nuclear and military cooperation accords.

Khatami said Iran wanted a second nuclear power plant after the completion of Bushehr.

On January 8, 2002, Former President Rafsanjani announced, "Iran is not seeking to arm itself with non-conventional weapons."

On August 15, 2002, the exiled opposition group, NCRI (also referred to earlier as the "MEK" or "PMOI"), revealed that Iran was building two secret nuclear sites—a uranium enrichment plant and research lab at Natanz and a heavy water production plant in Arak. President Khatami acknowledged the existence of Natanz and other facilities on Iran's state-run television and invited the IAEA to visit them.

On September 1, 2002, Russian technicians began assembling heavy equipment in the Bushehr reactor, despite U.S. pressure not to do so. The plant faced frequent delays in construction, often caused by late payments by the Iranians.

On February 9, 2003, President Khatami said Iran had discovered and extracted uranium in the Savand area and cited Iran's "legitimate right to obtain nuclear energy for peaceful aims." He indicated Iran's willingness to accept international inspections of its nuclear activities.

On May 6, 2003, Iran's Atomic Energy Organization presented the U.N. with a sketch of its nuclear program, insisting the program is peaceful.

On May 17, 2003, Tehran backed a proposal by Syria to rid the Middle East of weapons of mass destruction. (Four years later, the Israelis would launch an air strike against a Syrian nuclear facility secretly being built there with the financial assistance of Iran and technical assistance of North Korea. Syria—in order not to draw attention to what it was doing—would never seek international action against Israel for the attack.)

On June 19, 2003, an IAEA report failed to find Iran in violation of the NPT but said Iran should have been more forthcoming about the Natanz uranium enrichment facility and the Arak heavy water production plant. It later urged Iran to sign and ratify the Additional Protocol to the

Safeguards Agreement of the Nuclear NPT to allow inspectors more access to nuclear sites and the right for unannounced inspections.

On August 26, 2003, traces of highly enriched uranium at Iran's Natanz nuclear plant were found by IAEA which Iran claimed came from equipment imported from another country.

On September 19, 2003, disavowing an interest in nuclear weapons, President Khatami said:

> *"We don't need atomic bombs, and based on our religious teaching, we will not pursue them...but at the same time, we want to be strong, and being strong means having knowledge and technology."* (This statement was made long after Supreme Leader Khomeini had reversed his position on nuclear weapons, giving then President and later Supreme Leader Khamenei the go-ahead during the Iran-Iraq war to re-start Iran's nuclear program for fear Iraq would obtain such a weapon.)

On September 25, 2003, traces of highly enriched weapons-grade uranium were found by U.N. weapons inspectors at a second site near the capital city of Tehran. The IAEA set a deadline of October 31, 2003 for Iran to prove it was not making nuclear weapons.

On October 21, 2003, following talks with Britain, France and Germany (EU-3), Iran agreed to suspend uranium enrichment and processing activities and to open nuclear sites to unannounced inspections by the IAEA. It also agreed to sign the Additional Protocols of the Non-Proliferation Treaty and its Safeguards Agreement with the IAEA. (It should be noted Iran's cooperative attitude coincided with the presence of U.S. forces in Iraq and Afghanistan.)

On October 24, 2003, a (staged) protest was held by Iranians to denounce its EU-3 agreement.

On November 12, 2003, while concluding there was no evidence of a secret nuclear weapons program in Iran, IAEA expressed concern about Tehran's production of plutonium. President Khatami claimed the plutonium was used for manufacturing pharmaceuticals, arguing the small amount produced could not make a nuclear bomb.

On December 18, 2003, Tehran signed the Additional Protocol to the NPT's Safeguards Agreement granting IAEA inspectors' greater authority in their nuclear verification programs. Since then, Iran has at times voluntarily allowed more intrusive inspections, but the Iranian parliament has not yet ratified the Additional Protocol.

On February 22, 2004, Iran acknowledged secretly buying nuclear parts from international sources, but insisted its goal was production of electricity and not nuclear weapons. (Why then were the parts bought secretly?)

On April 7, 2004, as Iran declared plans to construct a heavy water reactor to produce radioisotopes for medical research, Western envoys warned the facility could reprocess the spent fuel rods to produce plutonium.

On August 28, 2004, President Khatami again insisted Iran had a right to enrich uranium and was willing to provide guarantees to the IAEA that it was not developing nuclear weapons. (It should be noted while the U.S. envisioned Khatami to be a "moderate," he was working hard to secretly move Iran's nuclear program forward.)

On October 6, 2004, Tehran announced it had produced tons of the hexafluoride gas needed to enrich uranium by converting a few tons of yellowcake uranium.

On November 14, 2004, in discussions with the EU-3, Iran accepted the Paris accord recognizing Tehran's rights to pursue nuclear technology for peaceful purposes and reaffirming Iran's commitment not to acquire nuclear weapons. Iran voluntarily agreed to the temporary suspension of uranium enrichment activities and to allow the IAEA to monitor it.

On November 15, 2004, the IAEA reported it had not found evidence Iran had tried to develop nuclear weapons, although it could not rule out the existence of nuclear materials that had not been declared.

On November 22, 2003, Iran invited the IAEA to monitor the suspension of all enrichment-related activities.

On November 30, 2004, Iran declared it had not abandoned its right to enrich uranium and the suspension was only temporary. European officials hoped to make the suspension permanent in return for trade deals and other incentives.

On December 22, 2004, Iran's intelligence minister announced the arrest of more than 10 people on spying charges. Tehran charged the spies were passing sensitive information on Iran's nuclear program to the Israeli Mossad and the CIA.

On January 13, 2005, IAEA inspectors were only given partial access to the Parchin military base near Tehran. (Under the NPT, Iran was not required to allow inspectors into its military bases.) But the Bush administration consistently expressed concern that Iran's failure to allow full access to its suspected military bases and facilities was linked to a secret nuclear weapons program.

On January 17, 2005, President Bush advised that military action against Iran remained an option, "if it continues to stonewall the international community about the existence of its nuclear weapons program."

On February 7, 2005, Iran's Minister of Defense Ali Shamkhani said in an interview that it was not in Iran's national interest to acquire nuclear weapons.

On February 28, 2005, Tehran and Moscow signed an agreement stipulating that Russia would supply nuclear fuel for the Bushehr facility and Iran would return all spent fuel rods to Russia to ensure the fuel was not diverted for other use.

On May 15, 2005, Iran's parliament approved a non-binding resolution urging the government to resume uranium enrichment for peaceful use.

On August 1, 2005, Iran informed the IAEA it had decided to resume activities at the Isfahan uranium conversion center. The IAEA urged Iran not to take any action that would prejudice negotiations with the EU-3 or undermine the inspection process.

On August 5, 2005, the EU-3 proposed the "Framework for a Long-term Agreement" to Iran. The deal offered assistance in developing peaceful nuclear energy in exchange for a binding commitment that Iran would not pursue fuel cycle activities other than for light water power and research reactors. It called for a halt on construction of a heavy water research reactor at Arak. Iran rejected the proposal as it required Tehran to abandon all nuclear fuel work.

On August 8, 2005, Iran resumed uranium conversion at the Isfahan facility under surveillance of the IAEA.

On August 9, 2005, Supreme Leader Khamenei issued a fatwa forbidding the "production, stockpiling and use of nuclear weapons." (It should be noted issuance of such a fatwa, while moving forward with a nuclear weapons program, would be in keeping with the Iranian practice of "taqiya"—detailed later but which basically allows Muslims to further their objectives against an enemy through the use of deception.)

On August 11, 2005, The IAEA urged Iran to suspend all enrichment activities and re-instate IAEA seals.

On September 24, 2005, The IAEA found Iran in noncompliance with the NPT Safeguards Agreement and decided to refer Tehran to the U.N. Security Council for further action. The decision followed Iran's repeated failure to fully report its nuclear activities. Tehran threatened to suspend its voluntary implementation of the Additional Protocol.

On November 20, 2005, Iran's parliament approved a bill requiring the government to stop voluntary implementation of the Safeguards Agreement's separate Additional Protocol, which allowed more intrusive and surprise inspections, if Iran were referred to the Security Council. The parliament did not move to block normal inspections required under the Safeguards Agreement, which had been ratified by parliament in 1974.

In January 2006, Iran broke open internationally monitored seals on the Natanz enrichment facility and two related storage and testing locations, clearing the way to resume nuclear fuel research under IAEA supervision.

On February 4, 2006, the IAEA voted to report Iran to the U.N. Security Council for its non-compliance with its NPT Safeguards Agreement obligations.

On July 31, 2006, the U.N. Security Council passed Resolution 1696 demanding Iran suspend its uranium enrichment activities within one month. Although no sanctions were imposed, the resolution warned of "appropriate measures" being taken in the case of Iranian non-compliance. Tehran called the resolution illegal.

On August 26, 2006, Iran's President Mahmoud Ahmadinejad inaugurated a heavy water production plant at Arak. The U.S. expressed concern the heavy water would be used in the reactor at Arak to produce plutonium, an ingredient in making nuclear weapons.

On October 2, 2006, President Bush signed into law the Iran Freedom Support Act, imposing economic sanctions on nations and companies aiding Iran's nuclear program.

On December 23, 2006, the U.N. Security Council adopted Resolution 1737, sanctioning Iran for its failure to comply with Resolution 1696 by halting uranium enrichment. The resolution banned the sale of nuclear-related technology to Iran and froze the assets of key individuals and companies related to the nuclear program.

On March 24, 2007, the U.N. Security Council adopted Resolution 1747, banning the sale of arms to Iran and increasing the freeze on assets.

On December 4, 2007, a U.S. National Intelligence Estimate on Iran's nuclear activities said there was evidence Tehran halted its nuclear weapons program in 2003, assessing with "moderate confidence" Iran had not re-started its nuclear weapons program as of mid-2007. These findings contradicted the 2005 U.S. intelligence assessment that Tehran was seeking a nuclear weapons capability.

On February 22, 2008, an IAEA report concluded Iran had not fully answered the international community's questions concerning its nuclear program and testing of new centrifuge technology for faster uranium enrichment. The report was based, in part, on intelligence acquired by the Bush administration that allegedly pointed to Iranian efforts to weaponize nuclear materials. The data was extracted from a laptop computer reportedly smuggled out of Iran in 2004.

On March 3, 2008, the U.N. Security Council approved Resolution 1803, imposing further economic sanctions on Iran.

On July 18, 2008, the Bush administration agreed to send U.S. Undersecretary of State William Burns to Geneva to participate with his European counterparts in talks with Iran about its nuclear program. But Iran again rejected the suspension or freeze of its enrichment activities.

On September 26, 2008, the U.N. Security Council passed Resolution 1835, reaffirming three earlier rounds of sanctions against Iran. No new sanctions were imposed due to objections by Russia and China.

On September 25, 2009, President Obama, French President Sarkozy and British Prime Minister Brown told a press conference Iran had a covert fuel enrichment plant near the holy city of Qom. Iran said it had already confirmed the construction of a new pilot enrichment plant to the IAEA in a letter four days earlier. Critics said Tehran disclosed the site once it discovered the facility was already under surveillance and would be reported soon.

On October 1, 2009, Iran met in Geneva with permanent members of the U.N. Security Council and Germany to discuss its nuclear program. The parties outlined a proposal for Iran to ship 80% of its stockpile of low-enriched uranium from Natanz to Russia. It would then go to France for further enrichment and fabrication of fuel rods for TRNR, which produced isotopes for medical use.

On October 19-21, 2009, the early October talks in Geneva were continued in Vienna with the IAEA present, on the transfer of Iran's low-enriched uranium. A consensus was reached on a draft agreement. The U.S., France and Russia approved the agreement, but Iran backed down due to domestic opposition.

On February 12, 2010, President Ahmadinejad announced that Iran had produced 20% enriched uranium, up from 3.5%, in a move marking a major increase in its capabilities. He said Iran had the capability to enrich the fuel even further.

On May 17, 2010, Turkey, Brazil and Iran agreed to a nuclear deal similar to the agreement outlined in Geneva in 2009. The proposal called for the transfer of 1,200 kg of low-enriched uranium (3.5%) to Turkey, in exchange for 120 kg of 20% enriched uranium needed to run the TRNR. The United States and Europeans rejected the deal because Iran had increased its uranium stockpile. The 1,200 kg then represented only about half of Iran's stockpile, rather than the 80% it had in the October 2009 deal proposal. Washington also believed the move was a delaying tactic to avert sanctions.

On June 9, 2010, the U.N. Security Council adopted Resolution 1929, imposing a fourth round of sanctions on Iran. They included tighter financial measures and an expanded arms embargo. President Ahmadinejad dismissed the sanctions as ineffective, saying they were a "used handkerchief that should be thrown in the dustbin," as they were "not capable of harming Iranians."

On June 24, 2010, the U.S. Congress approved the Comprehensive Iran Sanctions, Accountability, and Divestment Act of 2010, passing unanimously in the Senate and overwhelmingly in the House. It expanded existing U.S. sanctions on Iran and imposed extensive sanctions on foreign companies exporting refined petroleum to Iran or investing in Iran's energy sector. The legislation went well beyond U.N. Resolution 1929.

On July 6, 2010, Iran announced talks with the U.N. Security Council and Germany could begin in September.

On July 11, 2010, Iran announced it had produced 20 kilograms of 20% enriched uranium and had begun work on fuel plates. The fuel was to be delivered to the TRNR by September 2011, for creating medical isotopes. Western powers have repeatedly expressed fear Iran's capability to enrich to 20% would help it produce nuclear weapons material, which is around 90%.

On July 26, 2010, the EU passed sanctions banning technical assistance to Iran's oil and gas industry.

On August 13, 2010, the Russian Federal Atomic Energy Agency (Rosatom) announced the first reactor at Bushehr would soon be loaded with nuclear fuel, becoming Iran's first operational nuclear power plant.

On August 21, 2010, an official launch ceremony was held to mark completion of the Bushehr reactor, after years of delays. Iran began loading the plant with fuel, hoping to make it fully operational within a few months. As part of the deal, Russia supplied the reactor with fuel but Iran is required to return the spent fuel to Russia.

On December 5, 2010, Iran reports it will for the first time at a key nuclear facility use domestically produced uranium concentrates, known as yellowcake, cutting reliance on imports of the ingredient for nuclear fuel.

On December 6-7, 2010, Iran met in Geneva with members of the U.N. Security Council and Germany for negotiations over its nuclear program, agreeing to meet again in January 2011 in Istanbul.

On January 21, 2011, the five U.N. Security Council members—Britain, China, France, Russia and the U.S.—along with non-Security Council member Germany (a group that became known as the "P5+1) fail to make any progress in negotiating concessions from Iran. There are no plans for future meetings to discuss Iran's nuclear program.

On February 28, 2011, the Iranian Foreign Minister Ali Akbar Salehi reportedly held fruitful and frank discussions with his EU counterpart, which he hoped would lead to further talks.

On April 8, 2011, Iran's reactor at Bushehr is loaded again with nuclear fuel after several delays.

On April 28, 2011, Iran announces the production and testing of second and third generation centrifuges.

On May 24, 2011, the IAEA announces new information about possible military aspects to Iran's nuclear activities, also reporting Iran has amassed more low-enriched uranium, despite increased international sanctions.

On June 9, 2011, Russia and China finally join the other four P5+1 members in registering their "deepened concerns" with Iran's "consistent failure" to comply with U.N. resolutions. These concerns were raised once Iran boasted it would triple production of higher-grade uranium and shift it to an underground bunker to protect it from possible air strikes.

On July 12, 2011, Iran's Foreign Minister Salehi again claimed he had "very fruitful" talks with Yukiya Amano, the IAEA director general who replaced Mohamed ElBaradei, agreeing to explore ways to resolve outstanding issues. Amano did not seem as encouraging, indicating during the session he simply "reiterated the agency's position on the issues where Iran is not meeting its obligations."

On August 3, 2011, On an Iranian television program Ahmadinejad again announces Tehran has no intention of making a nuclear weapon and its program is purely for peaceful purposes.

On August 22, 2011, Tehran announces it is transferring centrifuges from its only enrichment plant at Natanz to a new underground, bunkered facility at Fordo with full observance of non-proliferation safeguards.

On August 23, 2011, Tehran permitted an IAEA representative rare access to a facility where it develops advanced enrichment machines during a tour of all of Iran's main nuclear sites.

On September 3, 2011, the Bushehr nuclear facility finally starts to provide electricity to the country's national grid.

On September 22, 2011, while at the U.N., Ahmadinejad offers to revive a 2009 fuel swap deal, by which Iran will stop producing 20% enriched uranium if guaranteed fuel for a medical research reactor.

On October 18, 2011, an Institute for Science and International Security report states, although Iran's nuclear program struggles with low-performing centrifuges, it would still be able to produce material usable in nuclear weapons.

On October 21, 2011, Iran is soon to start moving nuclear material to its underground Fordo site for the pursuit of sensitive nuclear activities. Also, the first batch of uranium hexafluoride gas (UF6)—material fed into machines to refine uranium—is to be transferred to the Fordo site near Qom in preparation for enrichment work there.

On November 8, 2011, IAEA reports Iran has worked on developing a nuclear weapon design, testing and other research relevant to nuclear arms development—some activities of which may still be ongoing.

Also in November 2011, the IAEA reported, there was intelligence input from ten governments of images, letters and diagrams—all suggesting Iran was secretly working on nuclear weaponry. Iran again asserts any nuclear development it is undertaking is for peaceful purposes and that any material evidence against it has been fabricated by the U.S.

In November/December 2011, Iranian protesters attacked the British embassy in Tehran after the U.K. imposed tighter economic sanctions. Britain evacuated its diplomatic staff and expelled all Iranian diplomats—although it did not sever its ties with Iran.

In January 2012, the U.S. imposed sanctions on Iran's central bank, the main clearing-house for its oil export profits, for which Iran threatened to block transit of oil through the Strait of Hormuz. Also, Iran began uranium enrichment at its underground Fordo plant as it seeks "further escalation" of the nuclear confrontation. The EU imposed an oil embargo on Iran due to its nuclear program.

On February 15, 2012, Iran announces nuclear advances, including new centrifuges able to enrich uranium much faster. The next day it proposed a resumption of nuclear talks with the P5+1.

On February 20-21, 2012, senior U.N. inspectors concluded another round of talks in Tehran without success as Iran continued to refuse IAEA access to inspect a suspect military site at Parchin, south of Tehran.

In February 2012, IAEA inspectors leave Iran after being denied access to the Parchin site. Despite Iranian threats to block the Strait, U.S., U.K. and French warships pass through unhindered.

On March 5, 2012, Iran tripled its monthly production of higher-grade enriched uranium, raising "serious concerns" by the IAEA about possible military dimensions to Tehran's activities.

On March 6, 2012, the EU accepts Iran's offer of new talks following a one year standstill. That same day, Iran announces it will allow U.N. nuclear inspectors to visit Parchin but only on the pre-condition a broader agreement on outstanding issues is reached.

On April 14, 2012, Iran held talks with the P5+1 in Istanbul, Turkey, which, again, proved inconclusive. Another round of talks are to be held in May.

During March-May, 2012, Iranian voters supported Supreme Leader Ayatollah Khamenei's parliamentary candidates over those of President Mahmoud Ahmadinejad, suggesting popular support for the country's nuclear program.

On May 21, 2012, IAEA Director-General Yukiya Amano traveled to Tehran to have talks with the Iranian negotiator. They proved to be both extensive and, temporarily at least, encouraging.

On May 25, 2012, Iran and the P5+1 again meet, this time in Baghdad, where they agreed to hold yet another session the following month.

In May 2012, U.N. nuclear inspectors found traces of uranium enriched at 27% at Iran's Fordo nuclear site.

On June 8, 2012, the IAEA reported no progress was made in its talks with Iran about suspected nuclear weapons research, calling the outcome "disappointing."

On June 11, 2012, Iran's chief nuclear negotiator agreed he would focus on the P5+1 demands at the Moscow talks scheduled for June 18 and discuss a proposal to curb production of high-grade uranium.

On June 18, 2012, talks were held in Moscow between Iran and P5+1 with no progress as a "gulf of mistrust" continued to permeate the discussions. Additional talks among technical experts are to be held on July 3, 2012. Iran insisted on the right to enrich uranium for what it claimed are peaceful purposes, insisting that right is non-negotiable and "there is no reason or excuse to have doubt regarding the peaceful aims of Iran's nuclear program." However, the P5+1 seek an Iranian compromise on uranium enrichment that will address their doubts about Tehran's intentions. It was demanded that Iran comply with prior Security Council resolutions and suspend all uranium enrichment. It was also demanded the Iranians ship the 20%-enriched uranium out of the country and shut down an underground enrichment facility.

In June 2012, the U.S. exempts seven major customers (India, South Korea, Malaysia, South Africa, Sri Lanka, Taiwan and Turkey) from economic sanctions in return for their cutting imports of Iranian oil.

On July 1, 2012, new sanctions against Iran went into effect to further isolate Tehran from world oil markets and the international banking system, with the EU implementing a full ban on Iranian crude oil and petroleum products.

On July 3, 2012, technical experts met to clarify various issues which, supposedly, were clarified. Another meeting is to be held on July 24, 2012.

On July 24, 2012, deputies to Secretary of Iran's Supreme National Security Council (SNSC) Saeed Jalili and to EU foreign policy chief

Catherine Ashton held day-long talks in Istanbul, Turkey with the norm achieved—i.e., no progress made.

On August 22, 2012, IAEA intensified efforts to get Iran to allow an inspection of its Parchin site after Tehran has denied access multiple times on the basis a visit will be granted only after extensive planning—which IAEA says is a stalling tactic to complete sanitization of the site after conducting secret nuclear weapons-related experiments. IAEA reports Iranian wrecking crews have removed buildings at the site; soil has been removed and other activities seeking to hamper future IAEA verification are being undertaken by Tehran. Additionally, IAEA notes Parchin activities "may have been undertaken related to the development of nuclear explosive devices" making early access "very important to clarify this issue."

On September 13, 2012, the IAEA's Board of Governors—clearly concerned over Iran's nuclear program—overwhelmingly adopted a resolution requiring Iran to cooperate fully and immediately with the IAEA on all outstanding issues.

In September 2012, the IAEA reported Iran doubled its production capacity at the Fordo nuclear site and had "significantly hampered" IAEA's ability to inspect the Parchin military site.

In November 2012—the most recent U.N. report (prior to this book's publication) on the status of Iran's nuclear issue—IAEA Director-General Yukiya Amano said Tehran continues not to cooperate on the probe. That probe has intensified in the year since the November 2011 IAEA report found "credible information that Iran had carried out activities relevant to the development of a nuclear explosive device. However, no concrete results have been achieved so far." Additionally, Amano reported, "Iran is not providing the necessary cooperation to enable us to provide credible assurance about the absence of undeclared nuclear material and activities. Therefore, we cannot conclude that all nuclear material in Iran is in peaceful activities." Obviously frustrated by a lack of progress with Iran, Amano cited a duty to tell it like it is:

> *"Throughout the past three years, we have obtained additional information which gives us a fuller picture of Iran's nuclear program and increases our concerns about possible military dimensions."* Accordingly, he added, *"I must alert the world."*

In addition to Iran's lack of responsiveness, Amano also noted Syria has failed to respond to inquiries about the nuclear facility under construction in 2007 destroyed in an Israeli air attack. He indicated the building was "very likely" a covert nuclear reactor site despite Syrian protestations it was not.

As a review of the above timeline indicates, Iran has consistently demonstrated absolutely no desire to make progress in resolving the nuclear issue. It consistently utilized negotiations for the sole purpose of buying additional time with which to continue moving forward with its nuclear program.

The P5+1-2 Confronts Iran and Sanctions Slowly Flow; Iran Announces It Has Achieved Completion of the Full Nuclear Fuel Cycle

As mentioned, by 2006, the six countries most intent on forging a diplomatic initiative to resolve the issue of Iran's nuclear program—the P5+1—began enduring the futility of Tehran's endless efforts in talking without offering substantive progress.

China and Russia's reluctance to pressure Iran to the extent the other four were willing to do so effectively made the "P5+1" group the "P5+1-2" group. Iran was able to use this divided support to repeatedly delay action from being taken against it while moving its nuclear program forward. As Ahmadinejad had his own agenda concerning Iran's nuclear program, he was not about to allow anyone else's to interfere with it.

In February 2006, the IAEA's Board of Governors voted overwhelmingly to refer Iran to the U.N. Security Council for its non-compliance. Russia and China continued to buy additional time for Tehran by supporting the referral but only on the condition no action be taken for another month.

Iran then immediately terminated any voluntary, non-legally binding cooperation with the IAEA.

Ahmadinejad's "in-your-face" confrontational attitude in dealing with the West was quickly evidenced by his statement at a televised news conference in April 2006 he was "officially announcing that Iran joined the group of those countries which have nuclear technology." Iran had attained successful completion of the full nuclear fuel cycle.

Despite international objections, Ahmadinejad declared there was now no going back as Tehran's uranium enrichment program was here to stay. He said the world should accept that and treat Iran as a nuclear power.

In a rather revealing chastisement of Iran's critics, Ahmadinejad added:

> "Our answer to those who are angry about Iran achieving the full nuclear fuel cycle is just one phrase. We say: Be angry at us and die of this anger."

However, it is not dying of "anger" with which people should be concerned now that Iran has achieved the full nuclear cycle.

Satellite photographs and other intelligence revealed Tehran was expeditiously continuing its tunneling activities.

As reported in the above timeline, a U.N. Security Council resolution in July 2006 ordered Tehran to stop all enrichment related activities, with a subsequent resolution in December of the same year imposing sanctions for its failure to do so. But the harsher sanctions the U.S. and European nations sought to implement were again watered down by Russia and China, both of which sought to preserve their special relationship with Iran. As a result, the sanctions did nothing to deter Iran from continuing its nuclear program. Dismissing the sanctions as "illegal" and imposed by "arrogant powers," Ahmadinejad claimed Iran will never be denied its right to enrich uranium and pursue the peaceful use of nuclear power.

One cannot help but wonder why Russia and China would break with other members of the U.N. Security Council to minimize the impact of various sanctions against Iran, providing Tehran with additional time to cross the nuclear "finish line."

Iran clearly embarked upon a lobbying campaign aimed at Moscow in October 2005 when Ahmadinejad established a headquarters to strengthen and align Iranian-Russian interests. (Whether Moscow was unaware of it or just chose to ignore it, at about this same time, Tehran was dispatching elements of its Qods Force to support Chechnya rebels in Russia.)

For Russia, some motivation for supporting Iran is Putin's general opposition to U.S. foreign policy despite the threat a nuclear-armed Iran poses to the world. The Russian mindset is, if Iran's foreign policy is focused on destroying the Great Satan, then that is of no concern to Moscow.

Prime Minister Vladimir Putin

Additionally, helping Iran enables Tehran to try to save its puppet regime in Syria—also a country of strategic importance to Russia. Under a 1971 agreement with Syria, Moscow maintains a naval base at Tartus on the Mediterranean Sea, providing port access for Russian vessels not having to return to Black Sea bases via the Bosporus Strait—controlled by NATO member Turkey. Much Russian pride and prestige is at stake in retaining what is the last Russian military base outside of the former Soviet Union so that Moscow will not have to submit to a NATO country's whims concerning access to the Bosporus.

As for Beijing, which similarly opposes the U.S. on general principle, China is also tied to Iran by several energy deals running into billions of dollars and extending well into the first quarter of the 21st century. Such arrangements prompted a senior Chinese general to declare, "China will not hesitate to protect Iran even with a third World War."

Iran has demonstrated its appreciation for China's support in various ways. This has included shipping off to Beijing for its own assessment a hard-to-detect U.S. drone that either crashed or was manipulated into landing deep inside Iran in 2011 while monitoring Iran's nuclear sites.

Former IRGC/ex-CIA Agent Kahlili provided his own insights on the lack of cooperation by Russia and China:

> *"From early on the Soviet Union and then Russia was deeply involved with this regime helping the Guards (IRGC) with their intelligence operators to consolidate power for the clerics. Then the Chinese got involved and they helped with the missile program and even the nuclear program by bringing the Islamic regime and North Korea together which continues the collaboration to this day.*
>
> *"The Chinese are helping the Islamic regime with the intercontinental ballistic missile technology that the regime will test very soon. They are sharing data on the nuclear detonations that North Korea conducted. Even that action is being financed by the Islamic Regime."*

When Iran first initiated its nuclear program under the Shah in the 1950s/1960s, there was an asset being used then that was terminated when the mullahs came to power in 1979. When the mullahs sought a few years later to jump start the program during the Iran-Iraq war, they failed to access the asset, undoubtedly causing them significant delays. While they still remain opposed to using the asset today, the good news is those continuing delays have bought a little more time for the West to attempt to negotiate a peaceful resolution to stop Iran's nuclear program.

That asset was very visible in a 1968 Iranian newspaper photograph taken of work being done at one of Iran's nuclear facilities. The caption of the photograph noted, "A quarter of Iran's Nuclear Energy scientists are women," with several posing in front of the TRNR reactor. All were said to have doctorate degrees—quite a tribute to Iran's push for equality of the sexes under the Shah and the educational system he established emphasizing the sciences.

But when Khomeini came to power in 1979, he held little regard for women and their mental faculties. In fact, one of his first acts as Supreme Leader was to dismiss all female judges as he believed they lacked the mental capacity to reason and apply Islamic law. (Under shariah, women were credited with only having half the mental capacity as do men—one reason why Islamic courts require the testimony of two females to balance that of one male.) Undoubtedly, the same attitude was taken towards any educated women, resulting in the dismissal of female scientists from Iran's nuclear program. Failing to make use of them probably slowed down the start-up of Iran's nuclear program considerably.

As the West monitored Iran's nuclear program timeline, the question continued to linger whether Tehran would toe the line and direct development towards a commercial application or towards a military one. For the West, a dark cloud continued to hang over Iran for more than a decade as the international community struggled to get Tehran to come clean with which direction it was heading.

The Contentious IAEA-U.S. Relationship

A brief detour is necessary to explain what was a rather contentious IAEA-U.S. relationship.

The Director-General of the IAEA, Mohamed ElBaradei, served three four-year terms as head of the agency. He was first appointed to so serve on December 1, 1997, with his last term ending in November 2009. ElBaradei spent a lot of time in the international spotlight in this position as his term in office involved two high profile WMD cases to ascertain whether nuclear development programs were being pursued. One involved investigating Iraq, which was resolved before he left office; the other involved Iran, which was not.

It was after the commencement of ElBaradei's second term in 2001 that the issue arose over whether Iraq had re-started its WMD program. An IAEA inspection led by the Director-General failed to identify any violations. In March 2003, ElBaradei reported to the U.N. Security Council that documents suggesting Iraq was trying to obtain uranium from Niger were not authentic.

While the 2003 U.S. invasion of Iraq took place out of concerns Iraq was ramping up its nuclear program—against ElBaradei's conclusion to the contrary—no such weapons were found by U.S. forces post-invasion. ElBaradei believed, therefore, he had been proven right.

It should be noted, however, the jury may still be out on whether or not WMDs really were in Iraq as the real truth may not be known absent the fall of Syria's Bashar al-Assad.

There has been ample evidence in the years after Saddam's fall his WMDs were actually transported to Syria prior to the U.S. invasion, where they were then hidden. This is supported by a number of different sources and events:

Saddam's No. 2 air force commander has reported this was the case.

At least two Syrian defectors over the years have verified this.

Also lending credence to this is Syria's effort to pick up where Saddam may have left off as it was determined in 2007 that Assad was secretly building a nuclear facility at al-Kibar. That facility was destroyed September 6, 2007 in a surprise air attack by the Israelis—an attack Syria chose not to turn into an international incident so as not to draw attention to its nuclear undertaking or to the fact it may have been the beneficiary of some part of Saddam's WMD effort.

Undoubtedly, the failure to find WMDs in Iraq bestowed a great deal of credibility upon ElBaradei, while leaving the U.S. suffering from a lack of it. ElBaradei had counseled after WMDs were not found in Iraq:

> *"We learned from Iraq that an inspection takes time, that we should be patient that an inspection can, in fact, work."*

After the U.S. failure to find WMDs, ElBaradie has pressed for an international criminal investigation of U.S. officials under President George W. Bush who planned the invasion.

For ElBaradei, 2005 was a very good year. He was awarded the Nobel Peace Prize in recognition of his "efforts to prevent nuclear energy from being used for military purposes and to ensure that nuclear energy for peaceful purposes is used in the safest possible way." Additionally, he was unanimously reappointed as Director-General of the IAEA—but only after the U.S. initially opposed him.

Thus, when the issue of whether Iran was developing nuclear weapons began seriously rearing its ugly head in 2007, it was ElBaradei who sat in the driver's seat. In making his call on whether Iraq had a clandestine nuclear program, ElBaradei was 1-0 in making his calls while the U.S. was 0-1. Thus, the U.S. was at a major disadvantage in pressing a position contrary to ElBaradei's as to whether Iran was developing WMDs.

The problem with ElBaradei, however, was, although an honest broker, he never seemed to find a dictator he would not trust. He adopted an approach of erring on the dictator's side—a dangerous direction to take if and when he was ever wrong. This approach, coupled with his acceptance of Tehran's pattern of delays, fed right into Iran's game plan to buy more time for itself to move forward with its real plans.

With the nuclear issue still not resolved, ElBaradei gave a farewell speech in June 2009 to the IAEA Board before ending his third term. Ever the optimist, ElBaradei continued to express hope a peaceful resolution with Iran was still possible:

> "The new initiative of the United States to engage the Islamic Republic of Iran in direct dialogue, without preconditions and on the basis of mutual respect," was encouraging to him and one hopefully to which "Iran will respond...with an equal gesture of goodwill and trust building."

Unfortunately, ElBaradei sent some encouraging words to Iran by sending some discouraging ones to those concerned about Tehran's intentions. He said in an April 2009 interview:

> "Israel would be utterly crazy to attack Iran... (as it would) turn the region into a ball of fire and put Iran on a crash course for nuclear weapons with the support of the whole Muslim world."

In another interview with encouraging words for Iran, ElBaradei said he wishes:

> "...to get people away from the idea that Iran will be a threat from tomorrow and that we are faced right now with the issue of whether Iran should be bombed or allowed to have the bomb. We are not at all in that situation. Iraq is a glaring example of how, in many cases, the use of force exacerbates the problem rather than (solves) it."

Despite being replaced as IAEA Director-General on July 3, 2009 by Japanese ambassador Yukiya Amano, ElBaradei—apparently never at a loss for words—continued to offer indirect support for Iran. In a July 12, 2010 interview, he was quoted as saying:

> "I do not believe that the Iranians are actually producing nuclear weapons... (I)n general, the danger of a nuclear-armed Iran is overestimated; some even play it up intentionally."

Amano has proven to be much more committed to holding Iran responsible for its failure to meet its NPT obligations.

Having initially tolerated Iran's delays in meeting these obligations, Amano took a different tack in September 2012. He advised Tehran "without further delay" to open up the Parchin military site. He informed them that despite Iran's covert clean-up efforts to cover it up, traces of suspicious materials had been detected.

Although Iran had undertaken activities to prevent the IAEA from conducting an effective verification at Parchin, Amano warned:

> "We have powerful tools to find and trace indicators of the activities. Nevertheless we can know for sure only when we visit the site and take samples."

NCRI Exposes Iran's Nuclear Program to the Light of Day

The most valuable intelligence to assess what activities are being undertaken in a country is human intelligence, known as "humint," which provides one with "eyes on-the-ground" to more accurately make an intelligence assessment. It is intelligence gained by a source's firsthand interpersonal contacts. When available, humint is very helpful in exposing clandestine activities to the light of day.

The U.S. was fortunate in August 2002 to have just such a humint source surface in Iran. It was an Iranian opposition umbrella coalition group known as the "National Council of Resistance of Iran" (NCRI). (This coalition group has an interesting history that includes broken promises by the U.S. government to protect its members, who are Iranian and residing in Iraq—all of which is detailed later.) The NCRI, able to continue its monitoring activities in Iran much to the mullahs' dismay, subsequently reported in October 2003 Tehran was operating what was its largest nuclear facility at Isfahan.

Based on its human assets operating within Iran, NCRI also produced evidence the Iranian government was covertly building two nuclear facilities—one, partially hidden underground, which was a uranium enrichment plant at Nantanz; the second a heavy water facility located at Arak.

The NCRI reports underscored the fact construction of *clandestine* nuclear facilities was a good indicator that Iranian intent was something other than the peaceful use of nuclear energy. Even prior to NCRI's disclosure, there were comments being made by Iranian leaders supporting an other than peaceful intention.

If One Bomb Can Destroy Israel, Iran Must Be Talking About Nukes

Prior to the public disclosure by the NCRI concerning a possible nuclear weapons program in the works by Tehran, a statement by former president Akbar Hashemi Rafsanjani in December 2001 was a strong indicator high level officials could not contain themselves from spilling the beans. Apparently, Rafsanjani was not just blowing smoke out of his hookah when he bragged:

> "One bomb is enough to destroy Israel...In due time the Islamic world will have a military nuclear device."

Later clarifying his statement that Israel's destruction would require but "one bomb," Rafsanjani explained:

> "Israel is much smaller than Iran in land mass, and therefore far more vulnerable to nuclear attack."

Thus, this supposedly "moderate" Islamic cleric rationalized nuclear war as an acceptable means of affecting Israel's destruction since the consequences of an Israeli retaliatory strike would only prove "damaging" to a much larger Muslim world with a greater land mass and population.

The December 2001 statement by Rafsanjani was the first time reference was made to the use of a nuclear weapon against Israel. Interestingly, as one critic points out, Rafsanjani's assertion about destroying Israel with one bomb shows a callous disregard for Palestinians living next door who undoubtedly would suffer a similar fate as their Israeli neighbors if Iran were to launch a nuclear attack. Ironically, while Iran has constantly voiced its support for the Palestinian cause, such a comment suggests the need to take Israeli lives is more important than sparing Palestinian ones. Ahmadinejad has openly communicated this in speeches prioritizing the destruction of Israel to the establishment of a Palestinian state.

Iranian Early Bird Failed to Catch the Computer Worm

As Iran's leadership sought to put its nuclear program on a fast pace to move forward, there were efforts being mounted by others to de-rail it.

While Iran awaited delivery of nuclear fuel at its Bushehr facility in late August 2010, international eyes turned to Israel. During two previous attempts by Middle East countries unfriendly to Israel to develop a nuclear capability, the Israelis never allowed development of a facility to reach that point. In both Iraq in 1981 and Syria in 2007, Israel initiated decisive military strikes to destroy the facilities before nuclear fuel could be transferred.

That deadline was self-imposed by Israel to avoid the risk during an air strike of releasing nuclear radiation into the atmosphere. As the transfer of nuclear fuel to Bushehr's reactor was completed with no Israeli attack, observers were surprised.

However, it now appears Israel's reason for not launching an airstrike was because it had already, the year before, launched quite a different attack on Iran's facilities. It was not until well after it was launched, Iran would realize it had been conducted with devastating impact.

Every attack Israel has launched to stop construction of another country's nuclear facility has always been uniquely designed—and this one was no exception. Within their quiver of options to stop Iran was a "computer-transmitted disease." And, like a sexually transmitted one, it was a "gift" that kept on giving.

Iran did not prove to be an early bird in catching the computer worm. It was not until June 2010 that a Belarus computer security firm identified the existence of a very mysterious malware known as "Stuxnet." Dubbed the "malware of the century," it was designed to infiltrate industrial control systems. Accessing its target, the virus was able to spy, re-program or sabotage a system and the equipment it operates.

Stuxnet is very complex, making identification of its architect extremely difficult—if not impossible. However, some indicators suggest an Israeli connection.

First, any single individual or group would have been hard-pressed to design such complex malware. Thus, it is believed, state support had to be involved.

Second, while most advanced nations have aired concerns about cyber wars of the future, few have taken the threat as seriously as has Israel. Its "Unit 8200" is a highly secretive cyber-warfare group established within its intelligence services that works not only on defending against cyber-attacks but launching them as well.

Third, as of August 2010, of nine countries hit by Stuxnet, the country most adversely impacted was Israel's nemesis, Iran—i.e., 60% of all infected computers worldwide were located there.

Fourth, a New York Times report suggested an Israeli link existed deep within the malware's code. In trying to peel back Stuxnet's complexities, the word "Myrtus" appeared. Debate continues as to this word's significance but one fingerprint possibility is a biblical reference to the Book of Esther.

Esther's birth name was "Hadassah," meaning "myrtle"—an evergreen shrub of the genus Myrtus, native to the Mediterranean region. A Jewish orphan, Esther was later taken as queen by a Persian king who did not know her ethnicity. Risking death, she subsequently revealed to the king, in a courageous effort to prevent a campaign to exterminate all Jews in Persia, that she was Jewish. Her effort was successful as the Jews launched a pre-emptive attack against their enemies. While some experts contend "Myrtus" is an Israeli calling card intended to cause the Iranians to question the ability to control their own nuclear program, others contend it was planted as misinformation.

It is uncertain when this cyber-attack was first launched. A few time stamps on pieces of the code suggest it was created in early 2009. While the worm may have been released then, it probably was programmed with a time-delay feature—allowing it to infect as many Iranian systems as possible before being activated to do its damage. This would make sense as it was in late 2009 the Iranians began encountering problems with their centrifuges, used to enrich uranium, at their main nuclear facility at Natanz.

As mentioned earlier, in the aftermath of Israel's 2007 air strike against Syria's nuclear facility, Damascus maintained a low profile—failing to even challenge Israel for violating its airspace—so as not to focus further attention on its nuclear program. Similarly, although Iran experienced a cyber-attack, Tehran perhaps maintained a low profile for this reason, as well so as to avoid giving credibility to Israel's cyber-warfare capabilities. Nonetheless, Stuxnet's impact appeared to generate a schizophrenic Iranian government's witch hunt for nuclear spies, as evidenced by several subsequently announced arrests.

The potential dangers from industrial control system failures triggered by malware are endless. On September 9, 2010, as an example of a malware's potential, the U.S. was on the receiving end of an accidental failure of a control system that was monitoring pressure in a gas pipeline under a residential community in San Bruno, California. The resulting explosion and fireball claimed eight lives, destroying dozens of homes.

In April 2012, after the Stuxnet virus had been identified, a scientist at Iran's Atomic Energy Agency sent an email to Mikko Hypponen—the Chief Research Officer of the Finnish computer security firm "F-Secure." It read as follows:

> *"I am writing you to inform you that our nuclear program has once again been compromised and attacked by a new worm with exploits which have shut down our automation network at Nantanz and another facility Fordo near Qom.*
>
> *"According to the email our cyber experts sent to our teams, they believe a hacker tool Metasploit was used. The hackers had access to our VPN. The automation network and Siemens hardware were attacked and shut down. I only know very little about these cyber issues as I am scientist not a computer expert."*

It was back. A computer virus with some Stuxnet-like features had hit Iran's nuclear facilities once again.

As if Stuxnet had not been confounding enough, an even more complex malware, known as "Flame," was identified, described by a representative of the company that detected the virus as "certainly the most sophisticated malware we encountered…(and) arguably, it is the most complex malware ever found."

Iran first detected this virus, not because it targeted its nuclear program, but because it targeted its oil industry.

The emergence of Flame suggested the back-to-back hits might be part of "the first sustained campaign of cyber-sabotage against an adversary of the United States…(which) secretly mapped and monitored Iran's computer networks, sending back a steady stream of intelligence to prepare for a cyber-warfare campaign."

It was determined Flame could be spread by means of a USB stick or over a local network.

Experts reported Flame "was designed to replicate across even highly secure networks, then control everyday computer functions to send secrets back to its creators. The code could activate computer microphones and cameras, log keyboard strokes, take screen shots, extract geo-location data from images, and send and receive commands and data through Bluetooth wireless technology…Flame was designed to do all this while masquerading as a routine Microsoft software update; it evaded detection for several years by using a sophisticated program to crack an encryption algorithm."

Most of Flame's infections took place in Iran, Israel, Sudan, Syria, Lebanon, Saudi Arabia and Egypt. It infected more than 1,000 machines. Because it shared code with Stuxnet, which seemed to specifically target equipment used by Iran's nuclear program, it was believed the same source originated both.

Although allegations have been made that the U.S. and Israel jointly developed Flame, there has been no independent confirmation of this. But there are some doubts as the U.S. seemed to be surprised by Flame's emergence.

As to the focus of Stuxnet and Flame, one former U.S. intelligence officer said:

> *"This is about preparing the battlefield for another type of covert action,"* adding, however, that *"Cyber-collection against the Iranian program is way further down the road than this."*

It is clear Stuxnet, followed by Flame, have raised concerns, as well as doubts, into the minds of those involved in the Iranian nuclear program. There have to be worries that Iran's enemies can pick the locks to its nuclear files at will to steal its secrets. Worse than that, concerns must be mounting in Tehran as to what else can be accomplished by such malware. Is there, for example, a capability to completely override or disconnect Tehran's control of certain equipment or facilities? It is coming to the point in Iran where the more that becomes known about the malware, the more fear there is of the unknowns.

The concerns have reached a point where Iran believes a partial solution to preventing these cyber-attacks may be to "unplug" the internet. In August 2012, Iran's Minister of Communication and Information Technology, Reza Taqipour, criticized the global Internet as "untrustworthy," announcing his intention to disconnect Iranian government agencies from the worldwide web.

Iranian Islamist cleric Hamid Shahriari—seemingly much more savvy than his religious robes would suggest—said in March 2012:

> "We have identified and confronted 650 websites that have been set up to battle our regime—39 of them are by opposition groups and our enemies, and the rest promote Western culture and worshiping Satan, and stoke sectarian divides. We are worried about a portion of cyberspace that is used for exchanging information and conducting espionage."

The plan is to disconnect Iran from the worldwide net, replacing it with a closed loop system making Iranians dependent on an intranet system.

Mahmood Enayat, Director of the Iran Media Program at the University of Pennsylvania's Annenberg School of Communications, notes the cyber-attack campaign has caused Tehran to undergo a perception change of the U.S. He says:

> "The regime no longer fears a physical attack from the West; it still thinks the West wants to take over Iran, but through the Internet."

Among those most frustrated by the cyber-attack campaign against Tehran has to be President Ahmadinejad who still believes the Prophet Muhammad has ordained him to lead Iran to closure on its nuclear arms program before the end of his second (and supposedly last) term in office. But with that term ending in August 2013, Ahmadinejad is in a race against the clock. He is undoubtedly putting significant pressure on his technicians and nuclear scientists to expedite implementing the necessary fixes to get the program on a fast track.

But, just as Ahmadinejad might have felt it was safe to get back on the computer, it appears there could now be another cyber-attack in the works—this one known as the three "Sister Viruses." Once again targeting Iran's computer banks and equipment associated with its nuclear program, it appears again to be brought to Ahmadinejad by the same designers who brought him Stuxnet and Flame.

The malware technology has enabled someone to place themselves inside the inner-workings of Iran's computers and equipment committed to the nuclear program to better understand where the program stands.

If only the West had technology to tap into the Iranian leadership's mindset to better understand how it functions.

CHAPTER SIX

Iranian Officials Indicted for Exporting the Islamic Revolution

Just as important as knowing whether Iran possesses nuclear weapons is knowing whether it intends to use them. That requires knowing everything possible about the propensity of the Iranian leadership's mindset to resort to violence. It involves knowing what makes the leadership "tick." It involves knowing whether that leadership can and will act extra-territorially to fulfill its constitutional mandate. It involves knowing whether it has a history for acting violently even if unprovoked.

If an assessment of the Iranian leadership's mindset raises a red flag because its behavior is not hindered by international pressures or norms, then, "Houston, we've got a (serious) problem!" And, if Iran is willing to act out on such violent tendencies while not in possession of nuclear weapons, imagine what it would prove capable of doing once it does possess them.

In the next chapter entitled, "Hezbollah—The Arms of the Octopus Reach to 9/11," several examples are given of Tehran's use of its terrorist proxy group Hezbollah to fulfill the extra-territoriality mandate of its constitution. In those examples, the U.S. was the target. However, Tehran is an "equal opportunity" terrorist state and has targeted other states in addition to its own opposition leaders living outside Iran.

One gets a flavor for Iran's lust in exporting the Islamic Revolution outside its borders by examining its strong anti-Israel sentiments exhibited over the years by random acts of violence.

In April 1991, Iran's representative cleric in Argentina, Imam Mohsen Rabbani, declared in a speech in an Argentinian convention hall that, "Israel must disappear from the face of the Earth."

Rabbani, supposedly providing services as the cultural and religious information officer at Iran's embassy in Buenos Aires, actually was involved in forming a terrorist network there involving both Hezbollah and the Qods Force. (Hezbollah got its start originally as a Shiite political organization in Lebanon; Tehran later helped the group acquire its terrorist credentials by providing it with funding, manpower from the Islamic Revolutionary Guard Corps [IRGC] in the early 1980s, and targets. It is an Iranian puppet group that ever since then has undertaken certain activities in which Tehran has opted not to get directly involved so as to avoid leaving behind its own fingerprints. Qods Force is a special unit of the IRGC. [Further details on both the IRGC and Qods Force are provided later herein.])

Imam Rabbani's declaration concerning the mandate Israel must "disappear" is especially noteworthy as he would make a subsequent symbolic attempt to do just that. His major role in undertaking terrorist activities against Israel was later revealed when an Argentine judge issued an indictment in 2003 linking him to a 1994 terrorist attack against a Jewish Community Center. It proved to be the single deadliest anti-Semitic incident since World War II.

Much of the information detailed in the lengthy indictment was based on secret testimony provided by a former high-ranking Iranian intelligence officer, Abdolghassem Mesbahi. He had defected to Germany in 1996 after becoming disillusioned by the government's efforts to kill Iranian dissidents both at home and abroad.

It was also the result of an extensive eight-year investigation which witnessed the collection of numerous telephone records—including conversations between Iranian embassy officials and Hezbollah members residing in the triangle area formed by the borders of Argentina, Brazil and Paraguay; immigration documents; false names on passports; etc. (There was also a 1992 terrorist attack initiated against the Israeli embassy which remains unsolved.)

The indictment ran 400 pages as it went into the intricate relationships of those involved and how they operated. Although there were only four high-ranking Iranian officials indicted, including Rabbani, the document detailed links establishing authorization for the bombings attributed at the highest possible levels—i.e., President Rafsanjani and Supreme Leader

Khamenei. Although neither Rafsanjani nor Khamenei were named in the indictment, allegedly both personally ordered the 1994 attack. Hezbollah was also named in indictment details but no single member of the group was identified at that time.

Despite a tidal wave of evidence, Tehran labeled the indictment as "groundless." (Later, international arrest warrants were issued for Rafsanjani, as well as for a Lebanese Hezbollah operative.)

Argentina was not the only country to issue arrest warrants for Iranian officials involved in terrorist activities.

In September 1992, two Iranian gunmen walked into the Mykonos Greek Restaurant in Berlin, Germany. Approaching a table where four diners were seated, the gunmen began shooting. When the gunfire stopped, four individuals lay dead (three Iranian-Kurdish opposition leaders and their translator) and the restaurant owner who was wounded.

The subsequent investigation by German police officials determined the plot to assassinate these men was approved by Iranian President Rafsanjani and Supreme Leader Khamenei. Three of the co-conspirators involved escaped—for whom international arrest warrants were then issued, along with warrants, as well, for Rafsanjani and other high level Iranian government officials.

(Rafsanjani's name has surfaced in a number of investigations into assassinations of Iranian dissidents in Europe, establishing a reputation for the cleric as one of Iran's chief exporters of terrorism.) Only two co-conspirators were actually tried—one a Lebanese Hezbollah member; the other an Iranian. After serving ten years in a German cell, both were returned to their native countries.

Hezbollah—The Arms of the Octopus Extend to 9/11

Imagine in the fight against Acquired Immune Deficiency Syndrome (AIDS), if medical science had known—at the time the disease first appeared in 1959—everything it knows today. Millions of lives could have been saved. Unfortunately, it would take decades for the medical community to determine AIDS is characterized by the progressive loss of certain lymphocytes, leading to severe immunosuppression and other complications linked to the human immunodeficiency virus (HIV). The first cases in the U.S. would not even be diagnosed until 1981.

Around this same time, the U.S. would be exposed to another disease proving just as deadly. It was Islamofascism which thrived on a different kind of HIV virus—one of Hatred, Intolerance and Violence. This HIV arrived in Iran in 1979 as Khomeini and his cohorts filled the power vacuum left behind by the Shah's fall.

Once Iran tested positive for HIV and put a constitution in place giving it the mandate to export Islamism, Khomeini only lacked a "carrier" to transmit the disease extraterritorially. Wishing to be able to claim "plausible deniability" by not using Iranian assets for such a mission, Khomeini saw his opportunity in 1982 and seized it.

Israel had invaded southern Lebanon to evict the Palestine Liberation Organization (PLO) which had been firing rockets into northern Israel. Syria, which then controlled Lebanon, reluctantly allowed a group of 500 Iranian Revolutionary Guards into the Lebanese city of Baalbek, providing the seed from which Hezbollah sprang forth. Shiite clergymen, educated in Iran and exposed to its HIV virus, founded an organization composed of smaller Islamist groups in Lebanon's Bekaa Valley that became known as "Hezbollah," meaning "Party of Allah."

The various subgroups under Hezbollah were motivated to unite as one to fight the Israeli occupation. However, Khomeini saw the opportunity to use Hezbollah beyond Lebanon's borders. This was where he saw the chance to train, arm and fund a terrorist group attack dog, but one Tehran could keep on a leash, responsive to its own attack commands. Ordering additional IRGC members into Lebanon, Khomeini began training Hezbollah on how to conduct a range of terrorist activities.

Fueled by HIV and Iranian funding, Hezbollah embraced Khomeini's long term plan to accelerate confrontation between the Muslim world and the West wherever the opportunity arose. Thus, from these early roots, Hezbollah became a puppet of Tehran's mullahs, carrying out their will outside Iran's borders and earning a reputation as a terrorist group in its own right.

Hezbollah became a Shia Islamic militant group and political party, as well as a resistance movement throughout the region. Coming to power as head of Hezbollah in 1992, Secretary-General Hassan Nasrallah remains there today.

It did not take long for Tehran to set its Hezbollah dog loose on American and other Western victims.

On April 18, 1983, the U.S. Embassy in Beirut, Lebanon, was destroyed in a suicide car-bomb attack, killing 63. Responsibility was claimed by the Islamic Jihad.

On October 23, 1983, U.S. and French peacekeeping forces in Beirut were targeted. In what was both the largest single non-nuclear explosion and the largest single-day loss of lives (241) of American military personnel since World War II, the U.S. Marine barracks at the airport was destroyed in a suicide truck-bomb attack. No sooner had the dust settled from that attack when a second bomber attacked the barracks of the French paratroopers in West Beirut, killing 58.

The U.S. ended up withdrawing from Beirut as a result of these terrorist attacks and failed to ever retaliate against Iran and Hezbollah. It was a valuable lesson for Iran—which would rely on it again. By being careful not to leave its own fingerprints on such attacks carried out by others at its direction, Tehran had a free pass to kill Americans.

While the earlier-mentioned unsolved bombing of the Israeli Embassy in Argentina in 1992 was believed to have involved Hezbollah, the 1994 bombing of a Jewish cultural center in Buenos Aires was known to have.

On June 25, 1996, the U.S. suffered yet another Tehran-orchestrated bombing attack—this one a truck bomb that exploded at the U.S. Air Force Khobar Towers housing complex in Dhahran, Saudi Arabia. Nineteen Americans were killed and more than 350 people wounded. Responsibility for the attack was attributed to "Hezbollah al Hijaz"—a Saudi Shiite group linked to the IRGC and Hezbollah in Lebanon. Retaliation against Iran was not taken for fear of escalation, although the Saudi chapter of Hezbollah was later shut down—possibly at Tehran's direction.

It would not be until September 11, 2001, however, that the "Mother of all Terrorist Attacks" against the U.S. took place.

The evidence collected in the years since these various attacks has now revealed Iranian fingerprints, in some form.

A U.S. Department of State report identified Iran as "the most active state sponsor of terrorism in 2003." Not much has changed about Iran since then.

On July 22, 2004, the 9/11 Commission Report was published. The Fall 2004 issue of the "Middle East Quarterly" provided an excellent analysis of the 9-11 Report in its article, "Iran's Link to Al-Qaeda: The 9-11 Commission's Evidence." (The analysis below follows that provided by the Quarterly.) The Commission did examine the 9/11 terrorist attack, as well as others against the U.S. Its Report clearly dispelled the old myth, erroneously believed for years by those in the intelligence field, it was impossible for Sunnis and Shiites to work together. They most certainly could—and did.

The Report identified a little known catalyst in the lead-up to 9/11 as Hassan Addullah at-Turabi—the Islamist movement leader of a group called Sudan's National Islamic Front. Having sheltered al-Qaeda's Osama bin Laden in Sudan, Turabi arranged meetings for him with Iranian officials. The relationship that evolved was described as follows:

> *"Turabi sought to persuade Shiites and Sunnis to put aside their divisions and join against the common enemy. In late 1991 or early 1992, discussions in Sudan between al Qaeda and Iranian operatives led to an informal agreement to cooperate in providing support—even if only training—for actions carried out primarily against Israel and the United States. Not long afterward, senior al Qaeda operatives and trainers traveled to Iran to receive training in explosives.*

In the fall of 1993, another such delegation went to the Bekaa Valley in Lebanon for further training in explosives, as well as in intelligence and security. Bin Ladin reportedly showed particular interest in learning how to use truck bombs such as the one that had killed 241 U.S. Marines in Lebanon in 1983. The relationship between al Qaeda and Iran demonstrated that Sunni-Shia divisions did not necessarily pose an insurmountable barrier to cooperation in terrorist operations."

Osama bin Laden relocated to Afghanistan in 1996 after the Taliban came to power, establishing terrorist training camps there. Reportedly, Islamists traveling to these camps did so by way of Iran. Al-Qaeda training attracted a steady stream of young Islamists, many of whom transited Iran. It was noted these travelers were exempted from having their passports stamped by Iranian authorities, which facilitated al-Qaeda operations as follows:

"Certain al Qaeda members were charged with organizing passport collection schemes to keep the pipeline of fraudulent documents flowing. To this end, al Qaeda required jihadists to turn in their passports before going to the front lines in Afghanistan. If they were killed, their passports were recycled for use. The operational mission training course taught operatives how to forge documents. Certain passport alteration methods, which included substituting photos and erasing and adding travel cachets, were also taught. Manuals demonstrating the technique for 'cleaning' visas were reportedly circulated among operatives. Mohammed Atta (a 9-11 hijacker) and Zakariya Essabar (an Al-Qaeda member whose U.S. visa was rejected, preventing him from participating in the 9-11 hijackings) were reported to have been trained in passport alteration. The purpose of all this training was twofold: to develop an institutional capacity for document forgery and to enable operatives to make necessary adjustments in the field. It was well-known, for example, that if a Saudi traveled to Afghanistan via Pakistan, then on his return to Saudi Arabia his passport, bearing a Pakistani stamp,

> would be confiscated. So operatives either erased the Pakistani visas from their passports or traveled through Iran, which did not stamp visas directly into passports."

While the U.S. was focusing on improving relations with Iran, Tehran—both directly and indirectly through Hezbollah—was continuously supporting the 9/11 terrorists as follows:

> *"While in Sudan, senior managers in al-Qaeda maintained contacts with Iran and the Iranian-supported worldwide terrorist organization Hezbollah, which is based mainly in southern Lebanon and Beirut. Al Qaeda members received advice and training from Hezbollah.*
>
> *"Intelligence indicates the persistence of contacts between Iranian security officials and senior al-Qaeda figures after bin Ladin's return to Afghanistan. Khallad (bin Attash, a high-level al-Qaeda operative) has said that Iran made a concerted effort to strengthen relations with al-Qaeda after the October 2000 attack on the USS Cole, but was rebuffed because bin Ladin did not want to alienate his supporters in Saudi Arabia. Khallad and other detainees have described the willingness of Iranian officials to facilitate the travel of al-Qaeda members through Iran, on their way to and from Afghanistan. For example, Iranian border inspectors would be told not to place telltale stamps in the passports of these travelers. Such arrangements were particularly beneficial to Saudi members of al-Qaeda. Our knowledge of the international travels of the al-Qaeda operatives selected for the 9/11 operation remains fragmentary. But we now have evidence suggesting that 8 to 10 of the 14 Saudi 'muscle' operatives traveled into or out of Iran between October 2000 and February 2001."*

The 9/11 Report notes in October 2000, a senior Hezbollah operative visited Saudi Arabia to coordinate activities there and to assist individuals in traveling to Iran during November. That travel involved a top Hezbollah commander and Saudi Hezbollah contacts. In October 2000, two future "muscle hijackers," Mohand al Shehri and Hamza al Ghamdi, flew from Iran to Kuwait.

"In mid-November, we believe, three of the future muscle hijackers, Wail al Shehri, Waleed al Shehri, and Ahmed al Nami, all of whom had obtained their U.S. visas in late October, traveled in a group from Saudi Arabia to Beirut and then onward to Iran. An associate of a senior Hezbollah operative was on the same flight that took the future hijackers to Iran. Hezbollah officials in Beirut and Iran were expecting the arrival of a group during the same time period. The travel of this group was important enough to merit the attention of senior figures in Hezbollah.

"Later in November, two future muscle hijackers, Satam al Suqami and Majed Moqed, flew into Iran from Bahrain. In February 2001, Khalid al Mihdhar may have taken a flight from Syria to Iran, and then traveled further within Iran to a point near the Afghan border.

"KSM (Khalid Sheikh Mohammed, the alleged mastermind of the 9-11 attacks who is now in custody and (Ramzi) Binalshibh (an al Qaeda operative captured in Pakistan a year after the attacks who acknowledged a planning role) have confirmed that several of the 9/11 hijackers (at least eight, according to Binalshibh) transited Iran on their way to or from Afghanistan, taking advantage of the Iranian practice of not stamping Saudi passports. They deny any other reason for the hijackers' travel to Iran. They also deny any relationship between the hijackers and Hezbollah.

"In sum, there is strong evidence that Iran facilitated the transit of al Qaeda members into and out of Afghanistan before 9/11, and that some of these were future 9/11 hijackers. There also is circumstantial evidence that senior Hezbollah operatives were closely tracking the travel of some of these future muscle hijackers into Iran in November 2000. However, we cannot rule out the possibility of a remarkable coincidence—that is, that Hezbollah was actually focusing on some other group of individuals traveling from Saudi Arabia during this same time frame, rather than the future hijackers.

"We have found no evidence that Iran or Hezbollah was aware of the planning for what later became the 9/11 attack. At the time of their travel through Iran, the al-Qaeda operatives themselves were probably not aware of the specific details of their future operation.

"After 9/11, Iran and Hezbollah wished to conceal any past evidence of cooperation with Sunni terrorists associated with al-Qaeda. A senior Hezbollah official disclaimed any Hezbollah involvement in 9/11. We believe this topic requires further investigation by the U.S. government."

What prompted the last sentence above from the Commission was that it had received additional information on the issue of Iran's and Hezbollah's linkage to 9/11 only a week before the Report was due and, therefore, was unable to process it in time. It would take a federal court civil lawsuit (as discussed later) to gain access to this documentation and to determine, once and for all, whether Iran and/or its terrorist puppet, Hezbollah, were involved in 9/11.

Concerning the June 26, 1996 truck bomb attack on the Khobar Towers housing complex in Dhahran, Saudi Arabia, it was reported the Saudi Hezbollah operatives involved were linked to an IRGC commander—Brigadier Ahmad Sharifi. The Commission underscored the fact the Iranians likely played a major role in the attack:

> "In June 1996, an enormous truck bomb detonated in the Khobar Towers residential complex in Dhahran, Saudi Arabia, that housed U.S. Air Force personnel. Nineteen Americans were killed, and 372 were wounded. The operation was carried out principally, perhaps exclusively, by Saudi Hezbollah, an organization that had received support from the government of Iran. While the evidence of Iranian involvement is strong, there are also signs that al Qaeda played some role, as yet unknown."

The evidence above concerning the Khobar Towers attack prompted Washington to advise Tehran the report was a "cause of deep concern." While Washington ideally wanted improved relations with Tehran, it said it could not allow the murder of U.S. citizens to go unaddressed. Such an empty "threat" obviously instilled no fear in the mullahs and, unsurprisingly, generated a response from Iran it had found no basis for the U.S. allegation.

The earlier mentioned federal court lawsuit over the issue of Iranian involvement in 9/11 was issued in December 2011. A ruling by Judge George Daniels held both Iran and Hezbollah responsible for 9/11 as, but for their assistance, the attack would not have happened. The Judge found the defendants had provided direct support for the hijackers and was the result of joint planning of both the defendants (Iran and Hezbollah) and al-Qaeda.

Further details of the court's decision are provided by Ryan Mauro, National Security Analyst for Family Security Matters and Founder of WorldThreats.com. He noted testimony was provided by three Iranian defectors—intelligence officers—who had firsthand knowledge of the events. Apparently the defectors independently provided very similar details on matters where they had witnessed the same thing. Testimony given also indicated al-Qaeda's then No. 2 man, Ayman al-Zawahiri, and other members of the group were in Iran to discuss the plot in January 2001. One defector, who worked in Ayatollah Khamenei's office, provided secret documents that mentioned a pending attack in September 2001.

Before one intelligence officer defected less than two months before 9/11, he saw a "target wall" at Iranian intelligence headquarters bearing photographs of the buildings hit that day plus others, with a missile overhead and "Death to America" written in Arabic.

The plot was entitled, "Satan on Fire," and had been in planning for years, with al-Qaeda and Iran contacts going back to the early 1990s. The plot was evidenced by Iran's receipt 18 months before 9/11 of a Boeing flight simulator—for an aircraft it does not even own.

In July 2012, the court placed a monetary value on the human loss the 9/11 attack caused the victims' families. The two terrorist groups—Hezbollah and al-Qaeda—and the one terrorist state, Iran, were all ordered to pay the victims' families $6 billion as "entities that carried out, or aided and abetted" in 9/11. It remains to be determined how fast collection on the judgment can, or whether it ever will be, made.

Late 2011 was not a particularly good time period for Iran as in November of that year, another federal court decision, this one by Judge John Bates, found Iran and Hezbollah complicit in providing training to al-Qaeda which admitted involvement in the 1998 embassy bombings in Sudan. The Judge ruled:

> *"Following the meetings that took place between representatives of Hezbollah and al-Qaeda in Sudan in the early to mid-1990s, Hezbollah and Iran agreed to provide advanced training to a number of al-Qaeda members, including shura council members, at Hezbollah training camps in South Lebanon. Saif al-Adel, the head of al-Qaeda security, trained in Hezbollah camps. During this time period, several other senior al-Qaeda operatives trained in Iran and in Hezbollah training camps in Lebanon. After one of the training sessions at a Lebanese Hezbollah camp, al-Qaeda operatives connected to the Nairobi bombing, including a financier and a bomb-maker, returned to Sudan with videotapes and manuals 'specifically about how to blow up large buildings.'"*

July 2012 also did not prove to be a good month for Iran either. In addition to the 9/11 damages of $6 billion awarded against Iran and its co-defendants, another federal judge levied an $813 million judgment against Iran for its involvement in the 1983 Beirut bombing attack that killed 241 U.S. servicemen.

U.S. District Chief Judge Royce Lamberth noted in his July 3, 2012 opinion that courts have so far awarded more than $8.8 billion in judgments against Iran for its role in the attack. He wrote, "Iran is racking up quite a bill from its sponsorship of terrorism." Iran's liability stems from its support for terrorists involved in it. Sadly, as the U.S. court system seeks to hold Iran and Hezbollah accountable, the U.S. executive branch fails to do so.

Clearly, much of the terrorist activity directed against both the U.S. and Israel since the 1979 Islamic Revolution can be counted on to contain either Hezbollah's or IRGC's DNA.

Yet, despite Hezbollah's long track record of violence, it would take until 1997 for the U.S. finally to put Hezbollah on its Foreign Terrorist Organization (FTO) list.

Based on all the evidence to date, there should be no question as to Hezbollah's and Iran's involvement and to the former's linkage to the latter.

Ali Akbar Mohtashemi was actively involved in the 1979 Islamic Revolution, later becoming Iran's Ambassador to Syria and then its Interior Minister. A dedicated follower of Khomeini, he is also considered a founder of Lebanon's Hezbollah as one of the Shia clerics who first helped organize it. Supporting exportation of the Revolution, he saw Hezbollah fitting Tehran's need to have a vehicle to export its revolution.

Mohtashemi could not have made the relationship between Hezbollah and Tehran any more clear. He described the organization as one of "the institutions of the ruling regime in Tehran and a main element of its military."

During the time of the 1983 Beirut U.S. Embassy and the barracks bombing attacks against U.S. Marines and French paratroopers, Mohtashemi was the Iranian Ambassador to Syria. It is believed it was in this capacity he coordinated the attacks with Hezbollah and actually received the last transmission from Tehran giving the "go ahead" for them.

As an original architect of violence for Hezbollah, Mohtashemi discovered such a job runs its risks. Turnaround apparently became fair play as he was targeted in an assassination attempt in 1984. Receiving a book on Shia holy places he had been sent as a gift, it detonated as he opened it up. In the ensuing explosion, his right hand was blown off and he was seriously wounded.

Mohtashemi would survive—to kill again. He was involved in the September 1984 attack against the U.S. Embassy annex in Beirut and later became a key player in the execution of U.S. Marine Lieutenant Colonel William R. Higgins, serving as the American Chief of the United Nations Truce Supervision Organization's (UNTSO) observer group in Lebanon. Higgins was taken hostage on February 17, 1988 by Lebanese pro-Iranian Shia radicals controlled by Mohtashemi. It is believed he ordered Higgins' death later out of concerns U.S.-Iranian relations might be on the verge of improving—a development to which he was opposed.

In 1989, he also made a ten million dollar payment to Libyan terrorists to blow up Pan Am Flight 103 over Lockerbie, England.

A former Hezbollah secretary general has confirmed Iran's direct ties as well, offering that "Hezbollah is a tool and it is an integral part of the Iranian intelligence apparatus."

In 2007, the group's deputy secretary general revealed that Hezbollah suicide operations were approved at the top level of Iran's government—initially by Supreme Leader Khomeini and, after his death, by Khamenei. This undoubtedly meant Khomeini personally gave the green light for the Beirut bombings.

It is said much is revealed about a person based on whom he claims as his heroes. By that measure, we can understand much by examining one of Hezbollah's heroes.

Hezbollah has long lusted for infidel blood—and it really has not mattered what the victim's age is as long as he or she dies. The organization includes among its "wall of heroes" Samir Kuntar. He participated in a 1979 nighttime raid into Israel. Seeking kidnap victims, Kuntar broke into an apartment where a young mother and baby hid as her husband and four-year-old daughter were led out to the beach. With the daughter watching in horror, Kuntar shot the father in the head execution style. Then, using the butt of his rifle, he smashed the daughter's head against a rock. Imprisoned for three decades, Kuntar was released in a 2008 prisoner swap—returning home to a Hezbollah hero's welcome.

In its strategic game plan to fight a future war with the U.S., Iran has most certainly been making long-term plans that include the deployment of Hezbollah members in America's back yard.

Based on the close relationship between President Ahmadinejad of Iran and President Hugo Chavez of Venezuela, Tehran has been able to pre-position Hezbollah forces there since 2006. More recently, the terrorist group has been joined by members of the IRGC's Qods Force. Their strategy is twofold.

The first part of Hezbollah's strategy south of the U.S. border has involved establishing itself in South and Latin America, as well as Mexico. It has been building networks to link up with drug cartels capable of accessing U.S. borders when war with Iran occurs.

Former IRGC/ex-CIA Agent Kahlili has provided information on the extent of Iran's and Hezbollah's reach in the Americas:

> "Many countries in Latin America are being infiltrated by agents of the Islamic regime with money and oil. Venezuela is a major hub for them. They have agents in Nicaragua, Ecuador, and Bolivia. They are arming and training cadres. The regime is using front companies based in these Latin American countries with the goal of helping to build homes, roads and infrastructure.
>
> "These front companies have approached not only the Islamic community in these Latin American countries but also impoverished indigenous populations. Many Latin American countries are in a dire financial situation. The front companies recruit local assets, send them back to Iran for training, bring them back and give them a mission.
>
> "In my book, 'A Time to Betray,' I reported on the lawless triangle where Argentina, Brazil and Paraguay meet. There is virtually no police presence there thus the zone enables Iran to infiltrate, transfer arms and provide cash

to recruit terrorists. They are currently sending cells to Paraguay, Guatemala, Nicaragua, Ecuador and Bolivia. This is a threat to the Western hemisphere."

When Iran gives the word, Hezbollah will be prepared to enter the U.S. and launch a series of devastating attacks on U.S. soil.

Representative Sue Myrick (R-N.C.) raised concerns with the Obama Administration about signs Muslim extremists and Mexican drug gangs have teamed up. These signs in Mexico included: Increased bomb-making sophistication based on the first time use of a cell phone-detonated car bomb; increased numbers of Mexican gang members arrested bearing tattoos in Farsi—the language of Iran; use along U.S. borders of new tunnel-digging techniques mastered in the Middle East; and federal court indictments revealing a drugs-for-weapons conspiracy involving Hezbollah and a cartel.

Hezbollah's base has become a pipeline, as one Western government expert put it, for moving "people and things" into the Americas—both South and North.

Former DEA operations chief, Michael Braun makes it clear:

"Hezbollah relies on the same criminal weapons smugglers, document traffickers and transportation experts as the drug cartels… They work together…One way or another, they are all connected."

Hezbollah has discovered in working with the drug cartels it can not only serve the calling of the Prophet, it can also make a profit from a very lucrative drug trade.

The Mexican government's war against the cartels is driving drug activity north where some areas on U.S. soil are now deemed unsafe. An Arizona sheriff shockingly reported cartels control some parts of his state. (Yet, tough new immigration laws by Border States like Arizona that seek to protect our country are met by federal lawsuits to prevent their enforcement—including the federal government reporting the state to the U.N. for human rights violations.)

The second part of Hezbollah's strategy south of the U.S. border has involved the construction in Venezuela by Hezbollah and the Qods Force of missile bases they will jointly operate. These bases will be armed with Iranian medium-range missiles, capable of reaching the U.S., and launchers manned by IRGC soldiers. In a far cry from President Kennedy's aggressive, and successful, actions more than a half century earlier to force an eviction of Soviet missiles secretly placed in Cuba in 1962, President Barack Obama has done nothing to challenge Iran on this threat to U.S. national security.

Venezuela has sought other ways to assist Iran, as well. In October 2009, Ahmadinejad's bosom buddy Hugo Chavez offered to assist Iran with its uranium exploration. Always eager to sound like he knows what he is doing, Chavez reported, "We're working with several countries, with Iran, with Russia. We're responsible for what we're doing, we're in control."

Chavez sought to help Iran skirt international sanctions by exploiting uranium not only in his own country but in Ecuador and other countries in the region as well. He also has facilitated Hezbollah terrorist contacts into Colombia and Brazil.

Additionally, to help evade sanctions, Chavez has assisted Iran in laundering in excess of $30 billion into Venezuela's economy.

While Hezbollah's foray into the Americas poses risks to the U.S., sadly Chavez fails to see the risk to which he is exposing his own people in the years ahead. For the moment, Iran's Ahmadinejad is embracing Chavez, but the two men are ideologically opposed to each other as the former is driven by his religious beliefs and the latter by his drive to retain power.

Ahmadinejad embraces Chavez for as long as he proves useful to Iran's strategic plan. But one day, the vibrant strain of HIV Chavez has allowed into his country will come back to haunt his people. Chavez, who is suffering from cancer, may be long gone by then, having served as

Ahmadinejad's useful tool in spreading Islamism into South America and beyond.

Hezbollah was also actively involved in Iraq to undermine U.S. stability there. The Karbala attack of January 20, 2007 is one such effort that became noted as the "boldest and most sophisticated attack in four years of warfare" in Iraq—an attack in which five Americans were murdered. U.S. intelligence sources determined that attack bore all the markings of a similar Hezbollah attack against the Israelis on Lebanon's border, triggering the 2006 war. It is believed the Karbala raid was prompted by Iran's desire for U.S. hostages to exchange for senior Iranian military leaders who had been captured earlier by U.S. forces in Iraq.

It took eighteen years for Israel to withdraw from Lebanon, thus ending its 1982 invasion and removing one of the initial reasons Hezbollah was organized. In the end, it was not blood but cost that necessitated Israel's withdrawal.

In the years since the withdrawal, Iran has actively been supplying Hezbollah with missiles and rockets—many of which have been used to randomly fire into Israel and also for the 2006 and 2010 wars against it. In preparation for a possible future war by Israel against Iran, Hezbollah has been resupplied by Tehran with thousands of additional missiles and rockets. Ahmadinejad believes he will see these missiles falling from the skies all over Israel from various directions as a welcoming gift for the returning Mahdi.

The Hezbollah of today is much more threatening to world peace than the Hezbollah that started three decades ago. The threat is no longer limited to Lebanon alone but extended to a global basis. Some of Hezbollah's goals remain unchanged as it is determined to turn Lebanon into a Shiite theocracy. But its approach for achieving this has changed significantly today as the group has joined the democratic process (officially doing so on June 13, 2011) to become a political party in the Lebanese government. While its religious platform is the same, it has now piggybacked itself upon the democratic process in hopes of driving its religious objectives home.

While Hezbollah was to disarm once Israel withdrew from Lebanon, that has not happened despite a June 2008 U.N. certification that Israel has withdrawn from all Lebanese territory.

Other objectives include Hezbollah's old party line of destroying Israel and eliminating Western influences in the region. Several years of exposure to the democratic process, however, does not yet appear to have mellowed the organization.

An important factor for any investor to consider is his "Return On Investment" (ROI). Iran has invested $100 million annually into Hezbollah. Based on the violence, death and destruction that organization has wrought, Iran appears to be enjoying a very good ROI.

Iran has proven to be an "equal opportunity" funder of HIV. While Shia beliefs have served as a natural ideological link between Tehran and Hezbollah, it is absent from Iran's link with Hamas in the Palestine Territories as that group is Sunni oriented. But despite the ideological gap between Iran and Hamas, Tehran's hatred for Israel motivates it to fund Hamas which, similarly motivated, willingly accepts the funding. In any future conflict with Israel, Iran looks to have Israel fighting on as many different fronts as possible.

In February 2012, in a very rare acknowledgement, Khamenei admitted Iran's assistance to militant groups like Hezbollah and Hamas. He said:

> "We have intervened in anti-Israel matters, and it brought victory in the 33-day war by Hezbollah against Israel in 2006 and in the 22-day war" between Hamas and Israel in the Gaza Strip.

Iran clearly uses Hezbollah as a playing piece for "Islamofascist Monopoly" as it seeks to add properties, such as Lebanon, from the world board of nations to the Islamofascist fold.

A retired Bahrainian general looking back on Iran's 1979 Islamic revolution suggested it gave birth to an "octopus"—with its head in Tehran but its tentacles reaching out far beyond its borders. The arms of the octopus are formed by groups such as the Qods Force, the IRGC, Hezbollah and Hamas. While they all function independently of each other, each arm moves at the order of the head. Severing a tentacle in Iraq, Afghanistan or elsewhere will not stop the octopus' pursuit in paving the way for Islamic extremism.

It is known the octopus has an amazing ability to regenerate a severed limb. The only way to kill it, therefore, is to sever the head. Similarly, Iran's designs on stirring up chaos around the world will only be brought to an end by severing the clerics' control of their people. Tehran's theocracy has to go!

Iran Takes an "All Talk/No Action" Approach to Negotiations; President Mahmoud Ahmadinejad Takes Office Creating International Incidents as Distractions

After the 2003 U.S. invasion into Iraq and as the U.S. became bogged down in pacifying the country, three of its European allies—England, France and Germany, known as the "EU-3"—took the lead in pressuring Iran to come clean with its nuclear program. But it became clear very quickly in efforts to obtain verifiable assurances from Tehran its focus was really commercial and not military, that "talk is cheap." Iranian negotiators soon learned to adopt an "all talk but no action" approach in negotiations based on their intentions of continuing to advance their nuclear weapons program.

Despite having agreed to the placement of IAEA seals on its enrichment equipment at Isfahan, Iran announced it was removing those seals on August 1, 2005. The IAEA reported Tehran's failure to meet its obligations under other agreement terms as well. For example, Tehran's importation from China of uranium went unreported as did its experiments with plutonium. It also denied the IAEA access for inspections. Iran began to press for its right to conduct uranium enrichment. The Europeans, however, insisted Tehran provide verification it was not diverting uranium for military purposes.

With Iran's sixth president—Mahmoud Ahmadinejad—taking office on August 3, 2005, the existing divide between Iran and the West in reaching agreement on Tehran's nuclear program only got wider.

Tehran removed the IAEA seals from its nuclear equipment at Isfahan. While Iran had only threatened, prior to Ahmadinejad taking office, to restart its enrichment program which had been temporarily halted, the new president carried the threat out. Ahmadinejad's message to all was clear: there was a new sheriff in town and the last thing on his mind was to undertake serious negotiations to resolve differences.

While Tehran is well schooled in its own right on how to use delaying tactics in negotiations, it has undoubtedly studied how North Korea successfully became a nuclear armed power. One of Pyongyang's often used tactics whenever it was being pressed to stop its nuclear program was to create a major international incident, totally unrelated to the program. As the international community shifted its focus to resolving the unrelated incident, it would take the spotlight off of the North's nuclear program long enough for Pyongyang to advance it.

North Korea has had a long history of using this tactic, even before it started its nuclear program, for other reasons, as well. As domestic problems arose, it was used to focus the population's attention on an outside threat and to pressure South Korea and the U.S. for various kinds of aid. Whether a violation of South Korea's borders, a naval engagement, an assassination (such as that of South Korea's First Lady) or assassination attempt (such as that of its President) either South of the border or in another country, the sinking of a South Korean warship, the seizure of a U.S. intelligence ship and incarceration of its crew, shooting down a U.S. aircraft—the list goes on and on—North Korea has embarked upon a foreign policy that has long sought to divert an adversary's attention from one issue by provoking another.

Undoubtedly, Ahmadinejad has noticed North Korea's success in pursuing such a foreign policy, especially as it related to moving its nuclear weapons program forward. Nor did it not go unnoticed by Ahmadinejad that, time and time again, the U.S. failed to take military action in response to the North's aggression.

Whether arresting and convicting innocent hikers who were seized near its border, or boats and their crews straying into Iranian waters seeking the internationally recognized right of safe harbor, arresting U.S. citizens who had returned to Iran to visit families and accusing them of spying, Tehran has never missed an opportunity to turn an innocent incident into a high-profile international one.

One such international incident—intentionally planned—demonstrates the extremes to which the Iranians will go and then attempt to justify, contrary to the facts, an unprovoked act of aggression. Interestingly, this particular incident occurred just as Iran's nuclear program was falling under the international microscope again in 2007.

On March 23, 2007, fifteen British Royal Navy sailors and marines were operating in an inflatable boat from the ship HMS Cornwall in Iraqi waters. The Brits were outside the mouth of the Shatt al-Arab waterway, a 125-mile channel separating Iraq and Iran. They had stopped to inspect a merchant vessel for contraband when they were swarmed by Islamic Republican Guard Corps (IRGC) boats and arrested.

The history of the waterway is that its center was agreed upon as the dividing line between Iraq and Iran in a 1975 treaty, abrogated in 1980 when Saddam invaded Iran. No new treaty had yet been signed by the new Iraqi government and Iran. But satellite positioning clearly placed the British on the Iraqi side, despite Tehran's claims they had entered Iranian waters in an act of "blatant aggression." The Brits operated in these waters with Iraqi authorization and pursuant to a U.N. mandate.

After the Brits were taken prisoner, the British government gave the Iranians their exact coordinates, which plotted inside Iraqi waters. The Iranians disputed the coordinates, providing a set of their own. When the Brits pointed out that even using the Iranian coordinates, they still plotted into Iraqi waters, the Iranians then modified and resubmitted another set of coordinates that finally plotted within Iranian waters. The Iranian objective was to create an incident by capturing the Brits and then molding the facts accordingly so Iran could provide a version justifying the seizure.

The fifteen Brits were held for thirteen days before negotiations ended with their release on March 28, 2007. One of the female sailors, Faye Turney, was forced under duress to sign a statement apologizing for violating Iranian territorial waters after Tehran made it clear such an apology might facilitate the captives' release. (Interestingly, unlike in an Islamic court where shariah law requires testimony of two women to equal that of one man, the Iranians did not demand testimony from a second British woman.) Ahmadinejad held a news conference announcing the release was a "gift" to the British people as Iran would not pursue its right to put them on trial.

It was an IRGC unit that captured the fifteen Brits in 2007, rather than Iran's regular naval forces. This lends credence to the belief its seizure was a pre-planned operation, carried out with authorization directly from either the Supreme Leader or president and was not simply a target of opportunity that presented itself to a nearby IRGC unit. For the IRGC to have made the capture required they have been pre-positioned to do so.

With the release of the British personnel on March 28, 2007, there was a sigh of relief that confrontation had been avoided. The incident succeeded not only in distracting attention from the more serious issue of Iran's nuclear program but also took the spotlight off of the arrest and trial of several Iranian dissidents—an event which just happened to coincide with the arrest of the Brits.

Tehran undertook a similar initiative in 2009 when it arrested the Iranian-American journalist, Roxana Saberi, who had been on assignment in Iran, allegedly for spying. Although she held dual U.S. and Iranian citizenship, Iran only recognizes its own citizenship in such cases. Convicted and sentenced to eight years in prison, she was released later that same year. Again, with international focus on an unrelated matter, Iran's nuclear program was given "breathing room" to move forward.

The Role of the Islamic Republican Guard Corps, Qods Force and Basij

As seen in the incident in which Iran took British sailors in Iraqi waters captive, Tehran has a tendency to view the world as its oyster, violating other nation's territorial integrity (as it did with the seizure of the U.S. Embassy) and disregarding other time-tested precepts of international law. The vehicle by which Iran effects much of its extra-territorial aggression is the Islamic Republican Guard Corps (IRGC), who regard themselves as "soldiers of the Mahdi," and a group subordinate to it known as "Qods Force." Another group, known as the "Basij," wreaks havoc on the domestic level whenever Iranian citizens demonstrate against their government.

Further detail on each follows.

During the days of the Shah, Iran depended on its regular military forces—army, navy and air force—to defend the nation. But with the Shah's fall and Khomeini's rise to power, the loyalty of the regular military came into question as far as its commitment to defend the Islamic Revolution.

A major purge of Iran's armed forces by the Islamists resulted in the forced retirement of all major generals and brigadier generals, the severance of 12,000 lower ranking officers out of the service and the execution of 85 senior generals—all this despite the military having taken a neutral position during the anti-Shah demonstrations.

Consequently, the IRGC was formed in 1979 as a carefully screened force of Islamic zealots whose unquestioned loyalty was both to defending the regime and to spreading the Islamic Revolution. The IRGC commander reports directly to the Supreme Leader, which is why it is the IRGC that is entrusted with responsibility for Iran's nuclear program.

Of note is President Ahmadinejad's particularly close relationship with the IRGC. He had served in it and, consequently, has nurtured a relationship with its members by directing lucrative government contracts to its construction division; quietly moving former IRGC commanders into prominent government positions; carefully assigning operational responsibilities of critical military facilities to IRGC cronies, etc. Such a relationship with the IRGC, despite its loyalty to the Supreme Leader, provides Ahmadinejad with some feeling of empowerment to deal with Iran's enemies as he sees fit and may be what emboldened him, during his second term in office, to lock horns with Supreme Leader Khamenei.

The Qods Force is a special operations command which has primary responsibility for exporting the Islamic Revolution outside Iran's borders. While experts are in disagreement with the exact numbers of the command's membership, there may be around 15,000. It was created during the Iran-Iraq war and, while subordinate to the IRGC, its commander reports directly to the Supreme Leader. It establishes networks with other militant Islamic groups throughout the world. It has been active in Iraq, Syria and Venezuela.

The importance Iran placed on the Qods Force interfering with U.S. efforts to stabilize Iraq was underscored by the establishment in 2004 of a command headquarters along the Iran-Iraq border, from where it could better launch operations into Iraq. (This was in violation of the secret agreement—discussed later—Tehran made with Washington in 2003 by which it agreed not to get involved in Iraq in exchange for certain U.S. guarantees.) To add insult to injury, the Qods Force also maintained a command presence in Tehran by occupying the building vacated by the U.S. as its embassy. During the U.S. war in Iraq, the Qods Force was responsible for thousands of American deaths as it distributed Improvised Explosive Devices (IEDs) to militants.

Apparently there was a quid pro quo extracted by the U.S. due to Qods Force activities conducted into Iraq. Reportedly, President Obama authorized U.S. cross border paramilitary operations into Iran to go after Qods personnel and coordinate with Iranian opposition groups. (This is also detailed later.)

Ahmadinejad's service in the IRGC was actually with the Qods Force during the Iran-Iran war. (The shockingly despicable role he played during that conflict while serving in the Qods Force is also detailed later.)

The "Basij" is a paramilitary volunteer militia force established in 1979. Its members believe the Supreme Leader to be Allah's representative on Earth—and by obeying him they will receive their individual reward in Heaven. The group was Supreme Leader Ayatollah Khomeini's brainchild, organized to be subordinate to the IRGC, but loyal to him.

During the Iran-Iraq war, Khomeini encouraged these civilian, and mostly very young, volunteers to contribute to the war effort. Its members have proven to be a very brutal and effective security force as evidenced by their suppression of the domestic riots that took place after Iran's 2009 presidential election.

The Basij have been called "Brown Shirts" as they have come to perform a very similar role for President Ahmadinejad as Nazi Brown Shirts performed for Adolf Hitler in the days before World War II. The Basij even use the same "Heil Hitler" salute as did the Germans. It is estimated there may be as many as eleven million Basij members.

There was a very notable role the Basij played during the Iran-Iraq war. Urged by Khomeini to participate, members became volunteers for special suicide missions, mostly to clear minefields.

The Iranians were taking heavy casualties in attempting to penetrate Iraqi defensive positions protected by these minefields. The Basij were trained to march through them in waves in order to trigger the mines to clear an approach route for the Iranian soldiers who would then follow behind them.

What is most disconcerting about this tactic is that many Basij members were mere children. They were assured by volunteering for this mission, they would be rewarded in Heaven. Part of the religious programming to which these children were subjected beforehand involved presenting them with plastic keys to wear around their necks with which they could then open the gates to Heaven upon reaching the afterlife. (Apparently, Khomeini ordered one-half million of these keys from Taiwan, although it is unknown how many were issued.)

Most children were too young to comprehend what the mines would do to them. For many, the realization bodies would be ripped apart or vaporized, along with their plastic key, only came as someone near them was killed or wounded by a mine.

It even caused some Islamist believers to question the practice due to the difficulty of recovering a child's remains for burial. Unbelievably, one proposed solution called for the children simply to wrap themselves in blankets and roll across the minefields, suggesting the blankets would keep the bodies intact once a mine was detonated.

Iraqi war veterans reported their disbelief in witnessing waves of young children, naively marching through the minefields, impervious to the horrible death awaiting them. The unfortunate ones were ripped apart upon stepping on a mine; the lucky ones were shot and killed by the Iraqis to prevent them from successfully clearing lanes.

It is of note that one of the members of the Qods Force responsible for organizing and sending these children through the minefields was Mahmoud Ahmadinejad. If Ahmadinejad and the mullahs had no concerns about sacrificing their nation's most valuable asset during the Iran-Iraq war in this manner, one can only imagine what sacrifice they have in mind for non-Muslims.

Israel's fourth Prime Minister, the late Golda Meir, made a very astute observation many years ago about Muslim violence and how long it will take before peace comes to the Middle East. While her original comment was in reference to "Arabs," its message is just as applicable to Iranians such as Ahmadinejad whose mentality includes a willingness to sacrifice the lives of children in the name of Islam.

Meir's observation was peace in the Middle East would only prove possible "when Arabs love their children more than they hate us." Amen.

CHAPTER SEVEN

Analyzing the Iranian Leadership's Mindset: "We Will Bury You"

In 1956, Soviet Premier Nikita Khrushchev threatened the West with the statement, "We will bury you." While some interpreted his remarks as threatening a nuclear attack, it was really a symbolic suggestion that communism would bury capitalism.

Ironically, today as one hears statements from Iran's leadership threatening destruction of the West and Israel, it seems to be the symbolism that is heard and not the threat the speaker clearly intends to convey. The world seems to hear what it wants to hear rather than what it should be hearing.

As the P5+1 continue to seek a diplomatic solution to the nuclear issue with Iran, they seem to not focus on understanding Ahmadinejad's and Khamenei's mindset as reflected by their own statements and beliefs. The world would do well to read their lips and listen precisely to what they are saying.

Ahmadinejad was an ardent follower of Supreme Leader Ayatollah Khomeini's reign and remains a devoted adherent to his beliefs long afterward.

In January 2006, Ahmadinejad said:

> "We don't shy away from declaring that Islam is ready to rule the world... We must believe in the fact that Islam is not confined to geographical borders, ethnic groups, and nations. It's a universal ideology that leads the world to justice... We must prepare ourselves to rule the world."

How is Ahmadinejad's view of a world ruled by Islam even possible if the Iranian leader has any intention of resolving the nuclear issue creating the great divide between his country and the P5+1?

Reflecting on the answer to this question is of keen importance in understanding the mindset of Ahmadinejad and Khamenei. It is of particular importance as they have clearly made known a contrary intent by both their words and deeds. It is an intent carved in stone from which they will not retreat. It forewarns of a chaotic world to come—a warning many Westerners choose to disregard as but a symbolic reference. But it is chaos the Iranians believe to be mandated by Islam and which, therefore, is unavoidable. As such, it is a fate to be imposed upon Israel and the U.S., using a tool of Iran's own making, to create global chaos to trigger an event that will change the world forever.

In analyzing the mindset of Iran's leadership, one need keep in mind a recurring theme raised as to what lies ahead for its two sworn enemies—Israel and the U.S. The following represent but a fraction of those comments which have repeated this theme over the past seven years of Ahmadinejad's rule and the past 23 years of Khamenei's.

Supreme Leader Khamenei said in January 2001:

> *"It is the mission of the Islamic Republic of Iran to erase Israel from the map of the region."*

President Ahmadinejad said on October 26, 2005:

> *"God willing, with the force of God behind it, we shall soon experience a world without the United States and Zionism... Israel must be wiped off the map."*

President Ahmadinejad in May 2006 sent a bizarre, somewhat rambling letter to President Bush and the American people. While the purpose of it was unclear to American readers, it was well understood by those familiar with Islamic tradition. The letter had a sinister motive: Prior to initiating war, an enemy must be offered a chance first to embrace Islam—an offer which, once rejected, empowers a Muslim nation to destroy its forewarned enemy.

President Ahmadinejad urged on October 20, 2006—a day marking the Iranian holiday of Quds—that Muslims prepare for a "great war" to destroy Israel.

President Ahmadinejad on June 2, 2008, commemorated the 19th anniversary of Supreme Leader Ayatollah Khomeini's death by saying:

> *"Today, the time for the fall of the satanic power of the United States has come, and the countdown to the annihilation of the emperor of power and wealth has started."*

Supreme Leader Khamenei said on May 4, 2008 concerning Iran's commitment to its nuclear program despite Western efforts to stop it:

> *"No threat can hinder the Iranian nation from its path."*

President Ahmadinejad said on June 4, 2008:

> *"Get ready for a world minus the U.S."*

President Ahmadinejad said in September 2009:

> *"The pretext (Holocaust)… is false… It is a lie based on an unprovable and mythical claim…This regime (Israel) will not last long. Do not tie your fate to it… This regime has no future. Its life has come to an end."*

President Ahmadinejad said in August 2011:

> *"Annihilate Israel."*

Supreme Leader Khamenei said on February 3, 2012:

> *Israel is a "cancerous tumor that should be cut and will be cut."*

Understanding Iran's "Path"

The May 4, 2008 comment above by Supreme Leader Khamenei defining Iran's ultimate goal concerning its commitment to its nuclear program—i.e., that "No threat can hinder the Iranian nation from its path"—represents the gist of the dispute between the P5+1 nations and Iran.

What really is Iran's "path" concerning its nuclear program?

The quickest and easiest way to ascertain this answer would simply be for Tehran to "open up its kimono" and, in accordance with the terms of the Non-Proliferation Treaty it signed, show the world exactly what it has underneath. Doing so and if, as Iran represents, it is pursuing the peaceful use of nuclear energy, conflict is avoided, sanctions can be lifted, the Iranian people can enjoy a better life and economy, the confrontation is over and both Iran and the West can turn their attention to other matters.

This easy resolution, however, is one Tehran adamantly refuses to accept, thus continuing to hide its nuclear-related activities while representing its focus is peaceful. This representation alone should raise concerns in the West as to why Iran refuses to take the easy route to resolve the issue and, instead, chooses to continue along the path of confrontation. What is it, then, that Iran is trying to hide?

Furthermore, Iran's representation of peaceful intent should raise concerns because of an Islamic tenet to which the Iranian leadership subscribes. As referenced before, the tenet is, in pursuing the goals of Islam, Muslims can deceive their enemies as to their true intentions. From a Western perspective, simply put, this tenet should give the West notice never to accept representations by Muslim leaders that cannot be verified independently. Therefore, it is unacceptable for the West to rely on Tehran's representation alone that its nuclear program is a peaceful one.

This presents the following problem: If Tehran continues to represent its nuclear program is for peaceful purposes while continuing to deny the West independent verification, how does one ascertain Iran's true intentions? The West is left to examine Iran's words and actions in an effort to piece together what its true intentions are.

It would be interesting to sit down with the P5+1 negotiators to see whether they truly recognize what drives Iran to lock itself into a position from which it refuses to retreat by not allowing the necessary independent verification to be conducted. These negotiators should understand, especially after years of frustration in unsuccessfully attempting to resolve the nuclear crisis. that Iran's leadership is driven by a religious "Belief" and "Goal" controlling every aspect of its decision-making process in its confrontation with the West over its nuclear program and its ultimate resolution. Based on its Belief, independent verification is not an option for Tehran as it would deny Iran its Goal.

Absolutely nothing the P5+1 offers will deter Iran from attaining the Goal based on its Belief. Everything Iran does is designed, based on the Belief, to reach the Goal regardless of the cost to either Iran or the West. And, allowing Iran to achieve the Goal will ultimately cost both sides dearly.

It is important, in examining the Belief and the Goal driving Iran's leadership, one not be lulled into applying Western logic to Islamic extremist thinking. The two mindsets are as different as night and day. The two have entirely different perceptions on the value of human life, adding to the distance of the great divide separating Muslim and most other non-Muslim cultures.

Thus, it is also important to recognize that, in trying to understand the Belief and the Goal, one cannot approach it from the "reasonable man" perspective as, ultimately, any reasonable man would seek a resolution favoring peaceful co-existence over the alternative. Again, such logic has to be set aside in dealing with Tehran.

It is imperative one understand the psyche of Iran's leadership and, in particular, of President Ahmadinejad—a non-cleric who, based on the way he has chosen to live his own personal life, exhibits more of a commitment to the Belief and the Goal than most of Iran's more materialistic mullahs do. Crawling inside Ahmadinejad's head, knowing he may well have his hands on a nuclear weapon before his current term in office expires, should shake a reasonable man to his senses.

For those who have closely followed Ahmadinejad's rants and raves since he became president in August 2005, he is a troubling psychological case study. To understand his psyche, one must study his words, his actions and the beliefs to which he is known to adhere.

The "Belief" and the "Goal"—Crossing Over from Reality to the Spiritual World of the Mahdi

Ayatollah Khomeini had laid out in the Constitution the absolute (almost) powers of the Supreme Leader. Interestingly, those powers only granted him "temporal" authority. Why "temporal?"

There are only three ways the Supreme Leader's authority, vested for life, is terminated under Iran's Constitution. The most likely termination is caused by death. The second, while possible but highly unlikely, is by an impeachment action of the Assembly of Experts. This is unlikely as the Assembly is indirectly influenced by the Supreme Leader and any such termination has yet to happen.

But there is one other way it could happen—by the occurrence of an event which Westerners believe is the most unlikely to occur in the near future while Iranian clerics believe it is the most likely. That event is set out in Article 5 of the Constitution which states the following:

> "During the Occultation of the Vali al-Asr (may God hasten his reappearance), the Velayah and leadership of the Ummah devolve upon the just (['adil] and pious [muttaqi]) faqih, who is fully aware of the circumstances of his age; courageous, resourceful, and possessed of administrative ability, will assume the responsibilities of this office in accordance with Article 107."

To better understand what Article 5 is saying, a few definitions are necessary.

"Vali al-Asr" means "he who is divinely guided"—a mystical figure in Islam known as the "Twelfth Imam" or "the Mahdi."

"Velayah" means "Guardianship."

"Faqih" means "an expert in Islamic jurisprudence."

"Ummah" means "the Muslim community throughout the world."

"Occultation" refers to the representation the Twelfth Imam is presently in a "suspended" state. Such suspension is why the Twelfth Imam is also known as the "Hidden Imam."

So, Article 5 suggests that when the Twelfth Imam emerges from Occultation, the Supreme Leader's powers will pass on to him.

Just as the U.S. Constitution provides for leadership succession, so too does the Constitution of Iran. There is one big difference—while both provide for succession of power between two human figures, Iran's also provides for succession from a human figure to a mystical one. This is important to recognize for it demonstrates Iranian Islamists merge the real world into a mystical one. As such, they make real world decisions with one foot embedded in the real world and one in the mystical one while reasonable men make their decisions with both feet securely planted in the former.

A more detailed explanation of this Islamist mindset—"the Belief"—is required to understand their mystical world.

As do other religions, Islam too has its own eschatological beliefs—i.e., those concerning death and "end of world" prophesies that determine mankind's ultimate destiny. Islam's eschatology is based on a messianic figure, as identified earlier, known as—the "Hidden" Twelfth Imam—Muhammad al-Mahdi—or "the Mahdi." Those believing in the Twelfth Imam are known as "Twelvers," who represent the largest branch of the Shia sect. (Of Islam's two major sects, Sunni and Shiite, it is primarily the latter that adheres to the belief of the Mahdi.) President Ahmadinejad is a devout "Twelver;" his "marja" (devout "source to imitate")—also a Twelver—was Supreme Leader Khomeini.

Doomsday: Iran

It is believed that since the death of the founder of Islam—the Prophet Muhammad—in 632 A.D., there have been twelve great imam descendants. The Belief is that the Twelfth (and last) Imam disappeared in 873 A.D. at the age of four or five to be hidden from the caliphs. The Mahdi then ascended into the first of two phases of occultation.

The "Minor Occultation," occurring between 873-941 A.D., was a period during which Shiites believe the Hidden Imam, while remaining in this state, communicated with his followers through a series of four successive deputies, who acted as his agents. Thus, when believers had problems, they would write to the deputy who, supposedly, after discussing the matter with the Mahdi, obtained a decision from him, with the deputy then communicating the message back to the believer.

In 941 A.D., the last of the four deputies announced he was informed by the Mahdi he was to die soon. The deputy's death would then launch the Mahdi on his "Major Occultation." Four days later, the deputy died, allowing the Mahdi to ascend into an occultation which, so far, has lasted more than a millennium. The Mahdi is not to be seen again by anyone on Earth until he is directed by Allah to reappear at some future date. As Mahdi's return becomes imminent, it is said he will reveal himself beforehand to an earthly being who has been chosen to assist in the Mahdi's return. The Major Occultation will occur just before Judgment Day.

Islamists, such as Ahmadinejad, believe the world is in its last days. The president has reported he has been visited by the Mahdi (as has Supreme Leader Khamenei and others) and believes the Major Occultation is in the works.

As the Belief goes, upon his return, the Mahdi will rule for seven years—a period of time known as the "Tribulation," restoring Islam to its former greatness. A global caliphate will then evolve, subordinating all other religions to Islam, with non-believers given the opportunity to convert—or die.

The Belief is further detailed in the Koran. It indicates before the Mahdi's return, there will be a tremendous persecution of Shiites for whom life around the world will become unbearable. Shiites will then confront their enemies, which will include Israelis and Sunnis, controlling the Muslim world between Iraq and Egypt. Furthermore, not until nine out of every ten persons of the global community die—either by fire or epidemic—will the Mahdi return. Stability will then be restored under that global caliphate.

There is one major condition precedent, however, to the Mahdi's return to Earth: he can only return if the world is in the midst of great chaos.

It is here that Shiites split on how the chaos is to occur. The vast majority believe it must evolve in the natural order of things. But a very small minority believes man can be a catalyst in hastening the Mahdi's return.

What is worrisome, however, is that President Ahmadinejad is thought to be of the latter mindset–a member of a cultist group known as "Hojjatiech." These cultists believe man can be an active player—i.e., become the "catalyst"—in creating the chaos necessary to trigger, and thus hasten, the Mahdi's return which, in turn, will hasten the conversion of all humanity to Islam. Ahmadinejad believes he is the "catalytic converter" to make this all happen. At least four of Ahmadinejad's Cabinet ministers are also believed to be members of this same cult.

Anti-Sunni, Hojjatieh cultists flourished as the Islamic Revolution swept over Iran in 1979. The group's views were so extreme, however, that even as brutal as Supreme Leader Ayatollah Khomeini was, he feared their influence, therefore, banning them in 1983.

Wielding influence over Ahmadinejad too is a Hojjatieh cultist known as Ayatollah Mohammad Taghi Mesbah-Yazdi—an ultra-conservative cleric whom some suspect of possibly being the real power in Iran. Yazdi has repeatedly praised Ahmadinejad's efforts to return to the foundation beliefs of the Islamic Revolution (as if conservatism there was not already at its most extreme).

Further demonstrating Ahmadinejad's crossover to the mystical world is his claim he and his Cabinet have even signed a contract with the Mahdi in which Cabinet officials have all promised to dedicate themselves to achieving the Mahdi's work. (This raises an interesting legal question as to who is authorized to sign such a contract on behalf of a not-yet-manifested mystical being!) The contractual work to which Ahmadinejad and his Cabinet have undoubtedly committed themselves is achieving the Goal (discussed below) required by the Belief.

It is against this background Belief Ahmadinejad's quest to develop nuclear weapons must be weighed. If one recognizes Ahmadinejad's adherence to this Belief and that he also seeks to expedite the Mahdi's return by creating the chaotic world necessary to usher it in, it should give one pause to reflect upon how desperate he is to possess nuclear weapons. It should not take a rocket scientist to predict then what that ultimate Goal must be. **It is the possession of nuclear weapons with which to create the necessary global chaos to trigger the Mahdi's return.**

There is a tendency among many in the West simply to dismiss Ahmadinejad's Belief as a grown man's fantasy lacking impact upon the rest of the world. That is a very reckless assumption to make when Ahmadinejad—soon to be, if not already, armed with a nuclear device—views it as a mission.

As mentioned above, Ahmadinejad's spiritual advisor who has helped train him in the "Mahdism" ideology is Ayatollah Mohammad Taqi Mesbah-e Yazdi. It was the influence of Yazdi and his group that helped maneuver Ahmadinejad, a relative unknown when he started his political career, into power.

In November 2005, Yazdi claimed Ahmadinejad's 2005 presidential election victory was made possible by the will of the Mahdi. The ayatollah indicated the Mahdi's return is imminent and that the election of Ahmadinejad to the presidency puts the Mahdi one step closer to his return.

Headquartered in France, the Internet daily "Rooz," written by independent journalists from Iran to provide insights on what is happening in their country, noted in its December 12, 2005 issue:

> *"Immediately upon assuming the presidency, Ahmadinejad began to assert his belief in the imminent return of the Mahdi as the basis for his political activities. Despite the traditional belief that no one can foresee the hour of the Mahdi's return, Ahmadinejad frequently stated that his coming was nigh, and even gave a more specific prediction. During a meeting with the foreign minister of an Islamic country, he said that the crisis in Iran 'presaged the coming of the Hidden Imam, who would appear within the next two years.'"*

While Ahmadinejad's two year prediction was not met, he still believes it is imminent as it will occur before his second term ends in less than a year.

Knowing Iran would not surrender its nuclear program with Ahmadinejad taking office in 2005, Yazdi made a frightening statement—perhaps a warning of things to come during Ahmadinejad's remaining time in office:

> *"We must wipe away the shameful stain whereby some people imagine that violence has no place in Islam."*

Yazdi remained as President Ahmadinejad's spiritual advisor. Soon thereafter, one of Yazdi's disciples issued a religious justification based on shariah to support the use of nuclear weapons.

The September 10, 2006 issue of the Iranian government newspaper "Kayhan" reported on the year's address given by Yazdi at the International Seminar on the Doctrine of Mahdism in which he explained:

> *"…the Mahdi's return would lead to the establishment of a single rule over the entire world, and that the present battle against the infidels and against 'the global arrogance' is preparing the ground for, and hastening, the coming of the Mahdi."*

On the occasion of the Mahdi's 2006 birthday and the failure of his still pending imminent return, Yazdi claimed certain obstacles were delaying the Twelfth Imam's return:

> "What are the obstacles delaying the appearance of the Mahdi? [They are] the [heretical] denial of the blessing [conferred] on society by the presence of the Imam, [as well as] ingratitude, insubordination, and objections [to the doctrine of Mahdism]...We must...limit the [control of the oppressors, i.e. of the Western powers] over the oppressed throughout the world -- both Muslim and non-Muslim. [This is what we must do] in order to prepare the ground for the Mahdi's coming. Thus, the greatest obligation of those awaiting the appearance of the Mahdi is fighting heresy and global arrogance."

It will be interesting to see if Yazdi, Ahmadinejad and other Islamists continue to use this excuse for the delay in the Mahdi's return or look for other excuses in the future.

There was a sense of euphoria among conservatives in Iran of Ahmadinejad's ilk as expressed in the Iranian weekly publication, "Parto-ye Sokhan," dated March 1, 2006:

> "...with the advent of the new government, and [due to] Ahmadinejad's singular devotion to the Hidden Imam and his heir, the people of the West and dissidents fear a rise in Mahdism not only in Iran but throughout the world... [They fear this] because they see Ahmadinejad taking every opportunity and using every platform to spread this doctrine... so that the blessed name of the Mahdi is reaching the ears of all the people of the world, [even] from the world's most exalted political pulpit -- the U.N. [Assembly Hall]."

There will be those who scoff at the Goal as explained above. They should, however, consider the following.

A very significant point was made by Rooz in its October 16, 2006 issue that explains why the West will never be able to negotiate with Iran on the nuclear issue:

> *"Some of those close to Ahmadinejad, who frequently speak [of the need], to prepare the ground for the Mahdi's return, explicitly link the [fate of] the Iranian nuclear dossier to this need… According to reliable information, they stressed, in various private meetings, that the [Iranian] opposition to global pressure [on the Iranian nuclear program] and its insistence on the right to utilize nuclear power are among the ways to prepare the ground for the return of the [Hidden] Imam."*

While the good news is there are clerics in Iran who disagree with Ahmadinejad on the Mahdi, the bad news is they lack the clout that Khamenei and Ahmadinejad together wield. It is reported:

> *"Ahmadinejad's messianic policies have drawn growing criticism from ayatollahs and senior religious figures in the religious seminaries in Qom who oppose the politicization of the messianic doctrine. Two articles published in the daily Jomhouri-ye Eslami, the newspaper of the religious seminaries in Qom which represents the views of important Ayatollahs from the seminaries, emphasized the danger posed to the Shi'ite faith by the encouragement of messianic messages and by their propagation by Ahmadinejad, his supporters, and, by implication, Ayatollah Mesbah-e Yazdi, as well—a group they label 'the spreaders of superstitions.'"*

There is one aspect of the Belief that lies beyond Ahmadinejad's control. Ideally, he would like to unify the Islamic world behind him—not by attacking first but by defending against an attack first launched against Iran. He will do everything within his power to trigger a first strike by the U.S. and/or Israel so that he can take the "high ground" of "defensive jihad" as outlined in the Koran. The advantage of defensive over offensive jihad is that other Muslim nations are required to come to the assistance of the former.

Islam's holy book goes on to indicate when the Mahdi reappears, he will lead an invincible army—one in which each soldier possesses the strength of forty men. The Mahdi's army will continue the struggle on Allah's behalf. And, when all is said and done, non-believers will see how corrupt their religions are. As such, they will be allowed to convert to Islam—or die. Thus, when Allah's will is finally done, Ahmadinejad believes, the only survivors will be believers—whom he more narrowly defines as Shiites, not Sunnis.

While Iran's leadership embraces a violent end for non-believers, the West embraces political correctness, contending the dispute with Iran is not one of Islam against Christianity. The West naively clings to this position as Ahmadinejad declares that differences with the West represent an "historic war between the oppressor (Christians) and the world of Islam."

Ahmadinejad told his senior national security officials in January 2006 a war of confrontation is being fought with the West. But, in reality, such a war started much earlier. It is a war Iran has been fighting against a Christian West refusing to recognize that war for what it is.

Beware of the Imposter—Awaiting "the Mountain of Gold?"

Obviously for Islamists awaiting the Mahdi's return, it is important they welcome the right Twelfth Imam. As the exact time of the "Qiyamah," or "Resurrection," is known only to Allah, it makes it difficult for believers to separate the "wheat from the chaff" as far as knowing whether one claiming to be him is, in fact, the Mahdi.

Prophet Muhammad supposedly indicated there would be certain observable signs that will precede the return of the true Mahdi. Muhammad allegedly said:

> "The world will not pass away before the Arabs are ruled by a man (referring to the Mahdi) of my family whose name will be the same as mine."

The problem in identifying the right Mahdi is complicated by the fact that numerous times there have been false claimants. Stepping forward, these imposters become contestants on "To Tell the Truth" as believers attempt to determine the truth concerning the claimant's identity—i.e., whether he is the Mahdi or an imposter.

The website "Inter-islam.org" mentions several such imposters:

> *"However, many people in the past falsely claimed to be Imam Mahdi. One of these false claimants was Muhammad bin Tumarat; a tyrant who spread corruption and even buried some of his companions because they did not believe that he was the Mahdi described by the Ahaadith of Rasulullah…Mirza Ghulam Ahmed Qadiani (the cursed) was also one of those who claimed to be the Mahdi, as well as many other people. Beside those mentioned there were many others who claimed the office of Mahdi, the most recent being somebody from Manchester who claimed the position for himself. It should be noted that none of the above or anybody else who claimed to be the Mahdi in the past fulfilled the conditions laid down by the Prophet."*

So that believers will not be misled by deceivers, Inter-islam.org lists some of the signs the Koran states will precede Imam Mahdi's return:

> *"1) A General Sign: There are many signs that will precede him; a general and very important sign is that he will come at a time when there is great confutation, intense disputes and violent deaths when people are afflicted by disturbance and experiencing great fear. Calamities will fall upon the people, so much so that a man shall not find a shelter to shelter himself from oppression. There will be battles and fitnaas (Islamic schism) before his appearance. Every time a fitnaa has come to end, another will start, spread and intensify. The people will be troubled to such an extent that they will long for death. It is then that Imam Mahdi will be sent. Abu Saeed Al-Khudri has reported that the Messenger of Allah said:*

"'He will be sent at a time of intense disputes and differences among people and earthquakes...'"

"2) The Double Eclipse In Ramadan: The Double Eclipse In Ramadan statement quoted from Darequtni is NOT verified, indeed it's authenticity is questionable. It is NOT to be considered as authentic Hadith."

"3) The Battle in Mina: Before Imam Mahdi emerges an inter-tribal fight will take place. In the same year hajis will be looted and a battle will erupt in Mina in which many people will be killed. Ameer bin Shauaib reported from his grandfather that the messenger of Allah said:

"'In Dhul Qaidah (Islamic Month) the tribes will fight, Hajis will be looted and there will be a battle in Mina in which many people will be slain and blood will flow until it runs over the Jamaratul Aqba. Their companion (referring to Imam Mahdi) will flee to a point between the corner and the Maqaam and will be forced to accept people's allegiance.' (Al-Fitan, Nuaim ibn Hammad)"

"4) The Euphrates will Disclose a Mountain of Gold: The Final Hour will not come until the river Euphrates (which flows through Syria and Iraq and finally opens in the Gulf) will disclose a mountain of gold over which people will fight and die. Abu Hurairah reported that the Messenger of Allah said:

"'This shall not occur until the Euphrates will disclose a mountain of gold, over which people will fight. 99 out of every hundred shall die, and every one of them shall say, 'perchance I shall be the one to succeed.'

"In another narration we have been told that whoever is present at the time when the Euphrates discloses a mountain of gold should not take the gold."

"5) Emergence of the Sufyani: The Sufyani (a descendant of Abu Sufyan) will emerge before Imam Mahdi from the depths of Damascus. According to some weak narrations, his name will be Urwa bin Muhammad and his kunniya 'Abu Utbah'. The Ahadith regarding the Sufyani specify that he is a tyrant who will spread corruption and mischief on the earth before Imam Mahdi. He will be such a tyrant that he will kill the children and rip out the bellies of women. When he hears about the Mahdi, he will send an army to seize and kill him. However the earth will swallow this army before it even reaches Imam Mahdi. Abu Hurairah has narrated that the Prophet said:

"'A man will emerge from the depths of Damascus. He will be called Sufyani. Most of those who follow him will be from the tribe of Kalb. He will kill by ripping the stomachs of women and even kill the children. A man from my family will appear in the Haram, the news of his advent will reach the Sufyani and he will send to him one of his armies. He (referring to Imam Mahdi) will defeat them. They will then travel with whoever remains until they come to a desert and they will be swallowed. None will be saved except the one who had informed the others about them.'"

While some of the signs—such as the Euphrates revealing a mountain of gold, should be quite easy to discern, others—such as the emergence of the Sufyani—may be open to interpretation. Arguably, the barbaric atrocities already committed against women and children during a number of the civil disturbances of the Arab Spring could suggest one or more Sufyanis have made their presence known.

The question remaining is whether Iran's mullahs will wait for all the signs to manifest themselves or act on the chaos element (i.e., the nuclear option) prematurely.

Islamists have an established track record of not adhering to the Koran and hadiths when it fits their own agenda (such as Osama bin Laden not having the credentials to issue his own fatwa), so one should not take particular comfort in the fact the Euphrates has yet to cough up its mountain of gold.

While a gambling man would bet the mountain of gold never appears, he should probably be unwilling to bet against Iran's mullahs not using a nuclear option once acquired—even before the signs of the Mahdi's return have manifested themselves.

Ahmadinejad Manifests his Belief the Mahdi is Coming

Ahmadinejad makes no secret as to what drives his foreign policy decisions over the nuclear issue. He noted during a meeting with religious leaders in November 2005:

> *"Our revolution's main mission is to pave the way for the reappearance of the 12th Imam, the Mahdi. Today, we should define our economic, cultural and political policies based on the policy of Imam Mahdi's return."*

Also, in a September 15, 2005 meeting in New York City with the foreign minister of France, Ahmadinejad shifted the focus of the conversation to ask a rhetorical question which he then answered:

> *"Do you know why we should wish for chaos at any price? Because after chaos, we can see the greatness of Allah."*

It should be evident, Ahmadinejad is firmly entrenched in his mystical world—from where all his decisions flow. Recognizing this should make it further evident in dealing with Iran's leadership, one must drop the reasonable man approach—for the reasonable man, in Ahmadinejad's mystical world, exists for the sole purpose of being taken advantage of to accomplish the Goal.

To assess how committed Ahmadinejad is to the Belief and preparing for the Mahdi's return, one needs to examine his actions.

In 2003, Ahmadinejad—virtually unknown in the Iranian political arena—was, surprisingly, selected to be mayor of Tehran. The next year in office, he commissioned the undertaking of various infrastructure projects. Most notable among these was one to widen a main boulevard in Tehran. The reason for the project was not traffic congestion but to accommodate the large crowds Ahmadinejad envisioned lining the parade route he had mapped out for the Mahdi's triumphant march upon his return to Earth.

Later, as president, Ahmadinejad committed millions of dollars in funding renovations for the Jamkaran Mosque, near the city of Qom. Within the confines of this mosque lies a well out from which, the Belief goes, the Mahdi will ascend upon his return. It is into this portal that Twelvers have been dropping messages over the years for the Mahdi. Those Twelvers included Mayor Ahmadinejad who deposited into the well his detailed plans for the Mahdi's return. Those plans also include construction of a train track for the Mahdi's transit directly from Jamkaran Mosque to Tehran for the parade. (It would seem having had the power to remain in a state of occultation for so long, the Mahdi would possess the power to "beam" himself up from one place to another rather than having to rely on public transportation!)

In speeches before domestic and international audiences, Ahmadinejad begins or ends his remarks with a very telling prayer. There is a sense of expectancy and urgency in his voice as he prays. Regardless of the forum, which in the U.S. has included audiences at the U.N. and Columbia University, he pleads for the Mahdi's expedited return.

> *"O mighty Lord,"* he said before U.N. delegates in 2006, *"I pray to you to hasten the emergence of your last repository, the Promised One, that perfect and pure human being, the one that will fill this world with justice and peace."*

The flip side of the message calling for the Mahdi's expedited return is one that tends to go unheard by audiences of non-believers—i.e., that they either convert to Islam or die in accordance with Ahmadinejad's Belief and Goal.

Ahmadinejad has claimed, while giving his 2006 U.N. speech:

> "One of our group told me that when I started to say 'In the name of God the almighty and merciful,' he saw a light around me, and I was placed inside this aura. I felt it myself. I felt the atmosphere suddenly change, and for those 27 or 28 minutes, the leaders of the world did not blink...And they were rapt. It seemed as if a hand was holding them there and had opened their eyes to receive the message from the Islamic republic."

Both Ahmadinejad and Supreme Leader Khamenei have gone as far as to tell others they have personally been visited by the Mahdi already—an indication his ultimate return is imminent. Ahmadinejad has eagerly told other Muslim leaders the Mahdi is soon to be revealed, possibly even before Ahmadinejad's presidency ends in August 2013.

Ahmadinejad truly believes it is he who has been ordained by the Prophet Muhammad to assist the Mahdi in making his return to Earth.

Most telling about Ahmadinejad's fervent religious beliefs is the lifestyle he has adopted as president. While many senior mullahs and presidents acquired enormous wealth either through corruption or other ways of accessing the public treasury, embarking upon a life of opulence, Ahmadinejad has waived all the material trimmings of his public office in favor of a life of austerity.

Islamic extremists whose strict beliefs have been tainted by the good life are less likely to invite Armageddon's total destruction—as they well understand it would include losing that very same lifestyle to which they have richly become accustomed. Among those who may have fallen victim to this mindset is Supreme Leader Khamenei, who enjoys lavish wealth, horse farms, etc. It is the truly untainted Islamist, living a humble life and prepared to serve the Mahdi by becoming the "catalytic converter" for his return who is more worrisome—especially when he has a hand on a nuclear trigger. But this is the life Ahmadinejad lives and the role he believes he is destined to play.

In May 2006, for the first time in 27 years, direct diplomatic communications with the U.S. were initiated by Iran when Ahmadinejad sent a letter to President George W. Bush through the Swiss Embassy. Although there was great hope the letter represented a new era in dialogue between the two nations, the letter proved to be bizarre, rambling and incoherent. It was yet one more indication the West was left to deal with an Iranian leader incapable of even communicating in a reasonable manner.

Three Stooges of Evil—the Movie: Coming Soon to a Theater Near You!

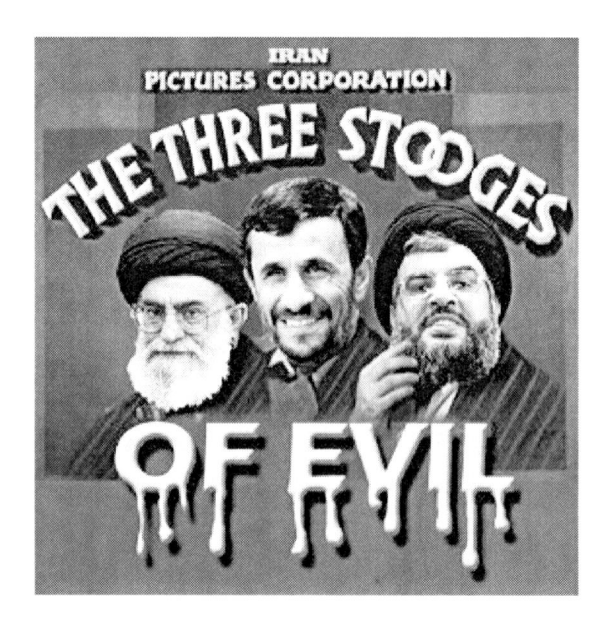

Despite all the signs that should put one on notice concerning Iran's future intentions, there will still be doubts among some who remain hung up on analyzing Tehran's true intentions towards the West from the "reasonable man" perspective. To what better source, then, can such doubters look to determine whether an autocracy is committed to walking down the path to peace or to war than a documentary film produced by its leadership detailing exactly how the future is to play out?

President Ahmadinejad brazenly produced such a documentary in early 2011 that does just that. What should worry any Western observer viewing it is there is absolutely no concern on Ahmadinejad's part about making this revelation of Iran's intentions known. Based on the West's past performance, its policy of appeasement and Allah's blessing, he believes no action will be taken to stop him.

The documentary, entitled "The Coming," reveals Iran spearheading the advent of Armageddon and the Twelfth Imam's arrival. Not only will Shiite Iran target the West and Israel, but Sunni Saudi Arabia and, specifically, Mecca—Muhammad's birthplace—is to be invaded, paving the way for the Mahdi's return. The film suggests all the stars are in alignment for the Twelfth Imam, thus indicating a pre-destined war with the West is "very close" in time.

It should be noted that as much hatred as the leadership of Shiite Iran has directed at the U.S. and Israel, it has immense hatred as well for Sunni Saudi Arabia. Some of it, perhaps, is jealousy over the location of two of Islam's holiest mosques in Saudi Arabia: Al-Masjid al-Haram in Mecca and Al-Masjid al-Nabawi in Medina. To the dismay of Iran's mullahs, Saudi Arabia is the protector of these mosques, the King having taken the title of "Custodian of the Two Mosques" in 1986. This was a particularly numbing experience for Iranian Islamists because the protector role is one traditionally reserved for the caliph under whose rule Islam is to be unified—which theoretically would shift responsibility as protector from Iran to Saudi Arabia.

Undoubtedly, the Iranians are particularly agitated by the Saudis' role of protector in light of recent developments in these two holiest of Islam's cities where the country's ruling Wahhabi sect is destroying some of ancient remnants of Prophet Muhammad's life there. The house of one of the Prophet's wives in Mecca was recently demolished to provide space for public bathrooms. His birthplace may also soon disappear as King Abdullah seeks to implement a plan to build a Grand Mosque.

In Medina, a mosque of the Prophet's grandson was destroyed with plans to tear down an additional three seventh-century mosques in the works.

Despite all the violence and anti-Western uproar that has followed publication of drawings of the Prophet in the West or destruction of Korans, there have been no similar protests by Muslims against the Saudis for their destructive actions. This provides yet another example of Islam's hypocrisy.

Khomeini's hatred of the Saudis did not allow him to depart this world without making one last scathing attack against his enemies. He left a 29-page will criticizing the Saudi King for spreading false (Sunni) Islam within the Kingdom and allying himself with the West. Khomeini's last will and testament is his last appeal for war and the return of the Mahdi which would then follow.

"The Coming" explains there are three men in the Middle East in positions of power and authority bonded together by a strong shared belief. All three see a world in complete disarray. Desperately needed to re-organize the world is a leader possessing mystical powers. They believe just such a leader has been pre-ordained for this role, with the ability to create a single global society—a leader who will effectively mold all of Planet Earth's inhabitants into a society answerable to but one God and one set of laws. Any one opposing such a world order under Islam would be put to death.

The trio believes this pre-ordained mystical leader has walked among Earth's inhabitants before. He was a descendant of a great religious warrior-leader more than a millennium ago, but disappeared as a child, ascending into a state of occultation. He still exists in this suspended state today, unable to return to Earth to lead this global unification fight until the right condition exists by which to release him and trigger his return.

The plot thickens as it is the trio alone who collectively hold the key to the occulted leader's release. Only by their joining forces and working together to achieve the necessary condition to free the leader from his occultation can his destiny be achieved.

The key for the trio in ushering in the Mahdi's return is world chaos. How that will happen, the viewer can surmise, is for one of the trio's members to obtain the necessary tool to create such global chaos—a goal from which he remains undeterred, regardless of the obstacles placed in his way.

The above may sound like intriguing fiction—but it is not. This is exactly how the real trio of leaders intends to use war to expedite the Mahdi's return. The stars of the film are identified as Iranian Supreme Leader Ayatollah Ali Khamenei, Iranian President Mahmoud Ahmadinejad and Lebanon's Iranian-sponsored Hezbollah's group leader, Hassan Nasrallah.

Khamenei is deemed "the preparer" for the Mahdi's return. The film claims Khamenei has already had a private meeting with the Mahdi who came down from his "occulted" state to reveal himself to the head mullah. During this meeting, Khamenei was allegedly told the Mahdi's official arrival will occur sometime before Khamenei's term as Supreme Leader ends (i.e., his death).

As "the preparer," Khamenei is to appoint a commander-in-chief 72 months before the Mahdi's return. Ahmadinejad became president in August 2005 and has continued in office for a second term by virtue of his theft of the 2009 election. Thus, that role is seen as Ahmadinejad's.

The last member of the prophecy's trio the film identifies is a military commander—a role played by Hezbollah's Nasrallah—who is to form the Mahdi's army with which to march into Mecca in Saudi Arabia. (As indicated earlier, this indicates the Mahdi's "three amigos" are targeting both Muslims and non-Muslims alike.)

A direct threat to the Saudis is made at the very beginning of the film which begins with the challenge:

> *"Whoever guarantees the death of King Abdullah in Saudi Arabia, I will guarantee the imminent reappearance of the Mahdi."*

This is an obvious invitation to assassinate the Saudi leader, yet another necessary pin to fall before the Mahdi's appearance. (The alleged 2011 Iranian plot to assassinate the Saudi Ambassador in Washington D.C. may well have been an effort to achieve the same symbolic result by assassinating the King's personal representative.)

It appears Ahmadinejad's intention is to use this documentary as an educational tool for preparing followers for the role "a nation in the east" (i.e., Iran) is destined to play in fulfilling the prophecy by leading the war against Islam's enemies to trigger the Mahdi's return. The film cites current events, such as the various Arab Spring uprisings, to explain that "the final chapter has begun."

Upon the documentary's release, it was immediately shown to top clerics, the IRGC and the Basij. It has been distributed to mosques and Islamic centers throughout the country. Ahmadinejad seeks to educate his own people as to what the future holds for them. Meanwhile, U.S. leaders do little to educate Americans on Iran's plans for the U.S. as set forth in the documentary.

If the trio above were characters in a comedy spoof, Western viewers would anticipate seeing the "three stooges of evil" stopped in time by a superhero. Unfortunately, the danger in the real life plot of "The return of the Mahdi" is the superhero role still remains unscripted. Absent such a superhero, Ahmadinejad has every intention of having this prophecy play out "at a theater near you."

Ironically, the war with Iran the West has so desperately sought to avoid is one Tehran, based on its own documentary, defiantly seeks to have play out. It cannot be made any clearer by Iran it is preparing for war. Yet the West seems to sleep through Ahmadinejad's movie. The brazen act of producing a film conveying one's evil intentions cannot be interpreted as anything other than Ahmadinejad's confidence of continuing Western complacency influenced by Allah.

The Sunni/Shiite split discussed earlier adds another dimension to the prophecy Ahmadinejad perceives will be fulfilled.

As indicated in the film, Islamists believe after Islam attains its manifest destiny and the Mahdi has re-established a global caliphate, harmony will follow. This harmony evolves, not because non-believers have "seen the light" and embraced the religion but, rather, because all who have refused to embrace it have been put to the sword. Thus, Ahmadinejad surmises, only believers will survive so that conflict is non-existent.

Basically, Islamists envision a once heavily populated "pool" of humanity being culled via forceful conversions or violent drowning of non-Muslims. But non-Muslims, again as perceived by Ahmadinejad, include all who are not Shiite, so that even their brother Muslim Sunnis would be put to the sword unless they agreed to convert to become Shia Muslims.

If Sunnis failed to convert to Shia in Ahmadinejad's mystical world, the peace he advertises, in an all Muslim world, could not exist. History's record of Muslim-on-Muslim violence shows conflict is unavoidable. Such violence prevails today in places like Iraq, Syria, Gaza, Yemen, Pakistan, Mali, etc. Muslim-on-Muslim violence during the twentieth century and through the early years of the twenty-first century accounts for far more Muslim deaths than those caused by non-Muslim-on-Muslim violence.

Iran Won't Be Kept from its Appointed Rounds—Not Even by MAD

As emphasized before, a natural tendency by Westerners in trying to understand the Iranian mindset is to apply the "reasonable man" approach. Doing so might tempt one to consider allowing Iran to have its own nuclear arsenal as, based on the success of the Cold War doctrine of "Mutual Assured Destruction," appropriately called "MAD," both sides restrained themselves from the use of such weapons for more than half a century.

During the Cold War, as the U.S. and Soviet Union continued adding to their nuclear arsenals, the national security doctrine of MAD evolved. In a nutshell, the rationalization of that doctrine was that both sides had so many weapons, it gave each an effective destructive retaliatory strike capability which then served to deter either side from launching a first strike. The reasonable thinking was in a nuclear exchange, once the missiles stopped flying, the devastation would be so extensive there would be no victors. Thus, reasonable men would be prompted to work toward a reasonable resolution to avoid a nuclear confrontation.

Despite an absence of logic on many occasions in dealing with Soviet leaders during the Cold War, one could take comfort in knowing they valued human life—even if it was just their own. Accordingly, they sought to preserve that life at all costs, reducing the likelihood of a U.S. nuclear retaliatory strike and its consequences. Thus, inviting self-destruction by initiating its own nuclear attack was never an option for Moscow. This was evidenced by the 1962 Cuban Missile Crisis—a confrontation that came close to nuclear war—but which was avoided due to this valuation as the Soviets backed down.

One should be able to recognize at this point that Ahmadinejad, in assessing the MAD deterrent, simply cannot be measured by the "reasonable man" standard. He does not fear nuclear retaliation for he believes the Mahdi will intervene to protect deserving Muslims who survive such a response. By his calculations, part of the Belief is 90% of mankind is pre-destined to die when the Mahdi returns so deaths caused in a nuclear exchange would be part of that equation. And, he believes, a nuclear holocaust is absolutely necessary to create the global chaos to trigger the Mahdi's return.

There is, therefore, a fatal flaw in believing, as a reasonable man, the MAD doctrine would work to deter Iran. That flaw was underscored in a bizarre 2009 PowerPoint presentation given by a senior year psychiatric resident and Islamist serving in the U.S. military at the time—Major Nidal M. Hasan—who later would be responsible for the Fort Hood massacre. While defending suicide bombing attacks and acts by Muslims of beheading, burning victims alive and pouring boiling oil down the throats of non-believers, Hasan concluded with a slide reading, "We (Muslims) love death more than you (non-Muslims) love life."

Hasan's observation was one near and dear to the heart of all Islamic extremists. As such, it permeates the Iranian leadership's mindset as to how it deals with the West. Hasan's presentation should have prompted his seniors to act, or at least investigate, his intentions; but, unfortunately, those seniors were blinded by political correctness. The failure to do so resulted in the worst shooting in history to occur on a U.S. military base. On November 5, 2009, Major Hasan killed 13 unarmed fellow soldiers and wounded 29 more at Fort Hood, Texas. Their crime, in his mind, was they were non-Muslims.

Similarly, from the combination of the words and actions of Iran's leadership, one should take notice of their intentions which were linked, as were Hasan's, to an intense hatred for non-Muslims and a belief in the Mahdi's prophecy. Like the U.S. postal service, nothing—not even MAD—will keep Iran's leadership "from the swift completion of their appointed rounds" in laying the ground work for the Mahdi's return.

If Hasan's mindset is not convincing enough, one should keep in mind the price Supreme Leader Khomeini made clear he was willing to pay in 1981 to ensure Islam's global dominance:

> *"I say let Iran go up in smoke, provided Islam emerges triumphant in the rest of the world."*

It is clear Iran's leadership puts no limits on what it is willing to sacrifice—including the motherland—to achieve the global Islamic domination it believes will follow the Mahdi's return.

Chapter Eight

Iran's Leadership Spreading HIV

One cannot listen to the diatribes of Iran's mullahs or non-cleric Islamist leaders without wondering what drives their venomous speech and mindset. What abuse have they suffered so as to program them with such negativity towards their fellow man? What is it in their psychological make-up that has infected them to the point they have lost all sense of humanity, not only towards those with different cultural backgrounds but those within their own culture who fail to mirror their own beliefs?

Somewhere in their life experiences, these leaders were exposed to an illness. Infected with this disease, they suffer its consequences now, while seeking to spread the disease globally. The disease from which they suffer is "HIV"—an affliction causing one to act out of Hatred, Intolerance and Violence towards anyone who is different.

The source of the disease is an extremist interpretation of Islam. It is an interpretation of human rights that has caused a great divide between the Muslim world and the world of non-believers. It is an interpretation choosing to cloak one religion as superior to all others—claiming it will one day rule all mankind.

Not Everyone is Invited to Humanity's "Pool Party"

The Islamist's HIV took firm root in 1979 in Iran as the people's will for democracy fell to the ill will of a theocratic leadership's belief system holding no room for "universal" human rights.

As the destructive wave known as the Islamic Revolution swept across Iran and the mullahs, under a brutal Supreme Leader Ayatollah Khomeini, stabilized their power, it was important for them to redefine what already had been defined and unanimously agreed upon decades earlier by the world community as the human rights gold standard.

A "supremacist" is a promoter or advocate who believes in the superiority of a particular group of which he is a member, over all other groups of humanity. Supremacists come in many different stripes whether based on color, sex, religion, etc. If a "pool party" were held for all humanity, the supremacist would move immediately to eliminate all the inferior "swimmers." The supremacist only wishes to "swim" with those he deems to be of equal status. All others must vacate the pool of humanity.

Accepting this understanding of a supremacist's mentality, one then needs to understand that Islamic supremacists in Iran empty the world community pool of "inferior" swimmers on the sole basis of not being members of their religious group. They cull the pool of inferior swimmers by defining human rights with a definition far more limiting than that applied by the rest of the world community.

To clarify, one must understand the initial reason the world community adopted, as a world body through a United Nations resolution, a "universal declaration of human rights."

In January 1941, President Franklin Delano Roosevelt delivered a State of the Union Address, identifying four all-important freedoms: freedom of speech, freedom of assembly, freedom from fear and freedom from want. After World War II broke out, the Allies saw as their objective in winning the conflict, securing these freedoms for all humanity.

In June 1945, the United Nations Charter was passed, referencing these freedoms and requiring them to be "universal." The Charter *"reaffirmed faith in fundamental human rights, and dignity and worth of the human person,"* requiring member states promote *"universal respect for, and observance of, human rights and fundamental freedoms for all without distinction as to race, sex, language, or religion."*

All 51 U.N. member states at the time eventually signed this Charter. It became effective October 24, 1945, following ratification by permanent Security Council members. Security Council members who signed included some states not particularly reputable for their support of human rights, such as communist China and the USSR. But by signing, Charter signatories also agreed all obligations made to the United Nations would have priority over any treaty obligations between or among any member states.

The revelation of the atrocities committed during World War II raised concerns the Charter should be revised to further define these rights. This gave rise to the "Universal Declaration of Human Rights" (UDHR), which was unanimously passed by the U.N. General Assembly (Saudi Arabia did not sign) in December 1948—a vote of approval cast by Muslim and non-Muslim member states together. Among the former was Iran.

It is ironic that the hatred and brutality of the Nazis during World War II that led to the deaths of six million Jews in the Holocaust was also what led to the UDHR initiative. The Nazi atrocities were recognized collectively by the world community, including Iran, all of whom supported the UDHR in hopes of preventing such brutality in the future.

Ironically, as Iranian President Ahmadinejad today continues to deny the Holocaust even took place, he fails to recognize it was the horrors originating from it that prompted his country initially to vote for the UDHR. The absence of any empathy on his part for such an abhorrent event was demonstrated by his insensitive initiative in 2006 to hold a contest to draw cartoons disparaging the Holocaust.

Interestingly, Supreme Allied Commander General Dwight Eisenhower took action when World War II ended to preserve evidence at the death camps so that future leaders, like Ahmadinejad, could not deny what had happened. Having walked through these camps, Eisenhower ordered the atrocities be captured on film and in photographs.

Eisenhower's words to his staff were:

> "Get it all on record now. Get the films. Get the witnesses. Because somewhere down the road of history some bastard will get up and say that this never happened."

Eisenhower undoubtedly believed in the logic of the "reasonable man"—i.e., that such evidence of past horrors would undermine future deniability by the ignorant. Unfortunately, Eisenhower's effort to collect evidence did not envision the "unreasonable man"—epitomized by Ahmadinejad today—whose hatred for Jews is so intense it blinds him from seeing the truth.

The Preamble of the UDHR and Articles 1 through 3 stipulate the following:

> "Now, Therefore THE GENERAL ASSEMBLY proclaims THIS UNIVERSAL DECLARATION OF HUMAN RIGHTS as a common standard of achievement for all peoples and all nations, to the end that every individual and every organ of society, keeping this Declaration constantly in mind, shall strive by teaching and education to promote respect for these rights and freedoms and by progressive measures, national and international, to secure their universal and effective recognition and observance, both among the peoples of Member States themselves and among the peoples of territories under their jurisdiction.
>
> "Article 1.
>
> "All human beings are born free and equal in dignity and rights. They are endowed with reason and conscience and should act towards one another in a spirit of brotherhood.
>
> "Article 2.
>
> "Everyone is entitled to all the rights and freedoms set forth in this Declaration, without distinction of any kind, such as race, colour, sex, language, religion, political or other opinion, national or social origin, property, birth or other status. Furthermore, no distinction shall be made on

> *the basis of the political, jurisdictional or international status of the country or territory to which a person belongs, whether it be independent, trust, non-self-governing or under any other limitation of sovereignty.*
>
> *"Article 3.*
>
> *"Everyone has the right to life, liberty and security of person."*

The UDHR left no doubt in 1948 the world community had approved a single universal standard for human rights. That standard was inclusive of all—i.e., everyone was a swimmer in the human rights pool and no one was required to vacate it. Clearly, the universal standard held all mankind to be equal.

As part of Khomeini's feint to fool the world as to his real intentions for Iran before coming to power there, he also claimed he supported the UDHR. Recognizing the Koran granted him the right of taqiya, i.e., to lie to non-Muslims to further the cause of Islam, he said:

> *"We would like to act according to the Universal Declaration of Human Rights. We would like to be free. We would like independence."*

But that was Khomeini's position on the UDHR before he had consolidated power in Tehran. Although for thirty-three years following the U.N.'s approval, no objections had ever been voiced concerning the UDHR by Iran, it only took two years after Khomeini came to power in 1979 for him to raise objections to accepting the position equal rights attached to ALL mankind under the UDHR.

However, not wishing to be labeled an Islamic supremacist, Khomeini couched his objection in a way that allowed him to exercise those beliefs without having to come right out and say the life of a non-believer was inferior to the life of a Muslim.

Iran simply took the position—and succeeded in getting the Arab world to agree—Muslim countries only recognized human rights as defined under shariah. Shariah only recognizes human rights equality among male Muslims followed, to a much diminished degree, rights for Muslim women. But shariah does not recognize human rights for non-believers. Thus, according to Islamic supremacists, Muslims are superior to non-Muslims in the human rights pool and all non-believers must vacate it. This translates as follows: Non-Muslims must either convert to Islam or die—which is the fate awaiting all non-believers upon the Mahdi's return.

There are 57 Muslim member states of the "Organization of Islamic Cooperation" (OIC)—an international group formed to have a single voice to represent the interests of all Muslims. In August 1990, led by Iran, foreign ministers of 45 of those states adopted the "Cairo Declaration on Human Rights in Islam" (CDHRI) to supplant their earlier UDHR approval.

The CDHRI is notable for recognizing human rights only as they remain compatible with shariah. Thus, Iran gave notice Muslim countries were changing their definition of the human rights standard from recognizing the UDHR's all-inclusive equality of all mankind—i.e., "everyone in the pool"—to the less-inclusive CDHRI's standard of equality only among those submitting to shariah—i.e., in other words "all you non-believers, not so fast into the pool." The 2000 CDHRI was subsequently approved by the OIC.

It must be kept in mind that this Islamic standard of non-equality for non-believers permeates the mindset of Iranian leaders negotiating with them. Therefore, non-believers are viewed by Iranians as non-entities, thus making meaningful negotiations virtually impossible.

In response to the OIC's retraction from the UDHR and the U.N.'s concern over a less acceptable standard, the OIC reported application of CDHRI was only considered "general guidance" for members. Additionally, it suggested the CDHRI prohibited "any discrimination on the basis of race, colour, language, belief, sex, religion, political affiliation, social status or other considerations." While it calls for the "preservation of human life," the CDHRI qualifies it within the context of "a duty prescribed by the

Shariah"—which, by that definition, does not equate a non-Muslim life to a Muslim one, denigrating the former.

The line being promoted by OIC to the U.N. was, again, an exercise of a Muslim's right to lie to non-Muslims to further his cause. OIC simply played the "general guidance" tune for the U.N.'s consumption while mandating member states strictly adhere to the CDHRI.

Concerning women, the CDHRI indicates women are given "equal human dignity" as men—a position absolutely refuted by shariah. Islamic law, for example, demands the testimony of two women to equal that given by one man. The OIC, in effect, speaks out of both sides of its mouth, claiming equality of the sexes but not practicing it.

Interestingly, the late Ayatollah Khomeini and his Islamist cronies, upon taking power in 1979, immediately removed all women judges for lacking the mental capacity to render legal decisions under shariah. Yet it is ironic while claiming women only have half the mental capacity of men, Islamists claim females have the mental capacity to marry at the tender age of ten—with an effort underway now to reduce the age to nine. What logic flows from not giving adult women, for lack of mental ability, equality with men in rendering testimony but claiming a female child has the mental capacity to enter into marriage at an age even younger than a male child (15)?

A member of the International Commission of Jurists has criticized CDHRI for endangering "inter-cultural consensus" on what constitutes human rights based on the 1948 UDHR, introducing serious discrimination against non-Muslim males and all women.

While Western sensitivities recognize the equality of all human life, Muslim sensitivities do not. If one accepts all that is written in the Koran, it is impossible for one to accept the universality of human rights. The Koran contains more than a hundred verses calling for violence against non-Muslims. These include the mandate in Sura 9:5 that followers "Slay the idolaters (i.e., non-believers) wherever you find them."

An article by Marguerite Del Giudice on Persia in the August 2008 issue of National Geographic makes a startling revelation about Iran past that is totally out of sync with Iran present. The author states:

> "The concepts of freedom and human rights may not have originated with the classical Greeks but in Iran, as early as the sixth century B.C. under the Achaemenid emperor Cyrus the Great, who established the first Persian Empire, which would become the largest, most powerful kingdom on Earth. Among other things, Cyrus, reputedly...freed the enslaved Jews of Babylon in 539 B.C., sending them back to Jerusalem to rebuild their temple with money he gave them, and established what has been called the world's first religiously and culturally tolerant empire."

This is quite a contrast to today's Iran which is recognized as one of the most brutal regimes, even against its own people. This is evidenced by the sharp increase in executions in 2011 as Tehran implemented a "judicial killing spree" in an effort to intimidate opponents to the regime. There is particular irony between Persia past and Persia present based on a relic Tehran proudly displays at the U.N. Headquarters in New York City.

With their rich history anchored in antiquity, Iranians treasure relics of their former empire. An ancient decree, written in the sixth century B.C. during the rule of the creator of the first Persian Empire, Cyrus the Great, was preserved over the ages on a small cylinder—aptly called the "Cyrus Cylinder."

National Geographic author Del Giudice reports the cylinder to be, "perhaps Iran's most exalted artifact," describing the document:

> "...as the first charter of human rights—predating the Magna Carta by nearly two millennia. It can be read as a call for religious and ethnic freedom; it banned slavery and oppression of any kind, the taking of property by force or without compensation; and it gave member states the right to subject themselves to Cyrus's crown, or not. 'I never resolve on war to reign.'"

It is truly ironic a Persian decree predating Muhammad by almost six centuries and granting greater human rights to people who lived 26 centuries ago is today displayed with pride by an Iranian theocracy that defies everything for which the Cyrus Cylinder stood.

When Shiites Need Not Play "To Tell the Truth"

In the early days of American television, a game show began in 1956 that became a popular hit with audiences. It was so popular, the program continued to be aired in similar form, although not regularly, over the next six decades. Entitled "To Tell the Truth," the show involved panelists who questioned three contestants—all claiming to be the person described in an affidavit the host had read. The panelists were given time to question each contestant but when their time was up would then have to guess, of the three, which one really was the person described in the affidavit. Only the contestant detailed in the affidavit had to answer panelists' questions correctly but the two others were not required to do so. At the show's end, panelists were well aware who had deceived them.

In negotiating with Shiites, and in particular with Iranians, there are elements of "To Tell the Truth" involved—with one significant difference: based on a religious practice, none of the "contestants" are required to tell the truth. It is a practice known as "taqiya." It is the equivalent of smiling at someone while simultaneously stabbing the person in the back.

Taqiya is the practice of deception by which a believer (read this primarily to mean a "Shiite") is permitted to deceive a non-believer (read this to mean either a "Sunni" or "infidel") for reasons of survival. Historically, this practice originated as a means of allowing vastly outnumbered Shiites to lie to Sunnis by revealing one intention while really harboring a different one. This practice evolved due to the great disparity in numbers between the two sects. It was a "free pass" to deny one's faith or else run the risk of persecution.

Taqiya later became an acceptable practice for Sunnis as well during times of persecution. For example, during the Spanish Inquisition of the late 15th and very early 16th centuries in which Jews and Muslims were required to convert to Catholicism or leave the country, Muslims would hide their faith by attending Catholic mass. Upon returning to the privacy of their own home, however, they would then wash the holy water off their hands. Taqiya gradually evolved into a justification for diplomatic deception as well.

Author Dore Gold explains taqiya as a concept initially designed to provide the Shiite with a survival mechanism against the much larger Sunni sect which has since been manipulated to dispel any need to be truthful:

> *"Using taqiya, Middle Eastern historians have written that Iranian Shiites facing oppression were able to protect their community from external dangers from the Sunni world. What Khomeini did was to make a virtue out of what had once been a necessity...* (It became) *part of Khomeini's ideological legacy for the Islamic republic to protect its nuclear program...one of the great problems with Iran's use of deception as a part of state policy is that many in the West refused to accept that they have been deceived."*

The Koran justifies deceit based on the following premise:

> *"Those who renounce Allah after they believe, if they were coerced, while their hearts are comforted with faith, but those who openly renounce Allah, upon them is wrath from Allah, and for them is a great punishment."*

In other words, taqiya was justified on the basis of renouncing Islamic faith only as a deception to save the believer from persecution for worshipping Allah. Taqiya, therefore, had limited application. However, Khomeini expanded its applicability to empower believers to deceive non-believers about the former's intentions to further Islam's goals.

Going hand-in-hand with taqiya is another practice known as "khod'eh." This is the process of fuzzing up an understanding sufficiently so as to "trick one's enemy into a misjudgment of one's true position." It does not necessarily involve lying but rather providing half-truths that become confusing. The late Secretary of State Warren Christopher became very frustrated in dealing with the Iranians, noting how they could quite readily disavow something to which they had already agreed.

Yet another sanction imposed by Islam supposedly allows Shiites to have discussions or undertake negotiations with unbelievers on the basis of a process synonymous with taqiya, known as "kitman." When used together, "taqiyya and kitman" are descriptive of the role Islam supposedly sanctions for the use of deception in Islamic terrorism. Kitman permits concealment of malevolent intentions and the use of "holy hypocrisy" against unbelievers.

It is such Islamic rationale that permits deception by Muslims by pretending to be a non-believer in order to gain access to a target.

Shiites believe lying is permitted in three situations: (1) A husband can lie to his wife to please her (as did the Prophet Muhammad); (2) Believers may lie to an enemy in times of war; and (3) Lying is not a sin when done while attempting reconciliation among one's people.

The sanctioning of deception towards a wife seems to be yet another indicator of the low esteem women are held under Islam.

Through the use of the above processes or a combination of them, historically many non-believers have been lulled into a false sense of security, only to meet their demise. As the online publication "6th Column Against Jihad" stated in a July 17, 2004 article on "Islam Practices to Deceive:"

> *"Like many Islamic concepts, taqiyya and kitman were formed within the context of the Arab-Islamic matrix of tribalism, expansionary warfare and conflict. Taqiyya has been used by Muslims since the 7th century to confuse and split 'the enemy.' A favored tactic was 'deceptive triangulation;' to persuade the enemy that jihad was not aimed at them but at another enemy. Another tactic was to deny that there was jihad at all. The fate for such faulty assessments by the target was death."*

An Italian diplomat who had the challenging task of negotiating an end to the Iran-Iraq war with Iranian officials said:

> "The problem is that the verbal dexterity they display is a mask to hide reality."

The practice of taqiya is one to which IAEA and Western negotiators have consistently been subjected as they attempt to resolve the issue of Iran's nuclear program.

In attempting to monitor communications by senior Iranian leaders, the CIA closely listens to what Khamenei says. Of course, the problem is, if shariah allows one to lie to his enemies, how can it be determined when Khamenei is speaking the truth and when he is not. (Like the old joke about how one can tell when an attorney is lying, one can tell Khamenei is lying when his lips are moving.)

It is confusing enough that the CIA must consider the numerous contradictory statements Khamenei makes, the various interpretations each can be given and the religious context in which it is given (which Khamenei often does when discussing nuclear issues), but having to factor in as well a taqiya element makes extracting intelligence from what the Supreme Leader says as vexing as trying to break a complex code.

In one statement, Khamenei said:

> "Iran is not seeking to have the atomic bomb, possession of which is pointless, dangerous and is a great sin from an intellectual and a religious point of view," even issuing a fatwa against acquiring nuclear weapons.

Fair enough, but Khamenei followed that statement with one chiding the late Libyan strongman Muamar Qadafi for surrendering his nuclear program, saying:

> "Look where we are, and in what position they are now."

Such a comment is open to interpretation but it seems Khamenei is suggesting he is glad Iran had not disclosed its own nuclear arms program.

Also, it must be kept in mind that when Supreme Leader Khomeini came to power in 1979, he immediately discontinued Iran's nuclear program—which was then known to be on track for peaceful purposes—because nuclear power, per se, was anti-Islamic. Khomeini was condemning all nuclear technology. What has changed to make what was un-Islamic in 1979, "Islamically-acceptable" today? Or, is Supreme Leader Khamenei simply feeding the West a piece of Shiite logic by practicing taqiya?

It should be noted as well, Khomeini reversed his decision on a nuclear weapons program during the Iran-Iraq war, only after Saddam had used WMDs against the Iranians and had attempted to start a nuclear program of his own. Saddam's effort was terminated by the Israelis in 1981.

In 2003, probably in response to the American invasion of Iraq—originally justified by the Bush administration on the grounds Iraq had WMDs—Ayatollah Khamenei ordered suspension of Iran's nuclear weapons program, although he did allow uranium enrichment efforts to continue.

At an emergency meeting of the IAEA in 2005, Iran's nuclear negotiator, hoping the West would accept a religious edict at face value, noted a fatwa had been issued by the Ayatollah Khamenei. He reported the religious edict declared, "the production, stockpiling and use of nuclear weapons are all forbidden in Islam" and, therefore, "Iran shall never acquire these weapons." Absent proof by Iran to substantiate this, the West was left to wonder whether it was "fact or taqiya."

During the television game show "To Tell the Truth," a large logo hung high above the three challengers, which consisted of a hand with two fingers crossed—a symbol indicating that not everyone on the stage was being truthful. Perhaps that same logo should be displayed above the heads of Iranian negotiators as a reminder to those sitting across from them, NO ONE on the Iranian side of the table is being truthful.

Even Islamic Extremists Need Love

Just as important in realizing that, in negotiating, the Iranian mindset accepts the deception of non-believers as an act sanctioned by Allah, so too does it justify an activity, deemed sinful under the Koran, simply by re-packaging it. As Islamists are in need of loving too, it is a tactic legally used to end run the Islamic prohibition against pre-marital sex by entering into a "temporary" marriage.

Under shariah, men can have a mullah conduct such a marriage ceremony known as "seeqeh." It is a legal union—the duration of which is not fixed. The marriage can run as short as an hour or any time longer. While the practice of seeqeh is discussed openly in Iran, the government has tried to lower the subject's profile on the internet so as not to expose it to international ridicule.

A researcher for women's affairs in Iran, Massoumeh Pareesh, conducted a study on this subject that was published by the Iranian news agency MEHR in 2010:

> "The average period for temporary marriages ranges anywhere between one hour and five months and financial issues is what drives women to submit to such conjugality. This study has been conducted in a qualitative fashion and is based on in-depth interviews with women who are either in temporary marriages or have been in one; the minimum period of the contract has been between one hour and 99 years..."

> "Most of these women either were experienced housewives or had worked in service careers such as nursing. Usually women who submitted to temporary marriages had experienced some kind of family trauma or had gone through serious divorce and domestic problems..."

Pareesh cites as the clear driving force behind a woman's willingness to enter into such a demeaning relationship with a man—seldom known to her but for the duration of the marriage—is the financial hardship created by divorce or some other source of loss of the bread winner. There is little option for such women, especially those with children, as there are no state welfare program benefits available to them.

Their temporary husbands usually lack adequate financial means as well so the temporary wife is left to accept whatever she can get. Many temporary husbands have permanent wives who, in the interests of maintaining marital tranquility with that wife, do not acknowledge a relationship with a temporary wife. And, those temporary husbands who do not have a permanent wife are reluctant to engage a temporary wife on a permanent basis.

Shariah does impose some restrictions upon temporary wives, such as a prohibition against entering into another temporary marriage for at least 45 days. Pareesh notes, however, that "women are forced to marry one man after another which has turned this into a career and a form of commerce. The issue is if this is compatible with Sharia law."

The fact that temporary marriage has become "commerce"—i.e., "legalized prostitution"—is supported by Pareesh's observation in her study:

> "The results show that neither religious nor non-religious women cite their reasons for temporary marriage as prompted by their beliefs."

Of note is that some temporary marriages are entered into with girls of a very tender age. The pre-1979 legal age under the Shah of 16 is being lowered to nine.

Mohammad Ali Isfenani, who is a member of the Iranian parliament, addressed the issue, saying:

> "We must regard nine as being the appropriate age for a girl to have reached puberty and qualified to get married. To do otherwise would be to contradict and challenge Islamic Sharia law... Before the (1979) revolution girls under 16 were not allowed to marry. Parents determined to get around the law would often tamper with their

> daughter's birth certificate. Under the previous constitution, people were legally regarded as adults when they were 18. After the revolution the age at which children were regarded as going through puberty was lowered to nine for girls and 15 for boys."

What is bothersome about Iran's initiative lowering the legal age of marriage for girls to nine is that such action was only taken three months after Saudi Arabia lowered the age to ten. It was as if Shiite Iran was in competition with Sunni Saudi Arabia—with no thought given to the health and safety of these young girls. (Statistics provided by the Mohabat News indicate over a period of just a few weeks, more than 75 female children under ten were forced to marry much older men and, in nearly 4000 cases, both the bride and groom were under the age of fourteen.)

While the timing of the initiative strongly suggests competition with Saudi Arabia was the reason for the age change, the Iranian government suggests otherwise, justifying it on the basis that the age of 16 approved before 1979 was "un-Islamic and illegal" and needed to bring civil law more in line with shariah. But this rationale totally ignores the sad reality, as determined by Baroness Jenny Tonge—charged with investigating the international issue of child brides on behalf of the British government—"that one of the major causes of maternal death is early marriage... the girls are married so young that their bodies are simply not ready for child birth."

Thus, in addition to legalizing prostitution, Iran has legalized sex with children.

The profound Islamic cleric Ayatollah Khomeini shared his sick religious wisdom concerning a Muslim man's right to have sexual relations with a young child, sanctioning abuse at an even younger age than that now permitted under Iranian law:

> "A man can have sexual pleasure from a child as young as a baby. However, he should not penetrate; sodomizing the child is OK. If a man penetrates and damages the child, then he should be responsible for her subsistence all her

life. This girl, however, does not count as one of his four permanent wives. The man will not be eligible to marry the girl's sister... It is better for a girl to marry in such a time when she would begin menstruation at her husband's house rather than her father's house. Any father marrying his daughter so young will have a permanent place in heaven."

These benchmarks of what is deemed "legal" and "normal" in Iran are ones to be kept in mind by Western negotiators struggling to find a common, rational ground upon which to resolve the nuclear issue. One is left to wonder, based on the above, whether such a common ground can ever be found.

Iran's Gender Pecking Order Hidden Under Cover of the "Wicked Double Helix"

It should be evident in Iranian culture women are denied equal status with their male counterparts. Women are unable to pursue the same livelihoods males do. Their access to education is much more limited. Additionally, they must tolerate polygamy, unfair inheritance laws, and custody rights in divorce settlements stacked in their husband's favor.

Every time during the 20th and 21st century there have been uprisings in Iran against the country's leadership, there have been women in the forefront of those protests. However, once the dust has settled, women have seldom benefitted from the fight to the same extent as their male counterparts have. Women have been locked into a vicious cycle of constant struggle for greater rights; sometimes followed by improvements which, inevitably, they then watch regress. While the Iranian government represents women have equal rights as men, it is taqiya at work again.

Even under the brutal rule of the mullahs, women have braved the consequences of pushing for greater rights. It has often led to arrests, kangaroo court trials and lengthy prison sentences or, in some cases, execution.

Persecution against women was, perhaps, at its greatest during the initial years after the 1979 Revolution as many had no idea what violated shariah—particularly as that law was being interpreted by Khomeini. It is estimated by Amnesty International that during the first three years of his rule, Khomeini executed about 20,000 women for a wide range of offenses—from extremely young girls on up. When some girls were deemed too young for execution, even by Iranian standards, they were simply kept in prison until they came of age to be executed.

The Iranian government's charge against women fighting for their rights is that their actions pose a threat to national security. Such a charge has attached to minor acts like taking photographs of protests and forwarding them out of the country. The serious nature of the charge reflects how serious Tehran is about maintaining inequality for women.

Additionally, with the mindset that "the sins of the father are visited upon the son," police have arrested some women in their homes along with their young children. Also taken to prison, the children are then forced to make confessions against their mother.

The unequal role to which Iranian women are relegated is extraordinarily reflected by the punishment of death by stoning afforded to women compared to men and the right to have the death sentence commuted. To carry out a stoning sentence, a hole is dug in the ground and the "criminal" is placed in it, with the hole filled back in. Under shariah, if the criminal should escape from the hole during the stoning process, the death sentence is commuted and the criminal set free. However, the difference between men and women in the application of this law is that the male criminal is only buried up to his waist; the female is buried up to her neck. Even in fighting for one's life, the cards are stacked in favor of the male.

Another shocking extreme is perpetrated against female virgins sentenced to death. Their execution is "illegal" under shariah. But to circumvent this and thus make it legal, mullahs perform "temporary" marriages in which the virgin is married to a prison guard. Her wedding night and night before execution are rolled into one, during which the temporary husband rapes his temporary wife. The next morning, the temporary wife—no longer a virgin—can be legally executed.

One prison guard, given this "honor" of raping female prisoners until his conscience got the better of him, shared his insights. As many of these women fought off the guards, they had to be given sedatives to make them more docile. He recalled hearing other women cry and scream during the attacks. Another clawed her own face afterward, leaving deep scratches. Most feared their "wedding" night more than their pending execution. But what perhaps really affected this guard was his observation, "By morning the girls would have an empty expression; it seemed like they were ready or wanted to die."

Roya Hakakian is an Iranian author who left her country in 1984 due to the oppression directed against women by the Khomeini regime.

She wrote a very insightful op-ed for the Washington Post on October 21, 2012, in the aftermath of the attempted murder by the Taliban of Malala Yousafzai, the 15-yar old Pakistani girl who had made headlines by pressing for a woman's right to pursue an education.

For being an education activist, Yousafzai was targeted for death by the Taliban's chief spokesman, Ehsanullah Ehsan, who accused her of becoming "a symbol of Western culture in the area; she was openly propagating it." While riding home from school with other children, the vehicle she was in was stopped—and she was shot. Initially treated in Pakistan, she was flown to a hospital in England for further treatment. Miraculously, it is believed she may make a full recovery. Having been shot twice—once in the head and once in the neck at point blank range—divine intervention must have played a role in saving Yousafzai from a savage act ordered by a religious fanatic applying his personal interpretation of Islam.

But for Roya Hakakian, the hell through which Yousafzai was put brought back memories of her own teenage years in Tehran under another breed of religious zealots. The title of her op-ed, "How Blaming the West Hides a War on Women," sums up how such Islamists seek to limit education for women for fear it will lead to independent thought rather than strict compliance with Islamic law.

Hakakian recalled how in 1982 women were being harassed by religious police for not observing strict dress requirements, scolding them—as Iran was fighting a war with Iraq—by ranting, "Our men are being martyred by Saddam to protect your virtue (suggesting)...the war was not over land or resources, but the honor of the nation's women."

But even as thousands of Iranians were dying in that conflict, Hakakian explains how Khomeini—using a ploy he often relied upon to take the spotlight off his true intentions (which she labels the "wicked double helix")—focused on reversing women's' rights earned under the Shah, including education:

> "The war with Iraq was not even the one the country was told to gird itself against. The bigger, bloodier but ultimately triumphant jihad was yet to come, Ayatollah Khomeini reminded us daily. It would be against 'world-devouring' U.S. imperialism and its proxies, the 'blood-sucking Zionists,' he said; they were at the root of all the world's evil.
>
> "That all-out war, forever looming, has never come. But the war on women has been raging ever since.
>
> "At the school gates every morning, we were greeted by our own Taliban, members of the morality unit, in charge of 'preventing vice and promoting virtue.' They rubbed the face of my rosy-cheeked classmate to the point of bleeding to make sure she was not wearing rouge and pulled at the long eyelashes of another to see if they were real. We missed months of math that year because schools were newly segregated by gender and there were not enough trained female instructors in the country to teach in the girls-only classrooms. Two months before the end of the year, a few of us signed up for private lessons given by a man who stared at the ceiling while teaching, lest he violate segregation laws by looking at us.

"The burning effigies of Uncle Sam, and the inflammatory rhetoric against modernity and the West, had done their work. The world cringed and turned away from Iran. Just then, the age of marriage was lowered to 9; the weight of a woman's testimony in a criminal trial was halved against a man's; divorce, abortion, inheritance and custody rights were slashed; several academic fields and careers were banned to women; and the Islamic dress code was reinstituted. Public spaces in Tehran, including buses, were segregated by gender, and the faithful's fists pumped into the air, punctuating Friday prayers with 'death to America' chants.

Credit for the discovery of this wicked double helix — the pairing of dramatic acts of anti-Americanism with an insidious assault on women, which subsequently infiltrated the DNA of fundamentalists throughout the region — goes to Ayatollah Khomeini.

"Early in his long career, he gave speech after speech about the 'toxic' influence of the Pahlavi monarchy on the nation's family values — the ayatollah's euphemism for the growing freedoms of women under the shah. But Khomeini's anti-feminist diatribe did not catch the public's imagination. What catapulted him to national stature began with his fiery criticism of a 1964 decree, known as the 'capitulation law,' that gave diplomatic immunity to non-diplomatic U.S. personnel working in Iran." (This law, referred to as the U.S. Status of Forces Agreement, is negotiated with all nations in which the U.S. has military personnel stationed. It defines their legal status on matters such as criminal and civil jurisdiction, the right to bear arms, etc. It seeks to protect U.S. personnel from a host country's laws that may not provide for U.S. constitutional guarantees. Iranian critics felt it was a capitulation by the Shah denying prosecution under shariah.)

"'They have reduced the Iranian people to a level lower than that of an American dog,' went one of the ayatollah's most memorable lines from the first of a series of speeches in which his anti-imperialist tenor steadily grew. By 1978, when his journeys through exile landed him in France, he no longer sounded like his misogynist self of a decade earlier.

"Now Khomeini casts himself as a nationalist in the image of Mahatma Gandhi, fighting the foreign powers that were plundering his motherland. His anti-Americanism lifted him to nationwide leadership, and he set to work on his earlier agenda. Days after his arrival in Tehran in February 1979, he issued an order to abolish women's freedom in dress and to bring back the mandatory hijab. After protests broke out and were widely reported by the international media, he retreated.

"Nine months later, the U.S. Embassy was seized in Tehran. As the news media became consumed by the fate of the 52 American hostages there, the ayatollah again ordered the dress code. This time, when all eyes were averted, he succeeded.

"Two factors have since veiled the U.S. perspective on the region: The first is the expression of anti-Americanism, which sends the rejected American psyche into a downward spiral of introspection over feckless U.S. policies and leads to inaction. The second is the use of Islam as a wall of privacy, behind which oppressors act with impunity. Both factors function, in great part, as a disguise. Behind them, where women are concerned, all the seemingly unbridgeable divides merge seamlessly to connect Sunni Saudi Arabia to Shiite Iran."

Hakakian noted that such undermining of women's rights has led to some acts of rebellion:

> *"In the Semnan region of Iran a few weeks ago, a cleric passing two women…told one to cover her head better, according to an Iranian news agency report. The woman, punching him to the ground, told him to cover his eyes."*

The Iranian women's rights activist revealed there is nothing to be gained by apologizing to Iran's mullahs for past grievances:

> *"Western politicians can apologize for crooked policies and retreat into passivity for fear of committing new errors, which are bound to be deemed as new sins by future generations. Yet none will change the elemental facts. The notion of an Islamic democracy is merely another euphemism for turning women into lesser citizens, and it ought to be deemed as unjust and anti-democratic as America before the end of racial segregation. 'Terrorism' is only one manifestation of the evil that the world hopes to root out from the region where part-time terrorists have always been full-time chauvinists.*
>
> *"The real enemy is misogyny. Malala Yousafzai is not just a teenager in Pakistan's Swat Valley but a victim of the greatest apartheid of our time, and a wounded warrior in feminism's newest front line."*

It is no surprise that in 2012 Iran placed 127th out of 135 countries listed in the Global Gender Gap Report, released by the World Economic Forum. Nor should it come as a surprise such a ranking represents a drop from Iran's 2011 placement of 125th. After all, it is hard for a government to work on improving women's rights when it is putting all its efforts into building nuclear weapons.

For the women of Iran and Pakistan, as is the case for women in most Muslim countries, the fight for equality is never ending.

CHAPTER NINE

Iranian Mullahs Destroying Persia's Roots

The 1979 Islamic Revolution that brought the ayatollahs and extremist leaders of a like ilk into power in Iran is referred to by those now subject to their brutal rule as the "second Arab invasion." Such a remark is not only historically accurate, but also very telling about how Iranians perceive their identity.

Iran's history goes back two and a half millennia—including a full millennium before Muhammad was even born. Long before Islam's existence, Persia had established its own culture, language (Farsi, which is one of the world's oldest) and religion (Zoroastrian). Long before Islam's existence, Persia had known the ecstasy of victory and the agony of defeat, having played the role both of conqueror and conquered. Long before Islam's existence, Persia was "regarded in some ways as one of the more glorious and benevolent civilizations of antiquity."

An article by Marguerite Del Giudice on Persia that appeared in the August 2008 issue of National Geographic is entitled, "Persia: Ancient Soul of Iran." It explains how Persia found itself in the path of invading armies but proved capable of retaining its identity, even when ending up on the losing end, as Islam's jihad spread to the northeast: "The earliest reports of human settlement in Iran go back at least 10,000 years, and the country's name derives from Aryans who migrated here beginning around 1500 B. C." The article states:

> "The empire once encompassed today's Iraq, Pakistan, Afghanistan, Turkmenistan, Uzbekistan, Tajikistan, Turkey, Jordan, Cyprus, Syria, Lebanon, Israel, Egypt, and the Caucasus region," Del Giudice notes. "Invaders have included the Turks, Genghis Khan and the Mongols, and, most significantly, Arabian tribesmen. Fired with the zeal of a new religion, Islam, they humbled the ancient Persian Empire for good in the seventh century and ushered in a period of Muslim greatness that was

> distinctly Persian. The Arab expansion is regarded as one of the most dramatic movements of any people in history. Persia was in its inexorable path, and, ever since, Iranians have been finding ways to keep safe their identity as distinct from the rest of the Muslim and Arab world."

This is why Iranians today identify themselves as Persians and not Arabs.

It was the seventh century assault by Islam that became Iran's "first" Arab invasion. But unlike other cultures of conquered nations that were stamped out by the conqueror's boot print, Persia has preserved its identity. Because of this, Iran embraces unique aspects of Islam not recognized elsewhere in the Muslim world.

> "Their conquerors were said to have 'gone Persian,'" continues the article. "Iranians seem particularly proud of their capacity to get along with others by assimilating compatible aspects of the invaders' ways without surrendering their own—a cultural elasticity that is at the heart of their Persian identity."

It is not surprising, therefore, that because Iranian people still identify with their roots and a history as one of the "more glorious and benevolent civilizations of antiquity"—an identity that clashes with the Iranian mullahs' Islamic extremist views—Tehran's rulers have attempted, unsuccessfully, to sever that connection.

One wonders if Iran's leaders have reflected at all—in their efforts to impose Islamic extremism upon their own people—on how far afield they have wandered from their original roots and the core beliefs of what was once among the world's largest religion.

Most Persians, at the time Islam was being promoted by Muhammad in the seventh century A.D., practiced Zoroastrianism. Accordingly, after securing most of Arabia, Muhammad's followers directed their focus on Persia in the year 634 A.D.—two years after the Prophet's death. Iran became the first nation to wage several battles against the Muslim jihad—a war which would last 17 years before Persia would finally be converted to Islam.

The conflict began with Muslim Arabs launching unprovoked attacks against Persian towns and their civilian population. Islamic jihad represented a different kind of warfare. Previously, enemies only engaged each other on a battlefield, where victory or defeat would be determined. The Persians, however, found themselves unable to fight a determined enemy, whipped up into a jihadist frenzy, who targeted the other side's civilian population rather than its military forces. It changed warfare as the world had known it for this enemy sought not to conquer land but to conquer souls. Victims had either to submit and convert to Islam or die at the hands of their Muslim Arab oppressors.

Ironically, just like Muhammad's followers oppressed the peace-loving Persians of antiquity, imposing Islam upon them, today Tehran oppresses peace-loving people elsewhere around the globe, imposing its extremist interpretation of Islam upon them. The victimized Persia of old, which resisted Islam, now seeks to be the Iranian conqueror of new, imposing Islam upon others.

Zoroastrianism, like Islamism, worships a single God. Teachings also emanate from a prophet—in this case, Prophet Zoroaster. It is believed to have originated in the eastern part of Greater Iran before the sixth century B.C. It was the state religion for Persians for several centuries. One major contrast between the two religions is that the God of Zoroastrianism is all loving and good; the God of Islam is one to be feared.

Additionally, Zoroastrians do not believe a need exists for a middleman—such as a mullah—to intercede on behalf of the believer in order to get to know Allah. Zoroastrianism is much more of a low-key religion, which the people could practice, or not, as they so chose. Ultimately, it became very influential, even influencing the world's three main faiths—Christianity, Judaism and Islam. But it began to deteriorate after Alexander III of Macedon invaded, along with Islam's expansion during the seventh century A.D.

Even with Zoroastrianism's decline, the Persians still retained some religious holidays as they forcefully embraced Islamism. The new year holiday of Nowruz is one such religious holdover from Zoroastrianism—almost a two week period of thanksgiving celebrated by eating, reciting poetry, dancing, etc. This holiday is one of those the mullahs have attempted to downplay or replace, so far without success. Perhaps for that reason, it is also the holiday U.S. presidents have recently selected to send an annual greeting to the Iranian people.

The majority of the Iranian people have learned a simple lesson from the 1979 Islamic Revolution: Be careful what you wish for! As Iranians longed to be released from the yoke of the Shah's rule—and were promised democracy by Ayatollah Khomeini should they cast it off—they wished for mullah control. While they understood mullahs would have their say on issues involving religion, they had no idea their view of Islamism would extend to every aspect of a citizen's life.

Actions Which Have Reeled-in Iran's Conduct

Interestingly, in the years since the Shah fell in 1979, there have only been two times the U.S. has succeeded in reining in Tehran's conduct under the mullahs.

The first time occurred in ending the Iranian Hostage Crisis.

After President Jimmy Carter tolerated more than fourteen months of it, President-elect Ronald Reagan made it clear the Iranians could expect a more aggressive policy once he took office. Not wishing to challenge the new president right out of the chute, Supreme Leader Khomeini decided to release the U.S. hostages just as President Reagan took office on January 21, 1981. The Supreme Leader would wait until he had a little better feel for Reagan's leadership before putting him to the test.

The second time Tehran's conduct was reined in was 22 years later.
Threatened by the U.S. 2003 invasion of Iraq, Tehran feared the U.S. might decide to continue the invasion eastward into Iran. With U.S. forces in position, Tehran approached Washington, through a third party, to suggest a confidential proposal.

Iranian President Khatami offered to end the country's nuclear program if Washington agreed not to invade Iran—an offer only made with Supreme Leader Khamenei's approval. But Tehran also sought, with U.S. assistance, retaliation against an Iranian opposition group.

Still furious over the NCRI's disclosure to the world of Tehran's nuclear activities at Nantanz and Arad a year earlier, Tehran sought U.S. help in disarming an NCRI member group residing in Iraq's Camp Ashraf located along the Iranian border. This opposition group—the People's Mujahedin of Iran (known variously as the MEK, PMOI or MKO)—had long been a thorn in the mullahs' side, as will be explained later. The U.S. apparently agreed both not to invade Iran and to disarm the MEK while Tehran promised not to intervene in Iraq. The U.S. would honor its agreement; Iran, exercising taqiya, would not.

Both the 1981 and 2003 rapprochement by Iran, though temporary, were triggered by U.S. commitment, backed by a demonstrated U.S. resolve, which Tehran found intimidating. Nothing short of Tehran sensing such U.S. commitment and resolve has successfully achieved a similar result.

There are also two times a third nation's actions have reeled-in Iran's conduct.

In 1982, two years into the Iran-Iraq war, Saddam Hussein offered Iran a peace treaty, which Tehran rejected. Six years later, he offered it again. Although Supreme Leader Khomeini loathed accepting it, Saddam threatened to conduct additional WMD attacks against Iran. Khomeini accepted a treaty on the exact same terms Saddam had previously offered in 1982.

Yet another time Iran's actions were influenced by external forces was in 1998 as it considered invading Afghanistan. The Taliban were responsible for "...the killing of 11 Iranian diplomats and the mass murder of thousands of Shia Muslims...Tens of thousands of Iranian troops amassed at the Afghan border in preparation for an attack. Iranian commanders, surveying the dusty, barren landscape, ultimately decided not to proceed...Tehran calculated that the cost of fighting the Taliban would far outweigh any benefit of occupying Afghanistan, at that time the poorest country in the world."

If one analyzes the history of U.S.-Iranian relations since the 1979 Islamic Revolution, it is a history of repeated acts of violence directed against the U.S. There is not one such incident that generated a forceful response from the U.S. to show Iran that violence begets violence. That has only succeeded in communicating a message of weakness to Tehran which has then become even more emboldened to escalate the confrontation. Undoubtedly, Iran's mullahs must believe Allah has been intervening to contain a U.S. response as nothing else could explain its failure to do so.

MEK: An Iranian Lion in Iraq

> *"For seventeen years before the U.S. invasion of Iraq, a lion there roamed the border with Iran, periodically foraying into Iran before returning to its Iraqi safe-haven. Its prey was formidable—the Iranian mullahs' elite IRGC force. It achieved tremendous hunting prowess in defeating its prey, until that March day in 2003 when the lion was caged. Ironically, it was captured by U.S. forces only as a gesture to placate those who feared it most—and hated the U.S. most: Tehran's mullahs."*

So began an article written in 2007 about an Iranian opposition group known as the as "Fighters for the People" ("Mujahedin-e Khalq [MEK]" or also known as the "People's Mujahedin Organization of Iran" [PMOI]). This is the organization that is the key component of the National Council of Resistance of Iran (NCRI), calling itself a "parliament-in-exile dedicated to a democratic, secular and coalition government in Iran." It is also the group identified earlier that first reported Iran's secret ambitions concerning its nuclear program in 2002. It is a group that symbolically identifies with the lion.

MEK has an interesting history in its three decade-plus struggle against Iran's theocracy. Tragically, however, the U.S. for some unknown reason has effectively done Tehran's bidding by de-clawing and keeping the MEK lion caged. It is ironic the U.S. embarked upon such a policy as MEK's own objective towards Iran's mullahs—regime change—is right in line with that of the U.S.

It is MEK's earlier activities many years ago under the Shah of Iran that earned the group a scarlet letter "T" for "terrorist"—but strangely not until years after such violence had ended. As its terrorist activities against the West waned and finally stopped, it unfortunately became a pawn in U.S.-Iranian relations that has caused it to suffer immense hardship ever since. Yet MEK continues to assist the U.S. in its effort to expose Tehran's nuclear weapons program, even though the U.S. continued to turn a blind eye to its own international obligations to protect MEK.

MEK is an ideological group, first organized in 1965 by students at Tehran University who opposed the Shah's rule, but who also objected to fundamentalist interpretations of Islam. It was during these early years that the group went on a terrorist bent, not only against the Shah, but also against the U.S. which was supporting him.

After the 1979 Islamic Revolution brought the brutal Ayatollah Khomeini regime to power, MEK began gaining popular support due to its anti-fundamentalist beliefs. With the U.S. out of Iran, MEK violence against American assets ceased.

A major rift between MEK and the mullahs occurred in 1981 when a peaceful MEK-sponsored demonstration against Khomeini's brutality led to horrific bloodshed. It was one of Iran's most severe human rights abuses. Security personnel, on Khomeini's orders, opened fire on half a million demonstrators, killing thousands and arresting others who were later executed in prison.

MEK provided an in-kind response to the government's violence, targeting IRGC elements and numerous Iranian government officials involved in the torture and execution of Khomeini's critics. As Khomeini cracked down on them, MEK's leadership was forced to flee to France. But Khomeini would not forget the challenge MEK made to his authority. He was determined to destroy the group, wherever it could be found.

MEK's residency in France would soon become an issue. The Iranian-sponsored terrorist group "Hezbollah" had taken some French citizens hostage in Lebanon in 1986. Khomeini, who had undoubtedly choreographed the hostage-taking incident for the purpose of resolving it at a price he already had in mind, informed the French he would "try" to negotiate with Hezbollah to gain the hostages release. But, since Hezbollah took their marching orders from Tehran, all Khomeini had to do was simply tell Hezbollah what to do. Khomeini told the French a deal for the hostage release could be negotiated but, in exchange, he wanted MEK expelled from France.

Hezbollah released the French hostages and France expelled MEK. Undoubtedly satisfied that he had forced MEK's departure from France, Khomeini could not have anticipated—in his wildest dreams—to where it would next relocate.

The homeless MEK received a surprising offer from Saddam Hussein to host the group in Iraq. Although Baghdad was engaged in a long war with Tehran at the time, in the spirit of "the enemy of my enemy is my friend," Saddam saw an opportunity to enlist MEK's help in fighting Iran. It made sense as there was one main objective now for Saddam, the U.S. and MEK: to force a regime change in Iran.

MEK re-located to Iraq in 1986. Saddam, who trusted no one, provided them with land on Iraq's eastern border with Iran—which became known as Camp Ashraf—and where MEK could be kept under a watchful eye. Located 44 miles from Iran's western border, it was a camp in name only. It was mostly barren land—a fourteen square mile area MEK eventually turned into a magnificent city.

MEK also proved to be an effective fighting force, making forays into Iran to take on the IRGC. Such forays often did not end well for the IRGC, from whom tanks and other military equipment MEK captured. MEK's numerous battlefield victories enabled them to build up an impressive military force.

MEK's battlefield successes also gave Khomeini yet another reason to seek the group's destruction. However, with his death in 1989, he would not live long enough to see it happen.

It is at this time that the U.S./MEK relationship took a strange twist.

With the Shah long gone from Iran, MEK had not targeted violence against the U.S. for more than a decade. MEK's actions were totally focused on Tehran's mullahs. Despite the ten plus year gap in time since MEK's last aggressive act against the U.S., the group suddenly found itself designated as a U.S. Foreign Terrorist Organization (FTO).

The designation came about as the mullahs had learned to play off of U.S. misperceptions, which Iran promoted, to its own benefit.

In 1997, Iranian President Khatami was perceived to be a liberal (moderate) in favor of improved relations with the U.S. It was suggested a good faith gesture by the U.S. to entice Tehran to move in that direction was to place the mullahs' hated enemy—MEK—on the U.S. FTO list. Spurred on by the U.S. FTO initiative, the United Kingdom (U.K.) and European Union (EU) also placed MEK on their FTO lists.

Although the Clinton Administration complied with Tehran's suggestion, this good faith effort was never reciprocated by Iran. It had all just been a ploy by Tehran to further isolate MEK.

Several former high ranking U.S. Government officials, such as Louis Freeh who was FBI Director when this happened, has stated that the listing was part of a failed political ploy that sought a possible rapprochement with Iran. However, the U.S. continued to keep MEK on the FTO list even after the U.K. and EU both later removed MEK from theirs.

This was where things stood between the U.S. and MEK as the U.S. prepared to launch its 2003 invasion of Iraq.

In 2003, another U.S. president fell for another Iranian ploy, again by President Khatami. Iran was obviously very concerned about the soon-to-be presence of U.S. troops on its Iraq border. Apparently, an initiative was taken by the Iranians, through the Swiss Embassy which was representing U.S. interests in Iran, to strike a deal with the Bush Administration.

Khatami proposed that, in exchange for a U.S. promise not to invade Iran, Tehran would agree to stay out of Iraq. Additionally, however, Iran wanted an additional promise from Washington. It wanted the U.S. to disarm MEK at Camp Ashraf. The U.S. promise would be kept; unsurprisingly (at least for those who understand the mullah mindset), once again Iran's promise would not.

True to its word, as the Iraq invasion kicked off, the U.S. immediately targeted MEK, which had declared its neutrality. But in what was perhaps most telling about the MEK in how it viewed the U.S. as a friend and not an enemy, it refused to fight back against attacking U.S. forces.

Surrendering without firing a shot, MEK signed a "voluntary consolidation" agreement with the U.S. in May 2003. It also agreed to disarm its forces in exchange for U.S. protection at Ashraf. All MEK's weaponry was turned over to the U.S. It submitted its members to an extensive 16 month U.S. investigation to ascertain if any were involved in terrorist activity.

Retired Brigadier General David Phillips, who supervised the investigation, said about those investigated, "A few had unpaid parking tickets, but nothing else." Thus, no charges against a single MEK member were ever filed. Finally, MEK agreed to be restrained at Camp Ashraf, or "caged" depending on how one looked at it. Limited to free movement only within the confines of the Camp in then volatile Diyala Province, MEK members were designated as "non-combatants."

Because MEK had surrendered to an "occupying force"—the U.S.—and had totally disarmed, it was granted "protected persons" status under the Fourth Geneva Convention by the U.S. Government on July 21, 2004. As such, it became a U.S. responsibility to guarantee MEK's protection.

Then Secretary of Defense Donald Rumsfeld made clear his written understanding for his approval of the "protected persons" designation:

> *"I understand that making such determination will assist in expediting the efforts of the International Committee of the Red Cross and the U.N. High Commissioner for Refugees in the disposition of these individuals in accordance with applicable international law."*

The MEK, before the U.S. invasion, had made a positive imprint on Diyala Province, winning over local tribesman there, which eventually helped secure the area after the invasion. Part of what had concerned Tehran was MEK's unifying impact among moderate Iraqis. MEK clearly made a very positive contribution to peace and stability in the region as evidenced in a petition signed by more than five million Iraqis.

As the U.S. began discussing a timeline for withdrawing from Iraq and as MEK sensed that Iraq was being subjected to Iranian influence, a defenseless MEK began worrying about its future. When MEK Secretary General Mojgan Parsai was asked in May 2007 what might happen, she warned:

> *"If the U.S. withdraws from Iraq before democracy is established in this country, it virtually means that it would hand over Iraq to the Tehran mullahs who are the godfather of terrorism; if a democratic government is in power in Iraq, then we should have no problem with the U.S. forces leaving."*

Parsai's warning was foreboding. It should have put the U.S. on notice that in order to meet its responsibilities to protect the MEK, action would have to be taken prior to any U.S. withdrawal. The U.S. failed to take notice. It would not take any action prior to withdrawal and it would leave a defenseless MEK to face the consequences of having entrusted the U.S. to protect it. Ironically, while keeping its promise to Tehran's mullahs, the U.S. would fail to keep its promise to MEK.

In January 2009, although U.S. forces remained in Iraq, they turned over responsibility for all military operations to the Iraqi government, with security for Camp Ashraf transferred the next month. The U.S. did continue to provide some security there by making regular visits while accompanying U.N. observers.

There were reasons why Parsai shuddered over MEK security at Camp Ashraf being turned over to the Iraqis. She was acutely aware of what had been taking place in Iraq for the past several years as revealed in the following statement by the NCRI:

> *"For the (Iranian) regime, Iraq is the gateway to the Islamic World. The most senior Revolutionary Guards commanders and thousands of members are focused on Iraq. They want to set up a puppet Islamic regime in Iraq. The regime has allocated billions of dollars to this mission. It has dispatched thousands of clerics to Iraq. It has been paying thousands of operatives on a monthly basis."*

She knew too that many Iraqis serving in law enforcement and the military—who would be responsible for MEK's security—were beholding to various Shia groups such as Badr Brigade, Mahdi Army and Iraqi Hezbollah because they were all being funded by Iran. Putting them in charge of MEK security was putting the fox in charge of guarding the hen house.

Also known was the fact thousands of Iranian Special Forces (Qods Force) were operating in Iraq.

Iran saw Iraq as an integral part of a militarized "Shia Crescent" to be formed from Iran, through Iraq, to Syria, Lebanon and the Hezbollah in Palestine, as well as from Iran to eastern parts of Saudi Arabia and Yemen. The Iranian focus on Iraq is evidenced by statements by both of Iran's Supreme Leaders that they should be the ultimate ruler of both countries. This is why Khamenei calls himself the "Supreme Leader of Muslims" rather than just the "Supreme Leader of Iran."

Five months later, the Iraqis struck.

In the short time before a tsunami strikes a shoreline, those in its path sense something terrible is about to happen. The clearest sign a tsunami is coming is the sight of a suddenly withdrawing sea, only to see it come roaring back. It was a similar sensation MEK residents at Camp Ashraf experienced on July 28, 2009.

U.S. forces, which had been in the area, suddenly and mysteriously were ordered to withdraw from the Camp by Iraqi authorities. Iraqi forces then came roaring up to the Camp's gate, allegedly to establish a police station at Ashraf, but with more force (2200 police and military personnel) than could possibly have been required to perform the job. They entered without any previous notice or coordination with MEK.

Video footage later released by MEK revealed the Iraqis employed small arms fire and other weapons to attack Ashraf's unarmed residents. Some victims were intentionally run over by Iraqi vehicles. Understandably, Iraqi forces did not allow journalists to accompany them to cover the event and monitor the operation.

By the time the dust settled, eleven MEK members were dead, two more lay dying, 400 were injured and 36 arrested. An Amnesty International report entitled "Iraq, Civilians Under Fire," published April 27, 2010, later described the incident as follows:

> *"On 28 July 2009, Iraqi security forces stormed Camp Ashraf, north of Baghdad, home to about 3,500 Iranian refugees and detained 36 residents. The 36 were subsequently reported to have been tortured, including by being beaten with batons and guns. Several people needed medical treatment for their injuries…The Iraqi government has continued to threaten Iranian refugees living in Camp Ashraf with forcible removal from the camp. On 28 July Iraqi security forces raided and took over the camp, in Diyala Governorate, which houses some 3400 members or supporters of the People's Mojahedeen Organization of Iran (PMOI), an Iranian opposition group."*

The report went on to condemn the Iraqis for violating MEK residents' human rights.

Because the Iraqis had ordered these attacks and thus were incapable of conducting an independent investigation of the July attack on Ashraf, an investigative court in Spain declared on November 26, 2009 it was competent to investigate possible crimes against humanity since MEK residents fall under the Geneva Convention protections. To investigate the massacre, a writ was sent to various senior Iraqi officials, including Prime Minister Nouri al-Maliki (who claimed he could not submit to the summons until out of office).

Later that year, on December 10, 2009, Baghdad announced it would relocate MEK members from Ashraf to Camp Liberty—a former U.S. military base near Baghdad International Airport. Baghdad claimed moving to Liberty was a necessary step in order to resettle them in other nations—and would result in Ashraf then being closed. Based on the inhabitability of Camp Liberty and its inability to house all 3400 MEK members, the relocation could only be seen as an intentional effort by Baghdad to make life as miserable as possible for them. Accordingly, MEK initially refused to comply with the order.

As Baghdad's efforts to close Camp Ashraf and relocate MEK residents elsewhere was seen by many Iraqis as simply a prelude to paving the way for MEK's extermination, more than a million Iraqi citizens signed a petition urging the United Nations to take measures to prevent this from happening. Some 94 members of Iraq's National Assembly, joined by senior officials including former Prime Minister Ayad Allawi and a Speaker of the Parliament, a vice president and a deputy prime minister, all made a similar appeal to Iraqi Prime Minister Nouri al-Maliki.

When MEK rejected the order to relocate to Camp Liberty, the Iraqi government sent security forces to Ashraf on December 15, 2009 to encourage compliance. Using loudspeakers and circulating pamphlets, the Iraqis threatened residents with deportation by the end of 2011, when all U.S. forces fully withdrew from Iraq.

MEK voiced concerns over the official status of its members and what protections would be afforded them. They were declared "asylum seekers" and "persons of concern" by the United Nations High Commissioner for Refugees (UNHCR), entitling them to certain humanitarian protections.

A December 10, 2009 French newspaper quoted al-Maliki as saying to improve relations with Iran he will "uproot" MEK residents, sending them to the desolate Neqrat as-Salman prison camp located in the southern Iraq desert, near the Saudi border.

Concerned about Iraq's intentions concerning the MEK, the EU adopted on November 25, 2010 a "Written Declaration on Camp Ashraf" for the U.S. and U.N. to provide urgent protection.

On January 7, 2011, another Iraqi raid took place at Ashraf that clearly revealed a Baghdad-Tehran connection concerning the MEK. Iraqis, who had either been hired by the Iranian government or who were accompanying Iranian agents, entered Camp Ashraf and attacked its residents, wounding 176. Medical treatment for the wounded, including 91 women, was barred by Iraqi forces. Interestingly, this raid followed a visit to Baghdad by the Iranian foreign minister.

The Iranian puppet masters still were not through, however, in manipulating their Iraqi puppets to further brutalize MEK.

Iraqi security forces again made a forced entry into Camp Ashraf on April 8, 2011. This time they came better prepared to inflict even more damage and injury. Equipped with bulldozers and armed with tanks, artillery and marksmen, they began wreaking havoc, destruction and death. Thirty-six MEK residents were killed, including eight women, most of which casualties Baghdad blamed on camp guards. However, an Amnesty International video again revealed the truth "appear(ing) to show Iraqi soldiers indiscriminately firing into the crowds and using vehicles to try and run others down."

Again, Iraqis allowed Iranians access to the area, where they installed communications gear to monitor conversations.

None of these Iraqi attacks was ever provoked by MEK.

Independent of any protected status MEK may have enjoyed pursuant to treaties or other agreements, international law also imposes upon a country the "responsibility to protect (R2P)" citizens from mass atrocities—and raises an international responsibility to do so should the state fail. Therefore, there was an obligation for the international community to act to fulfill its R2P duty when Iraq not only refused to do so but also was initiating the atrocities.

Of further worry to MEK was that the Iraqi prime minister continued to embrace Iran's mullahs. In April 2012, he visited Tehran where he was pressured to extradite 166 MEK members back to Iran for waging "war on God"—Iranian code for simply having opposed the ruling mullahs. It is believed several of these 166 members were identified when access was given to the Iranians and their agents during the January 7, 2011 Ashraf visit. It is also believed al-Maliki met with the head of Iran's elite military Qods Force while visiting Iran to discuss further suppressive measures to take against MEK.

In addition to vengeance against MEK, there were two other reasons Iran was so committed to destroying the group.

First, a fundamental difference in beliefs exists between MEK and Iran's mullahs. The former believes in man's right to exercise free will; the latter totally opposes it.

Second, Iran's biggest fear was of the Arab Spring becoming a Persian one, resulting in MEK members organizing domestic opposition in Iran.

For Shiite-dominated Iran, therefore, it was critical to gain influence over Shiite-dominated Iraq. Based on Tehran pulling al-Maliki's strings to destroy MEK, it most definitely seems that has happened as Baghdad plays the role of an Iranian puppet.

Iraq's continuing aggression at Camp Ashraf prompted Congressman Ted Poe (R-TX) to introduce an amendment, unanimously adopted in the House Committee, to the Foreign Relations Authorization Act, FY 2012 on July 21, 2011 after hearing testimony from a Camp survivor of the April 8, 2011 attack. That amendment stated that it was U.S. policy:

> *"...to urge the Government of Iraq to uphold its commitments to the United States to ensure the continued*

well-being of those living in Camp Ashraf and prevent their involuntary return to Iran in accordance with the United States Embassy Statement on Transfer of Security Responsibility for Camp Ashraf of December 28, 2008; take all necessary and appropriate steps in accordance with international agreements to support the commitments of the United States to ensure the physical security and protection of Camp Ashraf residents; and take all necessary and appropriate steps to prevent the forcible relocation of Camp Ashraf residents inside Iraq and facilitate the robust presence of the United Nations Assistance Mission in Iraq in Camp Ashraf."

Iraqi Prime Minister al-Maliki justified his actions against MEK based on the group's continuing FTO status. As such, he claimed MEK was in Iraq illegally and, therefore, should be dealt with severely.

The U.S. Department of State informed MEK that relocation to Camp Liberty was a condition precedent for being delisted as a FTO. Begrudgingly, the 3400 MEK members complied, making the relocation in a series of smaller groups. The first group of 400 departed on February 17, 2012. The Iraqis made the transit as difficult as possible for them, subjecting them to lengthy searches in the hot sun before leaving Ashraf, harassing them along the way, not allowing them to take many personal items that would make life a little more bearable at Liberty, etc.

International efforts were made to remove the FTO justification as an excuse for al-Maliki in his treatment of MEK by delisting it. But, it was a difficult road for MEK to travel to achieve this end as the one critical voice of support it needed was from the U.S. Government, which inexplicably refused to lend it.

MEK initiated an effort to have its name removed from the U.K., EU and U.S. FTO lists on the basis that it had renounced all violence in 2001 and was no longer involved in any kind of terrorist activities. The evidence it submitted to the U.K. and EU was sufficient to achieve that goal in 2008. On July 15, 2008, MEK submitted an appeal to the Bush Administration to be de-listed from the FTO on the basis of changed circumstances meeting the requirements for such de-listing. Just before leaving office, the Bush Administration rejected MEK's appeal on January 12, 2009.

As a result of this rejection, MEK filed a petition in the U.S. Court of Appeals that it had been denied due process by the U.S. Department of State in the face of evidence MEK had met the FTO de-listing requirements but the U.S. State Department had simply failed to apply the law.

When trial was held, because the U.S. Department of State would have to submit classified information to the Court, the courtroom was cleared after a public hearing. Logically, the intelligence U.S. Department of State gave to the court should not have been dissimilar to that which had been submitted during the U.K. and EU court FTO de-listing cases in which MEK had prevailed. MEK supporters were confident the U.S. Court of Appeals would reach a similarly favorable conclusion, ordering U.S. Department of State to re-consider.

Still, there were concerns about intelligence analysts whose assessments can change with the wind (sometimes political) as it has on various intelligence assessments about Iran. Concerns lingered too when weighed against the backdrop of an effective Iranian counter-intelligence campaign notorious for having "slimed" MEK on numerous occasions.

Incredibly, U.S. intelligence analysts in the past have relied on bogus Iranian counter-intelligence ploys. One report cites anonymous sources (immediately raising a credibility issue) as evidence MEK still held terrorist intentions—claiming MEK may have planned suicide attacks in Karbala (where Iran is active).

Even as late as 2007, bogus reports planted by Iran had the U.S. State Department taking the position that MEK retained "the capacity and will" to attack "Europe, the Middle East, the United States, Canada, and beyond." More recent reports included allegations MEK was active in violent acts in Karbala—an Iraqi city located a distance of 120 miles from Camp Ashraf where MEK members were imprisoned—as well as a city in which Iran's Qods Forces were known to operate.

Such allegations defy logic. Not only had MEK renounced terrorism in 2001, not only had MEK established a history of non-violent activity towards the U.S. both before and since then, not only had MEK voluntarily surrendered its weapons to the U.S. in 2003, not only did MEK lack the weapons and transportation necessary to conduct an attack in Karbala, not only did MEK lack the intention to conduct such attacks, but MEK was also under continuous 24-hour guard by U.S. forces at Camp Ashraf at the time, thus making any such operation impossible. The only logical source for such MEK allegations was Iranian counter-intelligence which, again, appeared to still be confounding U.S. analysts.

The U.S. Court of Appeals ruling was followed by calls to U.S. Secretary of State Hillary Clinton from over a hundred bipartisan members of Congress who urged her to act in favor of delisting.

Dozens of former high-level U.S. government and military officials also spoke out with support for MEK. As another allegation was circulated that MEK had a secret cache of weapons at Camp Ashraf, a former U.S. military commander in charge of Ashraf denied it, reporting the camp was thoroughly inspected and no weapons were ever found. That commander pleaded for the U.S. not to turn its back on MEK and renege on its responsibilities to protect its residents.

The U.S. Court of Appeals ruled in favor of MEK. It ordered the U.S. Department of State to revisit the MEK delisting issue, requiring a decision to be made by March 26, 2012. After considerable delay by the U.S. Department of State, another court ruling extended the decision deadline—either to grant or deny delisting—no later than October 1, 2012.

In Iran's effort to influence the U.S. decision on whether to keep MEK on the FTO list, the U.S. again was disadvantaged by a savvy Iranian intelligence service. In a word reminiscent of the code name of the most successful intelligence operation during World War II, the Iranians made "mincemeat" of U.S. intelligence assessments on the MEK.

Recounting World War II's "Operation Mincement" is important in understanding how critical it is to make an enemy think something to be true that is not. This will be followed by a very brief example of an Iraqi counter-intelligence operation aimed at Iran that went too well and, consequently for Iraq, terribly wrong.

When a Counter-Intelligence Operation Goes Well

It was described as "the most successful strategic deception in the history of warfare." In carrying out "Operation Mincemeat" during World War II, the man at the center of the plot never even knew he was the focus. Despite having died months earlier by his own hand, he would still prove able to save thousands of Allied lives. While the identity of "the man who never was," as he came to be called, is still debated, he is believed to have been Glyndwr Michael.

Michael's body, preserved in a morgue after his January 1943 death, became key to a British counter-intelligence plot. In April, dressed in the uniform of a British Army major, the body was given identification papers for a fictitious "Major Martin." Attached to Michael's wrist by chain and lock was a briefcase containing false "secret" documents of a bogus Allied invasion. Transported by submarine to the coast of Spain, the body was slipped into the sea. As hoped, it washed ashore and was discovered by the Nazis—who immediately examined the briefcase's contents.

While they knew an Allied invasion of Southern Europe was imminent, the Nazis did not know where it would occur. The Allies' counter-intelligence plan worked. The enemy was duped—diverting forces from Sicily, where the attack actually occurred in July, to Greece, where the documents falsely indicated it would take place.

When a Counter-Intelligence Operation Goes Too Well

Warfare—or preparation for it—is a constant battle to gain an edge over or to deceive an enemy. Depending on one's intent, the counter-intelligence game can be played to create a false perception either by showing a threat exists when one does not or one does not exist when it does.

Iran is attempting to use the latter against the West now; Iraq attempted to use the former against Iran earlier. Unfortunately for Iraq, its effort was too successful. Saddam Hussein made a major miscalculation which, ultimately, would cause his demise.

As a Sunni Arab leading a Shiite majority country, Saddam feared Shiite-majority Iran might one day suddenly announce it had nuclear weapons. In an effort to gain the upper hand, he initiated his own nuclear program, building a reactor at Osirak in central Iraq. The Israelis discovered the program and, in June 1981, launched a surprise attack, destroying the reactor.

Not one to give up easily, Saddam initiated a second effort to covertly develop WMDs. He had made substantial progress in this regard but made the mistake of misjudging the U.S. reaction to his 1990 invasion of Kuwait. The defeat of Iraqi forces during the Persian Gulf war put U.S. forces in the position to learn more about Saddam's second effort—one that had brought him much closer to success, until the U.S. shut it down.

In the aftermath of the Persian Gulf war, Saddam felt it important to keep Iran in line by convincing Tehran that Baghdad was still working on a nuclear weapons capability. Counter-intelligence operations were conducted to create this ruse. He did a very good job of conveying this deception, but also made a disastrous miscalculation. While Saddam sought to keep Iran at bay by convincing Tehran it had a nuclear weapons program, it was the U.S. that became convinced he was again working on a WMD program. In 2003, it invaded Iraq to terminate it. Ironically, in seeking to avoid another war with Iran, Saddam started one with the U.S., becoming the architect of his own demise.

The former director of Saddam's nuclear research program claimed Iraq's counter-intelligence effort was so effective, Saddam even believed he had such weapons. In a September 2004 New York Times opinion piece the former director wrote:

> "...the West never understood the delusional nature of Saddam Hussein's mind...(he lived in a) fantasy world...By 2003, as the American invasion loomed, the tyrant was...giving lunatic orders like burning oil around Baghdad to 'hide' the city from bombing attacks...(he kept

the country's Atomic Energy Commission alive but) staffed (it) with junior scientists involved in research totally unrelated to nuclear weapons, just so he could maintain the illusion in his mind that he had a nuclear program. Sort of like the emperor with no clothes, he fooled himself into thinking he was armed and dangerous. But unlike the fairytale ruler, Saddam fooled the rest of the world, as well, (although) our nuclear program could have been reinstituted at the snap of Saddam Hussein's fingers..."

Evidence that nuclear weapons were still a viable item on Saddam's "Bucket List" was evident in Iraqi documents captured during the 2003 invasion. Later translated, Saddam did have a plan to enrich uranium using a technique known as "plasma separation." But clearly, it was Saddam's very effective counter-intelligence plan that proved ultimately to be a miscalculation on his part. By trying to convince Iran he had such an active program, he also convinced the U.S., contributing to his own downfall.

Did Iran's Counter-Intelligence Operations Dupe the U.S.?

Based on the pressure placed on the U.S. Department of State by the courts to render a decision concerning MEK's removal from the FTO list, one can assume it was in Iran's best interests for the U.S. to come across intelligence suggesting MEK had not renounced violence. It can be assumed Iran mounted a counter-intelligence effort to create the false impression MEK was planning or otherwise involved in the conduct of terrorist operations in Iraq.

Through its manipulative relationship with Iraq, that is exactly what Iran did. Fraudulent documents were introduced to be "discovered" in Iraq that sought to give credibility to such claims which really emanated from Iran's counter-intelligence program.

It was here the U.S. Government should have applied the reasonable man test but failed to do so. Why, the reasonable man would query, with MEK having so much support for its effort to be de-listed from the FTO would it undertake violence after so many years of non-violence? It had nothing to gain and everything to lose by doing so.

Such counter-intelligence operations have duped the U.S. in the past, generating a 2007 National Intelligence Estimate in which the U.S. intelligence community reported, "We judge with high confidence that in the fall 2003, Tehran halted its nuclear weapons program." Our intelligence analysts—later believing Iran never halted work on its nuclear weapons program—prepared a new estimate in 2007.

But Iran's ability to confuse U.S. analysts on the nuclear issue has generated a sobering question from one U.S. Congressman. As he anticipated a new report from the U.S. intelligence community in 2010 and remained critical of the 2007 report, Representative Peter Hoekstra (R-Mich.) asked, "Why would I take the one in 2010 they are doing any more seriously, just because I like the outcome?"

The reality is the intelligence community has to make assessments in a part of the world that is extremely difficult to assess. And much of that difficulty is linked to an inability to understand the Iranian mindset.

Iran's counter-intelligence efforts have successfully cross-pollinated into Iraq. One example, illustrative of what Americans wrongly perceive is just a "cold" war with Iran while Iran knows otherwise, took place in Karbala—the city supposedly where violent activities by MEK were being planned.

On January 20, 2007, in what was called the "boldest and most sophisticated attack in four years of warfare" in Iraq, militants—dressed and armed as Americans, speaking perfect English and driving U.S. SUVs—infiltrated the provincial governor's compound where U.S. and Iraqi officials were meeting. Targeting only Americans, the militants killed one soldier and took four as prisoner.

With captives in tow and Iraqi police in hot pursuit, they headed for the Iranian border. But as their pursuers closed in, the militants abandoned their SUVs and uniforms—executing their captives. All four were found bound with gunshot wounds to the head.

The attack had Iranian fingerprints all over it. The evidence in support of this included a satellite photograph of a display on the ground of the Karbala compound at a base in Iran.

The MEK Pawn

The issue of whether the MEK lion was friendly or not to the U.S. was muddled when Tehran asked the Clinton Administration in 1997 to put it on the FTO. Various accusations against MEK had been made during the Shah's rule of terrorist attacks against U.S. citizens working in Iran, its cooperation with Saddam to put down post-1991 Gulf war uprisings in Iraq, etc.

An independent group, represented by former Congressman Dick Armey, assessed these allegations and the evidence upon which the Clinton Administration relied to reach that decision in 1997, finding it "fundamentally flawed." Far from being terrorists, Armey found MEK to be "a pro-democratic organization that for more than 40 years has worked to bring democracy and freedom to Iran…The MEK has repeatedly been a pawn…sacrificed in U.S.-Iranian and Franco-Iranian relations."

MEK was put on the FTO list in 1997 simply as a "goodwill gesture to Iran" — a country designated as the world's greatest state sponsor of terrorism. It was inconceivable MEK was listed at a time the U.S. failed to put other organizations on the list far more deserving. And, at a time MEK remained on the list having rejected violence years earlier, the most aggressive nation in its own region—North Korea—was delisted despite its blatant track record of terrorist activities directed at South Korea. Also inconceivable was MEK's presence on the list while a terrorist group responsible for continuing to kill U.S. and Allied soldiers in Afghanistan—the Haqqani network—remained off of it. (The Haqqani network was only added in September 2012 after political pressure to do so was exerted by Congress.)

MEK does have its detractors. Some say MEK's real preference is to establish a Marxist state along the lines of the Marxist-Islamist students who founded the group in 1965. MEK leader Maryam Rajavi, however, has called democracy "the spirit that guides our Resistance."

On balance, however, MEK seems to offer significantly more positive for Iran's future than negative. In major contrast to the mullahs, MEK incorporates women and human rights into its platform. And, MEK has demonstrated by its actions to date it is a needed ally in the fight for regime change in Tehran.

World War II's Operation Mincemeat demonstrated the West's ingenuity in implementing complex counter-intelligence plans. By successfully planting allegations of unproven terrorist intent by an MEK incapable of delivering on it—duping U.S. intelligence analysts and seeking to deny MEK FTO de-listing in the process—Iran has demonstrated the simple ingenuity of theirs.

MEK Update

The U.S. Department of State finally announced its court-ordered decision on MEK's request for de-listing. In a decision that rights an extreme wrong, imposed upon MEK fifteen years ago only to placate Tehran's mullahs, the U.S. Government de-listed the organization from the FTO designation effective September 28, 2012.

With its FTO status removed, MEK is now seeking support to be recognized as a legitimate advocate for democratic change in Iran. The head of the NCRI, Maryam Rajavi, noted that the group's delisting was the "greatest defeat" the mullahs have suffered since coming to power. She made clear what her organization's interests are:

> "Our people and the resistance's message is that, from the West, we seek neither money nor weapons. We only seek a definitive end to the policy of appeasement with the criminal rulers of Iran and the recognition of the Iranian people's resistance against religious fascism and for freedom and democracy.
>
> "This step is indispensable. This is the only answer to the mullahs who are striving for nuclear weapons. It is the answer to terrorism, fundamentalism and a regime, which as the primary supporter and partner of [Syrian

President] Bashar Assad, is directing the daily massacres in Syria."

As could be expected, the response from Tehran on MEK's delisting was not a positive one. The U.S. had indicated its decision was made in part on the voluntary departure from Camp Ashraf of the last MEK members and their relocation to Camp Liberty. Of this, Tehran said:

"The moving of the members of this terrorist group from Camp Ashraf to another place is not at all an acceptable excuse...for the terrorist nature of this group to be ignored.

"If America removes this group, with a long history of terrorist actions, from its list, it would be a breach of its international obligations and undermine global efforts to combat terrorism."

The mullahs have already claimed an October 3, 2012 protest in Tehran involving about 20,000 people was the work of MEK instigators—while totally ignoring the possibility it may have been the impact of devastating economic conditions at home.

Cable documents released by Wikileaks revealed the Iranian government desperately tried to prevent MEK from being de-listed as a U.K. FTO, threatening the U.K. government it could "endanger resolution of the nuclear issue."

MEK continued to move forward in its legal battle for de-listing while Tehran continued to make threats and denounce the MEK. It caused British Parliamentarian Lord Maginnis to note after MEK was successful in its fight to be removed from the U.S. FTO list:

"One fact that the mullahs' and apologists consistently ignore is that the PMOI (aka "MEK") has won victories in every court it has petitioned (18 in all), including those decisions in EU and U.K. courts. Those decisions are all a matter of public record, and were based solely on evidence. As the walls begin to close in around a regime

known for its outlandish lies and propaganda, it will continue to lash out in a desperate attempt to stave off the inevitable. Such reactions will not be of any surprise."

It was clear from the Wikileaks cables that Tehran feared the influence MEK might wield within Iran.

Iran had invested a great deal of money, time and international effort to contain and/or eradicate MEK in Iraq. Iran's hardliners see MEK's freedom and Iran's failed containment policy in keeping MEK on the FTO list as a major policy failure of Ahmadinejad's presidency. It also leaves Tehran wondering if this policy change by Washington will open the door to other anti-Tehran actions.

Although the MEK delisting decision was the result of a long, drawn out process that, in the end, was forced upon the U.S. Government, the decision should now serve as a wake-up call to Tehran: for the MEK, the gloves are off in the challenge to displace Iran's mullahs.

Tehran should start feeling the pain. The lion is free. It now seeks to help free the Iranian people who have been chained by their leadership to a seventh century ideology robbing them of independent thought.

The lion sleeps tonight but the mullahs do not.

Chapter Ten

Is It Already Too Late for the West—Has Iran Already Duped the World?

With the collapse of the Soviet Union on December 25, 1991, some Soviet Bloc nations were faced with an important decision. As newly independent states, they found themselves in possession of the nuclear weapons Moscow had left behind. "To be a nuclear power, or not to be—that was the question."

One of the countries having to make this decision was Kazakhstan. Based on its inheritance of thousands of missiles, it suddenly found itself possessing the world's fourth largest nuclear arsenal.

Fast forwarding to a nuclear security summit held in Seoul, South Korea, in May 2012, President Obama met with Kazakhstan President Nursultan Nazarbaev to congratulate him for having made the right decision twenty years earlier. Praising Nazarbaev, Obama said:

> "Twenty years ago, Kazakhstan made a decision not to have nuclear weapons. And not only has that led to growth and prosperity in his own country, but (Nazarbaev) has been a model in efforts around the world to eliminate nuclear materials that could fall into the wrong hands."

Nazarbaev wrote a March 25, 2012 op-ed for the New York Times entitled, "What Iran Can Learn From Kazakhstan." Nazarbaev encouraged:

> "Tehran to learn from our example," noting that Kazakhstan today is "a more prosperous, stable country, with more influence and friends in the world because of this decision."

At the time Kazakhstan made its decision concerning its inherited nuclear arsenal twenty years earlier, it was believed all the missiles had either been destroyed or sent back to Russia. Since then, it is believed some may have slipped through the cracks.

On October 27, 2011, a former IRGC spy who worked for the CIA, Reza Kahlili (who uses a pseudonym), wrote an op-ed for The Washington Times claiming some of those old Soviet missiles had gone unaccounted for, making their way into some very dangerous hands. This claim has been independently verified by other sources as well.

As if there were not enough already that is disconcerting about Iran's leadership, Kahlili's op-ed should keep people awake at night:

> "The pressure the United States and the West is bringing to bear on Iran to keep it from acquiring nuclear weapons is all for naught. Not only does the Islamic Republic already have nuclear weapons from the old Soviet Union, but it has enough enriched uranium for more. What's worse, it has a delivery system."

> "...In the early 1990s, the CIA asked me to find an Iranian scientist who would testify that Iran had the bomb. The CIA had learned that Iranian intelligence agents were visiting nuclear installations throughout the former Soviet Union, with particular interest in Kazakhstan.

> "Kazakhstan, which had a significant portion of the Soviet arsenal and is predominately Muslim, was courted by Muslim Iran with offers of hundreds of millions of dollars for the bomb. Reports soon surfaced that three nuclear warheads were missing. This was corroborated by Russian Gen. Victor Samoilov, who handled the disarmament issues for the general staff. He admitted that the three were missing from Kazakhstan.

> "Meanwhile, Paul Muenstermann, then vice president of the German Federal Intelligence Service, said Iran had received two of the three nuclear warheads and medium-range nuclear delivery systems from Kazakhstan. It also

was reported that Iran had purchased four 152 mm nuclear shells from the former Soviet Union, which were reportedly stolen and sold by former Red Army officers.

"To make matters worse, several years later, Russian officials stated that when comparing documents in transferring nuclear weapons from Ukraine to Russia, there was a discrepancy of 250 nuclear weapons.

"Last week, Mathew Nasuti, a former U.S. Air Force captain who was at one point hired by the State Department as an adviser to one of its provincial reconstruction teams in Iraq, said that in March 2008, during a briefing on Iran at the State Department, the department's Middle East expert told the group that it was 'common knowledge' that Iran had acquired tactical nuclear weapons from one or more of the former Soviet republics.

"Lt. Col. Tony Shaffer, an experienced intelligence officer and recipient of a Bronze Star, told me that his sources say Iran has two workable nuclear warheads.

"An editorial in Kayhan, the Iranian newspaper directly under the supervision of the Office of the Supreme Leader, last year (2010) warned that if Iran were attacked, there would be nuclear blasts in American cities."

The above announcement by Iran was timed to coincide with President Obama's Nuclear Security Summit held in Washington on April 13, 2010. Iran also announced it would join the nuclear club within a month. For the first time, Iran suggested with the statement below it might pass nuclear devices to terrorists capable of accessing U.S. borders to plant such devices. The specific statement was as follows:

"If the U.S. strikes Iran with nuclear weapons, there are elements which will respond with nuclear blasts in the centers of America's main cities."

As reported by DEBKAfile:

> "Without specifying whether those elements would be Iranian or others, Tehran aimed at the heart of the Nuclear Security Summit by threatening U.S. cities with nuclear terror. DEBKAfile's Iranian sources report that Tehran is playing brinkmanship to demonstrate that the Washington summit, from which Iran and North Korea were excluded, failed before it began, because terrorist elements capable of striking inside the U.S. had already acquired nuclear devices for that purpose.
>
> "The Iranian official's boast was run by the Fars news agency, published by Iran's Revolutionary Guards Corps."

Getting back to Kahlili's op-ed:

> "Despite knowing that Iranian leaders were seeking nuclear weapons, Western leaders chose to negotiate and appease with the hope of reaching a solution with Iran. Nearly three years into President Obama's administration, we must acknowledge that the policies of first a carrot of good will and then a stick of sanctions have neither stopped the Iranians with their nuclear program nor have they deterred their aggressive posture. The Iranian leaders today, despite four sets of United Nations sanctions, continue with their missile and nuclear enrichment program, and they have enough enriched uranium for six nuclear bombs, according to the latest International Atomic Energy Agency report.
>
> "The Revolutionary Guards now have more than 1,000 ballistic missiles, many pointed at U.S. military bases in the Middle East and Europe. The Guards also have made great strides in their intercontinental missile delivery system under the guise of their space program. As I revealed earlier, nuclear weapons-capable warheads have been delivered to the Guards, and Iran's supreme leader

has ordered the Guards to arm their missiles with nuclear payloads. Iran's navy also has armed its vessels with long-range surface-to-surface missiles and soon will expand its mission into the Atlantic Ocean and the Gulf of Mexico.

"History suggests that we may already be too late to stop Iran's nuclear bomb. Why do we suppose Iran cannot accomplish in 20 years of trying - with access to vast amounts of unclassified data on nuclear-weapons design and equipped with 21st-century technology - what the U.S. accomplished in three years during the 1940s with the Manhattan Project?" asks nuclear weapons expert Peter Vincent Pry, who served in the CIA and on the EMP Commission, and is now president of EMPact America.

"Mr. Pry concludes that Iran only needs a single nuclear weapon to destroy the United States. A nuclear EMP (electromagnetic pulse) attack could collapse the national electric grid and other critical infrastructures that sustain the lives of 310 million Americans.

"Are we ready to finally realize what the goals and the ideology of the jihadists in Tehran are and take appropriate action against them? The Iranian people themselves, who oppose the dictatorial mullahs, for years, have asked us to do so. Thousands of them have lost their lives to show us the true nature of this regime. We must act before it's too late."

Kahlili, in a September 2012 interview, shared some information on Iran's EMP capability:

"I received this information from an intelligence officer within the Guards who recently defected to a country in Europe. I passed that intelligence on to U.S. authorities and published it publicly. They have several neutron bombs.

"Now we know for a fact that North Korea has these super EMP bombs which are neutron bombs. The source told me that in a meeting of the security officials of the Guards, a plan was discussed where they would detonate these neutron bombs in the atmosphere.

"We know that they have successfully launched ballistic missiles off of a ship in the Caspian Sea, detonating the warhead in the atmosphere. The IAEA has confirmed such activity which is in line with an EMP threat, Electromagnetic Pulse attack.

"I also revealed that many of the Iranian vessels have been armed with long range ballistic missiles. This could be a commercial vessel under a third party flag with containers carrying a ballistic missile. A ballistic missile could be launched in less than 60 seconds...using a scenario involving a commercial vessel en route to Venezuela, Cuba, or Nicaragua.

"They could launch a successful Electromagnetic Pulse Attack on the U.S. Studies have been done for Congress showing that the devastation from a successful Electromagnetic Pulse attack on U.S. would be immediate. The U.S. could be sent back to the 18th century because our power grid is not protected. Telecommunication, water supplies and food distribution would be disrupted. Within weeks the study pointed out that Americans would be scavenging for food and water. One year after such an attack, two thirds of U.S. population could cease to exist.

"The Iranians have practiced a possible EMP ship borne attack. Arming their ballistic missiles with neutron bombs they could launch an Electromagnetic Pulse Attack on any country."

Is it possible Iran could have acquired nuclear weapons from Kazakhstan two decades ago? If so, the eventual target and means of delivery have long ago been thought out. With the available vehicles Iran has today, there are a number of scenarios for delivery that are plausible.

As Kahlili suggests, it could be placed on a SCUD missile launcher hidden on an innocent looking merchant ship to sail off the coast of the U.S. to create an airburst detonation to generate such an EMP wave capable of collapsing an entire region's electrical grid system.

It could also be placed on a missile launcher soon to be installed by the Qods Force in Venezuela. Or, it could be smuggled into the U.S. through the network Hezbollah has now established with drug gangs to access America's southern border.

If Iran obtained a nuclear weapon twenty years ago, could it have secretly maintained it ever since then without it being discovered?

With the Iranian opposition group MEK in the best position to provide humint and with the organization now finally de-listed from the U.S. FTO list, their assistance is needed more than ever before!

Turning Shiite Brother Against Shiite Brother: The Iran-Iraq War

Within the natural flow of Islamic sectarian differences, the 1980-1988 Iran-Iraq war should never have happened. Representing one-half the nations of the world with Shiite-majority populations, Iran and Iraq saw eye-to-eye on their sectarian beliefs.

As Arabs and Persians, the Iraqis and Iranians had had some disputes and had been historical rivals. There had been border disputes including one over waterway rights along the Shatt al-Arab river between the two countries—a major waterway linking the Persian Gulf with the Iranian ports of Khorramshahr and Abadan and the Iraqi port of Basra.

But none of these disputes reached the level of conflict justifying the eight year war the two countries fought between 1980-1988. Iraqi President Saddam Hussein named the conflict the "Whirlwind War"—expectations that were soon dashed by the war's long duration. It was a conflict that ultimately would claim one million casualties, of which approximately two-thirds were Iran's.

Because it involved the two major oil producing countries in a region where more than half the world's reserves are located, the conflict was one of the most strategically important of modern times.

How did it come to be that these nations defied the natural laws of Islamic sectarian hatred and friendship, giving rise to a Shiite-on-Shiite conflict between them? With Shiites so vastly outnumbered by Sunnis, what would have caused them to disregard their natural survival instinct to bond together and, instead, to turn on each other?

War would play out as one man's effort to promote an ideology collided with another's to promote himself—with both efforts manipulating Islam for its own benefit.

Saddam Hussein was born, fatherless and penniless, on April 28, 1937, in a village called "Al-Awja." It was located near his ancestral home of Tikrit, in northern Iraq. Influenced by an uncle, Kharaillah Tulfah, who was a devout Sunni, Saddam became active in politics.

He quickly learned success turned both on being cunning and brutal. He joined the Ba'ath Party at age 19, but was humiliated when denied entry to the military academy for not completing high school. (After gaining power in 1976, he would take a short cut to pursuing a military career by simply appointing himself a general.) Forming various political alliances, Saddam quickly climbed his way up the power ladder, officially consolidating his authority in 1979—the same year Ayatollah Khomeini was consolidating his next door.

Despite Iraq's dominant Shiite population, Saddam was a Sunni. That made him particularly sensitive to the fact he was considered an outsider among the very Shiites he sought to rule. The challenge by both Shia and Kurdish movements to his authority soon after his power grab undoubtedly contributed to paranoia on his part that continued to impact him for the rest of his life.

It was this paranoia which prompted him, once in power, to rely on his family members, who were also Sunnis, as advisors to help him maintain control over the Shiite masses. He brought into his close circle as well other Sunnis, such as tribe members from his birthplace in Tikrit, giving them various leadership positions. (These would be the same people to whom he would turn to hide him after the 2003 U.S. invasion; while they did, he was eventually found hiding in a "rat hole" in the village of Adwar, about nine miles from Tikrit.)

Saddam knew his tribal ties had helped him come to power and as soon as he was in a position to do so, promoted them as his governing tool to consolidate his power. He came to appreciate that the bonds of tribal and family loyalty were much stronger than those of the party. He slowly began introducing these tribal and family members into key security leadership positions that enabled him to isolate his opponents without having to watch his back as he had someone doing that for him.

During his formative political years, Saddam was heavily influenced by Egypt's Gamal Abdel Nasser and his efforts to promote pan-Arab nationalism. As Nasser's influence spread, monarchies in the Middle East began to fall. As Nasser became a unifying force for the Arab world, Saddam saw himself as Nasser's heir. Coming to power the year after Nasser died, Saddam began promoting this image as soon as he came to power.

But as Saddam was vying for this leadership position, he found he was being challenged by Iran's new leadership, led by Supreme Leader Khomeini. Although both countries were Shiite, Iraq followed a more secular form of government while Iran was implementing its theocracy. The different approaches to government were of concern to Saddam. He worried Iran's leadership would be viewed as more legitimate to Muslims than his own as Tehran's was tied to representing the best interests of Islam while his, as a secular government, represented the best interests of Saddam.

Saddam's ego clearly knew no limits. Once he became the undisputed leader of Iraq, he began promoting his country as the rallying point for the rest of the Arab world. He praised Iraq's rich history and his own leadership skills as warranting the role. He decried that the best interests of Iraq mirrored the best interests of the Arab world and Islam; accordingly, Saddam was strategically poised to deliver on all fronts.

Khomeini's Islamist image pressured Saddam into demonstrating the Iraqi leader was not an anti-Islamic atheist. Consequently, Saddam began "Islamizing" his position to at least give the appearance of being a good Islamist. This was a necessary ploy for Saddam. He had to appeal to his mostly Shiite army as he did not want to be out-Islamized by Khomeini and his possible appeal to them.

Saddam promoted himself as the true champion of Islam and promised victory for those who followed him. He stayed with this theme to increase his popularity among Iraq's majority Shiites even after the Iran-Iraq war ended.

While starting a war with Iran might have seemed as an irrational move for Saddam, it was logical to a leader who was paranoid. Since Saddam and the Shah were enemies, Baghdad originally supported the regime change in Tehran. But, four months after Ayatollah Khomeini returned to Iran, he was encouraging Iraqi Shiites to overthrow Saddam. Tehran began supporting Shiites in Iraq, which included an assassination campaign against Ba'ath leaders. Within the month of April 1980 alone, twenty Ba'ath leaders were assassinated.

Feeling threatened, Saddam threw out a peace offering by praising Khomeini in a speech he delivered on July 17, 1979, calling for a friendship agreement. But Khomeini, perhaps believing his Islamic Revolutionary train was unstoppable, ignored Saddam's praise and renewed his call for Shiites in Iraq to throw him out. (As will be detailed later, Saddam's fall and Iran gaining influence over Iraq was a key piece of the puzzle for Khomeini to pave the way for the Mahdi's return.)

Clearly, Saddam feared Khomeini's train was a runaway capable of crossing over the border into Iraq, triggering an Islamic Revolution there as well. There were probably a number of reasons at this point in time why Saddam saw war unavoidable and/or preferable.

Iran's pan-Islamism and revolutionary Shia Islamism were coming into conflict with Iraq's Arab nationalism—and something would have to give.

One of the most common ways a dictator takes the focus off domestic problems is to create an outside threat. Accordingly, for Saddam, Iran was the convenient target of choice as that outside threat.

Khomeini and company were not yet firmly entrenched in Iran. The government was still in disarray there and its military was in a weakened condition as its senior leaders had been executed and lower ranking officers purged. Thus, Saddam believed initiating a war against Iran would be a cakewalk.

Finally, with Iran being viewed by the international community as a rogue nation, war would also improve Iraq's standing as a regional power.

Tremendous oil reserves had brought significant amounts of cash into Iraq's treasury so as to allow Saddam to go on a spending spree. Much of the funding was spent on the newest equipment for his military.

Saddam perceived something the West has yet to grasp—the Iranians were fully capable of striking out at Iraq and were in the early stages of preparing to do so. Tehran posed a dangerous threat that could no longer be ignored by Baghdad.

Occasional border skirmishes with Iran were occurring in 1980. In April, Shiite animosity was triggered in Iraq when one of their most senior ayatollahs—Grand Ayatollah Mohammad Baqir al-Sadr—was hanged in a mass murder campaign by Saddam seeking to restore his control. The border skirmishes soon increased to becoming a daily occurrence.

Saddam believed this would be a good time to take action, justifying it on Iran's assassination campaign against Iraq's Ba'ath political leaders and its border attacks. Without a formal declaration of war, he launched a surprise air attack against Iran on September 22, 1980, followed by a ground attack the next day. The ground attack succeeded in making what would be the deepest Iraqi penetration into Iran before Iranian forces checked the advance. Iran immediately set out to reclaim its territory, achieving that goal by June 1982.

(It is interesting to note when Iran and Iraq went to war, one of the countries to come to Tehran's aid was Israel, which provided weapons. Israel saw Iraq as the greater threat and, therefore, sought to assist "the enemy of my enemy." Ironically, today Iran and Iraq are back together as friends and Iran and Israel back to being enemies. Israel's assistance probably sought to curry favor with Iran so it would protect Jews residing there.)

Due to pre-existing sanctions against Iran, Tehran was hard-pressed to acquire new weapons. It did develop both China and North Korea as suppliers, initiating a relationship with Pyongyang that would eventually lead to sharing nuclear and missile technology.

Many of the other Gulf States, however, saw Iran as the greater threat, and came to the aid of Iraq. Countries like Kuwait and Saudi Arabia made billions of dollars in loans available to Baghdad. The U.S., France and Russia also lined up on Iraq's side.

The Khomeini regime had already neutered its own army due to its purge, which caused the government to turn to the IRGC to step into the breach. Initially the IRGC refused to serve alongside the regular army but after experiencing several defeats, joint operations with the regular army were conducted. Iranian officers who had been imprisoned were released to fight and many junior enlisted found themselves promoted to the general ranks.

Although Iran had not contemplated its efforts to stir up revolution in Iraq would trigger an invasion, the mullahs welcomed it as a chance to help consolidate power and unify the country behind them—as well as to gain control over Iraq. It did not do anything, however, to help get Iran out of an economic free fall which had started with the 1979 Islamic Revolution. Foreign exchange reserves tumbled from $14.6 billion to $1 billion by 1981. Iran's leadership had gambled too that Iraq's Shiites would rise up against Saddam and join Iran's cause, but it did not happen.

Over the next six years, the two countries were involved in a slugfest. They would engage in a repeat of World War I's famous Maginot Line defense in which advancement progressed in terms of inches. The only blips in the fighting occurred when Saddam tried to break the stalemate by introducing chemical warfare—targeting Iranian soldiers, civilians and Iraqi Kurds.

(Note: While Khomeini and his fellow ayatollahs would preach a strict interpretation of the Koran, they never hesitated to bend those teachings when useful to do so. For example, Islam prohibits performing autopsies. However, in 1984, Khomeini offered up the corpses of Iranian soldiers killed on the battlefield by chemical weapons so independent proof could be established Iraq was using WMDs. Thus, even Muhammad's teachings could bend to Khomeini's agenda.)

Although outnumbered at the outset, Iran slowly balanced things out with members of an organization known as the Basij-e-Muzaffezin (Mobilization of the Oppressed), comprised of volunteers—as young as fourteen and as old as seventy—who joined for various reasons from religious belief to nationalism.

Eight days after the Iraqi attack starting the war, Iran—probably motivated more by a desire to humiliate Saddam than to further destroy an already inoperable nuclear facility—launched Operation Scorched Sword, an air attack, against his non-functioning nuclear facility at Osirak, which had already been destroyed by the Israelis earlier that year.

By the end of December 1981, Saddam had to withdraw his forces from Iran, feeling they could maintain a better defense on Iraqi soil.

In April 1982, Iran was able to toss a monkey wrench into Iraq's war effort by convincing Syria to close down an oil pipeline running from Iraq into Syria (Kirkuk-Banias Pipeline) which permitted Iraqi oil to reach the Mediterranean. That pipeline brought in about $5 billion per month to Baghdad, causing a severe financial burden for the country once it was shut down.

Just like his father cooperated with the Islamic fundamentalists in Iran during the Iran-Iraq war, Syria's Bashar al-Assad would do the same decades later.

To offset the financial loss of the Syrian oil outlet, Iraq would have to rely on Turkey's pipelines and on money provided by other Sunni states that feared an Iranian victory in the conflict. For those states, such as Saudi Arabia, Jordan and Kuwait, the decision was a "no-brainer" as Ayatollah Khomeini had declared all monarchies illegitimate and for their people to rise up against their rulers.

The Iranians had counted on intimidating the Saudis as the war with Iraq dragged on, hoping to get them to kowtow in the face of Tehran's aggressive stance. However, the Saudis refused to be intimidated, putting up a tougher front than the Iranians expected.

Two years into the war, Saddam finally realized the "cakewalk" invasion he had envisioned at the outset was not to be. He offered Khomeini a ceasefire. Khomeini countered with demands of his own which included Saddam's resignation and the installation of an Islamic government in Baghdad. (Again, the reason for this demand is detailed later.)

Knowing he would reject Saddam's offer, Khomeini held discussions with his staff concerning the efficacy of launching an invasion into Iraq. As is often the case, those not charged with fighting the war—in this case the hardline clerics including Khomeini and President Rafsanjani—opted in favor of an invasion. Those responsible for fighting it, however, such as Army Chief of Staff General Ali Sayad Shirazi advised against continuing a war that would only claim many more young lives.

Khomeini's mind was made up, however, and he ordered the invasion. (Note: This would appear to run afoul of the Koran's teaching in Qur'an 8:61 requiring:

> "But if the enemy inclines towards peace, do thou (also) incline towards peace, and trust in Allah. For He is One that heareth and knoweth (all things)."

Khomeini's decision would extend the war for six more years, only to be settled in 1988 on the same terms Saddam had offered in 1982. The loss of hundreds of thousands more lives in a war that achieved nothing would not concern Iran's highest ranking man-of-the-cloth. Khomeini rejected the ceasefire terms on June 21, 1982 and announced the invasion of Iraq the next month.

Having objected to an invasion and been overruled, the Iranian generals proposed launching a knockout punch against Baghdad. That too was not supported by the clerics who sought to take a much more protracted approach, conquering Iraq region by military region. They hoped such a campaign would trigger a domestic uprising upon Iraq's majority Shiite population.

It was a foolish call by religious zealots who believed donning clerical robes imbued them with a warrior's expertise. They soon discovered, however, Iraqis fighting Iranians on Iraqi soil were much more difficult to dislodge than were Iraqis fighting Iranians on Iranian soil. The massive casualties promised by General Shirazi quickly materialized. But, Iraq would spend the remaining six years of the war on the defensive.

The Iranians often launched large human wave attacks against heavily fortified Iraqi positions. The mounting casualties generated a requirement for an equal number of replacement forces. It was no wonder two Iranian soldiers were lost for each Iraqi. And, any effort for the Iranians to launch a surprise attack was often confounded by U.S. satellite pictures and aerial photographs shared with Iraqi intelligence in time for the Iraqis to defend against it.

It was in defense of a large Iranian attack against Basra, the Iranians began using the Basij child soldiers to march through the Iraqi minefields so the IRGC could follow behind them unimpeded.

Just like Adolf Hitler made military decisions during World War II that would have been better left to his generals, so too did Saddam. Having made himself a general overnight, Saddam failed—just as Iran's mullahs failed—to leave the fighting to those trained to do it. It was no wonder the war dragged on for years.

Over time, however, Saddam's interference with military operations caused a great deal of anger among his generals. After some of them courageously confronted him, however, Saddam backed down, allowing them to implement their own strategy.

It was a smart decision on Saddam's part to do so as his generals proved much more capable, recapturing all Iraqi territory held by the Iranians and eventually forcing an end to the war. However, after the war, an ungrateful Saddam purged those very same generals.

The last push in the war effort by the Iraqis required every available body they could press into service. To attract Iraqi Shiites to the military, Saddam implemented the same religious fanaticism as did the Iranians. He promoted the image of being a devout Muslim by having state television run footage of him praying or visiting mosques.

The television footage, however, belied Saddam's own perceptions of himself.

When U.S. forces combed through Saddam's numerous palaces following the 2003 invasion into Iraq, an interesting observation was made in one—"Believers Palace" in Baghdad. Located within an area which came to be known as the "Green Zone," the palace had a huge ballroom accessible through a foyer at ground level. The ballroom's ceiling opened up to a second level, from where one could look down upon the massive floor below.

On the wall at the second floor level, but large enough to be seen from the first floor, was an inscription. It consisted of two names, written in Arabic. One was Saddam's; the other was Allah's. While the appearance of the two names, together, is not particularly noteworthy, what was of note was the sequencing. Saddam's name appeared first—above Allah's, suggesting a superior position for Saddam over Allah. It was most telling about Saddam's arrogance, reflecting his personal belief that, despite being mortal (as he later found out), he stood above Allah.

Nonetheless, for appearance's sake, Saddam re-packaged himself as the new, improved "Islamized" Iraqi leader during the Iran-Iraq war. This initiative continued after that conflict ended as he declared that where Iraqi laws ran afoul of shariah, the latter was to control. Just prior to the Persian Gulf war to further his new image as a man of faith he added the words, "Allah Akbar" ("God is great"), to Iraq's national flag.

Some Iranian domestic opposition to the war began rearing its head in 1982. Former Prime Minister Mehdi Bazargan engaged in correspondence with the U.N., sending a telegram criticizing the war as un-Islamic and Khomeini for failing to have accepted the Iraqi ceasefire proposal. In a 1988 open letter to Khomeini, Bazargan said:

> *"Since 1986, you have not stopped proclaiming victory, and now you are calling upon the population to resist until victory. Is that not an admission of failure on your part?"*

Not holding back, Bazargan chastised Khomeini for slaughtering Iran's youth and bankrupting the country.

It was clear by late 1986/early 1987, a much weakened Iranian force had lost much of its fighting spirit. A year earlier, in 1985, the minor domestic protests against the war became major ones throughout much of Iran. The mullahs' response was to brutally put the protests down, executing many protestors. But, by 1988, it appeared even the mullahs had lost their fight, realizing a stalemate and war of attrition was no longer sustainable.

Another factor Iran weighed was that, with improved Russian weaponry and French training, the Iraqis were becoming a more effective fighting force, taking a deadlier toll on Iran. Also in the mix was the fact that the U.S. had launched Operation Praying Mantis, destroying several Iranian oil platforms in retaliation for continuing IRGC speed boat attacks against oil tankers. The Iranians realized they could not afford to simultaneously take on the U.S. and Iraq.

Iran's mullahs also remained discouraged that Iraq's Shiites had not turned against Saddam. Khomeini had lived in Iraq during most of his time in exile in the 1960s-1978. He did nothing to convince other Shiites that his view of Islamic utopia held enough promise for them to join him. As British journalist Patrick Brogan put it:

> "Even the Shiites of Iraq preferred the vicious tyranny of Saddam Hussein, Sunni though he was, to the Ayatollah's Shiite paradise: Hussein was an Arab, Khomeini a Persian, and 13 centuries of hostility are not to be dispersed by a Friday sermon."

Furthermore, the morale of the Iranian people was drained. Brogan also observed that by 1988:

> "The economy was collapsing. War and revolution had taken their toll. Only war industries survived, and the standard of living was dropping precipitously. There were no longer enough recruits for the Revolutionary Guards; the Iranian war machine was no longer capable of supplying the huge armies that had marched singing to war in the early days...

> "The country was sliding steadily into bankruptcy. Strict Islamic law forbids usury, and Khomeini interpreted that to mean Iran could not borrow against future oil revenues to meet the expenses of war. Iran paid cash, and when the reserves were exhausted, Iran had to rely on income from its oil exports. Oil revenue dropped from $20 billion in 1982 to $5 billion in 1988. At an OPEC meeting in June 1988, Saudi Arabia, who had broken diplomatic relations with Iran two months earlier, vetoed a last, desperate Iranian initiative to cut production and thus raise prices again."

But what may well have been the final nail in the coffin for continuing Iran's war effort was Saddam's public threat to use more WMDs against Iran. He had used them before on the battlefield and Khomeini knew he would do so again. However, he had no idea what kind of weapons Saddam might have left in his WMD arsenal.

The hardline clerics did not prove to be so hardline any more. However, Khomeini made clear his dissatisfaction with having to accept the U.N.

resolution while making his radio announcement of the ceasefire agreement on July 20, 1988:

> *"Happy are those who have departed through martyrdom. Happy are those who have lost their lives in this convoy of light. Unhappy am I that I still survive and have drunk the poisoned chalice…"*

How many lives could have been saved had Khomeini "drunk the poisoned chalice" six years earlier?

The loss of a million soldiers and $300 billion in costs for the war mattered not to Khomeini. In a "Letter to the Clergy" he later wrote to justify the eight year conflict, Khomeini justified the extension of the war and effort to throw Saddam out with this explanation:

> *"We do not repent, nor are we sorry for even a single moment for our performance during the war. Have we forgotten that we fought to fulfill our religious duty and that the result is a marginal issue?"*

Yet another indication the Iranian mullahs cared not about their people—even for those who had courageously fought for them—was their lack of effort to seek the return of their prisoners-of-war (POWs). The war officially ended August 20, 1988, but it would take an additional 15 years for the last POWs to return home.

Who Wants to be a Millionaire?

It is odd that what Muslim clerics in Iran and elsewhere tout as Islam's greatest strength, in reality, is its greatest weakness.

> *"And desire not corruption in the land. Indeed, Allah does not like corrupters." Sura Al-Qasas 28:77.*

There are at least fifty entries in the Koran forbidding corruption and addressing the need to combat it.

"Enrichment by illegitimate means and ways has been with us since the very beginning of the formation of human societies," said Seyyed Ali Mousavinejad of Iran's Mehr News Agency in July 2012. "Greed is at the heart of all these criminal activities," he continued. "Mere admonition and scolding will do no good. Leniency toward those who are harming the people is not appropriate. Prevention should from the very beginning stop plundering of people's wealth."

In March 2011, British Imam Anjem Choudary, who praised the 9/11 terrorists, was interviewed concerning his desire to come to the U.S. to push for the implementation of shariah. With such implementation already partially successful in the U.K. (for civil cases), Choudary was seeking to do the same in the U.S. (He is the same person who, in 2006, condemned the Pope to death for quoting a Byzantine emperor's negative observation about Prophet Muhammad.)

Choudary claimed in the interview the imposition of shariah is necessary to rid the U.S. of corruption. But the hypocrisy of such a claim is evidenced by implementation of shariah in its severest form in a country—Iran—where religious leaders have become among the world's wealthiest through unparalleled corruption.

Former IRGC/CIA Agent Kahlili was living in Iran—"a largely secular country under the late Shah"—and saw it transition into "an Islamic theocracy that returned the country to medieval tyranny under Shiite Mahdism." He reportedly saw "donkey-riding Islamic clerics living off meager contributions and handouts rise to become dictators suppressing Iranians, controlling the nation's economy..."

New York Times correspondent Elaine Sciolino's book "Persian Mirrors: The Elusive Face of Iran," published in 2000, details much of this corruption. She notes that the Supreme Leader controls foundations operating hundreds of companies accounting for about 40% of the country's economy. The foundations were established soon after the 1979 Revolution confiscating, "billions of dollars in assets of the former royal family, banks, and ordinary homeowners." Supreme Leader Khamenei has doled out wealth to other religious and non-religious leaders who have supported him. Their wealth continues to grow as the foundations are exempted from paying taxes.

Sciolino states:

"Two decades after the revolution, the foundations are among the biggest economic complexes in the Middle East... Most of them are the individual fiefs of powerful clerics, and their size crowds out smaller private competitors who might be more efficient, even as their corruption fuels resentment."

Supreme Leader Khamenei

In the August 2008 National Geographic article on Iran referenced earlier, it was noted that corruption in the country is "an open secret," that it is "worse than ever" and that it has become "institutionalized."

Derived from Turkish and Persian, the word "mullah" means an educated Muslim, trained in Islamic laws and doctrine, usually serving as head of a mosque or holding an official post. The mullah's role evolved as that of shepherd for Muslim flocks in need of guidance on how to live a Koran-compliant life.

While life for flock members is typically harsh and demanding, life for mullahs—of the extremist variety—has definite rewards. It provides significant financial security. Flock members normally tithe about 10% of their earnings to their religious leaders. For some mullahs, however, this is just not enough. In Iran, these holy men have been acquiring more money than Allah.

In August 2010, employees of an Iranian bank, apparently disturbed by the wealth many of their religious leaders had been acquiring and transferring to international banks, went public with information about the clerics' accounts. While stripping the people of their human rights and dignity in the name of Allah, these mullahs had been using their positions of power to strip the country of its wealth. Details later released by Iranian filmmaker and opposition spokesman Mohsen Makhmalbaf about the lavish lifestyle of the country's Supreme Leader indicated piety to be a characteristic in short supply among Iran's "rich and famous" mullahs.

Billions of dollars in cash have been deposited into personal international accounts of Iran's leading religious leaders. And that does not include billions more held in resources such as real estate, oil, state trading companies, etc. Apparently the title "Ayatollah" includes a license to steal.

Supreme Leader Ayatollah Ali Khamenei was shown to have several foreign accounts—with $100 million alone in a Geneva bank—representing just the tip of the iceberg. Meanwhile, he lives lavishly in several of the Shah's former palaces. An avid horseman, Khamenei also owns a multi-million dollar horse farm, with his prize horses flown to various locations around the country whenever desired. His estimated personal wealth is over $30 billion, with an estimated additional $6 billion held by his family.

Former Iranian president and current opposition supporter Ayatollah Ali Akbar Hashemi Rafsanjani must have mastered the power of prayer as Allah has been good to him as well. A man of modest means early in Iran's 1979 Islamic Revolution, he is now a billionaire.

Ayatollah Abolghassem Khazali, a former member of the powerful Guardians Council, enjoyed a similar rags-to-riches transition, now boasting assets of close to $300 million from his control of maritime trade.

Another cleric blessed by Allah, at least before his death in 2007, was Ayatollah Ali Meshkini who accumulated a fortune of $330 million, having parlayed his position as Speaker of the Assembly of Experts—the clerical body responsible for designating the country's Supreme Leader—into great wealth. For the people of Iran, the Islamic Revolution has brought a significant decrease in per capita income; for Iran's clerics, however, it has brought an astronomical per capita increase.

Part of Khomeini's justification in 1979 for clerical rule in Iran was that justice would always prevail, oppression by the strong over the weak would cease, and corruption would be eliminated. One can only wonder what Khomeini would think about today's Iran—a country where justice is an acceptable injustice if it preserves the clerics' powers; where the unchecked power of the strong rules over the weak opposing them; and where corrupt religious leaders enjoy the lavish wealth they have stolen from the national treasury.

Such high corruption obviously impacts on the country's economic freedom. For the period 2009-2011, Iran has consistently been ranked in the bottom third of 180 countries listed in the Corruption Perception Index; meanwhile it has fared worse on the Freedom Index, taking the 175th spot out of 179 countries.

Undoubtedly, Iran's clerics clamor for access to the Supreme Leader's inner circle of ayatollahs where the only question asked is, "Who wants to be a millionaire?" In light of these revelations of horrendous clerical greed, perhaps the title "mullah" in Iran should appropriately be changed to "moolah!"

Chapter Eleven

"Assad" State of Affairs in Syria

Just like the same sectarian beliefs of Shiite-majority Iran and Shiite-majority Iraq should have disinclined them to fight a war, the different sectarian beliefs of Shiite-majority Iran and Sunni-majority Syria should have disinclined them to be allies. Both relationships ran contrary to the Islamic sectarian norm. The Iran-Iraq relationship since the 1980 Iran-Iraq war has now aligned with that norm, growing even closer. However, the Iran-Syria relationship still remains contrary to the norm as Sunni-majority Syria has moved closer to Shiite-majority Iran and farther away from the Sunni-majority fold that contains states such as Saudi Arabia.

Understanding how this friendly relationship between normally unfriendly sects evolved requires understanding the background of the Syrian father/son al-Assad dynasty that has ruled the country for over forty years.

The al-Assads are "Alawites" or "Alawis," as they were later known. They are minority members of the Shiite sect living mainly in Syria. But it was the Sunnis, forming about three-fourths of Syria's population, who enjoyed control until 1971.

Considered by many Muslims to be heretics and thus non-believers, much of it due to their secret religious practices, the Alawites sought a legal decision to protect their status as Muslims from the Lebanese leader of the Ithnā ʿAsharīyah (Twelver) sect of Shiite Islam. Mainly as a result in 1971 of the accession to power of Syrian President Ḥafez al-Assad, followed by his son, Bashar al-Assad, in 2000, Alawites have prospered for more than four decades, becoming politically dominant in Syria.

Needless to say, the Alawites—as a minority in power—are not particularly cherished by the very large majority of Sunnis in the country. The Alawites consider themselves moderate Shiites and, thus, a Muslim sect distinctly different from the Sunnis.

Hafez al-Assad was absolutely brutal in putting down a challenge to his authority by militants of the Sunni Muslim Brotherhood that began in 1980. He mounted a 32-month anti-Brotherhood campaign after an assassination attempt by the Muslim Brotherhood against him failed.

He began the campaign by executing 1200 Islamist prisoners held at Syria's Tadmor Prison. Two weeks later, he initiated a military offensive known as the Siege of Aleppo (and site of another siege today by his son), leading to additional Sunni massacres.

In 1981, the Hama massacre, which claimed 400 Sunnis, occurred after a failed Sunni attack against an Alawite village. Most its victims were males over the age of 14, randomly selected from the city's population for execution.

In 1982, another massacre took place in Hama after members of the Muslim Brotherhood rose up against Hafez. He ordered his Alawite-led army into the city to brutally suppress the uprising. Estimates are between 20,000-40,000 civilians lost their lives—all killed in less than a month. In yet another example of Muslim-on-Muslim violence, it remains to this day "the single deadliest act by any Arab government against its own people in the modern Middle East."

Hafez al-Assad died in 2000.

After his father's death, Bashar al-Assad inherited the dynasty in July of 2000. He proved quite different from his father.

Assad the father proved during his rule he was basically his own man. As such, one of the last things he was trying to accomplish before his death was to negotiate with Israel for the return of the Golan Heights. When Assad the son took office at the age of 34, it was not only clear he lacked experience (having been an ophthalmologist in London for several years previously) but also the ability to be his own man.

Due to his inexperience, Bashar probably felt intimidated by his Iranian neighbors, whom he sought to please. This may be why he set out to consolidate his power by promoting radical and controversial positions.

He also became a major supplier of weapons to Iran's proxy in Lebanon—Hezbollah—and took to receiving high-ranking delegations from North Korea.

Tehran recognized Bashar as weak and saw an opportunity to manipulate the rookie leader into becoming an invaluable tool for building its militarized "Shia Crescent." Ostensibly this Crescent was to be formed with Iran, continuing through Iraq, into Syria, Lebanon and Palestine, as well as from Iran into eastern parts of Saudi Arabia and Yemen. Iran also began using Syria as another point of access through which to smuggle weapons and IEDs into Iraq after the U.S. invasion.

But Tehran had a bigger plan for Syria. It was one, fortunately for the West and Israel, which would be discovered when an Iranian general defected, proving to be an intelligence "gold mine." The fascinating story of what his defection triggered is related in a seven-part series published in the November 2, 2009 issue of Spiegel Online, authored by Erich Follath and Holger Stark.

Ali-Reza Asgari had served as head of Iran's IRGC in Lebanon in the 1980s and later as the country's Deputy Defense Minister in the mid-1990s. His career path came to an abrupt end after President Ahmadinejad came to power in 2005. While serving under Ahmadinejad's predecessor, President Khatami, Asgari had accused some senior military officers of corruption. Unfortunately for Asgari, those officers were friends of Ahmadinejad so, when Ahmadinejad took office, it became payback time for Asgari. As Asgari's life was in danger, he defected in late 2006.

Follath/Stark note Asgari immediately reported to his U.S. handlers that, "Iran was apparently funding a top-secret nuclear project in Syria, launched in cooperation with the North Koreans." While Asgari knew nothing more about the project, what he reported was enough to draw close scrutiny from Western and Israeli intelligence agencies.

Asgari identified the project was taking form at a place called "al-Kabir." Although the Israelis were unaware until Asgari's revelation about the purpose of the al-Kabir project, they were not totally in the dark. The location had been flagged starting in 2004 due to a high volume of phone communications taking place between Syrians there and North Koreans. Just about the time of Asgari's defection, additional intelligence had come in to suggest al-Kabir was going nuclear.

However, the renewed scrutiny left no doubt in the collective mind of the Israeli leadership by mid-2007 that a cabal consisting of Syria, North Korea and headed by Iran was working feverishly to build a nuclear facility. The Israelis had learned that Mohsen Fakhrizadeh-Mahabadi, who was head of Iran's "Project 111" to outfit Iranian missiles with nuclear warheads, had traveled to Damascus in 2005. He was followed in 2006 by Ahmadinejad who promised Bashar al-Assad $1 billion to undertake construction of the nuclear facility. In return, Assad offered up a site at al-Kibar for the project.

As Follath/Stark further report in Spiegel:

> "Al Kibar was to be a backup plant for the heavy-water reactor under construction near the Iranian city of Arak, designed to provide plutonium to build a bomb if Iran did not succeed in constructing a weapon using enriched uranium. 'Assad apparently thought that, with his weapon, he could have a nuclear option for an Armageddon,' says Aharon Zeevi-Farkash, the former director of Israeli military intelligence."

The Israelis knew they needed conclusive proof as to what was being built at al-Kibar. That necessitated putting Israeli agents on the ground in Syria to obtain soil samples. On an August 2007 evening with overcast skies, the Israelis sent in a commando team in helicopters to obtain those samples. The team was able to obtain some but not all the needed samples as they were forced to withdraw prematurely after being detected.

Still lacking definitive proof, it was decided the samples "provided evidence of the existence of a nuclear program." This plus other intelligence, such as North Korean ships transiting to Syria with suspicious materials—along with reports construction in Syria was being accelerated—made it clear the Israelis had to act sooner rather than later.

The U.S. declined an offer to join the Israelis in hitting the Syrian site. The Israelis therefore informed the U.S. it intended to attack al-Kibar. Since the site was only a few dozen kilometers from Turkey—a NATO partner—Israel wanted the U.S. to inform Ankara. The U.S. had to have given either direct or tacit approval to Israel to conduct the attack and, due to the NATO relationship with Turkey, would have notified Ankara as well.

The Israeli attack on al-Kibar, known as Operation Orchard, was launched on the evening of September 6, 2007.

Follath/Stark provide the following details concerning the air attack:

> "At 2:55 p.m. on that day, the Damascus-based Syrian Arab News Agency (SANA) reported that Israeli fighter jets coming from the Mediterranean had violated Syrian airspace at 'about one o'clock' in the morning. 'Air defense units confronted them and forced them to leave after they dropped some ammunition in deserted areas without causing any human or material damage,' a Syrian military spokesman said, according to the news agency. There was no explanation whatsoever for why such a dramatic event was concealed for half a day."

> "At 6:46 p.m., Israeli government radio quoted a military spokesman as saying: 'This incident never occurred.' At 8:46 p.m., a spokesperson for the U.S. State Department said during a daily press briefing that he had only heard 'second-hand reports' which 'contradict' each other."

> "To this day, Syria and Israel, two countries that have technically been at war since the founding of the Jewish state in 1948, have largely adhered to a bizarre policy of downplaying what was clearly an act of war. Gradually it became clear that the fighter pilots did not drop some random ammunition over empty no-man's land on that night in 2007, but had in fact deliberately targeted and destroyed a secret Syrian complex.

"Syria's response in the wake of Israel's bombing was curious. The regime sought no retaliatory measures. It did not even ask the U.N. Security Council to discuss or condemn the incident. Rather, satellite photos show Syria's efforts to scrub the site of any traces of the nuclear reactor that Syria denied having. Reuters reported that Syria bulldozed the area, 'removed debris and erected a new building in a possible cover-up.'

"International Atomic Energy Agency (IAEA) director Mohammed ElBaradei condemned the U.S. and Israel for their 'shoot first and ask questions later' approach. Nonetheless, the IAEA began probing Syrian nuclear activity, and Syria gave its inspectors access to the al-Kibar site in June 2008. (Syria later refused IAEA requests to revisit al-Kibar and examine three other related sites.)

"The IAEA released a report on November 19, 2008, containing a number of relevant data points. The report establishes that construction of the al-Kibar facility began between April 26 and August 4, 2001." (What is intriguing about this start date is the taqiya Syria and Iran pulled on May 17, 2003 when Syria submitted a proposal to rid the Middle East of weapons of mass destruction, which Iran supported.)

"Based on analysis of satellite imagery, the IAEA also noted:

"Imagery taken prior to and immediately after the bombing indicates that the destroyed box-shaped building may have had underground levels. Its containment structure appears to have been similar in dimension and layout to that required for a biological shield for nuclear reactors, and the overall size of the building was sufficient to house the equipment needed for a nuclear reactor of the type alleged.

> "The IAEA's on-the-ground evaluation also found a water pump and other adequate infrastructure to support a reactor. Environmental samples from the site also yielded a 'significant number of natural uranium particles' that were of anthropogenic origin. (Syria claimed that the particles came from the missiles Israel used to destroy the facility.)
>
> "Consistent with the caution for which the IAEA is known, its report did not conclusively state that the Syrian site was a nuclear reactor—but the implication was strong."

As to North Korea's involvement in al-Kibar, Follath/Stark note:

> "Post-attack analysis also highlighted North Korea's connection to al-Kibar. Shortly after Israel's strike, press reports suggested that the characteristics of the Syrian facility were similar to North Korea's reactor in Yongbyon. David Albright and Paul Brannan of ISIS confirmed this in April 2008. Specifically, they 'measured the footprint of the Yongbyon reactor building and compared it to that of the suspected reactor building in Syria and found the two footprints were approximately the same.' Prior to Syria's construction of al-Kibar, the Yongbyon model had been the only one of its type built in 35 years.
>
> "Video from inside the Syrian facility has also been described as 'very, very damning' by a nuclear weapons specialist who spoke to the Washington Post. The video demonstrates that al-Kibar's core design was the same as the Yongbyon reactor, 'including a virtually identical configuration and number of holes for fuel rods.' The video also shows North Korean personnel inside the site.
>
> "Subsequent investigations have revealed that key materials for al-Kibar were smuggled from China and

possibly Europe into Syria by Namchongang Trading, a North Korean firm."

In the aftermath of Syria's failed effort to build a nuclear facility, Damascus still remains a critical pawn in Iran's efforts to de-stabilize the region. Also, as a critical piece of the Shia Crescent puzzle, Iran is committed to helping Bashar al-Assad survive the insurrection against him.

Developments in the Middle East—from the perspectives of both the U.S. and Iran—have been a roller coaster ride.

Iran sat back and watched the U.S. remove one enemy—Saddam Hussein—on its western flank and contain another—the Taliban—to the east.

Iran rejoiced when the Arab Spring swept into Sunni-dominant Libya since Moamar Ghadafi had been cooperating with the U.S. The subsequent fall of Hosni Mubarak in Egypt was a plus for Tehran as well as it distanced the U.S. from a longtime ally, bringing the Muslim Brotherhood to power.

Ahmadinejad and Khamenei undoubtedly felt the Prophet smiling down upon them. But then, from Iran's perspective, the Middle East door through which the Arab Spring gained access swung open too far, gaining entry into Syria.

As peaceful demonstrations introduced President Bashar Assad to the "Arab Spring" in March 2011, he responded with brutal repression. A week later, the U.N. urged restraint, but civilian casualties mounted. Some courageous Syrian soldiers who refused to fire on unarmed civilians were executed by Assad's security forces. Those forces also began targeting mourners at funerals being held for opposition victims. Syrian intellectuals went into hiding; some army units began defecting. Assad's ally, Iranian president Mahmoud Ahmadinejad, began sending covert forces into Syria to bolster its Syrian puppet.

Perhaps dissatisfied that Assad's forces were not instilling sufficient fear into his people, Iran's Qod Forces began showing Syrian forces how to do it. Among the first Syrians victimized by the Iranians was a young boy who was arrested, tortured and murdered—his body later found with his face badly beaten. Such brutal treatment of children by the Iranians was sanctioned by Allah, the mullahs advised, as Syria played an important role in establishing the Shia Crescent.

For the uprising's duration, Iran has supported Assad with weapons to put it down, deploying thousands of elite Qods Force members into Syria. Iran knows it cannot afford to lose Syria as an ally and is committed to keeping Assad in power, regardless of what it takes to do so. As an example of the mullahs' commitment, senior Qods Force military personnel have been occupying a Syrian operational command headquarters.

Sunni-dominant but Alawite-controlled Syria provided the fertile ground by which the cabal consisting of Sunni Hamas, Shiite Hezbollah and Shiite Iran were all able to operate under Tehran's tutelage. However, as Syria's Sunni population rose up against its Alawite leader, it became more difficult for Sunni Hamas to continue supporting Bashar al-Assad over their fellow Sunnis. As Assad continued to murder his people, Hamas began distancing itself from the Syrian leader.

It was believed Iran had arranged for Hezbollah to assist Assad as well. Its direct participation in Syria against the Sunnis initially was speculative; however, reports in September and October 2012 provided indisputable proof. The combination of numerous Hezbollah funerals in Lebanon—staggered so as to draw less attention—as well as Syrian opposition taking over a dozen Hezbollah prisoners prove the organization's participation. While Hezbollah continues to deny its direct involvement, U.S. ambassador to the U.N. Susan Rice accuses the terrorist group of now being an active part of Assad's "killing machine."

This has caused problems for Iran in being able to continue supporting Hezbollah in Lebanon as Syria had been the transit route by which Tehran funneled arms and supplies to the terrorists.

With Iraq subjecting itself more and more to Iranian authority following the U.S. withdrawal, Tehran had envisioned a future in the region dominated by an Iran/Iraq/Syria alliance. However, a Syria controlled by Sunnis disrupts that vision. As a result, Iran is seeking to do everything it can to ensure Assad remains in power.

While sending its own forces into Syria, Tehran hypocritically calls for those foreign powers supporting the Syrian opposition not to interfere.

When former U.N. Secretary-General Kofi Annan sought to lay out a plan to stop the violence in Syria, Tehran coached Damascus on using the Annan plan only as a cover for giving the appearance of cooperating. The Iranians have proven grand champions at the process.

Iran's influence in the Syria uprising has contributed to violence being targeted against those who suffer most in times of war—children.

The U.N. human rights chief, Navi Pillay, has claimed Syrian forces are deliberately targeting children, employing "horrendous" tactics. She reported to the BBC that:

> *"They've gone for the children—for whatever purposes—in large numbers. Hundreds detained and tortured... Children shot in the knees, held together with adults in really inhumane conditions, denied medical treatment for their injuries, either held as hostages or as sources of information."* She added, if Assad would *"simply issue an order to stop the killings...the killings would stop."*

In the first ten days after Assad failed to implement Annan's plan, an additional 45 children died.

Meanwhile, the Syrian opposition has become more and more frustrated by an international community seeking "to pass the buck" on assisting them rather than providing meaningful support.

As Assad continues to play the role of the Prince of Darkness to his own people, such international inaction fails to take advantage of a weak link in his armor. It is one about which Assad is very conscious as evidenced by a very telling action he has undertaken.

What keeps Assad in power is an army that mirrors Syria's population—i.e., it is composed of a majority Sunni force controlled by a minority Alawite officer corps. It is the Sunni civilian population that is now suffering Assad's wrath. While Assad trusts his officer corps, he fears an unbridled army. This has been reflected by the decision to stop issuing weapons to new Sunni conscripts as many of these arms have been discovered flowing to the opposition from Sunni defectors.

The brutal tactics Ahmadinejad employed in putting down his own domestic unrest after his fraudulent re-election are being mirrored in Syria. Qods Force members have been involved in the brutal killing and torture of Syrian men, women and children. As the international community demonstrates less and less enthusiasm for stepping in, Assad and Ahmadinejad have gotten more and more confident they will have time to put the rebellion down.

Such confidence may have emboldened Assad to make a rare appearance since the fighting in Syria erupted 20 months ago. Demonstrating the bravado of one yet to feel personally threatened, he boasted in an interview with "Russia Today" released November 8, 2012:

> *"I am not a puppet, I was not made by the West for me to go to the West or any other country. I am Syrian, I am made in Syria, and I will live and die in Syria."*

Assad is not the first, nor will he be the last, to display such defiance from the safety of his "castle," only to break and run when the castle door breaks down and an angry citizenry starts rushing in.

Assad knows the international community failed to act decades earlier when his father killed over 25,000 Syrians in an uprising during his rule; the son has confidence that inaction by the international community will continue as the number of Syrians killed continues to climb.

While the outcome in Syria for Bashar al-Assad is still in question, the son—as did the father before him—demonstrates a callous ability to continue slaying his countrymen.

One of the last options the son will pursue in an effort to remain in power in Syria is to draw other states of the region into the conflict.

That option is already in progress as evidenced by the October 19, 2012 assassination of Lebanon's internal forces' intelligence chief, Brigadier General Wissam al-Hassan.

General Hassan was the victim of a car bombing in Beirut. As a Sunni and pro-Western member of the Lebanese government, he had actively sought—in the aftermath of the 2005 "Cedar Revolution" that drove Syria out of the country—to keep Syrian influence out of Lebanese affairs. There is little doubt who had the most to gain by Hassan's assassination and who, therefore, was the mastermind.

In an October 25, 2012 editorial, The Washington Post wrote about insights the general had shared about Assad during a meeting with its newspaper staff during a visit two months earlier.

The editorial noted:

> "Dictator Bashar al-Assad, he told us, still had a chance to outlast the rebellion against him, though 'it will take a couple of years and more than 100,000 killed.' For the Assad regime, he added, 'one of the solutions of the Syrian conflict is to move it outside Syria. He survives by making it a regional conflict'...Mr. Hassan warned us that the prolongation of the fighting in Syria would lead 'to sectarian war and a destroyed civil society.' He added: 'The (Syrian) Army will disintegrate, and after its collapse there will be chaos.'"

Seven weeks after his Washington visit, the general was dead as Assad, it is believed, fulfilled Hassan's prophecy in an effort to make the conflict a regional one, spreading it to Lebanon—most likely with the assistance of

Hezbollah. Little did the general realize he would be targeted as the vehicle for seeking to move the conflict "outside Syria."

As the Hassan assassination bears all the markings of the 2005 murder of another popular Lebanese Sunni leader, former Prime Minister Rafiq al-Hariri, Sunni resentment in Lebanon against Hezbollah is running higher than ever before. It took six years, but four members of Hezbollah were eventually indicted for Hariri's assassination by an international tribunal. However, as the outrage and fallout over Hariri's murder quickly subsided, Assad undoubtedly felt he could count on that happening with Hassan's assassination.

But that outrage has manifested itself once more in Lebanon as Sunnis again blame Assad. When Rafiq Hariri was assassinated, his son Saad Hariri assumed leadership. However, the son has drawn distant from his supporters as, to ensure his own safety from being targeted for assassination, he took up residence in Paris. It was necessary, his supporters say, to avoid the same fate now suffered by Hassan, but has resulted in a loss of authority. Therefore, Sunnis feel there is a vacuum in their leadership with no one in position to look out for their interests. As fighting erupted following Hassan's assassination, Hariri was unable to quell it by his pleas sent by Twitter. A Sunni leadership void now needs to be filled.

The revolution is having an impact in several other directions "outside Syria" as well. These include:

- The withdrawal of the Syrian army from the Kurdish dominant northeastern part of the country has freed up militant Kurds to become more aggressive in the war they have been conducting for decades against Turkey for their autonomy.

- Iraqi Shiites are now threatening to get involved on the side of the Syrian government, especially should Shiite shrines, such as Sayeda Zeinab, be damaged.

- Whether unintentional or not, Kurds and the Syrian Free Army have been fighting after the latter fired shots at the former in the Syrian city of Aleppo.

- Turkey has been threatening to respond in kind to Syrian aggression crossing over the border. Stray artillery shells have fallen in Turkey and Syrian aircraft have violated Turkish airspace. Ankara is eager to get other nations to back it up but so far has received little support, making a unilateral response by Turkey unlikely absent a more serious Syrian intrusion. The lack of international support and the humanitarian crisis created by Syrian refugees in Turkey has caused Ankara to solicit support from Iran to negotiate an end to the fighting.

- Syrian tanks entered the Golan Heights' demilitarized zone in early November 2012, resulting in a protest by Israel to U.N. peacekeepers. Although the action was not perceived as an immediate threat, continued transgressions may be viewed as such.

Clearly the situation in Syria is stretching Hezbollah's resources. The daily killings of Sunnis in Syria has not set well with Sunnis in Lebanon, who have begun to express their resentment towards the Hezbollah-controlled Lebanese government. Thus, Hezbollah has to deal with both Sunni threats—all at a time it could also be faced with having to assist Iran in attacking Israel should Israel undertake a pre-emptive strike against Tehran's nuclear facilities. Hezbollah's leadership has already warned against any international interference into an investigation of Hassan's assassination.

As Iran's and Hezbollah's efforts to suppress the opposition in Syria are further challenged, Islamic extremist groups of the al-Qaeda ilk are starting to gain favor with Syrians in their push to topple Assad. From the Syrian opposition's viewpoint, the extremist groups are becoming "the only game in town." The longer the fighting in Syria continues, the stronger the people's support becomes for the Islamists and the less likely the seed of democracy will sprout in Syria.

The range of diverse interests at play in Syria at this point, combined with the chaos there, leaves too many unknowns to predict what kind of government will eventually evolve there.

The chaos once limited to within Syria now spreads outside. An embattled dictator attempts to draw others in, hoping to trigger a collective approach toward containing the fires of revolution in his own country as others start to fear they will spread to theirs.

With so many influences at play in Syria, chaos runs rampant. While this is, in part, what Iran believes will trigger the Mahdi's return, the situs Syria is providing for the Arab Spring most likely is not one Tehran had anticipated.

However, once again, as with father, as with son, Syria finds itself in "Assad" state of affairs.

Iran's Motto: "What You Said is not What I Know I Heard"

For live programming, some broadcasters will impose a delay of a few seconds just in case there is a need to "bleep" out something inappropriate for broadcast—such as profanity—over the network. Obviously, it is more difficult to do this if no delay is involved—as when an audience is awaiting a translation.

It was August 26, 2012. It was the "best of times" for President Ahmadinejad as 118 members of the Non-Aligned Movement (NAM) were attending a summit meeting in Tehran. Many states, as well as international representatives such as U.N. Secretary-General Ban Ki-moon, encouraged by the U.S. not to attend Iran's one week long propaganda show, did so. However, before the week ended, it would also prove to be for Iran "the worst of times."

As expected, Tehran wasted no time putting the summit to use to criticize the U.S. Its foreign minister opened the proceedings accusing the West of terrorism.

A story by Ramin Mostaghim in the August 26, 2012 issue of the Los Angeles Times shared insights on the opening events:

> "Anti-Western symbolism was rampant across Iran's capital city on Sunday as the Islamic Republic welcomed attendees of a weeklong gathering of nonaligned nations, a Cold War-era movement that Iranian officials have embraced as a counterweight to U.S.-led efforts to isolate their country.
>
> "As the sessions began, a balloon with a message hailing Iran as a 'cradle of peace and justice' hovered near the site of the former U.S. Embassy, where Iranian militants held 52 people hostage almost 33 years ago.
>
> "At a major entranceway to the summit venue were arrayed three battered cars — the wrecks, officials said, of vehicles bombed to assassinate Iranian scientists. Iran blames Israel and the West for attacks that have killed at least five members of the nation's scientific community in recent years.
>
> "Security was extremely tight and authorities warned dissidents not to consider actions that might embarrass the government, despite calls for protests on social media and expatriate websites...
>
> "The Non-Aligned Movement traces its origins to the desire of such leaders as Yugoslav President Josip Broz Tito and former Egyptian President Gamal Abdel Nasser to chart a course independent of the Eastern and Western blocs in the 1950s and '60s.
>
> "...Tehran sees the group as a potential bulwark against international sanctions and the possibility of an Israeli or U.S. bombing strike aimed at its nuclear development program.

> "The gathering is shaping up as a global stage for Iran to thumb its nose at the United States and dispute Washington's insistence that Tehran is an isolated rogue state and sponsor of terrorism.

> "Iran, which is assuming the rotating presidency of the group, has highlighted the anticipated attendance of United Nations Secretary-General Ban Ki-moon — whose office says he is coming despite a personal plea from Israeli Prime Minister Benjamin Netanyahu that he stay away — and of President Mohamed Morsi of Egypt. Morsi would be the first Egyptian head of state to visit since the 1979 founding of the Islamic Republic.

> "Also expected to attend is India's prime minister, Manmohan Singh, whose nation remains a major oil client of Iran. The foreign minister of North Korea, an ally of Tehran, arrived here Sunday, Iranian news media reported...

> "'Many of us are victims [of] nefarious terrorist acts,' Iranian Foreign Minister Ali Akbar Salehi said in his opening remarks at the forum, accusing 'some Western powers' of promoting terrorism.

In the August 30, 2012 issue of The Guardian, Saeed Kamali Dehghan provided the week's coverage of the event:

> "To watch Iranian state television, you'd think the country was hosting the Olympics. Rolling television coverage included reporters at the airport covering the landing of diplomats as if they were top athletes and ongoing interviews with delegates being asked to comment on the hospitality of Iranians and their impressions of Tehran.

> "By devoting so much airtime to the summit of the Non-Aligned Movement, Iran's biggest international conference in three decades, authorities had one aim: to seize upon the

> rare presence of several heads of state and government to claim a diplomatic triumph in defiance of western-led efforts to isolate Tehran over its controversial nuclear dossier."

Dehghan explained the importance of the summit:

> "For Iran's leaders, hosting the summit represented an opportunity for an image makeover. In the face of the latest embargo against the import of the Iranian oil, it was also an effort to find new customers. They were able to depict an Iran that was a key-player in international politics but the unfortunate victim of a western-led campaign against its peaceful nuclear programme."

Apparently, the "makeover" for Iran was so important that it also sought to hide one thing it had no control over—the uncensored comments of the same guests they just welcomed. After Supreme Leader Khamenei spoke, carefully avoiding any specific mention of the uprising in Syria, first to embarrass the Iranians was Egyptian President Mohammed Morsi—the first Egyptian president to visit Iran in 32 years.

Morsi wasted no time in raising the issue that, in Khamenei's mind, apparently did not exist. As Morsi spoke, an Iranian interpreter simultaneously translated into Farsi his remarks, delivered in Arabic. There was no hesitation on the interpreter's part in providing a translation contrary to what Morsi said when what he said was unfavorable about Syria. The smooth, yet incorrect, translation given by the interpreter suggested he had been prepared for just such a possible embarrassment and had been instructed on how to deal with it—with authorization given at the highest levels to mis-translate.

> "...The Egyptian leader described the Syrian government as 'an oppressive regime that has lost its legitimacy'...and voiced support for 'the struggle of those seeking freedom and justice in Syria.' His remarks prompted a walkout by the Syrian delegation.

But in Iran, when one host such events, if something is said at such times that does not fit the image the host wishes to be portrayed, the host simply makes the words fit the desired image.

> "According to the reports, the simultaneous interpreter adapted Morsi's speech to fit in with the Iranian regime's rhetoric—according to which Assad's regime in Syria should not be criticized.
>
> "One website specializing in coverage of Iran's conservative media wrote that 'in an unprecedented action, the interpreter falsified part of Morsi's speech declining to translate Morsi's severe attack on the Syrian president's regime.'
>
> "The Iranian interpreter translated Morsi's criticism of Assad's regime as statements in support of Assad: 'There is a crisis in Syria and we must support the ruling regime in Syria,' he said, in complete contrast to Morsi's negative statements.
>
> "He then went on to add: 'It would be appropriate if reforms in Syria were renewed and that there is no external interference that is our stance.'"

Also, apparently, when the host country wishes to exchange—within the context of a guest's remarks—the name of a country the guest has not mentioned, the host country can take the initiative to do so:

> "When Morsi went on to discuss events in Arab states where the Arab Spring played a part, the translator exchanged the word Syria with Bahrain."

The September 1, 2012 "Daily News Egypt" detailed more of the shenanigans played by Iran with the Egyptian president's statements.

> "President Mohammed Morsi's speech at the Non-Aligned Movement (NAM) Summit in Tehran was mistranslated to

sound less critical of Syria. Al Jazeera showed video of Morsi speaking and ran a translation of the Farsi audio that accompanied it. Morsi clearly stated that those who are struggling for freedom are the 'Palestinians and Syrians.' However, the translation clearly said 'Palestinians and Bahrainis.'

"The tampered translations continue in a later part of Morsi's speech when he said, 'The Egyptian Revolution represents the cornerstone of the Arab Spring.' The Iranian translator replaces this with the words 'Islamic Awakening,' a term that would bring Iran into the revolutionary fold and also add an exclusively religious label to a movement embraced by seculars and Islamists alike.

"The switch from Syrians to Bahrainis is likely born out of Iran's steadfast defense of the Bashar Al-Assad regime's violent repression of the largely Sunni rebels, while Iran voices support for protestors in Bahrain who are largely Shi'a. Still, the willingness to tamper with Morsi's words will not help the growing camaraderie between Egypt and Iran.

"Lately, Iran has seemed almost desperate to ally with Egypt, with its foreign ministry giving a sycophantic interview to the Egyptian press. However, the translation debacle shows that Iran is having difficulty engaging honestly with their fellow Muslim powers. It is reminiscent of a fake interview published by the Fars state news agency soon after Morsi's election that claimed the newly elected leader was seeking closer ties with Iran and that he was interested in revising the Camp David accord. Not only did Morsi have to ensure the international community that the interview was false, but he had to deal with the backlash that was elicited entirely outside of his control.

"The manipulation of words during Morsi's NAM speech wandered into the realm of irony and outright offensiveness when his words 'Our solidarity with the plight of the Syrian people against a repressive regime that has lost its legitimacy is not only a moral duty but one of political and strategic necessity,' was translated to, 'Our solidarity with the Syrian people against the conspiracy.' Al-Assad's regime has long attributed the uprising to an international conspiracy against itself, calling the rebels themselves 'terrorist mercenaries.'

"The mistranslations were compiled by Hassan Hassan, a columnist for U.A.E news outlet The National.

"'The absurdity of such despotic regimes is beyond comprehension,' Hassan told the Daily News Egypt. 'What is interesting is the translator's ostensibly quick judgment to distort the speech in such a coherent way, replacing the word Bahrain with Syria and maintaining the official narrative of Tehran. I imagine they had known or guessed Morsi's speech and prepared for it.'

"Hassan said that this belligerent stance is typical of such regimes. But he adds that there could have been more intentionally behind the word-swaps, 'It could be a smart move by them to say that the same could be said about Bahrain but President Morsi chose to speak about Syria's situation, not Bahrain's. By doing so, they say it does not matter if we distorted his speech or not, compare the two situations.'"

Perhaps if Morsi had been the only speaker in whose mouth words were placed, it would not have been so bad. However, the Iranian interpreters also undertook their wordsmithing with U.N. Secretary-General Ban's remarks.

Ban took President Ahmadinejad to task for denying the Holocaust took place.

Returning to The Guardian's Saeed Kamali Dehghan account of events:

> "'I strongly reject threats by any member state to destroy another or outrageous attempts to deny historical facts such as the Holocaust,' Ban said, albeit without mentioning Iran. 'Claiming that Israel does not have the right to exist or describing it in racist terms is not only wrong but undermines the very principle we all have pledged to uphold.'
>
> "Ban is said to have raised concerns about the nuclear programme in his meeting with Khamenei on Wednesday. His full remarks were censored, and the image from the meeting that dominated Iranian media shows a humble secretary general sitting face-to-face with a smiling and authoritative Ayatollah unleashing a tirade of reproach.
>
> "For the Iranians, the image makeover was complete."

Supreme Leader Khamenei did not waste his stage time at the session. He used his opportunity to toss out clever but meaningless phrases such as, "Our motto is nuclear energy for all and nuclear weapons for none," following up with assurances making nuclear weapons was a "sin."

Yet, as Khamenei spoke, the IAEA was preparing its latest report on Iran's nuclear program, which reveals it has increased its "potential capacity to refine uranium by installing more than 300 centrifuges at an underground uranium enrichment facility, despite U.N. calls for more clarity over its activities."

(Specifically, examples of Iran's lack of cooperation noted by the IAEA included: (1) For one year now, Iran continues to deny access to its Parchin site (a military base) where it is believed weapons-related testing was conducted and satellite photos reveal major efforts are now underway to "cleanse" it; (2) a lack of "concrete results" despite "intensified dialogue" between the parties; (3) Iran's breach of several U.N. Security Council resolutions requiring a "halt to all enrichment work;" and (4) the addition of 644 more centrifuges at Fordow "completing the site where

Iran enriches uranium to 20 percent purity – a few technical steps away from weapons-grade of 90 percent.)

It boggles the mind that in such a public arena where it is hosting the event, Iran would dare deny a participant his own voice in addressing fellow participants where the forum is one in which all are supposedly to be treated equally. Iran has demonstrated to the other members of NAM it not only cannot deal truthfully with its foes, but also with its friends.

Perhaps a better motto for Iran's Supreme Leader to have shared with his audience is, "What you said is not what I know I heard"!"

Iran's Influence In Iraq

There is a very subtle message Supreme Leader Ali Khamenei is communicating about what he has in store for Iraq. His predecessor, Ruhollah Khomeini, also conveyed the message in 1982 when he tried to negotiate Saddam Hussein's removal from office during the Iran-Iraq war.

The late Supreme Leader Ruhollah Khomeini originally was awarded the title "Leader" under Iran's 1979 Constitution as the country's senior religious and political figure. Perhaps feeling inadequate as a mere "Leader," Khomeini later had the title modified to add "Supreme" to it. Since the inception of the Islamic Republic of Iran in 1979, there have just been two "Supreme Leaders"—Khomeini who died in 1989 and Khamenei who serves today.

There is probably very little difference between the authority Khamenei wields as Supreme Leader and that Joseph Stalin or Adolf Hitler did as dictators of the Soviet Union and Nazi Germany respectively. Of the three, two already have served for life while Khamenei will probably continue to do so.

All three dictators held absolute authority. All three cherished preservation of personal power over the welfare of their own people, denying to them the freedoms upon which democracies are built. All three depended on a propaganda machine and a security apparatus to ride to power. All three rose to the top of a governmental structure two helped build (Hitler and Khomeini)—selling the design to the people but then instituting a "bait and switch," thereby getting them to unknowingly accept something entirely different—and the other (Stalin) inherited.

But, as egotistic and self-aggrandizing as were Stalin and Hitler, their personal titles never exceeded the boundaries of their own country. Stalin's title of "General Secretary of the Party's Central Committee" and Hitler's of "Fuhrer" failed to convey any extra-territorial ambitions, although history would most certainly demonstrate their intent was otherwise.

The point is they did not advertise such claims in advance of their efforts to stake them.

A visit to Khamenei's website, however, suggests—having secured authority in Iran—he is now promoting an extra-territorial title. As mentioned, "Supreme" had been added to the title to distinguish the "Leader" from any other domestic run-of-the-mill leader but, it seems, Khamenei now wants—just like his predecessor before him wanted—a more powerful or expansive title.

Apparently "Supreme Leader of Iran" was not acceptable but "Supreme Leader of Muslims" is.

By this title, Khamenei seeks to be the Shepherd of the Muslim Flock. But who exactly does he seek to include within it—i.e., exactly over whom does Supreme Leader Khamenei seek to rule?

As a Shiite, his Flock would obviously include all Shiites in Iran. But Shiites consider Sunnis non-believers. Therefore, the question arises whether Khamenei includes Iranian Sunnis within his Flock? As the word "Muslim" normally is all inclusive of both sects, it would seem Khamenei would be including Sunni "non-believers" as well.

But it is here Khamenei seems to make a jump. Just like the program "Doctors Without Borders," Khamenei seems to have adopted a program of "Supreme Leader of Muslims Without Borders." Just like Iran's Constitution gives the Supreme Leader the mandate to export the Islamic

Revolution outside the country's borders, Khamenei seems to claim he is empowered to serve as Supreme Leader of all Muslims both inside and without Iran's borders—in effect, a self-appointed global Pope of Muslims.

But a question still remains as to his intentions to include under his tutelage as Supreme Leader of Muslims both Shiites and Sunnis, everywhere.

A close examination suggests the answer lies next door in neighboring Iraq.

One of the reasons an agreement was not reached on the 1982 ceasefire proposal Saddam Hussein offered during the Iran-Iraq war to Supreme Leader Khomeini was the latter's requirement Saddam step down as president. Saddam obviously refused to do so, resulting in Khomeini fighting on for an additional six years—with the war finally ending in a stalemate. When an agreement was finally signed in 1988, Khomeini was not a happy camper to see Saddam remain in power.

But it was not jealousy that generated Khomeini's anger—it was his begrudging acceptance of the fact he had failed to bring Iraq into his Flock. Had Iran defeated Iraq or had Saddam otherwise stepped down from power, Khomeini saw his own "Supreme Leadership" extending into Iraq. As such, Khomeini would have been recognized by history as the unifying force in bringing together the two biggest Shia-majority populated countries in the world—to form part of the Shia Crescent and thus pave the way for the caliphate which one day would rule the world.

In the documentary film mentioned earlier released in April 2011 by Iran's leadership, it made clear that the Mahdi is to rule the world **from Iraq**. Therefore, it follows that the Supreme Leader wants all Iraqi Muslims within his domain—the entire country under Iranian guardianship to ensure the Mahdi can rule from Iraq.

Khomeini never lived long enough to see his dream of a unified Iran and Iraq under his Supreme Leadership come true. However, his successor still believes a unified Iran-Iraq partial Shia Crescent ruled by one

Supreme Leader is still achievable. It is a goal, therefore, upon which Khamenei is still focused on achieving.

An article to which Wesley S. Morgan contributed based on "The Endgame: The Inside Story of the Struggle for Iraq, From George W. Bush to Barack Obama," by Michael R. Gordon and Lt. Gen. Bernard E. Trainor, details how Iran set up Iraq as an area of responsibility for its Qods Force commander.

It was of such importance for Iran to bring Iraq into its Fold that it gave responsibility for it to the commander of Iran's Qods Force—Major General Qassim Suleimani—awarding him "sole authority for Iranian actions in Iraq" as per the orders of Supreme Leader Khamenei. Suleimani was a busy man as he also was later given responsibility for providing military support to Syrian President Bashar al-Assad to help put down his revolution.

While serving in Iraq, General David H. Petraeus came to know of Suleimani, describing him as "a truly evil figure" in a letter to then Secretary of Defense Robert M. Gates.

Ironically, for eight years of the Iran-Iraq war, Suleimani had tried unsuccessfully to fight his way into Baghdad; now, due to a successful U.S. invasion of Iraq in 2003 and transfer of control to Iran-friendly Iraqi Prime Minister al-Maliki, Suleimani can simply walk in.

Former U.S. Ambassador to Iraq Ryan Crocker offered the following about the Qods commander:

> "For Qassim Suleimani, the Iran-Iraq war never really ended. No human being could have come through such a World War I-style conflict and not have been forever affected. His strategic goal was an outright victory over Iraq, and if that was not possible, to create and influence a weak Iraq."

Having failed at the former strategic objective, Suleimani focused on the second. It was here he had better success, playing a major role in building up anti-U.S. resentment and forcing the U.S. to realize the futility of extending its nine year effort there.

Suleimani developed a reputation for not only being able to stir up trouble in Iraq among the local Shiite militias, but also being able to then tone it down.

In 2007, through the head of Iraq's intelligence service—Shirwan al-Waeli—Suleimani tried to negotiate with Petraeus on the release of the leader of a Shiite militia—Qais al-Khazali, who had been captured by the British in March—in exchange for Suleimani's promise to reduce militia attacks in Iraq. As Khazali was responsible for the Karbala attack that killed five Americans, it was clearly "no deal" for Petraeus, who told Suleimani to stop supporting the Shiite militias in Iraq.

General Petraeus demanded that the Qods Force stop training and arming Shiite militants there.

In a letter to Secretary Gates, Petraeus wrote:

> *"To provide a bit more jolt, I said that I am considering telling the president that I believe Iran is, in fact, waging war on the United States in Iraq...For what it's worth, I do believe that Iran has gone beyond merely striving for influence in Iraq and could be creating proxies to actively fight us, thinking that they can keep us distracted while they try to build WMD and set up JAM (aka "the Mahdi Army") to act like Lebanese Hezbollah in Iraq."*

Petraeus got word to Suleimani if the attacks did not stop, the U.S. would increase its attacks against Qods Force proxies and agents in Iraq by a secret U.S. commando unit established to counter Iranian influence. Although the Shiite militia attacks stopped for more than a year, they re-started later, continuing until the U.S. withdrawal from Iraq.

Between 2003-2012, Coalition force losses in Iraq totaled 4804. That was a heavy price to pay to free a country of a brutal dictator, to introduce it to democracy, to restore it to relative stability, to train its security personnel and to turn the state over to that country's democratically-elected government—only to see it start slipping under Iranian influence.

The hand-over by the Americans to the Iraqis was a memorable moment. More than two centuries earlier, a young America, having just won its freedom from England, debated how best to be governed. Benjamin Franklin, in September 1787, while exiting the Constitutional Convention, was asked by a citizen what form of government had America decided to embark upon. Franklin was said to have responded, "A Republic, if you can keep it!" He had no illusions that what was given to the people, absent their rapt attention to preserve it, could be lost.

With a price tag of nearly 5000 Coalition casualties, the U.S. gave Iraq a democracy—but can the Iraqi people keep it?

Iranian influence is responsible for a number of different factors at work in Iraq that will impact on Baghdad's future. Understanding them is critical.

Khamenei Seeks to Mirror in Iraq Khomeini's Success in Iran

The months and years ahead will determine whether the Iraqi people can keep their democracy or, similar to what Khomeini was able to do in Iran in 1979, if Khamenei will prove successful in a sleight-of-hand to sell the Iraqi people on a "Supreme Leader of Muslims."

In Khamenei's "world," Iran has such an influential footprint in the region—culturally, politically and religiously—that any issue concerning the Muslim world requires Iran's participation to resolve it.

The battle for Iranian control of Iraq has been ongoing for a while—starting soon after the U.S. invasion of Iraq and accelerating with the U.S. withdrawal.

Khamenei is now using two approaches "to win the hearts and minds" of the Iraqi people to get them to join the Flock.

Doomsday: Iran

One approach we see by Khamenei is the "Smiley Face" approach.

Thousands of posters of a smiling, Santa Clause-like Khamenei were distributed in August 2012 in half a dozen Shiite neighborhoods in and around Baghdad. This was part of an annual pro-Palestinian observance started several years ago by Tehran. The posters generate the air of a single candidate political campaign. Even billboards in the area depict the smiling Supreme Leader. No other country in the region markets within its own borders the leader of another.

Based on much of the hatred and venom Khamenei has been spouting towards the West and Israel, especially at a time he should be toning down his virulent rhetoric as tensions mount over Iran's nuclear program, a Smiley Faced Khamenei is something difficult to grasp—even when staring one in the face. It is doubtful the people of Iraq are getting a balanced picture of "the-man-who-would-be Iraq's Supreme"—as Khamenei seeks to pull a "Khomeini" with the Iraqis.

As Khamenei knows, if enough enthusiasm and support can be generated for a Supreme Leader, the people get caught up in the euphoria and fail to focus on the snake oil he is selling. As it worked for Khomeini in Iran, Khameini seeks to have it work for him in Iraq.

What is interesting, however, is—despite the beaming poster smile—Iraqi municipal workers responsible for taking them down after due time are not doing so. Why? Because they know and fear what is standing behind the smiling old man—the violent Shiite militias that hung the posters up and who wait to dole out retribution to anyone removing them.

This then is the second approach we see used by Khameini. Dropping the Smiley Face sham, he reveals his true face of fear and intimidation.

In her September 25, 2012 article "Iran Ayatollah Is Poster Boy for Influence in Iraq" for the Associated Press, Lara Jakes reported one of these militias—Asaib Ahl al-Haq—"even boasted that it launched the poster campaign, part of a trend that's chipping away at nearly a decade's worth of U.S.-led efforts to bring a Western-style democracy here."

One of Asaib Ahl al-Haq's officials claimed, "they distributed some 20,000 posters of Khamenei across Iraq…Khamenei enjoys public support all over the world, including Iraq, where he is hailed as a political and religious leader."

Estimated to be about a thousand strong, the militia is the same one that "carried out deadly attacks against U.S. troops before their withdrawal last year." Their leaders are believed to actually reside in Iran.

Jakes also reports intelligence officials believe Iran is sending approximately $5 million in cash and weapons monthly to underwrite the effort for the militias to gain ground for Khameini—using fear where being nice just does not get the job done.

Despite some lingering tensions from the Iran-Iraq war, Jakes notes "Iran's clout with Iraq's Shiites picked up after Saddam Hussein's fall from power in 2003, and, in many ways, accelerated since the U.S. military pulled out." The same acceleration will undoubtedly be seen in Afghanistan too when U.S. soldiers depart as the Taliban there, like the Shiite militias in Iraq, will add to their own Flock through fear and intimidation.

Iran is funding other Shiite militias in Iraq too. All are helping to promote a governmental system similar to Tehran's.

Iraq has its own well respected senior religious leaders, such as Grand Ayatollahs Ali al-Sistani and Mahmoud Hashemi Shahroudi, of whom Sistani, 81, is the elder. Sistani believes it is not the cleric's position to get involved in politics; it is his position to be available to the people only as spiritual advisor. This is the role of the cleric that most Sunnis and Kurds prefer as well.

However, due to Sistani's advanced age, he may soon be replaced by Shahroudi, who, unfortunately, does favor rolling the political and religious leader roles into one—ala Khomeini.

The question therefore remains whether Iraq will fall under the Iranian spell, losing its own identity and ability to operate independently of the

Supreme Leader of the Muslims. Will Supreme Leader Khamenei come to wield enough power in Iraq so as to control decisions there as to whether he or Shahroudi take title as overall Supreme Leader?

One measure as to whether Khamenei's influence has sufficiently spread in Iraq is to see what fate befalls his detractors. In Iran, criticizing the Supreme Leader can earn the speaker a prison sentence. Even Khamenei's younger brother—who has spoken out about reform and Khamenei's excessive powers—has incurred the Supreme Leader's wrath. He has been repeatedly beaten and denied the right to run for office again.

Should Iraqis start encountering similar fates, it will be a strong indicator that Khamenei's influence is spreading.

Iran Gaining Ground in Iraq

There are clear indications in the struggle for influence in Iraq that Iran is making a great deal of progress.

First, in Iran's efforts to destroy the Iranian opposition group MEK which had been given refuge by Saddam in 1986 to fight the mullahs during the Iran-Iraq war, Baghdad's government headed by Prime Minister Nouri al-Maliki contributed immensely. MEK had been disarmed by U.S. forces during the 2003 invasion, leaving it defenseless. After the U.S. turned over responsibility for MEK at Camp Ashraf, where they were confined, to the Iraqis, al-Maliki had it attacked several times by armed Iraqi soldiers—undoubtedly at Iran's request. Dozens of MEK members were slaughtered.

Second, the Iraqis have been helping Iran end run economic sanctions imposed against Tehran for its nuclear program. It was such an effort by an Iraqi bank, the Elaf Islamic Bank that caused the U.S. to bar it from doing business with the American banking system. Elaf may well just be the tip of the iceberg in an Iraqi financial network filtering cash to Iran. Allegedly, Iran has control of four commercial banks in Iraq through Iraqi agents, providing Tehran access to the international financial system. Al-Maliki seems to be ignoring payment of noncompliance penalties by these institutions. Additionally, Iraqi officials seem to be turning a blind eye to oil smuggling operations into Iran and to the possibility al-Maliki's close associates may be involved and profiting from some of these end run operations.

Third, Baghdad has allowed Iran to fly supplies and weapons through Iraqi airspace to Syria. When the issue was raised, the Iranians simply re-routed the planes a different way.

Fourth, again in deference to Iran, Iraq raised no objections last year when Tehran violated Iraqi territory in the north to attack the Kurds.

Fifth, Iraq has interfered with arrest warrants issued in the names of individuals supported by Iran.

Sixth, Ali Musa Daqduq was a senior Hezbollah operative who had been captured in Iraq two months after the deadly January 20, 2007 Karbala attack that left five Americans dead—four slain execution style after being taken captive. Since his capture, Daqduq had been held by the U.S. which, upon its withdrawal from Iraq in 2011, requested the terrorist be kept in Iraq's custody. However, al-Maliki released him in November 2012. Now purportedly in Beirut, Daqduq will undoubtedly return to his killing ways to help Iran pursue its agenda.

While there are Iraqis who support Khamenei, there are those who do not. Many desire Iraqi nationalism to be the top priority. Others express concerns the Khamenei self-loving posters are too much of a reminder of the days of Saddam Hussein's self-promotion.

One Iraqi government worker upset about Khamenei's posters chastised his country for becoming "a total Iranian stooge."

In October 2012, Prime Minister al-Maliki pressed the U.S. for faster deliveries of weapons it has ordered, including tanks and F-16 fighter jets. As Iraq continues to fall under the shadow of Iran's leadership, the U.S. might want to reflect on whether such weapons could one day be used against it by Iraqis defending its Iranian ally.

U.S. Turnover to Iraq—Tehran Was Ready But Was Baghdad?

As the deadline for the 2011 U.S. withdrawal from Iraq approached, a critical debate arose as to whether the Iraqi army and security forces were fully capable of doing the job of replacing U.S. troops. If it was determined they were not, there was talk about some U.S. forces being left behind to continue training the Iraqis to improve their performance.

Whether the Iraqi forces were ready or not depended upon to whom one spoke.

On October 21, 2011, President Barack Obama announced:

> "I can report that, as promised, the rest of our troops in Iraq will come home by the end of the year. After nearly nine years, America's war in Iraq will be over."

But for several months prior to that announcement, the U.S. was feverishly trying to negotiate an extension agreement with the Iraqi government to allow U.S. trainers to continue training Iraqi military and security forces who were not prepared yet to completely take the mission on. The negotiations failed because the Iraqi government refused to give those U.S. forces remaining behind immunity from prosecution in Iraqi courts in the event a criminal offense was committed.

Clearly, in a country where shariah would be the law of the land for prosecutions in Iraq against Americans, the U.S. could not leave military personnel behind who would be subject to such an arbitrary set of laws. If the Iraqis would not allow prosecutions of U.S. personnel to take place under U.S. law, there was no choice but for the U.S. to withdraw all its personnel.

However, trying to negotiate a training agreement up to the very end was an acknowledgement that the Iraqis did require more time and training. The President denied this, as did his Deputy National Security Advisor Denis McDonough, the latter reporting:

> "One assessment after another about the Iraqi security forces came back saying these guys are ready; these guys are capable; these guys are proven; importantly, they're proven because they've been tested in a lot of the kinds of threats that they're going to see going forward. So we feel very good about that."

"So, to sum up," said Obama in his closing remarks about the withdrawal, "the United States is moving forward from a position of strength."

This statement stood in stark contrast to the assessment of retired U.S. Army General John Keane. Keane played a pivotal role in providing strategy and oversight on the wars in Iraq and Afghanistan. In pulling no punches, he stated the impact of the scheduled U.S. withdrawal would be "an absolute disaster."

An Iraqi brigade commander, Colonel Salam Khaled, did not share Obama's optimism either, saying:

> "Our forces are good, but not to a sufficient degree that allows them to face external and internal challenges alone. The loyalty of the forces is not to their homeland; the loyalty is to the political parties and to the sects."

And it is the Iraqi soldier's loyalty to his own sect upon which Khamenei is relying.

What Obama failed to address with his announcement of the U.S. withdrawal was that Iraq would now be open season for Shiite majority Iran to finally achieve what it had failed to do by not winning the 1980-1988 war against Saddam—dominate its Iraqi neighbor.

Just as Tehran has succeeded in influencing events in Lebanon through its control of the terrorist group Hezbollah, it also seeks to influence events in Iraq. But while Supreme Leader Khamenei's influence presents one option for doing this, Tehran has two other options available. They involve two Shiite leaders who have spent considerable time in Iran being groomed by the mullahs just for this opportunity.

The convergence in the careers of these two Shiite leaders has been an important catalyst in helping Iran to gain influence in Iraq to date.

Iraq's Prime Minister al-Maliki—Friend or Foe to Iraq?

The first option involves Iraq's current prime minister, Nouri al-Maliki.

In 1979, al-Maliki was a Shiite dissident living under Saddam Hussein. After discovering al-Maliki was a member of the outlawed Dawa Party, Saddam imposed the death penalty upon him. Al-Maliki went into exile for 24 years—first to Jordan, then Syria, then to Iran, then back to Syria where he remained until the 2003 U.S. invasion of Iraq. He spent a total of two years in Jordan, thirteen in Syria and eight in Iran. While living in Syria, due to his affiliation with the Dawa Party there, he established a very close relationship with Hezbollah. Thus, of al-Maliki's 24 years in exile, 22 were spent under the influence of Iran or its Hezbollah proxy.

Parliamentary elections took place in Iraq in 2005, with Ibrahim al-Jaafari nominated as the first post-war prime minister. But when he proved ineffective, a push was mounted for a new prime minister. Four candidates evolved from a vetting process in which the U.S. was involved. Among them was Nouri al-Maliki, who won the position. Astonishingly, despite al-Maliki's 22 year affiliation with Iran, of him it was said he had a reputation "as someone who is independent of Iran." In May 2006, al-Maliki presented his Cabinet.

It was al-Maliki who on December 30, 2006 signed Saddam Hussein's death warrant. He dismissed a stay of execution request, declaring there would be "no review or delay." In a somewhat distorted interpretation of human rights, al-Maliki said, "Our respect for human rights requires us to execute him." While such a comment conveyed the deep hatred held for Saddam, it also provided some insights into al-Maliki's perception of human rights.

Al-Maliki proved much more effective than his predecessor as prime minister. He took on the Mahdi Army of cleric Moqtada al-Sadr—which played a dominant role in the deadly 2006-2007 sectarian war—driving it out of Basra. The next year he negotiated a peace agreement with al-Sadr.

(Al-Sadr—the second option Iran has available today to wield influence in Iraq—is discussed in a subsequent section.)

In the 2010 national elections, al-Maliki failed to take a majority of seats. Gridlock arose as the three parties involved could not work out an alliance among themselves. It was only after a surprise move by al-Sadr in throwing his support behind al-Maliki that the prime minister was able to gather the necessary majority to move forward.

It was a surprising move by al-Sadr as al-Maliki's aggressive action against the Mahdi army in 2007 had not endeared al-Maliki to al-Sadr. It is more likely, therefore, al-Sadr's support for al-Maliki was not voluntary but action he was pressured into taking by Tehran.

As prime minister, al-Maliki exhibited occasional streaks of independence—as he had done in 2007 with taking aggressive action against al-Sadr's Mahdi Army. However, al-Maliki also felt somewhat beholding to Iran for having given him refuge from Saddam. This was demonstrated as the U.S. and Iraq attempted to negotiate an extension for U.S. troops to remain behind and train Iraqi soldiers. This was not something Tehran wanted to see happen and used its influence to ensure it did not. It proved successful although many Iraqi legislators, recognizing their troops could use more training, favored the extension.

Despite appearing serious about negotiating an extension, al-Maliki was heard boasting after it failed to go through that he was the one who had succeeded in ending the U.S. occupation. It would appear, therefore, that al-Maliki subordinated the best interests of his own people (i.e., ensuring his military was adequately trained) to the best interests of Iran.

In most countries, such men are called "traitors."

Is Iraq Being "Saddamized" by Al-Maliki—The Man Who Would Be Dictator?

There is another possible role al-Maliki might play in Iraq's future based on some of his more recent actions. It raises the question of whether Iraq is being "Saddamized" by al-Maliki who quietly—and with little apparent objection from the U.S.—may be maneuvering the country into a dictatorship.

Several articles in April 2012 began flagging the possibility al-Maliki may be leading Iraq down this path.

Alice Fordham of the Washington Post raised concerns in an April 4, 2012 piece entitled, "In Iraq, Concern Over Shrinking Rights." She cites a trend that developed only four months after the U.S. withdrawal:

> "The Iraqi government is debating proposed laws that would impose strict controls on freedom of speech and association, prompting fears that the authorities are playing a growing and increasingly oppressive role in citizens' lives.
>
> "As the country settles into its new identity as a sovereign state, about four months after the departure of the last American troops, some Iraqis are nervous that the government is moving back toward the heavy-handed monitoring of citizens that was a hallmark of life under dictator Saddam Hussein.
>
> "In parliament, there has been fierce debate of several draft laws. One would carry harsh penalties for online criticism of the government. Another would require demonstrators to get permission for any gathering.
>
> "Local and international human rights groups say the proposed legislation is vague and would give the government power to move against people or parties critical of the government.
>
> "'In Iraq, we need to respect all the ideas,' said an activist and blogger known as Hayder Hamzoz who is campaigning against a proposed information technology law that would mandate a year's imprisonment for

anyone who violates 'religious, moral, family, or social values' online.

"The proposed law also contains a sentence of life imprisonment for using computers or social networks to compromise 'the independence of the state or its unity, integrity, safety.'

"Hamzoz...said the legislation is intended to allow the government of Prime Minister Nouri al-Maliki to control social media. The government essentially did just that more than a year ago, when it swiftly smothered an uprising inspired by the Arab Spring revolts sweeping the region.

"'It's to attack the activists,' Hamzoz said.

"Activists and nongovernmental organizations have criticized the proposed laws that would impose rules on gatherings and forbid meetings in religious establishments, universities, and government buildings for anything other than the facilities' primary purpose.

"The Center for Law and Democracy, a U.S.-based advocacy organization, produced a report in December criticizing Iraq's government for proposing a 'number of legal rules which do not meet basic constitutional and international human rights standards...'

"Basma al-Khateb, a women's rights activist, said some of the government's moves reminded her of the harsh controls under Hussein, before he was ousted in the 2003 U.S.-led invasion. She said she feared the new democratic system had brought to power groups with autocratic tendencies and conflicting religious and political loyalties.

> "'At least with Saddam, we had one red line,' she said. 'Now everyone is Saddam. We have 300 Saddams, each with his bloc and his party.'"

The Washington Post's Liz Sly agrees with Fordham's assessment. In an April 8, 2012 article entitled, "U.S. Policy on Iraq Questioned as Influence Wanes, Maliki Consolidates Power," she notes the down side of Iraq's relative calm as oil is being pumped at record levels:

> "But the appearance of calm that has endured for four months has come at a price, many Iraqis say, in the form of Iraqi Prime Minister Nouri al-Maliki's increasingly authoritarian behavior. Maliki, they say, has been moving steadily to consolidate his control over the country's institutions and security forces with the apparent acquiescence of the Obama administration.
>
> "Since U.S. troops withdrew in December (2011), Maliki has extended his reach to take on his political rivals, drawing accusations from Iraq's Sunni and Kurdish minorities that he is intent on establishing a dictatorship. An arrest warrant issued just days after the U.S. pullout for Vice President Tariq al-Hashimi—the top Sunni official in Iraq's Shiite-dominated government—has been followed more recently by challenges to the autonomy enjoyed by the Kurdish region in the north, provoking threats by Kurdish leader Massoud Barzani to sever ties with Baghdad.
>
> "Sunnis and Kurds, angered by what they see as Maliki's efforts to exclude them from power, accuse the United States of doing little or nothing to restrain his excesses or to press him to implement agreements under which he pledged to share power..."

One final article that same month (April 17) by John Glaser of Antiwar.com entitled "Iraqis Accuse Maliki of Dictatorship After Arrest of

Top Election Official" agrees al-Maliki may be straying down the dictatorial path:

> "Iraqi leaders from across the political spectrum are accusing Prime Minister Nouri al-Maliki of seeking to rig the country's electoral system after he arrested the official in charge of administering elections.
>
> "Maliki, increasingly denounced by Iraqi voices of all stripes as a ruthless dictator, seems to have taken to arresting anybody he disagrees with, including his own vice president, Tariq al-Hashemi.
>
> "Now, the top elections official, Faraj al-Haidari, and another election commissioner, Kareem al-Tamimi, are jailed inside the Salhayah police station in Baghdad on charges of corruption, despite a court ruling in their favor two months ago.
>
> "The arrest of Haidari 'is undemocratic and illegal,' said Muaid al-Tayab, a member of parliament. 'We call it political revenge.'"
>
> "Maliki had previously clashed with Haidari after the 2010 elections resulted in the prime minister's party losing out to the Iraqiya bloc, a clash that led to months of impasse as Maliki contested the initial outcome. As the head of the Independent High Electoral Commission (IHEC), Haidari rejected Maliki's petition to have thousands of votes for Iraqiya thrown out.
>
> "Maliki now seems to be teaching Haidari a lesson: never oversee an election that provides Maliki with fewer votes than others.
>
> "'The person who gave the specific order for this arrest, he is brother Nouri al-Maliki,' said a written statement issued

> by the cleric Moqtada al-Sadr. 'This arrest should be done under the law, not under dictatorship.'"

> "Khaled al-Alwani, a senior member of parliament in the Iraqiya bloc, accused Maliki and his backers of trying to target and marginalize his political opponents, and secure an unrivaled dictatorship. 'They will push out Haidari by any means necessary,' Alwani said.

> "The Obama administration has kept largely quiet about Maliki's behavior, aside from about $2 billion in annual aid and tens of billions in military assistance to support this drive to authoritarianism...

> "'Maliki is heading towards an incredibly destructive dictatorship, and it looks to me as though the Obama administration is waving him across the finishing line,' said Toby Dodge, an Iraq expert at the London School of Economics. 'Meanwhile, the most likely outcomes, which are either dictatorship or civil war, would be catastrophic because Iraq sits between Iran and Syria.'"

If al-Maliki is taking a walk down the path of dictatorship, the question then becomes whether he is taking it alone or with Iran's mullahs doing some hand-holding. Either way does not bode well for the Iraqi people.

On September 19, 1796, the world watched to see if George Washington who, having sipped the elixir of power, would freely yield that power to another. History is replete with examples of leaders choosing not to do so. But there was no hesitancy on Washington's part—his reason was made clear in his Farewell Address:

> "Of all the dispositions and habits which lead to political prosperity, Religion and Morality are indispensable supports."

Religion and morality were the pillars of Washington's journey to power; they also were the strengths obligating him to surrender that power when the end of his legal term in office dictated he do so. His relationship with the American people was one of a bailment in which he held the power of the presidency in trust for them. The power of the presidency was not his to own but merely to hold for them as they had intended by voting him into office.

Iraqis can only hope al-Maliki will recognize the same difference when his legal term in office as prime minister dictates he do so.

The Day Baghdad Died and No One Would Listen

Should al-Maliki succeed in converting Iraq to a dictatorship, with the benefit of hindsight one may see the day democracy died was when a message forewarning of such a fate—sent "to whomever listens"—fell on deaf ears.

Hadi al-Mahdi was home alone at his Bagdad residence on September 8, 2011. According to the ominous entry he made on his Facebook page reporting his life was in danger, it was approximately 2:30 pm. He was right—he had but minutes to live. An Iraqi journalist, Mahdi hosted a three-day-a-week radio program—"To Whomever Listens"—on which he voiced concerns that the fear and intimidation so much a signature of Saddam Hussein's regime was returning under Prime Minister Nouri al-Maliki.

Soon after Mahdi's last Facebook entry, there was a knock on his door. He apparently recognized his visitor(s), inviting him/them into his home. He went into the kitchen to pour water for his guest(s). As he did so, someone came up behind him. The last sound Mahdi heard was the report of a small handgun as two bullets were fired into the back of his head. He fell to the floor, still clutching the water jug in his hand. His last worldly act of kindness towards a guest in his home was reciprocated with a cowardly, violent act to silence the journalist forever.

It was a bitterly ironic end for Mahdi as he always sought to preserve life and avoid violence, even by those supporting the concerns he voiced over the radio. In February 2011, riots erupted in Baghdad over widespread corruption and lack of services. Demonstrators began throwing rocks at police who attacked them. Mahdi led an effort to form a human chain, interlocking arms with one another, to separate the two groups and restore calm. For his peaceful efforts, he was arrested, blindfolded, interrogated, tortured and threatened with rape. He was forced to sign a criminal confession and to agree not to participate in future demonstrations.

Released the next day, Mahdi continued organizing and participating in weekly protests to focus the al-Maliki government on issues of social inequality. For these efforts, he began receiving numerous warnings, followed by threats. Despite these, he organized a major protest for the end of Ramadan, to take place on September 9—the day after he was shot.

Mahdi's last Facebook entry revealed his fear and frustration, as well as his determination to give power to the people:

> *"Enough...I have lived the last three days in a state of terror. There are some who call me and warn me of raids and arrests of protesters...I will take part in the demonstrations, for I am one of its supporters. I firmly believe that the political process embodies a national, economic, and political failure. It deserves to change, and we deserve a better government...I do not represent any political party or any other side, but rather the miserable reality in which we live...I am sick of seeing our mothers beg in the streets and I am sick of news of politicians' gluttony and of their looting of Iraq's riches."*

Iraq has proven to be one of the most dangerous places to be a journalist. A 2010 UN report indicated within a four year period, 77 journalists lost their lives while countless others were threatened or attacked. While some simply were in the wrong place at the wrong time, a concerted effort appears underway to silence those seeking to awaken the Iraqi people to groups trying to maximize their control at the expense of minimizing the freedoms of the people.

Another journalistic critic of the al-Maliki government, Emad al-Ebadi, suffered a violent attack in 2009. Despite three gunshots to the head and a fourth to the neck by unknown attackers, he miraculously survived the attempt on his life.

Each time a journalist has been attacked or killed, a call has gone out for an investigation. However, just like in countries such as Russia, where powerful people seek to murder their journalistic critics, the calls for investigation go unheeded or are undertaken without any intention of solving the crime.

There are three groups that benefitted from Mahdi's death and should have been targeted for investigation. Interestingly, all shared an Iran connection.

First, al-Maliki and his supporters were clearly possible suspects. He was in the process of solidifying his control at the time so the last thing he needed was an independent journalist spotlighting his lack of interest in the welfare of the Iraqi people. Stirring up social unrest with protests such as the one scheduled for September 9 ran contrary to al-Maliki's interests.

Second, involvement by Tehran is possible. As the withdrawal date of all U.S. forces from Iraq drew near, al-Maliki had drawn closer to Iran's President Mahmoud Ahmadinejad. He had unabashedly become his puppet in trying to help Tehran get rid of the Iranian opposition group—MEK—residing at Camp Ashraf in Iraq. As majority-Shia Iran sought to dominate majority-Shia Iraq through al-Maliki, any journalistic attacks against the Prime Minister and Iran ran contrary to this interest. Special units of Iran's paramilitary Qods Force operated freely in Iraq—thus, the Iranians had both the motive and the opportunity to conduct such an assassination.

Third, also suspect in the murder was one of the most influential religious and political leaders in Iraq—Sayyid Muqtada al-Sadr (the name "Sayyid" indicating he is a direct descendent of the Prophet Muhammad), whom Mahdi had criticized. Al-Sadr was no stranger to murder. Although out of the country at the time of the crime, he still maintained a network of operatives in Baghdad.

The month after Mahdi's murder, a memorial was dedicated in Washington D.C. to honor American hero Reverend Dr. Martin Luther King. Reverend King was a man who embraced nonviolent resistance in the 20th century fight he led for social equality. Like Mahdi, King had a dream "to make justice a reality to all of God's children." Like Mahdi, King's nonviolent push for equality met with an act of cowardly violence when he was gunned down in 1968.

Perhaps Iraq's future holds a memorial dedication in Baghdad to honor Hadi al-Mahdi—a martyred hero who embraced nonviolent resistance in the 21st century fight he led for social equality. If so, it will be despite the violent efforts of al-Maliki, Ahmadinejad and al-Sadr to ensure such a day never happens.

Mahdi's life and death sends an important warning "To Whomever Listens."

Al-Sadr—Iraqi Nationalist or Shiite Islamist?

As mentioned earlier, the second option Iran has to manipulate its influence in Iraq is through Moqtada al-Sadr.

Moqtata al-Sadr

Al-Sadr's father was a most revered religious leader, Grand Ayatollah Mohammad Sadeq al-Sadr, who was murdered by Saddam in 1999 for voicing opposition to him after the Gulf war. After the 2003 U.S. invasion, the younger al-Sadr—largely on the reputation of his father—emerged as one of the most important Shiite leaders.

He headed a militant group, the Mahdi Army which, at various times, engaged U.S. forces in Iraq, the Iraqi army and rival Shia groups. A firebrand cleric, he was also known to support Shia death squads that targeted Sunnis, claiming over 1300 victims. As head of the Sadrist movement, the cleric had a tremendous following among the Shiite poor in Sadr City—a district in Baghdad named after his late father.

After U.S. forces arrived in Iraq, al-Sadr quickly demonstrated his propensity for violence. The month after the U.S. invasion, a moderate Islamic, Imam Abdul Majid al-Khoei, who was a rival of al-Sadr's, sought to mediate a sensitive issue involving control of the shrine of Imam Ali. He was attacked by al-Sadr supporters. Bloodied and semi-conscious, Khoei was dragged before al-Sadr who directed the mob to execute him. They did.

It took a year for an arrest warrant to be issued for al-Sadr and his lieutenants by an Iraqi judge, only to then have it sealed by the Coalition Provisional Authority—undoubtedly as enticement for al-Sadr to lower his profile. As al-Sadr later became active again in stirring up violence, he felt more secure directing it from the safe haven provided by Iran.

In the aftermath of the 2007 surge into Iraq, al-Sadr went on a three year, self-imposed exile, to Iran—ostensibly to undertake religious studies. He quietly and unexpectedly returned to Iraq in January 2011. When he departed three years earlier, al-Sadr had vowed not to return again until the Americans had departed. Yet, with 45,000 troops still in Iraq in January 2011, he did return. He claimed he wanted foreign forces out and an "Islamic democracy," similar to Iran's, established. This suggested either his definition of "democracy" was different from the Western concept or he meant the term in the same sense as Supreme Leader Khomeini meant it, i.e., as a sham to impose theocratic rule.

A similar claim of Islamic democracy had been made in 1979 by Iran's Ayatollah Ruhollah Khomenei as he sought to replace Iran's Shah. To appeal to Westerners, "Islamic democracy" has become code for "theocracy."

Al-Sadr had been labeled by the U.S. as "the single greatest threat to U.S. military and economic control of Iraq." He was still wanted for questioning in the murder investigation and for encouraging violence against Coalition forces. When he returned, the Americans vowed to take him dead or alive. However, al-Sadr quickly decided to make his stay in Iraq a short one, returning again to Iran to continue his religious studies.

The vehemently anti-U.S. al-Sadr gave his first major Western television interview in 2003 to Bob Simon of "60 Minutes." It provided some interesting insights into the cleric's thinking.

When Simon asked him to comment about the American invasion of Iraq earlier that year which had toppled Saddam, ending the dictator's brutal rule over he and his fellow Shiites, al-Sadr responded (in reference to Saddam and the U.S. respectively), "the little serpent has left and the great serpent has come."

Al-Sadr was then asked, since the "great serpent" rid him of his enemy Saddam, doesn't that make "the enemy of your enemy your friend?"

Not wanting to say anything positive about the U.S., he responded:

> *"Just because we are rid of Saddam and the evil Ba'athists does not mean the occupation is a good thing. Our salvation from Saddam was only with the Grace of God."*

Why then, queried Simon, did God wait for the U.S. to come in and do that job.

To this, al-Sadr responded:

> *"All praises to Allah. He works in mysterious ways."*

One could say the same thing about how al-Sadr thinks.

In July 2012, al-Sadr returned, again, to Iraq—and his old stomping grounds of Najaf. The question arises, "why?"

Unlike he did as head of the Mahdi Army, he came this time bearing no arms. It appears as if the cleric relocated to have a go at the political process since the Americans are no longer there "to kick around anymore." He returns to Iraq eager to do battle, only this time of a political nature, against al-Maliki.

Al-Sadr reports he is in Iraq to move the country forward as it is, once again, suffering from gridlock. And, while he is at it, he does want to run for office. Interestingly, the cleric who so despised America for its occupation of Iraq now seeks to make use of the democratic system it left in place at the sacrifice of thousands of American lives.

It appears al-Sadr is seeking to shed some of his extremist militant clothing by inviting non-Shiites to join his Sadrist party. Just like the smiling picture of Khamenei, it is difficult to envision a picture of al-Sadr embracing Christians and Sunnis in such a manner.

It also seems difficult for al-Sadr's own followers to accept this as well. A National Democratic Institute poll taken in April 2012 revealed the cleric's popularity falling. One worker at a shop in Sadr City, sensing the shift, noted:

> "People criticize him more than before. They are not accepting of what is happening."

Perhaps having preached the old hatred, intolerance and violence (HIV) theme to so many for so long, al-Sadr has been hoisted by his own petard.

In his 2011 interview with "60 Minutes," al-Sadr had rejected the adage Simon raised about the enemy of my enemy being my friend since the U.S. invasion had driven Saddam from power. Obviously not remembering that response, al-Sadr, in explaining to followers what he was doing nine years later by opening up his party to non-Shiites, intoned:

"Part of politics is that you make your enemy your friend, and people don't understand that."

It sure seems neither does al-Sadr.

Al-Sadr's about-face on violence should be taken with a heavy grain of salt—and only after serious reflection on whether his actions now are part of a grandeur Iranian blueprint for Iraq that needs to be understood by non-Muslims: His should not be a personality change simply accepted at face value.

There has been some thought that another reason for al-Sadr's return to Najaf is to position him for the eventual death of Iraq's leading and elderly Shiite cleric—Ayatollah Ali Sistani. Sistani, who is a "gentler, kinder" version of his Iranian ayatollah counterparts, has struggled to maintain his influence over Iraq's Shiite population as Iran's ayatollahs have sought to pull them into the Flock.

There was a very telling comment al-Sadr made to an interviewer's question in July 2012. Asked if he would consider leaving Iraq to return to Qom—the holy city of Shiite scholarship in Iran where he had spent years studying—al-Sadr responded:

> *"After this crisis (gridlock), if it were the last crisis, I would. But I know there will be more crises in another time."*

Heart is where the home is. There is little doubt, for al-Sadr, it is not Iraq but Iran where his heart lies. That speaks volumes about his loyalties.

That probably explains Saddam Hussein's last words before he was hung on December 30, 2006.

Three masked guards led the toppled dictator, dressed in a black trench coat, to the gallows. As one placed a noose around his neck, he told Saddam his rule had destroyed Iraq. A defiant Hussein argued with him. Hussein was offered a hood, which he refused.

The cloud al-Sadr might cast over Iraq's post-Saddam push for democracy was not lost on the soon-to-be executed dictator. Someone yelled out, "long live Moqtada al-Sadr!" The last words by a sneering Saddam were to repeat the cleric's name in a mocking tone, as if to make the point Iraqis would rue the day they rid themselves of one dictator only to replace him with a more brutal one.

Where Do Their True Loyalties Lie?

The question arising over whether the true loyalties of al-Maliki and al-Sadr lie with Iraq or Iran or with themselves brings to mind the great Roman statesman, lawyer, scholar and writer Marcus Tullius Cicero. He sought, unsuccessfully, to preserve the republican principles in the civil wars that ultimately led to the Roman Republic's destruction. In the throes of the fall of Rome, he made an observation then just as applicable today to Iraq should democracy fail there because its leaders opt for power over republican principles:

> *"A nation can survive its fools, and even the ambitious. But it cannot survive treason from within. An enemy at the gates is less formidable, for he is known and carries his banner openly. But the traitor moves amongst those within the gate freely, his sly whispers rustling through all the alleys, heard in the very halls of government itself. For the traitor appears not a traitor; he speaks in accents familiar to his victims, and he wears their face and their arguments, he appeals to the baseness that lies deep in the hearts of all men. He rots the soul of a nation, he works secretly and unknown in the night to undermine the pillars of the city, he infects the body politic so that it can no longer resist. A murderer is less to fear."*

Chapter Twelve

Shiites and Sunnis: Using Different Roadmaps But Heading to the Same Destination

It is important to realize Islamists do have a game plan in place by which they intend to gain real estate on the global Monopoly board.

For the Shiites, this plan has been mapped out in the chapter of this book entitled "The 'Belief' and the 'Goal'—Crossing Over from Reality to the Spiritual World of the Mahdi."

But many Sunnis also adhere to this same Belief and Goal, with one significant difference—they believe the chaos necessary to launch the Mahdi's return must evolve naturally. Therefore, Sunnis disagree with Ahmadinejad's interpretation that man can be a catalyst in creating the chaos necessary to release the Twelfth Imam.

That means both Shiites and Sunnis believe the Mahdi will return to lead Islam to greatness and to make all other religions subservient to it. Ultimately, all non-Muslims will be left to decide either to convert to Islam (as to whether such conversion would be to Shi'a or Sunnism turns on which sect prevails in the ultimate battle between them) or to be put to death.

But a common ground for all Islamists, whether Shiite or Sunni, is that democracies do not appear on either sect's roadmap. A democracy has to be transitioned into subordinating itself to shariah, and thereby into joining the Flock.

But this poses a problem for Islamists because a democracy, by its very nature, nurtures something anathema to Islamist thinking—independent thought. Therefore, a democracy requires a special approach to overcome that independent thinking, which necessitates using a democracy's own freedoms against it. A democracy has to be undermined from within in a way that allows shariah to creep in.

The Cordoba Initiative—Symbol of Islam's Greatest Victory

Such a "shariah creep" approach is not too dissimilar from that attempted when an effort was made to build the Ground Zero Mosque near the site of the World Trade Center destroyed on 9/11.

Obviously, there were certain American sensitivities to having a symbol of Islam constructed so close to a site where Islamism had manifested its hatred. Were roles reversed and Christian zealots were seeking to build a church in a Muslim country nearby to where a similar attack had been conducted, there should be no debate that effort would not be tolerated by any Muslim government, let alone its people. Such a church, if built, would be destroyed and its membership slaughtered. After all, it is still virtually impossible for any Christian group to get a church built in most Muslim countries. The destruction of existing churches and persecution of Christians in Muslim countries combined with the tolerance for all religions in democracies has resulted in a direct correlation between the decline of Christians in the former and the increase of Muslims in the latter.

This is the card—i.e., the tolerance of democracies—that Islamists well understand can be played to get the Islamist's camel's nose under a democracy's tent, paving the way for the acceptance of shariah in the latter to follow.

Do not think it is impossible—because the paving has already started in the U.S. It involves playing the political correctness (PC) card to a hilt, to make those non-Muslims who dare question a Muslim's motives, feel the critical sting of PC advocates for doing so. The opposite (a non-Muslim trying to inflict a similar sting upon a Muslim for questioning a non-Muslims' intentions) simply does not work.

U.S. concern for PC could well have cost thousands of American lives during World War II had not common sense intervened.

The PC concept feeds on the Golden Rule—treat others as you would have them treat you. In 1929, it was such thinking that prompted Henry Stimson, as Secretary of State, to dismantle the nation's only cryptographic facility, rationalizing "gentlemen don't read each other's mail." Later, as Secretary of War prior to and during World War II, preparing to face a brutal and committed enemy, he quickly realized his folly. Giving cryptography a high priority, he enabled the U.S. to break Japan's code prior to hostilities, saving an untold number of American lives by foiling the enemy's war strategy.

In an ideal world, it may be nice to be PC; however, in the real world, when an enemy uses it to challenge a country's survival, PC must be sidelined in the interests of national security.

But it was with World War II long forgotten by a generation of Americans proud of its PC orientation and with insensitivity toward an American public still in shock over 9/11 that the Ground Zero Mosque initiative was proposed.

Ironically, while Muslims never hesitate to react violently when their sensitivities are offended—whether it is publication of a cartoon of Muhammad or a non-Muslim handling the Koran without gloves—there was no similar non-Muslim concern demonstrated by this initiative based on the name given it. A tolerant society like the U.S. just did not understand the importance an intolerant one attached to the initiative's name—Cordoba. (That significance is shared later.)

If one feels it is only the Islamists who attach such significance to this victory, one need only recall the images of euphoria depicted in many Muslim countries around the world as news of the 9/11 attacks spread. Thousands of Muslims were seen rejoicing over the violent deaths of more than 3,000 innocent victims. While Islamic extremists had dealt the devastating blow, more than just Islam's extremists joined in the celebration over the pain and suffering inflicted upon non-believers.

At some point after 9/11, photographs of the New York City landscape near the World Trade Center began circulating on the Internet in Muslim circles. Cropped into the photographs were the minarets and domes of numerous mosques dotting the area surrounding the 9/11 site.

Many Muslim believers understood the symbolism—the assault against a key bastion of the non-believer's world had started. The push to place that bastion under Islam's world caliphate umbrella by establishing a foothold upon territory 9/11 had made hallowed to Muslims was now in progress.

If we choose not to blame Islam for the violent acts of Islamists—instead accusing extremists of having hijacked this religion of peace—we should at least listen to the insights Islam's supposed "moderates" have to say about their religion.

Turkey is among the most moderate of Muslim states today. As such, it was welcomed into the NATO alliance as sharing some of the values of its Western members. But comments by Turkish Prime Minister Recep Tayyip Erdogan on his beliefs about Islam and the symbolism its mosques represent should give us pause for concern. He has said:

> "The mosques are our barracks, the domes our helmets, the minarets our bayonets and the believers our army."

Nothing in this description of Islam by "moderate" Muslim Erdogan suggests it is a religion of peace.

Furthermore, Erdogan takes offense at even using the term "moderate" to describe Islam. Such a description, the prime minister asserts, is:

> "...very ugly, it is offensive and an insult to our religion. There is no moderate or immoderate Islam. Islam is Islam and that's it."

By Erdogan's definition, Islamists and moderates are of the same ilk. If so, a dangerous mindset now permeates NATO's den.

But, back to the Cordoba Initiative.

Imam Feisal Abdul Rauf and his wife Daisy Khan head the American Society of Muslim Advancement (ASMA). ASMA led the effort to build a $100 million, 13-story mosque, less than 200 feet from the World Trade Center. Both Rauf and Khan also are described as "moderate" Muslims.

Such a label suggests a tolerance for Western culture and beliefs but their actions/inactions reveal something far different.

An organization known as Former Muslims United (FMU) launched a campaign to appeal to Muslim leaders to repudiate shariah's more extremist views—i.e., such as executing Muslims who leave Islam for another religion. FMU asked Rauf and Khan to sign a "Muslim pledge for religious freedom and safety from harm for former Muslims." ASMA failed to do so.

During a live radio interview, Rauf refused to condemn violent jihadist groups as terrorists.

While refusing to admit Muslims carried out the 9/11 attacks, Rauf did not hesitate to condemn U.S. policies as the root cause.

In 2004, Rauf wrote a book entitled, according to the English translation, "What's Right with America is What's Right with Islam." Such a title again suggests a moderate perspective is taken. However, the book's Arabic translation—"The Call From the WTC Rubble: Islamic Da'wah From the Heart of America Post-9/11"—suggests otherwise. Rauf, denigrating the loss of American life in calling it "rubble," seeks to use 9/11 as a springboard for selling Islam to America.

Also closely linked to Rauf's AMSA is a charitable organization, Carnegie Corp., which topped its list of supporters. It is headed by Iranian-born scholar Vartan Gregorian who, in his own book, espouses the Islamist goal of world domination. Thus, both Rauf and Gregorian promote replacement in America of the U.S. Constitution with shariah.

This is quite evident by Rauf's assertion:

> "Throughout my discussions with contemporary Muslim theologians, it is clear an Islamic state can be established in more than just a single form or mold. It can be established through a kingdom or a democracy. The important issue is to establish the general fundamentals of shariah that are required to govern."

In re-reading Rauf's comment about Islamic democracy, similar references by Ayatollah Khomeini made in 1979, who promoted democracy as a sham to implement theocracy, and Moqtada al-Sadr made in 2012, should be kept in mind.

Never clarified by AMSA was the source of the $100 million funding for the mosque initiative. AMSA never disclosed how an organization with a relatively dry financial well was suddenly flush with cash. While it was critical the source of the funding be disclosed and verified to ascertain it had no link to the same groups to which Rauf refused to attach a terrorist label—such as the violent Muslim Brotherhood to which Rauf had ties—this was never done.

As non-Islamic religious houses of worship flounder in Muslim nations prohibiting freedom of religion, mosques flourish in non-Islamic states promoting such freedom. Muslim moderate leaders, such as Turkey's Erdogan, seek to achieve the goal of their extremist brethren of subjugating the West to shariah—the only difference being they have cloaked their ultimate objective under what the West chooses to call a "moderate" label.

Muslims understand symbols. That is reflected by the name initially selected for the Ground Zero Mosque building effort. It was named "Cordoba House." While few Americans understand this significance, many Muslims do. Cordoba is a Spanish city where a victorious Muslim army destroyed a church, building a mosque in its place. It was the site of Islam's greatest victory over the West, perhaps until 9/11. Similarly, the construction of a Ground Zero Mosque would symbolize another Muslim victory.

In 2001, President George Bush initially referred to the war on terrorism as a "crusade"—later apologizing for the negative connotation it had for Muslims and never using it again. Reference to the word crusade offended Muslim sensitivities. Yet in naming the Ground Zero Mosque effort after Cordoba, Muslims purposefully referenced a name that had a very negative connotation for non-Muslims. No similar apology for doing so or offer to change the initiative's name was ever forthcoming.

Building the Ground Zero Mosque would have symbolized a victory for Islam over Western values. Yet, it was a project a tolerant society was prepared to allow.

Sunnis Take the Fork in the Road for the Mahdi's Return

As mentioned, Shiites and Sunnis agree on Islam's final destination; they just do not agree on how best to get there.

Therefore, while Shiites and Sunnis are using different roadmaps on how to get to that final destination, one cannot focus on the Islamist Shiite's map to the total exclusion of the Islamist Sunni's map. It must be kept in mind the only difference is, while Islamist Shiites and Islamist Sunnis seek to arrive at the same destination, the Islamist Shiite seeks to get there sooner.

Thus, since the ultimate destination of Islamist Shiites and Islamist Sunnis is the same, and since the Shiites' plan for getting there has already been detailed herein, one must understand how Sunnis intend to get there as well. They too envision creating a Mahdi-friendly world to await the Twelfth Imam's arrival.

Accordingly, both sects journey the same road until they come to a decisive fork in the road where, as that great baseball philosopher Yogi Berra once advised, they take it.

Islamist Sunnis' Holy Grail Undermining Democracy— Opening the Door to Shariah "Creep"

The Islamist Sunnis' plan of attack against democracies is written out. It was found hidden at a location just miles from the heart of the Nation's capitol. Written in Egypt seventeen years before its 2004 discovery, the document remained hidden away as the "Holy Grail" for undermining the fundamental beliefs of non-Muslims living in a democratic state to open the door for their acceptance of shariah.

Obviously, the document was meant as "eyes only" for the Sunni leadership implementing it. While its disclosure initially worried Sunni leaders it might spark anti-Islamic sentiment, they soon realized there was nothing to fear—the Holy Grail document would not be taken seriously by those who should be heeding it. Accordingly, Islamist Sunnis continue to implement the plan which focuses on undermining democracies from within (both new ones, such as Iraq, or older ones, such as the U.S.).

In 2004, a car was traveling along the Chesapeake Bay Bridge in Maryland. The action of an occupant attracted the attention of two Baltimore off-duty police officers following behind. The front seat passenger was videotaping the structure—filming close-ups of cables and other features that were "integral to the structural integrity of the bridge," seemingly with no interest in filming the picturesque view available.

The vehicle was stopped and the driver, Ismail Elbarasse, 57, was initially detained. It was determined he had an outstanding material witness warrant to appear before a federal grand jury in Chicago. The warrant involved a racketeering case in which one of the highest-ranking leaders of the terrorist group Hamas—Mousa Mohammed Abu Marzook—was indicted. Elbarasse was arrested by the police officers.

A subsequent indictment specifically naming Elbarasse, described him as a "co-conspirator" in an international fraud scheme that had been going on for five years, laundering "substantial sums" of money for the terrorist organization Hamas.

Married with children, Elbarasse was a Palestinian American who had lived in the metropolitan Washington, D.C., area for twelve years. At the time of his arrest, he was residing in Annandale, Virginia. He had been incarcerated in Otisville, New York, for not responding to a grand jury subpoena in connection with his job as comptroller of a Saudi-funded school in northern Virginia.

Additionally, in 1992, Elbarasse had been involved in the transfer of funds to the military wing of Hamas. He was linked to criminal action taken after 9/11 against the largest Muslim charity in the U.S.—the Holy Land Foundation for Relief and Development—due to its ties to Hamas. That action resulted in the charity being shut down and its assets frozen.

A former board member of the Islamic Association for Palestine (IAP), Elbarasse also served on the Palestine Committee, created by an Islamist organization known as the "Muslim Brotherhood." The Committee was organized in the U.S. to help Hamas politically and financially.

From his past numerous run-ins with the law, Elbarasse was someone intimately and frequently involved with Hamas. Additionally, this tied him in as well to the Muslim Brotherhood—one of the most active Sunni Islamist organizations in the world and one eager to bring the U.S. under Islam's umbrella. The Brotherhood's official motto is most telling of the kind of world order it seeks:

> "Allah is our objective/The Prophet is our leader/The Quran is our law/Jihad is our way/Dying in the way of Allah is our highest hope."

This Muslim Brotherhood is this same organization that came to power in Egypt's 2012 presidential election.

A brief segue is needed to better understand why Hamas is designated a terrorist group and how it ignores cultural taboos and the laws of common decency to ensure its mandate to do violence to non-Muslims is fulfilled.

By December 2006, senior Palestinian military intelligence officer and Fatah loyalist Baha Balousheh had twice been the target of assassination attempts by Hamas due to a crackdown he had conducted on that group a decade earlier.

Unable to locate Balousheh, Hamas assassins targeted, what for them, was the next best thing—his family. On December 11, as his three children, aged three, six and nine, were being driven to school along the streets of Gaza City, they were brutally murdered, along with their driver.

While the murder of all four was despicable, what was most disturbing was that one of the children had been shot in the head—not once, but ten times. Such violence clearly reflected a deep-seated hatred on the part of the killers. But, even armed with such hatred, how could these killers be so detached—directing it against three innocent children, shooting them in cold blood, pumping round after round after round into the head of a child?

This incident did not involve the normally intense and long-running hatred Muslims have for Jews; this was hatred between Muslims; this was hatred between Muslims of the same sect; this was hatred targeting innocent Muslim children of the same sect—none of whom were even born at the time Balousheh had committed his alleged offenses against Hamas ten years earlier!

But it was this kind of Muslim-on-Muslim hatred that Elbarasse's illegal transfer of funds helped to fuel in the Gaza Strip.

It was Elbarasse's arrest by the Maryland police that ultimately led to the discovery of the Muslim Brotherhood's Holy Grail.

After Elbarasse's arrest, the police obtained a warrant to search his home in Annandale, Virginia. While searching the basement, a hidden entrance to a sub-basement was found. Inside was discovered a treasure trove of Islamist documents. Translations of the documents revealed them to be the archives of the U.S. branch of the fundamentalist and militant Muslim Brotherhood. Their contents indicated a conspiracy was in the works to take control of America, using the introduction of shariah as the vehicle for doing so.

Four years later these documents would prove invaluable in the prosecution of five officials of the Holy Land Foundation who were found guilty of conducting illegal money transfers to Hamas.

At this point, some background on the Muslim Brotherhood is helpful.

Founded in Egypt in 1928, today the Brotherhood is the world's most influential Islamist movement. Its slogan "Islam is the solution" is not limited in application just to the Arab world in giving Prophet Muhammad's holy book and sayings a global reach. Its ultimate goal is that all non-believers convert to Islam—or face the consequences of a global Islamic society that is intolerant of those who do not. (If this sounds a lot like the same Shiite mantra, it is.)

There is debate over whether or not the Brotherhood embraces violence to achieve its goals. While it allegedly has renounced violence, it is fair game for Muslims—both Shiite and Sunni—as mentioned previously about the practice of "taqiya," to lie to or otherwise deceive non-believers about their true intentions when necessary to further the cause of Islam. While giving the appearance of renouncing violence, the Brotherhood has given birth to many splinter groups that do embrace it—of which Hamas became one in 1987.

(The charter for Hamas recognizes it was founded to liberate Palestine from Israeli occupation and to establish an Islamic state in the place of Israel, the West Bank, and the Gaza Strip.)

Unfortunately, this debate has created some confusion, sadly even at the U.S. national security level. Astonishingly, in his February 2011 Congressional testimony, Director of National Intelligence James Clapper described the Brotherhood as "largely secular"—which it clearly is not. As it is now doing in Egypt, it simply uses secularism as a vehicle to achieve indirectly what it has failed to do directly. While Clapper's statement chose to downplay the organization's religious underpinnings, the CIA's website more accurately describes it as a "religious-based" party.

In September 2010, a non-partisan panel of national security experts issued a report entitled "Sharia: The Threat to America." It quoted one of the documents, dated 1987, found hidden in Elbarasse's basement containing the Brotherhood's strategic plan by Brotherhood member and senior Hamas leader Mohammed Akram. Although it details the

Brotherhood's mission in America, the strategy is applicable to a young democracy, such as Iraq, as well:

> *"The process of settlement is a 'civilization-jihadist process' with all the word means. The Ikhwan (brothers of an Islamic religious militia) must understand that their work in America is a kind of grand jihad in eliminating and destroying the Western civilization from within and 'sabotaging' its miserable house by their hands and the hands of the believers so that it is eliminated and God's religion is made victorious over all other religions."*

The report described this Islamist strategy:

> *"...for destroying the United States is to get us, specifically our leadership, to do the bidding of the MB (Muslim Brotherhood) for them. The Muslim Brotherhood intends to conduct Civilization Jihad by co-opting our leadership into believing a counterfactual understanding of Islam and the nature of the Muslim Brotherhood, thereby coercing these leaders to enforce the MB narrative on their subordinates."*

The non-partisan report urged the White House to make clear what the document states—radical Muslims are using Islamic law to subvert the U.S. But, the Obama Administration has yet to do so out of a ridiculous concern that mentioning an Islamic link will offend "moderate" Muslims.

According to the report, the Brotherhood's document calls for the Islamist's strategy plan to be slowly implemented in phases that enable shariah to "creep" into U.S. culture. To work, it requires Muslims gain influence in various ways including: expanding Muslims' physical presence in the U.S. via high birth rates, immigration and refusing to assimilate; keeping locals "in the dark" over human right infringement by ensuring they do not study shariah doctrine and its impact; controlling the language Muslims use to describe non-Muslims as the enemy lest it raise non-Muslim concern; forcing compliance with shariah at local levels; employing the offensive use of lawsuits and threats of lawsuits to silence critics of Islam; claiming Muslim victimization; subverting the U.S. education system through the introduction of dominant U.S. Middle East studies programs; demanding the right to practice shariah in segregated Muslim enclaves and demanding its recognition in non-Muslim spheres; and (ultimately) demanding that shariah replace Western law.

Every single one of these tactics has been employed to date by members of the Muslim community promoting the Brotherhood's agenda:

- In 2002, two U.S. universities accepted $20 million dollar donations from a Saudi prince in exchange for a commitment to establish programs in Islamic studies.

- In 2010, a New Jersey criminal court judge applied shariah law to find a Muslim husband not guilty of having raped his Muslim wife as Islamic law demands a wife submit to her husband's sexual desires.

- In Minneapolis, home to a large community of unassimilated Somali immigrants, Muslim taxi drivers refuse to transport passengers carrying alcohol and other Muslim communities are seeking the application to them of shariah.

- As Rep. Peter King (R-NY) sought in 2011 to hold hearings on Islamic extremism and how it radicalizes Muslims, he became the target of Muslim groups' claims of religious prejudice.

There is an eerie similarity between the revelation of the Muslim Brotherhood's war plans against the U.S. on how it strategically plans to defeat the U.S. and of Japan's war plans against the U.S. during World War II. The difference, however, is in how that knowledge was applied.

After Japan's devastating surprise attack against the U.S. at Pearl Harbor on December 7, 1941, concerns arose over the ability of a seriously wounded American Navy to defend the homeland against a future attack, let alone challenge Tokyo's control of the Pacific. Over the following three and a half years, those concerns proved unwarranted.

The U.S. became very effective at taking the fight to the Japanese, who—in launching their military strategy—never again achieved the tactical surprise they did at Pearl Harbor. While the resolve and courage of U.S. fighting forces was a factor, so too was America's success—unbeknownst to the Japanese—in having broken their naval code. Accordingly, almost every move the Japanese navy made on its tactical chessboard was eventually checked by an Allied counter-move, leading to one Japanese naval defeat after another.

Clearly, when an enemy secretly lays out its strategic and tactical plans on how it intends to defeat the U.S., and the U.S. learns of them before the enemy can employ them, it provides the U.S. with an enormous advantage.

In the Islamist war against the U.S., Washington has once again been given a secret "code" for how Islamists seek to destroy America from within. It could not be made any more clear by an enemy seeking to destroy America that those Muslims sent to the U.S. to do so *"must understand that their work in America is a kind of grand jihad in eliminating and destroying the Western civilization from within and 'sabotaging' its miserable house by their hands and the hands of the believers so that it is eliminated and God's religion is made victorious over all other religions."* With the Muslim Brotherhood code broken, the West should be working feverishly to check such advances by Islamists. However, it has failed to do so in the manner that was successfully achieved against the Japanese in World War II.

By failing to do so, the West allows the Islamist strategy to gain traction. The first signs of its success are already visible.

One can rest assured similar tactics are in play in Iraq, as well.

Iran Fans the Flames of Violence in Afghanistan

There's a somewhat chilling insight shared about one of Afghanistan's elite commando units.

A highly effective fighting unit, it has benefitted from high level training provided by foreign trainers. Ironically, these have included not only U.S. Special Forces, but also Iran's IRGC—interesting dichotomies since IRGC are Shiite and Afghans are Sunni.

Two scholars, Amir Bagherpour—a former U.S. Army officer—and Asad Farhad—a Defense Language Institute instructor and former Afghan minister—spent several weeks in Afghanistan in late 2010 to determine how extensive the Iranian influence is there.

The two men established a friendly relationship with some of the commandos. Two of them, who were Tajiks (98% of Tajikistan is Muslim of which 95% of the 98% is Sunni and 3% Shiite), revealed under their uniforms, they wore necklaces bearing a portrait of Iran's late Supreme Leader Khomeini. One commando told the scholars:

> "We have close relationships with the Iranians, but the biggest challenge to stability is the Afghan government itself."

Thus, key personnel the U.S. has been endeavoring to influence for the past decade are already firmly in the Iranian camp.

In further exploring Iran's influence, the researchers learned from a key advisor to Afghan President Hamid Karzai:

> "They (Iranians) are highly involved officially and unofficially. I do not think this government can succeed unless Iran is at the table. Although there is some animosity toward the Iranians, it is far less than any animosity shown toward Pakistan and perhaps America."

Bagherpour and Farhad's article entitled "The Iranian Influence in Afghanistan" published August 9, 2010 paints an interesting picture of an Iranian presence where, interestingly, there are some mutual overlapping interests shared with the U.S.

They write:

> "As neighbors with similar dialects and much in common historically, the cultural ties between Iran and Afghanistan run deep. Afghanistan's third largest city, Herat, situated just 80 miles from the Iranian border, was the capital of the Persian Empire in the 15th century. More recently, Iran has extended its electricity grid to the city, funded cooperative highway projects with India, and is even partnering with NATO members on construction of an Iran-Afghanistan railway."

They note the problem of opium production in Afghanistan has impacted on Iran:

> "As opium production has risen in Afghanistan, so too has usage in Iran. The Iranian government is faced with a population of nearly four million opium addicts—a number that continues to rise. A recent world drug report estimated that Iran accounts for nearly 40 percent of global opium usage. Aside from fueling this addiction problem, profits from the opium trade provide funds for Taliban insurgents."

In 1998, an incident in Afghanistan came close to triggering an invasion by Iran into the country:

> "...the killing of 11 Iranian diplomats and the mass murder of thousands of Shia Muslims by the Taliban nearly prompted Iran to invade. Tens of thousands of Iranian troops amassed at the Afghan border in preparation for an attack. Iranian commanders, surveying the dusty, barren landscape, ultimately decided not to proceed.

> "In the final analysis, Tehran calculated that the cost of fighting the Taliban would far outweigh any benefit of occupying Afghanistan, at that time the poorest country in the world. By practicing restraint in this circumstance, the Iranians demonstrated that they were rational political actors, a fact rarely reported at a time when President Mahmoud Ahmadinejad's remarks make them appear anything but."

What should be taken from the above is some hope that an Iranian mindset operating beyond the bounds of reason **may** be brought back on track only when confronted by an opposing commitment which seeks to extract a greater price for Tehran's recalcitrant attitude than Tehran is willing to pay.

Iran undoubtedly was most concerned when U.S. forces simultaneously occupied Iraq and Afghanistan. With American forces as bookends on either side of Iran, Tehran worried about the possibility of facing a two front war if hostilities erupted with the U.S. It prompted Iran to keep its own forces along both borders as a precaution. With the U.S. now out of Iraq, Iran's focus has been to leave its forces on its eastern border.

Bagherpour and Farhad point out, although most Afghans are Pashtun Sunnis, in the days when the Taliban came to power and ever since, Iran's policy has been:

> "...a strategy of supporting Afghan minorities, both Shia and Sunni...Iran commands significant influence over the Shia population, which accounts for 19 percent of the country's people. Furthermore, the Iranians have established a network of support among Hazaras, Uzbeks, and Tajiks—together; the three ethnic groups make up 30 percent of the population. This network played a central role in the overthrow of the Taliban following 9/11. Although no foreign or domestic player commands the loyalty of a majority in the country, Iran is a long-term player in Afghanistan with influence at least equal to and

arguably greater than that of Pakistan or the United States.

> "Over the past 30 years, Iran has craftily managed its relationship with its eastern neighbor. The border is relatively stable and secure compared to the unruly, highly volatile frontier Afghanistan shares with Pakistan. Whether opposing Soviet occupation or responding to Taliban rule, Iran has acted carefully. It has a policy of, first, minimizing the cost of conflict and, second, maximizing the chances for success—known as the minimum-maximum strategy. This strategy is exemplified by its arming and training of guerrilla forces, even as it avoids conventional military engagement. Pakistan's support for the Taliban, reflecting a similar strategy, has not proved as fruitful. And although the Afghan-Pakistani border involves complex tribal networks plagued with extremist ideologies, Tehran has clearly been more wise in dealing with Afghanistan than has Pakistan, with its destabilizing, self-destructive behavior.

The authors address the irony of Afghanistan's two neighbors—Pakistan which is a U.S. ally but operates contrary to U.S. interests and Iran which is a U.S. foe but has interests similar to the U.S. there:

> "The recent leak of classified U.S. Department of Defense documents has exposed the thinly veiled fact that Pakistani intelligence has been arming and supporting the Taliban and other anti-American elements. This places the United States in a precarious position. Afghanistan's largest neighbor and supposed U.S. ally is actually opposed to the American effort and the current Karzai government. Though on the surface, the United States maintains a partnership with Pakistan, after peeling away the propaganda it is clear that their preferences are in stark opposition.

"By contrast, Iranian desires in Afghanistan are much more aligned with vital U.S. interests. Iran opposes the Taliban and other Sunni extremists just as much as the Americans do. In addition, Tehran prefers a stabilized Afghanistan that will curb the flow of refugees and ultimately reduce its need to maintain security forces at the border. The Ahmadinejad regime is also opposed to the opium trade that is financing insurgent groups while further fueling the addiction problem in Iran.

"The point is that cooperation with Iran can benefit Afghanistan and the United States in ways that partnering with Pakistan simply has not and cannot. But over the past year, the war drums have begun to beat once again, raising the possibility of military conflict between Iran and the United States over Tehran's controversial nuclear program. And although cooperation could benefit both countries in unprecedented ways, historical grievances and mutual distrust have locked the United States into a mindset that makes cooperation impossible to conceive."

Meanwhile, Iran continues to be battered by economic sanctions and internal political strife.

This does not suggest Iran would not target the U.S. for violence whenever the opportunity presents itself—as it did on February 21, 2012.

On that day, a security sweep of an Afghan prison turned up numerous Korans that were being used by the prisoners to illegally communicate. About 500 of the holy books were collected and, against the advice of Afghan soldiers, were taken to an incinerator at Bagram Air Force Base. Although most of the books were saved when a quick thinking Afghan guard shut down the incinerator, the incident sparked riots in Afghanistan and elsewhere.

Once word of the incident reached the grapevine, Iran ordered its agents in Afghanistan to stir up anti-U.S. protests.

Analyzing Iranian actions in the aftermath of the Koran burning has provided "a mixed picture of Iranian capabilities" according to an article co-authored by Thom Shanker, Eric Schmitt and Alissa Rubin on April 4, 2012.

> *"With Iran's motives and operational intentions a subject of intense interest, American officials have closely studied the episodes. A mixed picture of Iranian capabilities has emerged, according to interviews with more than a dozen government officials, most of whom discussed the risks on the condition of anonymity because their comments were based on intelligence reports.*
>
> *"One United States government official described the Iranian Embassy in Kabul as having 'a very active' program of anti-American provocation, but it is not clear whether Iran deliberately chose to limit its efforts after the Koran burning or was unable to carry out operations that would have caused more significant harm.*
>
> *"In offering an overall view of the threat from Tehran, Gen. John R. Allen, the senior allied commander in Afghanistan, told Congress in recent public testimony that Iran continued to 'fuel the flames of violence' by supporting the Afghan insurgency. 'Our sense is that Iran could do more if they chose to,' General Allen said. 'But they have not, and we watch the activity and the relationships very closely.'*
>
> *"The most visible rioting that American officials say bears Iranian fingerprints occurred in Herat Province, along Afghanistan's western border with Iran. In a melee after the Koran burning, 7 people were killed and 65 were wounded, Afghan and American officials said. That violence peaked when a police ammunition truck was hit by gunfire from a rioter and exploded.*

"Iran has denied any government-backed effort to foment unrest in Afghanistan, but American officials see a pattern of malign meddling to increase Iran's influence across the Middle East and South Asia. Iran appears to have increased its political outreach and arms shipments to rebels and other political figures in Yemen, and it is arming and advising the embattled government of President Bashar al-Assad of Syria.

"Those activities also reflect a broader campaign that includes what American officials say was a failed plot to assassinate the Saudi ambassador to the United States in October, and what appears to have been a coordinated effort by Iran to attack Israeli diplomats in India and Georgia this year. Iran has denied any role in the attacks, which caused several injuries but did not kill anyone...

"Intelligence analysts emphasize that Iran can still tap the formidable resources of Hezbollah, the Lebanese Shiite militant group. And some American officials are wary of viewing the plots as a sign of Iran's diminishing ability to stir violence...

"...In Afghanistan, according to American officials, Iranian assistance to militants and insurgents is limited to training, money, explosive material, small arms, rockets and mortars.

"But General Allen, in two days of testimony before Congress, disclosed that NATO forces were watching for an infusion of more-advanced weapons—in particular a high-powered roadway bomb called an explosively formed projectile, or E.F.P., which can pierce American armored vehicles. These bombs proved their deadly effectiveness when Iran funneled them to Shiite militants during the height of the sectarian violence in Iraq.

"'So we're going to keep a very close eye on those signature weapons,' General Allen said, 'because we think that that will be an indicator of Iran's desire to up the ante, in which case we'll have to take other actions.'

"Iran has long faced a quandary in shaping an Afghan policy. It has wanted to target the Americans fighting in Afghanistan, and the best mechanism for doing that is the Taliban insurgency. But at the same time, Iran has little interest in the return of a Taliban regime. When they were in power, the Taliban often persecuted the Hazara minority, who, like most Iranians, are Shiite, and whom Iran supports.

"What Iran has pursued more relentlessly is an effort to pull the Afghan government away from the Americans, a strategy that has included payments to promote Iran's interests with President Hamid Karzai.

"One American intelligence analyst noted that Iran had long supported Afghan minorities, both Shiite and Sunni, and had built a network of support among Hazaras, Uzbeks and Tajiks. Iran has exercised other means of 'soft power,' the analyst said, opening schools in western Afghanistan to extend its influence. The Iranians have also opened schools in Kabul and have largely financed a university attached to a large new Shiite mosque.

"Iran is thought to back at least eight newspapers in Kabul and a number of television and radio stations, according to Afghan and Western officials. The Iranian-backed news organs kept fanning anti-American sentiment for days after the Koran burnings."

One area in which Iran seeks to diminish U.S. influence in Afghanistan involves shaking the trust element that normally develops among forces fighting together.

Over the past two years the number of insider attacks—i.e., attacks by Afghan soldiers on Coalition force soldiers, also dubbed "green-on-blue"—has drastically increased. For January thru August 2012, insider attacks accounted for more than 50 Coalition casualties.

Interestingly, these attacks began to accelerate in 2011, soon after President Obama announced his plans to withdraw U.S. forces in 2014. While the most significant numbers of these attacks are committed in Helmand and Kandahar provinces, where the Taliban is strongest and poppy production is highest, the influence the Iranians have on other members of Afghan's armed forces leave them in a position to influence such killings as well.

Iran has also established charitable Non-Governmental Organizations (NGOs) in Afghanistan which have received funding from the West. Some were later determined to be offering cash bounties to the Taliban for killing U.S. troops. Meanwhile, the beat goes on as IEDs provided by Iran to the Taliban continue to claim more lives of U.S. servicemen than do battlefield engagements with the enemy.

For the U.S., the good news on Afghanistan is that the eventual withdrawal of its forces will not leave the country as vulnerable as Iraq is to Iranian influence; the bad news is it will leave Afghanistan vulnerable to instability fostered by a return of the Taliban.

The "Wild Cards" in Iran's Future

There are two possible "wild cards" that may play out in Iran's future.

One is a strike by the Israelis.

Whether that happens sooner or later turns on U.S. participation. Should the U.S. be willing to join the Israelis, the Israelis may prove willing to wait a little longer before launching an attack. If they have to go it alone, they will know best how much longer they can wait. As has been Israel's trademark in such operations, when it comes, it will be one maximizing the element of surprise and, most likely, will prove highly effective. But it will not be accomplished without great human sacrifice to Israel should it be conducted without U.S. assistance as Israel will have to deal with counter-attacks from multiple sources.

The Iranians realize the Israelis—in operations such as Entebbe, Iraq's nuclear facility at Osirak and Syria's nuclear facility, etc.—have always managed to establish that element of surprise, even when an adversary knew an attack might be forthcoming. That has made the Iranians somewhat nervous and gun-happy as their concerns rise that an Israeli attack may be imminent.

Iran has picked up unidentified aircraft entering its airspace and taken them under fire, only to later learn they were their own military planes or friendly commercial aircraft. Some were taken under fire by surface-to-air missiles and anti-aircraft batteries; others were intercepted by Iranian jet fighters.

A U.S. intelligence report noted:

> *"Iranian air defense units have taken inappropriate actions dozens of times, including firing antiaircraft artillery and scrambling aircraft against unidentified or misidentified targets."*

Inadequate training and communications have made misidentifications a major problem for Iran's air defense command.

Targets included planes, known to be commercial, but which appeared to be on a spy mission. Perhaps this incident provided the Iranians with better insight as to how the USS Vincennes could have accidentally shot down an Iranian passenger plane.

For Iran's air defense, it has been both good news and bad. The bad news is it has fired at several of its own aircraft and drones; the good news is it has failed to hit any—which, in itself is both good news and bad news.

Israel has received some quiet assistance from Greece. Any pre-emptive attack against Iran will have the Israelis confronting one of the most effective radar missile defense systems in the world—Russia's S-300—

which was recently delivered to Iran. It is capable of simultaneously tracking hundreds of targets while engaging at least ten. Greece has access to the same system, obtained through a mutual defense pact with Cyprus. In a well-reported joint Israeli-Greek air exercise over Crete in mid-2008 which was viewed by international observers as an exercise to conduct a long distance attack—which it was—it also provided Israel with invaluable information on how best to penetrate the S-300.

Needless to say, the Iranians were none too happy about Greece providing such access, lodging an official complaint with the Greek government.

While the Greek's version of the S-300 is not as updated as Iran's, nonetheless, it did provide Israel with insights on how to defeat the system—a technique which Israel undoubtedly has built upon during the past four years.

Also, Israel has had to develop a technique for destroying Iranian targets buried deep underground. It has practiced attacking a target with successive sorties. A second plane conducts a precision drop of its ground-penetrating bomb into a crater already created by a previous airplane's ground-penetrating bombing run, thus enabling the second bomb to penetrate much deeper.

But even if successful in its attack against Iran, Israel will then have its hands full defending against Iran and its Hezbollah and Hamas proxies. The good news is it may not have to worry about Syria entering the fray on Iran's behalf as Assad continues to have his hands full dealing with his civil war.

In early November 2012, Prime Minister Benjamin Netanyahu made it clear as long as he is in office, Iran will not go nuclear.

"We are serious," he said in an interview. "This is not a show. If there is no other way to stop Iran, Israel is ready to act."

Two years earlier, the Prime Minister had put his country on "P Plus" alert—code for a pre-attack mode on Iran, later backing off due to opposition from his Chairman of the Joint Chiefs of Staff. As the window of opportunity for striking out at Iran gets smaller, it will be interesting to see who backs down in the months ahead.

As Iran has drawn closer to developing a nuclear weapons capability, an interesting dichotomy has manifested itself in regards to allies and non-allies assisting either Israel or the U.S. in a pre-emptive strike against Tehran.

While not acknowledging publicly it will do so, Saudi Arabia has enough of a concern about a nuclear-armed Iran simply to look the other way should Israel violate Saudi airspace to conduct such an attack.

Meanwhile, in a stunning response to an unofficial U.S. request for global access to U.K. airbases to stage its aircraft for such an attack, London has said "no."

In an October 25, 2012 article in The Guardian, reporter Nick Hopkins indicated the U.S. request was denied as secret legal advice warned a pre-emptive strike might be in breach of international law on the basis that Iran does not yet represent a "clear and present threat." It is unclear whether such a threat manifests itself when Iran acquires a nuclear "bullet" or whether the bullet has to be heading toward a U.K. target to so qualify.

The assumption by the U.K. is that it will only become involved in an ongoing conflict but not in an effort to start one. And, with a "see no evil, speak no evil, hear no evil" approach to the possibility of a pre-emptive strike, London prefers not even to be told if one is to be launched. The U.K.'s Foreign Office has made clear that it "does not believe military action against Iran is the right course of action at this time, although no option is off the table." In any event, as the West wastes time spinning its wheels trying to define what constitutes a threat, Iran continues to build it.

Iran has warned the U.S. an attack by Israel will be considered an attack by the U.S. as well, making U.S. targets subject to Iranian retaliation. Of course, based on the marksmanship of Iran's surface-to-surface missile launcher and antiaircraft battery crews to date in missing misidentified targets, the U.S. may not have much to worry about.

As another indicator of Iranian influence over Baghdad, Iraqi Prime Minister al-Maliki has informed the U.S. that Washington would be held responsible for any violation of Iraqi airspace by Israeli planes.

It seems fairly obvious that regardless of what the U.S. does or does not do, it will be held responsible as if it is involved. It is too bad neither Iraq nor the U.S. hold Iran responsible to the same standard on actions for which Tehran has actually been responsible.

The second wild card that could come into play is an uprising by the Iranian people.

There comes a point in time in the history of most autocracies when the people have had enough—i.e., they finally reach their breaking point. Marie Antoinette and Louis XVI of France discovered this the hard way in days of old, as did Moamar Ghadafi and Hosni Mubarak in modern times. The Arab Spring's run through the Middle East has been a chain reaction of these breaking points where one country's revolution sets off another's.

That the region was a tinder box of these breaking points on the verge of igniting was evidenced by how easily the chain reaction began.

Years from now, few people will remember the name of Tarek al-Tayeb Mohamed Bouazizi—a frustrated street vendor in Tunisia who on December 17, 2010 set himself on fire after his wares were confiscated and corrupt authorities harassed him for money to get them back.

His sacrifice released the pent up emotions of an entire nation, followed by those of a region. The revolution Bouazizi ignited toppled, in less than one month, a dictator who had ruled Tunisia for 23 years. Had it been known by the end of 2010 the impact Bouazizi's act of sacrifice would have on the entire Middle East, he would have been a worthy candidate for Time magazine's 2010 "Man of the Year."

But what Bouazizi and all those who rose up in protest after him have proven is that the people of a nation hold the key to their own destiny. Sometimes it just takes reaching that breaking point to realize they do have that power. That breaking point is reached when one realizes what one has to gain far outweighs all one has to lose—including one's own life.

The Arab Spring has shown the world there are millions of Middle Easterners who have done this calculation and opted to act against their undemocratic governments.

Do the Iranian people have another revolution in them? Former IRGC/CIA agent Kahlili says "yes." In a September 2012 interview he reported:

> "…regime change is earnestly desired by many people in Iran who despise its rulers and Islamic doctrine for their lack of basic freedoms and reduced economic status."

He added, those in power represent a:

> "…minority who are the true believers in Islam and take everything literally from the Quran… (welcoming) martyrdom… with open arms."

There does appear to be fight left in the Iranian people as evidenced by a mass protest that took place on October 3, 2012.

In an October 8, 2012 article by Reza Fard entitled "Iran's Political and Economic Crisis," the author hits on the crux of the unrest that had 20,000 protestors on the streets of Tehran within a few hours:

> "The anti-government demonstrations on October 3 in Tehran following Iran currency's free fall unveiled a grave crisis in the country. Analysts correctly point to the economic sanctions as a partial cause of the problems the regime is facing. But this is not the complete story. What transpired in Iran during the past week is the result of grave political and economic crises reflected in a widespread and deep popular discontent.

"The regime's authorities claim that the demonstrations did not just involve the Bazaaris (bazaar merchants and workers) but also rioters. The term 'rioter' is a reference to young protesters of the 2009 uprisings. According to the international media, including Reuters and CNN, Iran's main merchant association said last week that the demonstrations had been arranged by the Mujahedin-e Khalq (MEK), which was removed from United States' terrorist organizations list last week.

"The demonstrations manifested profound disenchantment among Iranians which had been simmering, albeit beneath the surface, following the deadly suppression of the 2009 uprisings. In fact, due to the severity of unemployment and inflation it has only deepened. The expression of protest by the Bazaaris, traditionally considered the regime's economic backbone, is an indication of the depth of the crisis.

"The protests first began with calling for the reduction in foreign currency rate but soon turned political and against the regime. The protesters screamed at the authorities to 'leave Syria alone and think of a solution for us.' YouTube clips show that the crowd is shouting 'down with Khamenei.' The Boston Globe wrote that people carried signs 'we don't want nuclear energy.' When the regime began a brutal crackdown, the protesters set fire to trash cans and attacked government offices and banks.

"Events of the past week, particularly the anti-government slogans during the protests, underscore the following three facts:

"The nature of the Iranian crisis and the popular discontent and their aspirations for change;

"The necessity of strengthening sanctions and to close all loopholes to further pressure the regime;

"The necessity to complement the sanctions with a new approach to the Iranian opposition to facilitate a fundamental change in Iran. In other words sanctions, alone, will not be sufficient.

"What caused the eruption of the protests was not the currency free fall. That was only a contributing factor. A more fundamental factor is the political crisis which Supreme Leader Ali Khamenei has tried hard to contain but has failed. The crisis in and of itself displays a rift that has appeared at the top of the regime.

"A day before the demonstration, during a press conference, Mahmoud Ahmadinejad publicly slammed on the Speaker of the Parliament, the head of the Judiciary and even the IRGC, all under Khamenei's command. A few days earlier while in New York, Ahmadinejad's media advisor was arrested and jailed in Tehran. And in the wake of the currency crisis, the Parliament Speaker blamed Ahmadinejad for the situation.

"For two years, Iran's economy has been in recession and crisis. According to a study done by the World Bank, in 2012 Iran's economic growth has been calculated at -0.7. Authorities have declared the inflation rate to be 22 percent. The rate is the highest across the Middle East. Nevertheless, independent economists estimate the rate of inflation at 50 percent based on various indications. This, in today's world, is only comparable to the economic situation in Zimbabwe."

Unemployment, according to official reports, stands at 13 percent but various other estimates suggest that it is closer to 30 percent. Since last year, the price of gas (the main energy source used in most Iranian households) has gone up tenfold; electricity sevenfold and diesel fuel 21-fold. A large part of the country's population has fallen below the poverty line.

"Iran's foreign currency began to fall in early 2011. The fall was moderate at the beginning. But in recent months it dropped repeatedly at an unprecedented rate...

"The sanctions have undoubtedly had their effect. Oil revenue is halved since last year and the government cannot inject foreign currency into the market like last year. But the sanctions are only a catalyst. From an economic point of view, the first reason for inflation is high liquidity in the country following many years of high oil revenues...

"The second factor (is) the investment capital leaving the country. People want to transfer their capital abroad. That is because they have no hope for the future...

"Meanwhile, the political infighting at the top is denying the regime the ability to manage and control the crises, including the currency crisis. By taking wrong measures and obstructing the efforts of other factions, they only provide fuel to the fire.

"Currently, the regime faces five major challenges for which finding a solution seems impossible:

"Discontent in the country ready to erupt at any opportunity;

"The prospect of Assad's overthrow in Syria that will mark the collapse of Tehran's regional front, Hezbollah's disarmament, and vulnerability against possible Israeli attack;

"Factional feuding at the top of the ruling clique;

"Economic downfall; and

"Tensions created by the nuclear program in the regime's relations with the West."

It appears Iran's mullahs recognize their people pose a problem to their rule as a possible wild card. It was enough of a concern that in early July 2012, they pulled 275 members of their Qods Force out of Syria and back to Iran due to a deteriorating domestic economic crisis.

It is not known whether the driving motivation for withdrawing the Qods Force was financial (it is estimated Iran has spent $5 billion to support Assad at a time its cash is being depleted due to significantly reduced revenues) or lack of confidence by Tehran's leadership in Assad's ability to survive.

Ahmadinejad delivered a speech before the U.N. General Assembly in New York City on September 26, 2012—his last as Iran's president—offering a nine-point plan concerning the resolution of its nuclear program which, as usual, provided no significant break-through. It stood out as the first speech he has given that was somewhat mellow compared to his others, although the mellowing did not last long. The Holocaust-denier returned to his old self, accusing the West of nuclear "intimidation and claimed Iran is under threat of military action from 'uncivilized Zionists.'"

As Ahmadinejad spoke about his vision for a "new world order," he told delegates:

> *"God willing, a new order will come together and we'll do away with everything that distances us. I do believe the system of empires has reached the end of the road. The world can no longer see an emperor commanding it."*

It was odd to hear such a statement emanating from one constantly preaching that the Mahdi is returning to do just that.

In a slap in the face to Ahmadinejad and reflection of the living nightmare he has created in Iran, while he was speaking at the UN, his cameraman, Hassan Gol Khanban, was applying for asylum in the U.S. Undoubtedly embarrassing for the brutal dictator, it could not have been more appropriately scripted as a final farewell for the Islamic blowhard.

While there may be a range of factors involved in creating a breaking point for a nation's people as frustrations continue to mount, it would appear many are found in Iran today. And, with additional sanctions possible for Iran's gas exports, the distance to that breaking point may be further reduced.

It cannot be denied the sanctions imposed on Iran have had a drastic impact on its economy, creating immense hardship on its people and edging them closer and closer to their breaking point.

As additional sanctions kicked in for Iran on July 1, 2012, it was noted that oil revenues for July were less than one-third what they were the previous year—down from $9.8 billion to $2.9 billion, as reported by Rhodium Group partner, Trevor Houser.

But Houser made a very astute observation:

> *"The challenge is it doesn't seem to have much of an impact [on Iran's behavior]."*

The most recent IAEA report supports this, stating Iran has doubled its capacity to produce higher-enriched uranium in an underground facility.

Ironically, although Iran is a country sitting atop oil and gas reserves estimated to total $10 trillion, it becomes the third country of the 21st century (joining Zimbabwe and North Korea) to experience hyperinflation (i.e., an economy experiencing a monthly inflation rate of 50% or more) and the first country in the Middle East to do so.

Iran's currency has plummeted, losing more than 80 percent of the value it had at the end of 2011—falling from 13,000 rials per U.S. dollar to 35,000. The tumble seems to be gaining momentum as it dropped 17% within a 24 hour span in September 2012. The quick pace of the depreciation has shocked Iranians. Many foreign companies are refusing to deal with Iranian companies. Impacting frustrations in Iran as well is a high inflation (23% before the latest dive of the rial) and unemployment rate (22.5% in 2012).

Ahmadinejad is personally feeling the heat of the economic tailspin.

The Iranian parliament in early November 2012 sent him a summons to answer their charges of his mismanagement of the economy and the currency crash—giving him a month to respond. The parliament also wants to investigate charges of unauthorized and illegal luxury car imports at a time only vital goods like medicines were to be imported.

This will be the second such interrogation he has faced this year as in March he was interrogated over his cabinet appointments and his confrontational relationship with Khamenei.

Later, after Ahmadinejad had a confrontation with a Khamenei-appointed official heading Iran's judiciary, Sadegh Larijani, over Larijani's demand Ahmadinejad obtain his authorization before visiting a political ally imprisoned at the Erin prison facility, Khamenei finally announced that political infighting would be viewed as treason.

Ahmadinejad subsequently agreed to obey Khamenei's orders—but not without getting in one last dig at Larijani. Ahmadinejad noted in the letter he remained "the highest official rank after the Supreme Leader."

Interestingly, one area of Iran's economy that has blossomed under the sanctions is tourism. While the average growth of tourism worldwide is 3.2%, Iran's has almost quadrupled during the last year to 12.7%. More than three million tourists contributed over two billion dollars in badly needed currency. Most come for religious purposes as only about 20,000 came for non-religious reasons. Most tourists falling into the non-religious category included Chinese and German visitors.

Another factor contributing to the frustrations of the Iranian people is living life in a real world dystopia, where they feel dehumanized by a leadership that thrives on instilling fear in their daily lives.

The 20th century witnessed yet another factor that contributes to a population's frustrations, eventually manifesting itself in an outbreak of civil disturbance.

In his 2002 report entitled "The National Security Implications of Global Demographic Change," CIA Inspector General John L. Helgerson considered a factor known as the "youth bulge."

This is the theory a youth bulge occurs when 30%-40% of a country's population falls within "fighting age"—i.e., ages 15-29. It occurs when a country's fertility rates have hit 4-8 births per woman, followed by a 15-29 year delay. The convergence of these events increases the likelihood the frustrations of the young people in this age group will generate civil disturbance.

It is estimated about one-third of Iran's population today is within this category with more than half its population under 35 years of age.

Interestingly, the fertility rate as of the 1979 Islamic Revolution was 6.2, hitting 6.5 in 1982, before heading into steady decline. By 1993, the birth rate had fallen under the minimum 4.0 births per woman to meet the youth bulge requirement and by 2009 had tumbled all the way down to 1.7 births. This was well under the 2.1 births necessary for a population to maintain its current level. The 1.7 birthrate also reflects the population's loss of hope in bearing children who would be ruled by such a brutal leadership. But, with the 15-29 year delay, the youth bulge still exists as a contributing factor in Iran today.

Because this generation was born after the Islamic Revolution, it is known as the "The Generation of the Revolution" (1979-1994).

Other factors contributing to the volatility of the youth bulge is a lack of regular, peaceful employment opportunities with a high literacy rate (80% for Iran in 2007). With fewer jobs available, the younger generation spends more time pursuing further education—but still suffers from high unemployment even though it is very well educated.

Ahmadinejad has already felt the sting of an angry youth bulge when a 2006 speech he gave at Amirkabir University of Technology in Tehran was cut short after students shouted him down with "Death to the dictator." Used to shouting such a chant at "the Great Satan (the U.S.)," Ahmadinejad was jolted when he found himself on the chant's receiving end.

This generation is beginning to push the edge of the envelope by testing how far they can contest existing restrictions, everything from anti-government activism to the size of women's veils.

The 2009 presidential election in which Ahmadinejad was awarded an unearned victory by Supreme Leader Khamenei generated numerous protests by the people. A government that would not tolerate opposition crushed a population that would not receive aid or support from the U.S.

An American hero, Dr. Martin Luther King, recognized the importance of having a breaking point, noting:

> "Our lives begin to end the day we become silent about things that matter."

Hopefully, the voice of the Iranian people—having reached their final breaking point—will once again be heard.

Conclusion

In April 2010, a British Petroleum (BP) oil rig exploded in the Gulf of Mexico, triggering the largest accidental marine spill in petroleum industry history. Oil flowed continuously into the sea, polluting the environment for three months until the leaking well was capped.

What if BP's efforts to address the leak focused simply on cleaning up and containing the oil spewing out of the well rather than on capping the well from which it spewed?

Obviously, such an approach—attacking the aftereffects of the spill rather than the source causing them—would have proven foolish, a waste of resources, and brought no resolution to the one problem responsible for causing so many other environmental issues. Damage created by the well would simply continue to occur until it ran dry.

It is logical, therefore, to recognize, where several other problems stem from a central one, the most effective solution involves attacking the latter so it will stop generating the others.

Why then not apply such logic to the conduct of U.S. foreign policy—specifically to a country like Iran so sick with hatred, intolerance and violence that it has become a cancer spreading to many other parts of the world, where it spreads its disease?

A retired Bahrainian general made the analogy that Iran's 1979 Islamic revolution gave birth to an "octopus"—with its head located in Tehran but its tentacles reaching far beyond its borders. Those tentacles stretch to Iraq, Afghanistan, Lebanon, Yemen, Gaza, the West Bank, Venezuela, Syria, Sudan, etc. To whatever length Tehran's tentacles stretch, trouble for the Western world brews.

But severing a tentacle in one hot spot will not stop the Iranian octopus from pursuing elsewhere the destabilization it seeks to pave the way for Islamic extremism. The octopus has an amazing capability to regenerate a severed limb, so even a policy of attacking its extremities will not solve the problem. The only way to stop its destructive ways is to go to the source—by severing its head.

For Iran, this means regime change. Tehran can no longer exist as a theocracy tied to a dangerous Belief and Goal because it is endangering the entire international community. Tehran's HIV regimen can no longer be tolerated. Tehran must, therefore, be forced to undergo regime change for it will never surrender its Goal.

This book has focused on explaining what drives the Iranian leadership to embark on a journey to a destination from which it refuses to be re-directed. The West has attempted to stop Tehran's transit but has only succeeded in slowing it down.

There are only three loves for which the risk of life is justified: love of human life; love of country; and love of God. Iran's leaders have demonstrated they lack the first two. It is their love of Allah based on their contorted view of Islam—manifested in the belief the Madhi will soon create a new world order in accordance with their distorted vision—that drives them toward their final destination. But what empowers them to defy logic and all other threats—whether economic or military—is the additional belief they, and they alone, have been ordained to deliver believers to the Twelfth Imam—their final destination.

Because those attempting to negotiate with Iran do so guided by a sense of reasonableness, they fail to understand no reasonable deterrent is capable of stopping the Iranian leadership's journey. Former IRGC/ex-CIA Agent Reza Kahlili has said as much in a September 2012 interview:

> "I think the central delusion of Western leaders is that they refuse to understand the ideology behind the actions of the

> *Islamic regime. Basically the ideology of the radicals in Iran is to stand against every principle of Western society...They believe that the Islamic regime was put in place by Allah and that the end of days are at hand and their studies of the hadiths, which are centuries old sayings by prophet Mohammed and his descendants, are representative of what is going to take shape in the world."*

Kahlili added concerning Iran's nuclear program:

> *"There is nothing you can do to bring about a change of behavior and therefore the failure of the approach that every U.S. Administration has taken...They have shown that they are not logical people by Western standards. They are not rational people as some U.S. officials have suggested."*

It is said the definition of insanity is doing the same thing over and over again, expecting a different result. The West continues to negotiate with Iran over and over again, despite the fact there has been no change in its commitment to develop a nuclear weapon.

If reason were a factor in the Iranian leadership's thinking, why did it not come into play on their own behalf to save the lives of Iranian children used to clear minefields during the Iran-Iraq war? Why did it not come into play to cut that war short by six years? Why does it not come into play to stop a domestic execution rate in the world second only to China?

(Note: For 2011, the total number of prisoner executions in Iran was more than 600. Many have been charged with "moharbeh" which is the crime of "waging war against God"—i.e., code for "waging war against the mullahs." Thirteen prisoners were hanged within a four day timeframe in September 2012. The rate of public executions can be expected to increase further as economic conditions worsen and the mullahs fear a massive uprising. Furthermore, evidence of Iran's total lack of concern about its high execution rate was demonstrated in 2007. U.N. High Commissioner for Human Rights Louise Arbour attended a Non-Aligned Movement event in Tehran. Following Arbour's appearance, Iranian officials crowed that the

U.N. had "taken part in the conference at the highest level"—and then proceeded to execute 21 people the day after she departed.)

While Iran's lack of reason has been demonstrated in its dealings with non-believers, it is its lack of reason in dealing with its own people that should most concern non-believers. If the killing of hundreds of thousands of their own people does not give the leadership pause to reconsider its journey, what will, and what does that say about what they are willing to do to non-believers?

Iran runs a serious risk of duplicating—on a vastly larger scale—a tragedy occurring more than three decades ago making headlines that left many people shaking their heads in disbelief: mass suicide.

A self-declared minister, Jim Jones, had started a religious cult in the U.S. However, when its actions came under investigation by the U.S. Government, Jones convinced his followers in 1977 to accompany him to property the "church" had purchased in Guyana. It was being developed as a camp where Jones sought to escape American capitalism and U.S. Government scrutiny, practicing a more communal life. The Guyanese colony was known as Jonestown.

After Jones and his flock departed, families back in the U.S. of cult members who relocated raised concerns about their loved ones' health and safety at Jonestown. It triggered a visit by U.S. Congressman Leo Ryan of California. When some cult members sought to return to the U.S. with Ryan, they were gunned down, along with the congressman, while trying to board his plane.

Realizing his dictatorial utopia would soon end, Jones assembled his 912 followers. He told them the only way to preserve their church was to make the ultimate sacrifice—"revolutionary suicide" by taking their own lives en masse.

Large vats of Kool-Aid, laced with poison consisting of cyanide, sedatives, and tranquilizers, were set out. Parents were instructed to give it to their children first and then drink it themselves. One-third of those who died were children in what, until 9/11, was the largest single loss of civilian life in a non-natural disaster. As the bodies of the cultists twisted in painful death contortions, Jones took the easy way out—putting a bullet through his head.

In an audio recording of the massacre (it is called a "massacre" although most participation was voluntary), Jones is heard feeding church members conspiracy theories about intelligence organizations conspiring against Jonestown and commandos who would parachute in on them and kill "our innocent babies." The hypocrisy of killing all their babies themselves to avoid such a far-fetched fate by the commandos was lost upon cult members who obediently gave their children the poison.

Hypocrisy never seemed to be a problem for Jones as his followers never questioned his use of it. As an example, four years before he led his congregation to Guyana, Jones had been arrested and charged with soliciting homosexual sex in a public men's room. Later, he claimed to be "the only true heterosexual" in the congregation. He proceeded to sexually abuse a male member of the church to prove the man's own homosexual tendencies!

That so many parents would have so willingly and so blindly followed Jones's mandate for "revolutionary suicide," sacrificing their lives and those of their children based on the ludicrous claims of such a false prophet, is very disturbing. Although in 1978 the occurrence of a voluntary mass suicide was thought to be impossible, today we know differently.

But is it possible for a nation to commit "revolutionary suicide?" Will that too prove to be an event today we believe to be impossible, only to find out differently tomorrow? Iran's future holds the answer.

Little difference exists between the Jonestown leaders and Iran's.

Both preached conspiracy theories to masses who believed/believe them. Both placed/place little or no value on human life, not even that of a child.

Both have played/play the religion card to make followers do what each needed/needs to have done. Jonestown's poison was in the form of Kool-Aid; if Iran's comes, it will come in the form of nuclear retaliation.

Former IRGC/ex-CIA agent Kahlili provides certification as to the madness of the Iranian leadership:

> *"The Supreme Leader...believe(s)... (he is) mandated to create an environment for the coming of Imam Mahdi...one or two nuclear weapons launched against Israel would destroy Israel. There would be retaliation and millions of Iranians would die, innocent Iranians who oppose this regime and then there would be chaos throughout the world...at that time Imam Mahdi would return. This appears to Westerners who have lived with logic and the consequences of the bad behavior, not to make sense. We all automatically refute this and believe that nobody is that crazy. However, they are."*

Like children in the West in anticipation of Christmas morning gifts, Kahlili says about the anticipation of the Mahdi's arrival by Iran's leadership:

> *"They are very excited with what's happening in the Middle East because they believe these are signs spoken of centuries ago that the end of times is near. The triggers are needed to create that environment for Imam Mahdi to come.*
>
> *"Ayatollah Khomeini, the founder of the Islamic Revolution said it himself. He had three goals for the revolution. One was to topple the Shah and the Monarchy, two was to establish an Islamic state and three was to pass the flag of Islam to Imam Mahdi. It was said that within the circles of the top officials in Iran that Ayatollah Khamenei is the one*

who is going to pass the flag of Islam to Imam Mahdi so they truly believe in this."

While the unfortunate fate of the Jonestown followers has played out, Iran's has yet to do so.

A common thread links many of the world's current problem areas. Anti-Americanism and/or international instability is fostered in places like Iraq, Afghanistan, Gaza, the West Bank, Lebanon, Yemen, Somalia, Bahrain, Venezuela, Mexico, etc., by a common source. That source, Iran, is so committed to the annihilation of America and Western culture, it has proven capable of doing something Western scholars of Islam once thought impossible: setting aside centuries of sectarian violence to cooperate in a common cause against the West.

During the Cold war, the Soviet Union fostered similar anti-Americanism and instability. But major differences exist between Moscow's and Tehran's approaches. The Soviets knew limits existed as to the actions they could undertake either directly and indirectly — and acted accordingly. When the U.S. made it clear, for example, that a national security line had been crossed with the 1962 placement of Soviet missiles in Cuba, Moscow backed down. Iran is not similarly constrained, only becoming more and more brazen in its violent actions against the U.S.

When Islamic extremists came to power in Iran in 1979, they immediately made it clear—with the seizure of the U.S. Embassy in Tehran—confrontation was the order of the day, with international law and tradition posing no obstacle to Iran's leadership.

Evidence clearly shows Tehran was involved, either directly or indirectly, in the 1983 suicide truck bombing of the U.S. Marine Barracks in Lebanon, in the 1996 Khobar Towers attack in Saudi Arabia and in the 9/11 attacks. In Afghanistan and Iraq, thousands of U.S. casualties have been claimed by Iranian IEDs or, in the case of the Karbala attack—the direct action of Iranian special forces. Meanwhile, Iran prepares to do battle in America's backyard as its terrorist puppet organization, Hezbollah, has deployed to Venezuela where it is building a missile base and linking up with drug cartels to be able to penetrate the U.S. border—possibly carrying a nuclear device as Kahlili has forewarned.

Iran is clearly a country at war with the U.S.

Iran's leadership has reached a high confidence level in acting against the U.S. because it believes Allah is running interference for it. The Iranians also see the West so committed to an appeasement policy that it remains clueless on how to stop Tehran's nuclear juggernaut.

Historically, U.S. perceptions of Iran's leadership have been overly optimistic. The evolution of relations between Tehran and Washington since the Islamic revolution has witnessed an enormous gap with little, if anything, in common to bridge it.

This has been evidenced by completely contrary objectives in Lebanon, Iraq, the Israeli/Palestinian conflict and Sudan. It would be irresponsible, therefore, after a long chain of Iranian presidents pretty much cut from the same cloth in their total disregard for citizens' rights both inside and outside Iran, to allow oneself to be fooled by the perception such a chain might be broken with a dynamic new leader evolving from within the same theocratic infrastructure. The idealist wants to believe it; the realist simply cannot afford to.

The message from Iran's leadership as to its future intentions is clearly visible: "Sign, sign, everywhere a sign." The West refuses to accept those signs as warnings.

Ahmadinejad has his gun sights set on nuclear war with the U.S. Just as the signs were there of Major Hasan, the Fort Hood shooter, being predisposed to undertake violence before he did on November 5, 2009, they are there for Ahmadinejad as well. There should be no confusion here, as there was with Hasan, that, in Ahmadinejad, we are dealing with a serious radical extremist threat determined to rain violence upon us. Like Hasan was then, Ahmadinejad is now a "ticking time bomb" waiting to go off. But this time, unless action is taken to cut the fuse beforehand, the big difference will be when it detonates, it will be of nuclear proportion.

An October 8, 2012 National Review Online article entitled "Obama's Iran Policy: A Timeline" by Anne Bayefsky details the President's "approach to the preeminent danger to world peace—Iran." She notes:

> "Here is a timeline of the Obama administration's Iran policy, as the world's most dangerous nation and leading state sponsor of terrorism moves inexorably towards acquiring the world's most dangerous weapon."

Bayefsky tracks some of the Administration's comments made over the past three years made to "intimidate" Iran into cooperating on the nuclear issue:

- "My expectation would be that if we can begin discussions soon, shortly after the Iranian elections, we should have a fairly good sense by the end of the year as to whether they are moving in the right direction..." President Obama, May 18, 2009, Washington, D.C.

- "The opportunity will not remain open indefinitely." Secretary Clinton, July 15, 2009, Washington, D.C.

- "[W]e are not going to keep the window open forever." Secretary Clinton, July 22, 2009, Bangkok, Thailand.

- "[T]he Iranians may simply try to run out the clock." Defense Secretary Robert Gates, July 27, 2009.

- "Our patience is not infinite. We're not willing to let this go on forever." State Department Spokesman Ian Kelly, September 14, 2009, Washington, D.C.

- *"If Iran does not take steps in the near future to live up to its obligations, then the United States will not continue to negotiate indefinitely...Our patience is not unlimited."* President Obama, October 1, 2009, Washington, D.C.

- *"We are in what we hope is an intensive diplomatic phase now. It will not be open-ended."* Office of the Press Secretary, October 1, 2009, Geneva, Switzerland.

- *"I don't think that there's a hard-and-fast deadline...What we have said all along is that this is not an open-ended process, we are not in this just to talk for talk's sake...[W]e expect prompt, concrete steps to be taken over the next couple of weeks."* State Department Spokesman Ian Kelly, October 2, 2009, Washington, D.C.

- *"We are running out of time."* President Obama, November 15, 2009, Shanghai, China.

- *"Time is running out for Iran to address the international community's growing concerns about its nuclear program."* Press Secretary Gibbs, November 29, 2009, Washington, D.C.

- *"Iran has to live up to its international obligations...The president has said that our patience is not unlimited."* State Department Spokesman Ian Kelly, November 30, 2009, Washington, D.C.

- *"[T]he window is closing."* National Security Advisor Jim Jones, December 2, 2009, Washington, D.C.

- *"Iran's nuclear program...there was going to be a time limit..."* President Obama, March 30, 2010, Washington, D.C.

- *"We've said to the Iranians all along...we still remain open to diplomacy. But it's been very clear that the Iranians don't want to engage with us."* Secretary Clinton, September 19, 2010.

- *"We want to see the Iranians engage, and as you know, we have attempted to bring about that engagement over the course of the last three-plus years. It has not proven effective."* Secretary Clinton, December 12, 2011, Washington, D.C.

- *"To resolve this issue will require Iran to come to the table and discuss in a clear and forthright way how to prove to the international community that the intentions of their nuclear program are peaceful...[T]he question is going to be whether in these discussions they show themselves moving clearly in that direction."* President Obama, March 6, 2012, Washington, D.C.

- *"[T]hat window is closing."* President Obama, March 25, 2012, Seoul, Republic of Korea.

- *"[T]ime is short."* President Obama, March 26, 2012, Seoul, Republic of Korea.

- *"Iran's window of opportunity...will not remain open forever."* Secretary Clinton, March 31, 2012, Riyadh, Saudi Arabia.

- "They assert that their program is purely peaceful...We want them to demonstrate clearly in the actions they propose that they have truly abandoned any nuclear weapons ambition." Secretary Clinton, April 12, 2012, Washington, D.C.

- *"[T]hat window is closing...Now, the clock is ticking...[W]e're not going to have these talks just drag out in a stalling process... [W]e haven't given away anything—other than the opportunity for us to negotiate."* President Obama, April 15, 2012, Cartagena, Columbia.

- *"We will not engage in an endless process of negotiations."* UN Ambassador Susan Rice, September 20, 2012, New York.

- *"Iran...has failed to take the opportunity to demonstrate that its nuclear program is peaceful...time is not unlimited."* President Obama, September 25, 2012, New York."

- As to what the President seems to accept as negotiations with Iran, a critic notes, *"History has another name for such delusional diplomacy—appeasement."*

Such non-intimidation of Iran has resulted, during Obama's term in office, in Iran going from possessing 3.5 percent low-enriched uranium *"sufficient for a nuclear weapons breakout capability in February 2009, to the production of 190 kilograms of 20 percent enriched uranium at the Fordo underground nuclear site this August (2012),"* according to the IAEA.

U.S. foreign policy towards Iran—through numerous administrations—has been one of conflict avoidance. It has involved burying one's head in the sand, hoping the problem will go away, as Iran continues to kill more Americans. It has been one of offering Tehran time, economic incentives, apologies, etc., to which there has been no reciprocal response. It has been one of Tehran using U.S. overtures as a basis for moving forward with its ultimate Goal.

In a 180 degree turn from the 2007 National Intelligence Estimate made during George Bush's administration which indicated Iran had stopped its nuclear weapons program, an Israeli newspaper reported the following in August 2012:

> *"President Barack Obama recently received a new National Intelligence Estimate report on the Iranian nuclear program, which shares Israel's view that Iran has made surprising, significant progress toward military nuclear capability."*

Concerning this report, Israeli Defense Secretary Ehud Barak responded:

> *"As far as we know it brings the American assessment much closer to ours ... it makes the Iranian issue even more urgent and (shows it is) less clear and certain that*

we will know everything in time about their steady progress toward military nuclear capability."

In August 2012, the Israeli Ambassador to the U.S. warns time is very short in being able to take action against Iran:

> "A combination of truly crippling sanctions and a credible military threat — a threat that the ayatollahs still do not believe today — may yet convince Iran to relinquish its nuclear dreams. But time is dwindling and, with each passing day, the lives of 8 million Israelis grow increasingly imperiled. The window that opened 20 years ago is almost shut."

In late September 2012, Iran's efforts to make the IAEA verification process—to determine the true intentions of Tehran's nuclear program—as confusing as possible received yet another "tweak."

The head of Iran's Atomic Energy Organization, Fereydoon Abbasi, acknowledged Tehran has lied to the IAEA on its reports. It sought to justify doing so by the fact British intelligence was spying on the program and Tehran simply sought to protect it. It indicated it reported some strengths as weaknesses and vice versa. While the fact the lying was acknowledged is a surprise, the practice of doing it—known as "taqiya" as explained earlier—is not.

As recently as October 21, 2012, France's foreign minister reported experts "have established in an absolutely indisputable way...(Iran is) on track to reach the ability to produce a nuclear weapon by the first half of next year."

That assessment suggests a little longer fuse exists than did a November 17, 2011 assessment by IAEA Director General Yukiya Amano.

After issuing a very scathing report concerning Iran's efforts to develop nuclear weapons based on research and experiments it has been conducting, Amano warned Tehran is on track to have one in less than a year. The assessment was made by IAEA experts putting together a *"clear, coherent and consistent picture"* on Iran's activities.

The IAEA assessment was extensive as Amano reported:

> *"Throughout the past three years, we have obtained additional information which gives us a fuller picture of Iran's nuclear program and increases our concerns about possible military dimensions."* Accordingly, he added, *"I must alert the world."*

Weeks after Amano felt obligated to "alert the world" about Iran's intentions, new evidence came to light of at least two more additional sites, previously unknown to the outside world, where Tehran was undertaking development of a nuclear weapon.

An IRGC spy reported one site was just outside the city of Shahrokhabad in Kerman Province codenamed "Fateh1," meaning "victorious." It was reported that uranium ore at the facility is processed into yellow cake for further conversion into enriched uranium.

Another source reported Iran is "operating another nuclear site at which scientists are testing a neutron detonator and implosion system for a nuclear bomb as well as on a nuclear warhead design and enrichment to weaponization levels."

Former CIA official Peter Vincent Pry sees this evidence as ominous, noting, "If any of these allegations (concerning two new sites) is even partially true, the whole timeline for Iran developing a nuclear weapon must be recalculated. The advent of a nuclear-armed Iran is much nearer than assumed by the Obama administration."

Those concerned about Iran obtaining nuclear weapons forewarn that the impact will be a true Domino Effect on the region as Tehran threatens Sunni states to capitulate to the mullahs' demands or face the consequences. Already sensing they are losing the U.S. as a loyal ally, several Middle Eastern states have started re-arming and are considering nuclear weapons programs of their own to be able to respond to an Iranian threat.

In nature, many animals mark their territory to warn males of the same species not to cross over a certain demarcation line. That line is either respected or disregarded at the violator's own peril.

Similarly, a demarcation line—called by some proponents as a "red line"—is needed to forewarn Iran there is a point beyond which it proceeds at its own peril. Tehran needs to be put on notice crossing that point will immediately be deemed by the West as a declaration of war by Iran (although Iran's conduct to date indicates such a declaration has already been issued) based on its hostile intent to use nuclear weapons. While the decision to cross that line is Iran's, it should have no doubt what the cost of exercising it will be.

Allowing Iran to step over that line without taking action permits Tehran to then establish a "zone of immunity"—a point at which Iranian uranium enrichment facilities will have been buried so deep underground that US or Israeli bombs would be unable to penetrate to such a depth.

Israeli Prime Minister Netanyahu stated at the U.N. in September 2012 where he draws his red line—experts say it is the point that Iran amasses enough uranium, enriched to 20%, that could quickly be enriched further to produce a nuclear device.

One of the better known quotes by the 18th century Irish statesman Edmond Burke is, *"All that is necessary for the triumph of evil is that good men do nothing."* The same is applicable to nations.

In his October 11, 2012 article entitled "Netanyahu's speech and the Ostrich Syndrome," Efraim Inbar of The Jerusalem Post makes a diagnosis as to an illness from which the international community suffers. He predicts its response to the Israeli Prime Minister's U.N. speech calling for a red line to be drawn for Iran's nuclear program will be to stick its collective head in the sand. Suffering from Ostrich Syndrome, the international community will do nothing:

> *"Most states prefer to ignore the bad news of nuclear proliferation. This happened with North Korea and it is being repeated in Iran. Members of the international community are reluctant to admit the stark reality because such an admission requires action, which they are hardly ready to take.*
>
> *"Indeed, most states ignore the extreme revolutionary nature of the Iran regime. Since 1979 a revolutionary outlook has sprung on top of an imperial tradition in Tehran. The mullahs want to export their radical Shi'ite version of Islam, and adopted a jihadist agenda. But we are told that they are rational just like us.*
>
> *"The Iranian leadership was responsible for killing Westerners in Lebanon and Saudi Arabia... and we are told that they are rational just like us. The Iranian leadership entertains the idea of bringing Andalusia (Spain) back into the Islamic fold... and we are told that they are rational just like us.*
>
> *"Iran plotted to assassinate the Saudi ambassador in the US... and we are told that they are rational like us.*

> *"Iran's President Mahmoud Ahmadinejad expressed his desire to remove Israel from the map... and we are told that he is rational just like us.*
>
> *"Ahmadinejad spoke to God and even got answers... and we are told he is rational just like us.*
>
> *"Similarly, the international community has ignored for more than a decade the progress in Iran's nuclear program and adheres to the illusion that talks will eventually dissuade them from building a nuclear bomb."*

Inbar notes, as the international community clings to its desperate belief there is always time for negotiations to achieve meaningful results, it is overcome by events:

> *"...The inevitable conclusion from the behavior of the international community is that it consistently opts for an easy, harmless transition from 'there is still time to do something' to 'it's too late to do something.'*
>
> *"A large part of the international community belittles the wide-ranging repercussions of a nuclear Iran.*
>
> *"Concerns about Iran 'Finlandizing' the oil producing nations in the Gulf and the Caspian Basin; nuclear proliferation in the Middle East; Iran nuclear terrorism; a security threat for states within a radius of 2,500 kilometers; the loss of Western credibility after repeated declarations that 'a nuclear Iran is unacceptable' are all dismissed as Israeli exaggerations or unfounded alarmism.*
>
> *"Western rationalist experts point out that Iran is 'rationale' and can be deterred. This is wishful thinking and reflects the prevalent ostrich mentality. There are numerous examples where Iran was undeterred even before owning a nuclear bomb.*

"Did the U.S. deter Iranian influence in Lebanon? No. Hezbollah took over the country. Did the U.S. curtail Iranian influence in Palestinian politics? No. Hamas took over Gaza in 2007. Did the U.S. deter Iran from turning Iraq into its satellite? No. Did the U.S. deter Iran from meddling in Bahrain? No. Did the U.S. deter Iran from assisting Assad stay in power in Syria? No. Did the U.S. deter Iran from establishing a presence in its backyard, in Venezuela, and penetrating Latin America? No.

"And all this inconvenient evidence is ignored by the Ostrich Syndrome-stricken strategists and statesmen.

"Deterrence works only if threats to use force are credible. Iran paused its nuclear program when the U.S. attacked Iraq in 2003. Unfortunately US President Barack Obama is not feared – with good reason. He is viewed in the Middle East by friends and foes of the U.S alike as a lightweight weakling. Obviously the Europeans hardly instill any fear in Tehran. The Tehran zoo provides a good picture of how ostriches behave."

Inbar reaches a stark realization by concluding:

*"At this late stage, after so many years, **nothing will stop the nuclear program except for the use of force**"* (emphasis added).

"The Iranians are smart enough to diagnose the international community with the Ostrich Syndrome and their prognosis is that they can get away with building a bomb, just like North Korea did. In the absence of a quick recovery from the Ostrich Syndrome, we are doomed to live in a more brutish world."

Critics knowledgeable about Iranian negotiating tactics have endeavored to educate U.S. negotiators about them:

> "The purpose of negotiations for an Iranian diplomat may not be to resolve a crisis or reach an agreed outcome, but rather to outsmart and get the best of one's adversary…the Persian term 'balie' can be translated 'yes' but real meaning depends on intonation, so one could be saying 'no.'"

> "Iranian diplomatic strategy is based on a completely different logic of outright strategic deception—language is used not to clarify but to intentionally confuse; if one party believes in building credibility by dealing above board with his counterparts and the other party uses deception and false pretense as part of his modus operandi, then diplomacy is bound to fail."

> "As the years passed and the West continued to attempt diplomatic engagement with Iran rather than fully confronting their deceptive diplomacy, Tehran had no incentive to change its approach."

Albert Einstein observed:

> "The world is a dangerous place. Not because of the people who are evil; but because of the people who don't do anything about it."

Einstein was making two observations: evil people exist in the world and such evil will prevail lest good people take action to eliminate it.

This was an appropriate observation by one who bore witness to the dangerous world that evolved prior to World War II as good people did nothing. Turning a blind eye to the evil of Nazism, they naively clung to British Prime Minister Neville Chamberlain's promise of "peace in our time."

What conditions give rise to such a dangerous world where good people do nothing? One of two factors prevails: either they are conscious of the threat but fear taking action against it; or they are unconscious of it, lacking a knowledgeable basis for acting in their own best interests. As to Iran, the U.S. Government fails to act out of fear; the American people fail to demand action from their government out of ignorance.

Thousands of years ago, in the days of the Sumerians who inhabited the flood plain of the lower reaches of the Tigris and Euphrates Rivers, the concept of the "lugal" evolved. It referred to a leader both feared and revered by his people. Having lived with this concept for almost five millennia, it has been a concept surviving into the 21st century.

Leaders like Saddam Hussein, Moamar Ghadafi, Bashar Assad—all are viewed in the light of the lugal. Where an enlightened leader might choose to eschew brutality, he would not be viewed as a lugal, but as a weak leader. The perception that has been handed down from the days of the Sumerians is that "nice guys finish last." It is the nice guy, who is overly trusting in dealing with one who is overly deceitful, that is taken advantage of to the latter's benefit.

Therefore, the numerous entreaties offered by President Obama to Iran have failed to have the impact he had hoped. Instead, it has had the opposite impact by conveying the message to the Muslim world American leaders are weak.

The failure of every U.S. president since the Islamists came to power in 1979 to retaliate for unprovoked aggression against the U.S. by Iran has only strengthened Tehran's resolve that it is on a religious mission to carry out Allah's will.

The U.S. failed to retaliate when U.S. servicemen were murdered in the Marine Barracks bombing in Beirut; or when U.S. servicemen were murdered at Khobar Towers in Saudi Arabia; or when U.S. civilians and servicemen were murdered on 9/11. Although, in many cases, it took years to find Iran's fingerprints on these and other acts of terrorism, the U.S. chose each time to do nothing other than warn Tehran not to do it again.

With its belief it is ordained by Allah to fulfill its mission, Tehran can only interpret such failures for the U.S. to retaliate as a sign Allah has intervened on its behalf—protecting Iran by tying the hands of the world's only superpower thus making it powerless to act.

In the Bible, God reportedly answered Daniel's prayers—sending an angel to protect him when King Darius placed him in a den of lions. The angel sealed the mouths of the lions shut. Similarly, the Iranian leadership believes Allah has answered its prayers by neutralizing America's ability to retaliate.

Despite Iranian tentacles reaching into Syria, Iraq, Afghanistan and elsewhere, President Ahmadinejad continues to blame the U.S. and Israel for the world's problems. On August 17, 2012, he declared Israel's existence an "insult to all of humanity." Only weeks earlier, he suggested to a group of Muslim diplomats in yet another example of hypocritical wordsmithing, *"anyone who loves freedom and justice must strive for the annihilation of the Zionist regime"* which would serve to *"solve all the world's problems."*

Perhaps Ahmadinejad sought to build upon Supreme Leader Khamenei's February 2012 statement encouraging Muslims to: *"Kill all Jews, annihilate Israel."* Sounding a bit "nuclear," he claimed he had a plan to wipe Israel out in just nine minutes and justified genocide as a moral obligation.

As The Miami Herald's Frida Ghitis noted in her August 8, 2012 article "Listen to What Iran is Saying" concerning the leadership's increasingly belligerent rhetoric:

> *"The Iranian regime has emerged as the world leader in Judeophobic conspiracy theories and incitement. Verbal taunts, smears and calumnies often include vicious attacks and libel against Americans, the U.S., and the West as a whole. Those who thought Ahmadinejad's words had been incorrectly translated in 2005 when he called for Israel to be 'wiped off the page of time,' have now heard ample and repeated clarification. That was exactly what he meant."*

Ahmadinejad is an Islamist so full of hatred for the West that were he given a button to push to eradicate all of Western civilization, he would do so without hesitation. And why should he hesitate when he has told the world what fate awaits non-Muslims in messages he has delivered in speeches, prayers, and documentaries. Why does the international community fail to heed these warnings?

In August 1996, Osama bin Laden issued his first of three explicit declarations of war (fatwa) against the U.S. A second was delivered in February 1998 to include the West and Israel. A third, given three months later, seemed to be more of a clarification of the earlier two, advising Muslims to focus their main attacks against the U.S., with a chilling forewarning about civilians being fair game:

> *"It is far better for anyone to kill a single American soldier than to squander his efforts on other activities…We believe that the worst thieves in the world today and the worst terrorists are the Americans… We do not have to differentiate between military or civilian. As far as we are concerned, they are all targets."*

(In what has become customary among Islamists, they do not require they comply with strict Islamic practice. For example, in issuing a fatwa, such a declaration is supposed to represent an interpretation of Islamic law by a respected Islamic authority—which Bin Laden was not. And, while he issued his fatwa from a cave in Afghanistan, perhaps to give his war declaration the appearance of David taking on Goliath, all the heavy equipment he used to dig the cave and the communications gear and other comfort items he outfitted it with, was in violation of strict Islamist practice that one live one's life as did Muhammad in the 7th century.)

The bottom line is that it mattered not whether Bin Laden issued one, or two, or three declarations of war because each was received by the U.S. with the same level of indifference.

Perhaps the seriousness of Bin Laden's warnings was dismissed at the time as being no more than the 1996 equivalent of the comedy film "The Mouse That Roared," in which a mythical small country declared war against the U.S. in hopes of immediately suing for peace to get U.S. financial aid. Similarly, Bin Laden's threat was given no credence. But, on September 11, 2001, the "mouse" came roaring back like a lion.

While more than a decade has passed since 9/11, it is as if it has faded from America's collective memory as, once again, the U.S. is threatened by an Islamic extremist—Ahmadinejad—to whom no heed is paid. There is extreme danger in simply dismissing Ahmadinejad as "the mouse that roared."

An interviewer asked news reporter Tom Brokaw as he was retiring in 2004 if there was ever a story he regretted not reporting. He responded it was his failure to do a pre-9/11 story that connected the dots on terrorism. The dots were all there but blind ignorance prevented the West from seeing the connection. Unfortunately, blind ignorance is at it again.

There are more subtle "dots" that should be connected to indicate the Iranian leadership truly clings to a Belief the Twelfth Imam will be coming soon (meaning, from its perspective, so too will the end of the world for non-Muslims).

In July 2010, Tehran's Supreme Leader Ayatollah Ali Khamenei, made an outlandish declaration. If the news media fully understood this religious fanatic's mindset, Khamenei's declaration should have been the topic on every major news program in the Free World. But in a Western world totally out of touch with the realities of the evil of which man is capable of perpetrating upon his fellow man, stories about Hollywood generate more attention from the public.

As previously explained, Khamenei and Ahmadinejad, as believers in the Twelfth Imam's return, seem locked in a competitive struggle as to who is more spiritually "in tune" with the Mahdi's return.

As president, Ahmadinejad went as far to suggest he is a messenger of Mohammad. He has confided in some Arab leaders the Mahdi will return before his term ends. Prior to delivering his first speech at the United Nations in 2006, he could be heard praying to the Mahdi. Following his U.N. appearance, he told Iranian religious leaders he saw himself engulfed in a "halo" as he spoke—a sign of his spiritual alignment with the Mahdi (although the halo apparently was visible only to the Iranian president).

Not to be outdone, however, Supreme Leader Khamenei reported to his advisors the Mahdi visited him, sharing the news his return will occur before the Ayatollah's death. (Khamenei has reportedly been suffering from terminal cancer since 2009.) Whether Khamenei viewed this visit, just prior to his 71st birthday, as a birthday gift from the Mahdi, we do not know. But his motivation for making the statement should have been a topic for analysis by the press.

One possible explanation was that Khamenei, worried that only Ahmadinejad was experiencing a "Mahdi moment," felt compelled to "create" his own. The "halo" story had already been claimed by Ahmadinejad, so Khamenei had to be a little more creative. If the motivation was not a product of creative license, two other possible motivations exist.

1) Khamenei really believes he was visited by the Mahdi as a result of the opium-based painkillers he is taking for his cancer treatment. (The hospital where he receives treatments bears the name of the Mahdi—the 12th Imam Hospital—so that his surrounding conditions may have been ripe for such an hallucination.)

2) Khamenei, free of any drugs that might have impaired his thought process, may truly believe the Mahdi paid him a visit.

With a cancer-ridden body, Khamenei may not have many years left. Therefore, if he did not create the experience and he believes the Mahdi is to return before he dies, Khamenei may believe Earth is soon to be looking at the world chaos necessary to trigger the Mahdi's re-appearance.

With a nutcase like Ahmadinejad serving as Khamenei's wingman, either is capable of taking the final action to create that chaos. With Iran probably having a nuclear capability soon, if it does not already, the reality of the death and destruction this dynamic duo of diehards could render starts to set in.

Khamenei's vision prompted him to make a declaration he never before claimed.

Shortly after his vision, he announced his rule is a direct succession to that of the Prophet Mohammad. Although Shi'ites only account for about 15% of all Muslims, he claims to be ruler of the Muslim world. While such claims have been made before by other mullahs on behalf of their Supreme Leader, this was the first time such a claim has been made personally by the Supreme Leader himself.

It is a claim demonstrating control over Iraq which the late Ayatollah Khomeini was unable to make during his lifetime which Khamenei feels is appropriate to make during his. It is a claim made to represent to a real world and the mystical one of the Mahdi that the Twelfth Imam's "throne" in Iraq is ready to receive him. As reported earlier, in 2006, Ahmadinejad wrote a long rambling letter to President George Bush that some interpreted as a warning. In April 2010, Ahmadinejad wrote to President Barack Obama. In another nonsensical diatribe, Ahmadinejad told the news media he informed him, "Obama has only one way to remain in power and be successful. This way is Iran," suggesting the President should "start cooperation with Iran in practice." Never one to waste words on specifics that might tie him down, Ahmadinejad failed to elaborate anymore.

Another "dot" to consider is that it is believed the Mahdi will not return in an odd-numbered year. It may well have been in Tehran's game plan—until Stuxnet and Flame malware delayed it—that 2012 was to be the "Year of the Nuke" to trigger the chaos necessary for the Twelfth Imam's return. But, for the Islamist, compliance with Islamic practice is not necessary if it furthers one's own agenda. Bin Laden did not comply with it and Iran's leadership will not feel a need to do so either, thus not necessarily committing it to an even-numbered year.

In October 1962, during a Cuban Missile crisis that lasted thirteen days, the U.S. came closer to nuclear war than any other time in Cold War history.

Obviously, as the crisis heightened, no one knew how it would play out. On October 22, 1962, President John Kennedy gave an eighteen minute statement to the American people on the Soviet arms buildup in Cuba. It was concise, to the point, and forewarned of the dangers and challenges that lay ahead:

> *"...Neither the United States of America nor the world community of nations can tolerate deliberate deception and offensive threats on the part of any nation, large or small. We no longer live in a world where only the actual firing of weapons represents a sufficient challenge to a nation's security to constitute maximum peril. Nuclear weapons are so destructive and ballistic missiles are so swift, that any substantially increased possibility of their use or any sudden change in their deployment may well be regarded as a definite threat to peace.*
>
> *"...The 1930's taught us a clear lesson: aggressive conduct, if allowed to go unchecked and unchallenged ultimately leads to war. This nation is opposed to war. We are also true to our word. Our unswerving objective, therefore, must be to prevent the use of these missiles against this or*

any other country, and to secure their withdrawal or elimination from the Western Hemisphere.

"...My fellow citizens, let no one doubt that this is a difficult and dangerous effort on which we have set out. No one can see precisely what course it will take or what costs or casualties will be incurred. Many months of sacrifice and self-discipline lie ahead—months in which our patience and our will, will be tested—months in which many threats and denunciations will keep us aware of our dangers. But the greatest danger of all would be to do nothing."

"The path we have chosen for the present is full of hazards, as all paths are—but it is the one most consistent with our character and courage as a nation and our commitments around the world. The cost of freedom is always high—and Americans have always paid it. And one path we shall never choose, and that is the path of surrender or submission.

"Our goal is not the victory of might, but the vindication of right—not peace at the expense of freedom, but both peace and freedom, here in this hemisphere, and, we hope, around the world. God willing, that goal will be achieved.

"Thank you and good night."

In his statement, Kennedy conveyed several important points to Americans:

1) The need to deal with a danger to the U.S.
2) History has taught the world the danger of unchecked aggressive conduct.
3) The greatest danger of all is to do nothing.
4) Never choose surrender.

By taking action decisively, Kennedy defused a crisis quickly and removed a nuclear threat to America.

The Iranian nuclear crisis has been around for more than a decade, yet nothing has been done to remove the danger it presents. It remains "the greatest danger" today precisely because nothing has been done about it.

Almost half a century ago, a television ad—airing only once—became the most famous political commercial of all time. During the 1964 U.S. presidential race, Lyndon Johnson's campaign ran the "daisy" ad.

A young girl—perhaps 4 years old—is viewed plucking petals off a daisy while attempting to count: "5, 7, 6, 6, 8, 9." Her voice fades, overridden by a man's voice counting down a missile launch.

Zooming in on the little girl's iris, the camera cuts to a nuclear mushroom cloud. President Johnson then says, *"We must either love each other or we must die."* The narrator ends with, *"Vote for President Johnson on November 3. The stakes are too high for you to stay home."*

Having its intended shock value, the ad served to create voter concerns that Republican challenger Barry Goldwater was advocating reckless nuclear testing.

Not since the early 1960s has the concern of a nuclear exchange been so great. While President Johnson's campaign ad did much to raise the American public's awareness about that, little is being done a half century later to educate Americans on the Iranian nuclear threat.

Perhaps America's ignorance is part of why Supreme Leader Khamenei and President Ahmadinejad believe the planets are falling into alignment for the return of the Mahdi.

It may well be, therefore, that they are now programming 2013 into Iran's Doomsday Clock as the year of the Mahdi's return and looking forward to the day the Iranian octopus will have achieved a global reach.

As the West, with blind ignorance, still attempts to feel its way through the fog of Iran's nuclear intentions, the minute hand of Tehran's Clock moves closer to midnight.

The Clock is ticking...

Also from James G. Zumwalt

Bare Feet, Iron Will – Stories from the Other Side of Vietnam's Battlefields

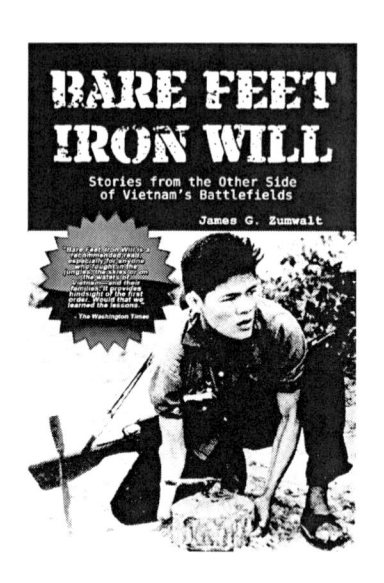

The Vietnam war left an indelible mark on America. Not since the American Civil War has a conflict so divided her people. And, a generation after the war in Vietnam ended; many Americans are still haunted by its memory.

In warfare, it is a universal tenet that both sides suffer. Neither the victor nor the vanquished emerges unscathed. Tragedy, hardship and suffering are universal to the warrior regardless of which side of the battlefield he stood; they are universal to the family awaiting his return; they are universal to the civilian population supporting the warrior's cause. "Universality" is a simple principle—it recognizes the commonality of suffering so that, once the fighting ends, a fertile ground can be plowed in which the seeds of friendship are then sown. It is a principle of which I, in my own sense of loss, lost sight.

I think there are veterans, like me, who have had difficulty in accepting the suffering the Vietnam war brought on us. It was my return to Vietnam however, in which I was able to come to terms with the internal struggle of my own personal tragedy of the war, which inspired me to write this book.

While we may not agree with the political motivations to which those on the other side of the battlefield adhered, we must respect their commitment and belief to die for them.

Living the Juche Lie – North Korea's Kim Dynasty

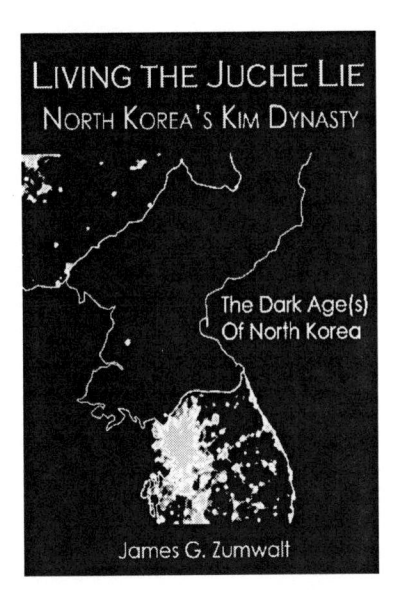

From a writer who has made ten trips to North Korea and seen things first hand...

The author takes a complex situation; one that factors greatly in US geopolitical decision and policy making and turns it into an understandable and easy read. It is an insightful analysis of the current situation in North Korea and how the past has led to the present and has significant impact on the future.

The Evolution of Power to Yet Another Generation of Kims—And the Conditions Giving Rise To It

The December 28, 2011 photographs of tens of thousands of North Koreans lining the streets of Pyongyang, uncontrollably mourning the passing of their leader, Kim Jong Il, as his hearse drove by, underscore the Kim family's success in its uninterrupted 63-year rule of the country. It stems from their mastery in molding the psyche of the masses they have led. The process began with the rise to power of Kim Jong Il's father and the nation's founder, Kim Il Sung, who, before his death in 1994 at age 82, had taught his son well. The family's future success in continuing its rule now turns on Kim Jong Il's youngest, most favored son and "Crown Prince," Kim Jong Un, mastering the same process. Should he fail to, turbulent times could be in store for the peninsula.

CPSIA information can be obtained at www.ICGtesting.com
Printed in the USA
BVOW022255301212

309372BV00002B/19/P